THE JOKER

THE JOKER

Twenty Years Inside The SAS

Pete Scholey

André Deutsch

First published in Great Britain in hardback in 1999
by André Deutsch Limited
This paperback edition published in 2000
by André Deutsch Limited
76 Dean Street
London W1V 5HA

www.vci.co.uk

A catalogue record for this book is available from the British Library

ISBN 0 233 99866 7

Typeset by
Derek Doyle & Associates, Liverpool
Printed and bound in Great Britain by
Mackays of Chatham plc, Chatham, Kent

1 3 5 7 9 10 8 6 4 2

This book is dedicated to:

My wife, Carolyn, daughter Amy and son David whose undaunted love and support have guided me throughout my career and since.

CONTENTS

ACKNOWLEDGEMENTS

My thanks to Ingrid Connell, Andrew Lownie and Jack Hughes for their help and advice in editing and publishing *The Joker*.

Special thanks, too, to my friends Mark Howarth and Colin Wallace for their unfailing support and encouragement.

CHAPTER ONE

The Radfan mountains and the jungles of Borneo are a world away from where I grew up, and if you'd told me back then that I was going to be a career soldier for nearly thirty years, and that most of those years were going to be spent slogging around some of the wildest parts of the world, with a bergen on my back and a rifle in my hand, I'd have said you were mad. It just didn't happen to little lads like me from Brighton. We turned out like my dad: buying and selling, wheeling and dealing, doing whatever we could to keep the wolf from the door and the family together.

And what a family we were! I was number six out of eight children. Pat and Mary, my sisters, were the eldest; then came George; then Jean, another sister; then Tony, and then me. I appeared on 25 July 1936, born in the little flat above the corner grocery that Mum and Dad were then running. Nineteen thirty-six was a good year: Edward VIII was on the throne, briefly anyway; Fred Perry won the All England Lawn Tennis Championship at Wimbledon for the third year running; and the *Queen Mary* crossed the Atlantic on her maiden voyage to New York (funnily enough, I saw the real Queen Mary, mother of the King, a few years later in Brighton). When I was born, Mum and Dad were taking a

1

break from the family watercress business, which normally occupied my aunts and uncles, and several of my cousins as well.

It was a strange business, this watercress. It was grown near Chichester and then loaded onto a little train that chugged over to Brighton where the whole family got involved in sorting it, packing it and sending it off to our customers around the country. We didn't go as far as machine-gunning the competition, or putting horses' heads in their beds, but we were a kind of Mafia. Watercress was our thing, and you didn't mess with the Scholeys. Well, we were Catholics: we always had numbers on our side!

The first big event I can remember was the war: no surprise there. We were living in the Milner flats in Brighton by then and Dad went off to join up, leaving us six kids in the care of my mum (the last two boys were born after the war, but six was enough to be going on with).

Dad joined the RAF, and when he'd finished his basic training he was based at the Royal Naval Air Station at Ford. His job was to fly as crewman on the mail-runs going up to Scotland and back. He told me later that he used to spend every flight perched on this little seat behind his pilot, clutching a spanner in case anything went wrong with the plane. Not to fix it or anything like that: the cockpit of the plane was so small that they couldn't wear parachutes. They had to unclip their 'chute packs from the harness and store them in a rack, but it was only really possible to reach one of them easily. No, Dad wasn't going to fix the plane, he was going to fix the pilot: *thwack!*

One of Dad's early exploits happened soon after he'd joined up, when the German bombing of Britain was at its height. Heading back to his billet after a raid, he spotted a hole in the turf, put two and two together, and reported an unexploded bomb. All the accommodation was evacuated and they waited for some hours as the overworked bomb-disposal squad made their way through their nightly list of tasks. Mind you, it didn't take all that long for them to clear Dad's rabbit-hole. Well, it could have been dangerous – someone might have tripped over it in the dark.

Even though it was a tight squeeze for a family of eight, the great thing about being in Milner flats was that most of the rest of the family lived there as well, so my aunts and cousins were able to help out when they could. However, having such a lot to cope with got my mum down, and she had a miserable time. In one of my little flashes of memory from that time I can see her shaking with fright at the sound of the air-raid warning siren, before we were all bundled downstairs to the Anderson shelter next to my granny's flat on the ground floor.

Mum's fears weren't helped by all the horrible rumours that were going round: one of these claimed that any German bombers that hadn't dropped all their bombs on London would offload them over Brighton on their way home. Another – even more frightening – maintained that the Germans thought that our block of flats, and the one next to it, was a barracks, and that Hitler had ordered a special raid to destroy them. Neither of these stories was true, of course, and we weren't ever directly bombed, but they were just about believable, and they were certainly enough to contribute to the panic of civilians who only wanted to protect their families against the threat of the Luftwaffe.

But even though Hitler never did score a direct hit on the Scholeys, he came very close. When I was about four or five years old, I was at home one day after my brothers and sisters had gone off to school. I was sitting on the big old brass bed that the five youngest of us slept in, playing with my toy cars and planes, when a bomb hit the clinic next to the flats, not more than thirty or forty yards from where I was. Most of the people inside it were killed or badly injured, and the blast brought down several nearby buildings, and damaged many others, of which ours was one.

I have a very vivid memory of a loud bang, and looking up to see the entire window, frame, glass and all, coming straight towards me. I had the sensation of being lifted bodily from the bed, thrown against the wall and falling to the floor. After that, I only recollect lying there, and the feeling that I couldn't move.

Sometime later an ARP warden found me, trapped beneath a wardrobe covered with wreckage and debris. Many years later I learned from my mother that I did not cry out, which is why it took some time to locate me. The wardrobe had fallen onto the bed, creating a small sheltered space and saving me from the falling rubble. Next day I stood with Mum and a big group of neighbours looking at one of the destroyed buildings lying in ruins in front of us, listening to them discussing how a man had been decapitated by a panel of corrugated iron blasted from the roof. As I scuffed my feet in the dust and rubble, I found a sixpenny piece. I didn't think about it then but I suppose it belonged to one of the people who had been killed or injured. Nearly sixty years later it remains a powerful memory.

Dad was given thirty-six hours' compassionate leave and arrived home in the evening, looking strong and handsome in his RAF uniform with its brightly polished brass badges and buttons. As soon as he walked in, he picked me up and gave me a big bear hug. He used to wear one of those side-hats decorated with an RAF badge, and he would let me put it on. Then I would bury my face in it and smell the Brylcreem from his hair (still pretty much obligatory in the RAF, even now). When he was away, I missed him terribly, as we all did, but sometimes I would catch that smell – clean hair, Brylcreem and an RAF side-hat – and it was as if he was there with me. It still happens from time to time.

Around this time, a great big low-loader parked outside the Dome in Brighton, carrying the wreckage of a German bomber. This was quite an attraction for the few hours it was there and I, along with most of the other small boys in the area, spent some time staring at it. Funnily enough, a couple of years ago I was looking at a book, *Sussex at War*, which featured a photograph of this scene and I'm sure if it was enlarged you would be able to see the small short-trousered Scholey lurking in the crowd. A few weeks after the appearance of the bomber my sister Mary took me with her on a mission to buy a couple of pence-worth of bacon bones for my mum to make into soup. As we walked along the main road, we heard a roar and looked up to see two German planes zooming past so low we could see the pilots' faces. They weren't going to shoot us or anything but Mary had the presence of mind to pull me back into a shop doorway just in case.

The bombing of the clinic made my mum decide that it would be better to get us out of Brighton for the summer and so she took us all off hop-picking near Goudhurst in Kent. Well, that's not quite accurate: she picked the hops, earning eightpence a bushel, while us kids played about. Still, at least we were out of harm's way in the countryside, sleeping on straw in a barn and eating food cooked on big twig fires.

One incident remains in my mind from this summer. One morning a German bomber came over very low, trailing smoke from both engines and obviously badly shot up. I ran out of the barn with the other kids to see what would happen and promptly collided with the legs of a big, fat lady carrying a bowl of boiling hot water, which she spilled all down my back. My sister Jean took me up to the first-aid post (where they also used to make pies, for some strange reason) and they fixed me up so well I was left without a mark on me.

Jean was a resourceful girl. One of the biggest problems for us kids in wartime was the shortage of sweets because of rationing. One solution was to hang around the American soldiers who began to appear around 1942, because they always had plenty of chewing gum and Hershey bars to hand out if you asked them nicely, and my older sister Pat used to go out with an American, so that was handy. Jean was more systematic, though.

For some reason, a lot of cancelled ration coupons used to be dumped on one of the municipal tips round Brighton and Jean discovered that some of them were in good enough nick to be cleaned up, dyed to the colour of the month, then used in the gloomy little sweet shop just across from where we lived. It was run by an old boy who was too short-sighted to see what we'd done.

Despite the rationing, I don't ever remember being hungry or going short of food as a kid. Dad used to send little parcels home: stuff he pinched from the cookhouse, I expect. And the family made sure that us kids had enough to eat. At that time, we were allowed one fresh egg a week which we'd have for tea on Sunday afternoon, but often I'd ask Mum for my Sunday egg a couple of days early, and usually she would give it to me. Despite this, every Sunday I'd still have an egg in my egg-cup and it took a long time for me to work out how this was possible: of course, Mum was giving me hers.

We wouldn't be cold either. Five of us kids slept in one big bed, and in the winter, as well as the blankets, Mum would pile all the coats in the house on top of us, from her own overcoat to the little baby's jackets, and although most of them had rolled off by the morning, it got us off to a nice warm start.

I suppose the arrival of the Americans signalled the beginning of the end of the war. I remember just before D-day, when I was eight years old, seeing all these trucks parked along the seafront, nose to tail, stretching as far as the eye could see. Some of us smaller kids tried walking along the top of them, jumping from truck to truck to see how far we could get without putting our feet on the ground. Some of the older boys reckoned you'd be able to get all the way to Hastings. But then, a few days later, they were all gone; and many of the happy, smiling GIs who'd joked with us and given us their chocolate bars were dead in the dunes of Omaha beach and the hedgerows of Normandy.

Only a couple of months later, we all heard a strange rumbling sound and rushed out to watch wave after wave of Dakotas, some towing gliders, as well as their fighter escorts, heading off – as we later discovered – to the Arnhem catastrophe. I was too small to realize it at the time, but I expect that this close proximity to the war – and for nearly five years, if you lived on the south coast, you were pretty much on the front line – later made it seem natural to me that I should follow a military career, or, at least, serve in the armed forces.

When the war came to an end and Dad came home there was no great song and dance. My sister Pat had eventually married a Canadian soldier called Robbie, and had a baby, and when he was demobilized she went back to Canada with him. Being good Catholics, though, Mum and Dad didn't let the grass grow under their feet and there were soon more children on the way.

Sadly, when Pat left, it was the last time I ever saw her. Twenty years later she came back to see the family, and they had a big party, but I was away on operations in Aden and I missed it. Unbeknownst to all of us, she was suffering *r* by then and died before I could get to see her

We were all pleased to have Dad back because we've always been a very close and loving family, but he wasn't the sort of man to want to dwell on what he'd been through. As far as he was concerned, he'd done his bit and that was the end of it. He threw his uniform away, and didn't bother to apply for any campaign medals, as far as I remember. Then he began to look around for some way of supporting his large brood. The watercress business had been sold when all the male Scholeys joined up so he needed to find something new.

Although nobody was being killed any more, the end of the war didn't change things a lot. Winston Churchill had lost the election and left office, making Mr Attlee the Prime Minister, but for one reason or another the Labour government clung on to rationing and lots of the rules that had come with the war, like conscription, so there was still an atmosphere of emergency and regulation, as well as a thriving black economy. Being the kind of chap he was, this was where Dad scented success.

One thing I remember about Dad coming back from the war was the large roll of banknotes he was carrying – well, it seemed a lot to me at the time – which I suppose must have been a combination of savings and a gratuity. And this provided the float for his first enterprise: unlicensed bookmaking.

Being the sort of family we were, it wasn't surprising that we all got involved. Dad's office was in my gran's flat downstairs, and my role was to act as a runner, getting the cash and betting slips squirrelled away in case of a police raid. Soon after he started, Dad gave me a good piece of advice, which I can't say I've always stuck to but which has always seemed sensible. He was doing his accounts at the end of one day, getting ready to do his round of paying out to the successful punters, and he showed me two piles of money.

'Son, this pile is what I owe to all the winners who've had a bet with me today, and this one is my money. Now, which one's bigger?'

'Your money, Dad.'

'Exactly son. You can't beat the odds, that's why I'm in the business.'

But, of course, he wasn't for very long. In a small town like Brighton the police soon got to hear about what he was up to, and while he never got caught in the act, their interest persuaded him to try his hand at something else, and he started selling fruit and veg off a barrow.

In those days you were allowed to set up on any street corner up to ten in the morning and then you had to move on. But provided that you were moving, you were okay, and this gave the rest of us yet another part to play in his business. Dad would be up at four in the morning and down the market, looking for nice cheap stuff to sell on. Then we would spend an hour or so helping him get the barrow set up and nicely arranged and he was off, racing the other barrow boys for the best pitch. Once he was started, we would come into our own, acting as lookouts, watching out for the shiny silver decoration on top of the policemen's helmets as they made their way through the crowds.

But the fruit and veg business was pretty cut-throat with so much competition about, and certainly not the most secure way of bringing up a family, so Dad's next step was to set up as a totter, a kind of rag and bone man, pushing his barrow around town collecting all sorts of old rubbish and sorting it out so that he could sell it on. He'd get eightpence for a trilby hat; sixpence for a rabbit skin; a halfpenny each for jam jars; a few pence for a pound of white wool, and so on.

Meanwhile, I'd started my education at St John the Baptist Secondary Modern, our local Catholic school and the place you were sent if you'd failed your eleven-plus exam, like I had. It was now that I first encountered a problem that was, in some ways, to shape my life. Back in the 1940s there was no mucking about with 'child-centred education' and the nuns who taught us were strict and unrelenting. I had no problem with reading and writing, but for reasons that I couldn't then explain, figures meant nothing to me. If I looked at a page of sums, after a couple of seconds the numbers on the page would seem to swim around, as if I was looking at a jigsaw with the pieces all jumbled up, and I couldn't see any way of putting them back together.

Well, nowadays 'dyscalculia' is a recognized condition, related to dyslexia. But in those days, as far as my teachers were concerned, it was because I was thick and not trying hard enough. My own reaction made things worse. Frustrated by my inability to do the work, I resorted to pratting about, with the result that I spent so long standing in the corner, I knew all the spiders by their first names.

Being the class clown is all very well, but after a while nobody wants to know you, and I ended up as something of a loner and also, I'm ashamed to admit, a little bit of a bully. I was helped in this by the fact that the only sport I was any good at was boxing. My two mates were the other two class dunces, Rudolf Syfflet (not the best surname for a schoolboy) and George Geady, and we got our laughs from coming out of school at lunch time, walking down the main street and taking the mickey out of everybody in sight. Even between ourselves we behaved stupidly. One time I was winding George up by slapping him on the legs below his shorts, and he responded by pushing me over, picking up half a brick and thumping me on the head with it. As if that wasn't bad enough, I took a swing back at him and managed to splatter his nose halfway across his face. That dropped both of us in the shit and we were soon in front of the teacher, getting six of the best across the backs of our knuckles with a big metal ruler.

Now a clip round the ear or a rap on the knuckles is understandable if you've been fighting, but what used to get me down was the beltings I'd get when I couldn't do the work. We'd be sitting there in rows at our little wooden desks, scratching away with the old-fashioned dip pens, or in my case staring at the big inky blot that had formed on my exercise book. Then the teacher would come up behind and *thwack*! In wintertime, I would spend the rest of the day with my knuckles in my mouth or under my arms, rocking backwards and forwards, crying and giggling at the same time, trying to make the pain go away.

We even got a clout for missing church. We had Mass every Wednesday at school, but if you missed it on a Sunday, you had to bring a note in from your parents to explain why. The old Irish priest would come around on Monday morning, and if he suspected you hadn't shown up, you'd go through his own little version of the catechism: 'Were you at Mass on Sunday?' 'Which church did you go to?' 'Who took the Mass?' 'Scholey you're a bloody liar! Get outside the door.' *Thwack!*

But I was saved from all this by one of the few teachers I came across who had any time for me. Mr Liddle was a history teacher who'd been in the Royal Flying Corps in the First World War and had decided, just after the Second World War had finished, to set up an Air Training Corps unit at our school. Mr Liddle saw that I was never going to be an academic superstar, but he also recognized that I lacked confidence and a focus for my life, and that was what the ATC provided. Once a week, we would put on our uniforms, and go and do a little drill, followed by something like first-aid training, or aircraft recognition, and then a few team games or sports. Not much perhaps, but better than hanging around on the streets getting into trouble.

One of the highlights of the year was the Shoreham Air Display, where we would act as guides and runners on the airfield. In the run-up to the display, my unit became involved in selling tickets and programmes, and seeing my enthusiasm, Mr Liddle would let me out of school an hour early so that I could go home, put on my uniform and make a start on my sales campaign.

One summer this became a sort of obsession for me. I'd leave the school at three and then walk from Rottingdean as far as Hove or even Shoreham itself, calling in at the big hotels, knocking on doors and flogging the programmes at a shilling a go. When the display finally arrived, I'd sold over 800 programmes and my reward was promotion to acting corporal and my first ever flight in an old Avro Anson, all the way from Shoreham, round Beachy Head and back. Well, that was that for me. I knew what I wanted to do with my life. I wanted to be in aircrew.

I suppose I was only about fourteen at this point, but I went to see Mr Liddle and told him that I had decided to volunteer for the Royal Air Force. Although he told me that he didn't think I was ready for it, he agreed that I should have a go. Then I told my dad, who was all for it, and finally I went off to get the forms from the RAF recruiting office.

A couple of weeks later saw me at the RAF College at Cosford for my initial selection for a twelve-year RAF apprenticeship. I'm sorry to say that I lasted four hours. I sat in front of a series of test papers, and they stared back at me, and that was it. I couldn't do them, so home I went. I slunk into the house and told Dad, and he was very nice about it, but I was struck with the thought, 'What am I going to do now?'

The answer was to try again. A year or so later I volunteered for adult service starting at the age of sixteen, and once more I went off for my assessment, this time at the old airship base at Cardington, which by then had been converted into a recruiting station. I did better this time – I managed to last a whole day – but my scores in the tests were hopeless, even though I'd lowered my sights and was only trying to obtain a basic three-year engagement. It began to dawn on me that I was never going to make it into the Royal Air Force.

But, of course, this was the beginning of the 1950s, and although I might not be going to join the Royal Air Force, I was going to have to do my National Service when I got to the age of eighteen, and in the meantime I needed to find work and earn some money. Looking back, I'm amazed at how many jobs I had over the next two years. I dug holes for the Borough Surveyor; I dug holes for the Electricity Board; I dug holes for the Gas Board; I baked bread; I delivered bread; I delivered newspapers; I was a plasterer's mate; I was a builder's labourer. All in all, more than thirty different jobs in less than two years.

Next time you pass through Gatwick Airport, you can console yourself with the fact that I spent four days working there for my brother-in-law, pushing a barrow full of cement through the muddy building site and unloading bricks from the back of a truck, with eyes full of brick-dust and fingers blunted like hammerhead sharks. And if you live in the early housing estates in Crawley, I helped build those as well.

But all the time I was doing these crummy jobs, I was hating it: none of them lasted more than a few weeks and some were only a couple of days. My drifting did finally lead to some tension with my family who had understandably begun to think of me as a bit of a waster. By now Dad had acquired a proper pitch and was back to selling fruit and veg, and doing quite well, but I think he was keen that we should all settle down and stand on our own feet as soon as possible. I knew that I was set on a career in the military but my record so far didn't necessarily indicate that I was going to be able to stick with it. Still, it passed the time until the fateful day when the little brown envelope plopped through the letterbox 'On Her Britannic Majesty's Service' to tell me that my attendance would shortly be required at a National Service medical board.

I had a choice. Either I could wait for my appointment and go with the flow, or I could take myself down to the local recruiting office and volunteer, thus short-cutting the whole procedure, and that's what I did.

It wasn't plain sailing, though. The recruiting centre for the army was at the Oddfellows' Hall in Brighton, where I signed all the forms and then had a medical, which was where the snag arose. This strange collection of half-dead looking doctors weighed, measured, prodded and probed before pronouncing me 'grade three' and a borderline case, because of a scarred eardrum. I did my best to persuade them and eventually they agreed that, as I was a volunteer, they would give me the benefit of the doubt.

So there I was, eighteen years old and off to join the army.

CHAPTER TWO

I don't suppose that joining the army as an eighteen-year-old National Serviceman in the mid-1950s was all that different from joining the army nowadays. It's a huge culture shock, of course, but at the same time it's a ritual that every soldier who has ever joined the British Army has been through, and although there have been some superficial changes, I don't imagine that much of it would come as a surprise to someone joining up in the year 2000 either.

I and about forty other ill-assorted herberts rolled up at the Royal Army Service Corps camp at Blandford in Dorset and straight away we were into the swing of it. Doubled over to our accommodation: eighteen-man rooms in wooden huts; a steel bedframe and a locker to call our own; a stove with a coal fire to keep the place warm.

Then *wham*! Doubled to the barber – Paddy the Chop – out come the clippers: *zhmm zhmm zhmm*. Suddenly I've only got an eighth of an inch of hair left. Then doubled over to the clothing store for: battledress, two sets; big leather-soled and studded ammunition boots, two pairs, 1937 pattern webbing, a great collection of canvas straps covered in ominous-looking brass buckles, together with berets, duffel bags, PT kit and a hundred and one other things that I would never have imagined I needed, but now found I did.

Then back to the accommodation to find out how you put it all on.

If, like me, you'd come from a working-class background where money was short but, at the same time, had experienced the fierce discipline of a Roman Catholic secondary school, then the shock to the system wasn't too severe. One feature of National Service – one of the better ones in my view – was that it was a melting pot. You got kids like me, you got lads who'd been at public schools and you got some people who'd been at university. You also had a selection of villains and nutcases as well – people who didn't want to be there and had no intention of knuckling down and making the best of it. In the first few weeks we had people trying to hang themselves in the bogs, we had people drink cans of Brasso in an attempt to poison themselves and one evening I watched a lad cut all of his kit into postage-stamp-sized pieces with a pair of scissors. On the other hand, a lot of these conscripts were magnificent, and you only had to look at the success of the British troops who fought in Korea, Kenya, Malaya and elsewhere during the fifties to see that the majority were just as good as any other soldiers Britain has produced in the last fifty years.

One of the big features of life during our first twelve weeks of basic training, apart from all the square-bashing, weapon training and so forth, was the amount of time we spent cleaning, ironing and polishing our kit. You still hear soldiers complaining about this today, of course, but I can assure you that this is an area where there has been a big improvement. Take boots, for example: when I joined, the standard boot for British soldiers was what was called the 'ammunition boot'. This was a sturdy ankle-length, black leather design, which also featured leather soles into which were hammered steel studs to improve their grip. In a perfect world, this kind of boot, although old-fashioned even in those days, could be made supple and waterproof by being regularly dubbined or polished. In combination with the canvas gaiters we wore, it would have been perfectly effective for general field-soldiering. Unfortunately, this kind of common-sense approach was unthinkable. Instead, we all had to go through the ritual of 'bulling' to try to achieve a perfect mirror-like shine all over our best boots, and on the toes and heels of our everyday pair. The first 'problem' with the boots was that the leather they were made from was covered in little tiny pimples, and to get a mirror finish the leather needs to be smooth. This was achieved by heating the handle of a metal teaspoon over a candle and using it to press the pimples flat. Of course, applying red-hot teaspoons to it is not really conducive to preserving the leather for extended use, but never mind. The next step was to coat the boot liberally in Kiwi polish, allow it to dry, and then repeat the process until the whole boot was covered with a smooth, thick layer. Finally, with a clean, damp duster, you gently apply tiny quantities of polish in a circular motion, polishing the layer of polish, rather than the actual leather, thus achieving a shiny surface in which you can, literally, see the reflection of your face.

Of course, at the same time as you achieve the ultimate shiny boot, you are also ruining it for anything other than parades, guard duties and so forth, when a high degree of bullshit is required. It's all very well to look smart but I wonder if it's worth, in effect, destroying kit to do so. A friend of mine, who had served in Korea, later told me how, after several weeks hard soldiering in their 'field' boots, members of the Glosters had only their best boots to change into when their first pair began to wear out, and as soon as these were exposed to field conditions, they fell to pieces: bad news when you have half the Chinese People's Liberation Army on your tail!

With our webbing equipment, the problem was slightly different. All the belts, straps, pouches and packs were made out of a sort of yellowy-green cotton canvas material which looked horrible in its raw state and absorbed water, mud and filth like a sponge. The army's solution to this was blanco, a green paste you applied to the webbing which made it a uniform colour. Well, again, it did make everything look smarter, but I have to say it would have been easier if they had adopted the obvious solution they worked out a few years later, and simply dyed everything the colour they wanted to achieve in the first place.

After the initial basic training I moved on to begin to learn my trade with the Royal Army Service Corps. The RASC, which subsequently became the Royal Corps of Transport and is now the Royal Logistics Corps, was responsible for moving all of the army's heavy equipment and stores to wherever they were required, whether by land, sea or air. There were, and still are, plenty of units in the Corps that do the exotic stuff – air despatching, maritime operations, and so on – but I was a truck driver, pure and simple. I learned how to drive on a 3-ton Bedford, and soon had experience on a broad range of now forgotten military vehicles: the Austin Champ; the Willys Jeep; the Stalwart; you name it, I drove it. And that, broadly speaking, is how I spent my National Service: ferrying men and equipment round the training areas, camps and garrisons of the south of England.

I came out of the RASC as a qualified military driver with a £70 gratuity, a railway warrant home and the determination to re-enlist in the army as soon as possible. I went home to

Brighton, spent a couple of weeks staying with my family then took myself down to the recruiting office to sign up again. I'd enjoyed myself in the RASC, but I was pretty sure now that I was ready to move on, and this time I fancied a crack at something difficult: I wanted to join the Guards.

I'm not sure if I entirely remember why I wanted to do this, but it certainly had something to do with the smart uniforms and cheese-cutter caps they wore. That sounds silly now, but I was still in the grip of a complex about my wasted schooling, and I wanted to show people, and my family most of all, that I could hack it.

Unfortunately for me, with National Service in full swing, the army wasn't short of private soldiers, as the recruiting sergeant informed me. While he promised he would try his best, he couldn't guarantee to get me into a Guards regiment. Well, that's what he told me anyway, and I certainly believed him. Two or three days later, I returned to the office to be told that there were no vacancies in the Guards but that he could get me into the Royal Regiment of Artillery. The Gunners.

I thought about this for a few moments and decided, 'Yeah, that'll do me nicely.' Although, I'd just spent eighteen months as an RASC driver, I was still pretty naïve. I didn't have a clue what the Gunners were about, but it sounded all right, and pretty soon I was signing the forms for a three-year engagement and collecting another rail warrant to take me to Park Hall Camp in Oswestry.

Basic training in the RASC wasn't easy, but I tell you, for the first sixteen weeks in the Royal Artillery my arse didn't touch the ground. Even though I was supposedly a trained soldier, I started at the beginning again, spending the first four weeks square-bashing as a member of 148 Meiktila Battery (which is now a highly specialized commando forward observation unit but was then a recruit training unit) and then going on for continuation training at Kimmel Park Camp in Rhyl, north Wales.

Once again I was selected as a driver and went through another training course with Royal Artillery instructors, but I was also trained as a crewman on the old 25-pounder field gun and on the 5.5 inch heavy anti-aircraft gun, just for good measure. Finally, at the end of this second bout of basic training, I was posted back to Oswestry as a member of the newly formed 27 Guided Weapons Regiment, Royal Artillery.

The arrival of nuclear weapons and ballistic missiles at the end of the Second World War had a profound effect on military thinking. For a while, it seemed as if the Americans' possession of the atom bomb made them more or less invulnerable to attack from the Soviet Union, which had begun shaping up as the only credible enemy almost as soon as the Germans were beaten in 1945. But then the Soviets got their nasty hands on nuclear weapons as well and the arms race started. As part of the British response to all this, 27 Regiment was designed to use tactical guided missiles in the event of a Soviet invasion of Europe.

It had been decided that, because we were going to be one of the first two guided-weapons regiments in the British Army, they would trawl the rest of the Royal Artillery to find the best drivers, the best signallers, the best mechanics, and so on, to staff it. That was the idea anyway. Whenever the army decides to do something like this, the response is always the same: everyone agrees, 'What a good idea!' and then all the drongoes, deadheads and weirdos who've not got past the rank of Gunner for fifteen years suddenly get a promotion to Lance Bombardier and a posting into whichever new 'élite' is being formed.

Still, they weren't a bad bunch of lads and I had a good time with the regiment. My first big trip away with them was to the missile range at Benbecula on South Uist in the Outer Hebrides. I was part of a team sent to St Kilda with monitoring gear to track the course of the missiles. The first time that the missiles – an American design called the 'Corporal' – were fired, they'd gone all over the place, the reason being that they'd placed them on concrete launch pads, which caused vibration when the rocket motor fired. In these tests they were fired from sand, which caused no such problems.

After three months of tests we returned to Oswestry for the regiment to begin the process of working up to operational readiness and eventual deployment in Germany. Before this happened we made a temporary move to Crookham camp near Aldershot in Hampshire, and from there we took part in build-up training: exercising on Salisbury Plain and the other training areas of the south of England.

But, as it happened, I didn't accompany the regiment to Germany. One of the many British Army formations which was then based around 'the Shot' was the 16th Parachute Brigade: Britain's airborne forces.

The focus of 16 Parachute Brigade was, of course, the battalions of the Parachute Regiment who formed the main striking force within it, but it also included the supporting arms: Engineers, Signals, Gunners, as well as services like doctors, cooks, bottlewashers, and so on, all of whom had to be Para-trained. Being based at Crookham brought me into contact with 33 Parachute Light Regiment Royal Artillery and so, with around a year of my contract left to run, and by now a bombardier (the Artillery equivalent of a corporal), I decided that I needed a more adventurous challenge and volunteered for service with the airborne forces.

Most armies don't get too fussed about parachute training: if you're daft enough to volunteer to do it, you get a quick physical check (though it's always struck me that a mental one might be more appropriate), you do your parachute training and that's it: you're airborne. Somehow, though, the British Army could never do things that simply. Instead we had the whole process of P Company to get through.

P Company is a series of tests designed to check out the airborne volunteer's fitness and determination before he gets on to the serious business of parachuting. Basically you turn up at the airborne forces depot, you're given a great big rucksack and a few other bits of kit and then spend the next three weeks charging around with said rucksack, now filled to weigh thirty-five pounds, firmly attached to your back. The tests included forced marches, assault courses, stretcher races and milling, where we all punched the living daylights out of each other while the instructors checked for suitable signs of aggression. As all the lads started mixing it – and some really knew how to box – I found it best to drop to the floor and bite ankles. Equally unpopular was the trainasium, a rickety scaffolding frame designed to see if you wet your pants when faced with heights. And it's only at the end of this that you're actually allowed to go off and do the parachuting!

As well as P Company, transferring to the airborne gunners also meant retraining on the specialist guns and equipment they used, and particularly the lightweight 105-mm Pack Howitzer, and it was while I was doing this that my contract came to its end. In the normal course of events the process of re-enlistment would be a formality, particularly for a junior NCO like me who was obviously keen on a long-term military career, but in truth I was having doubts. I went in front of the commanding officer for an interview and laid my cards on the table.

'Bombardier Scholey, have you decided whether you want to continue to serve with the Royal Regiment?'

'I've made my decision, sir, and I would like to leave.'

'What? Why on earth do you want to go now? You haven't even done your para course yet . . . '

'Sir, the thing is, I don't want to be a parachute gunner, I want to be a thoroughbred. I want to join the Parachute Regiment itself.'

As you can imagine, that went down like a fart in a space-suit and I had an uncomfortable few days. You can't blame them: almost everyone in the army is convinced that their regiment or corps is the only place to be and they were most likely astonished that I wanted to go elsewhere. Still, there you go.

Being based in Aldershot, demob presented me with an easy choice. I walked down Queen's Avenue from North Camp to the Parachute Regiment Depot, presented myself at the gate, explained what I wanted, signed on and, as luck would have it, joined a squad starting their basic training that same day.

Of course, by now I'd actually spent the best part of five years in the army and although there were a few problems of adjustment – the Paras did foot drill slightly differently from the way I'd been taught, for example – the basics were second nature to me. After a couple of weeks, the squad officer, Lieutenant Peacock, sent for me and told me: 'Scholey, it's ridiculous you doing all this again. You know your stuff with the weapons. So we're moving you up a squad.'

This was excellent news: now all I had to do to pass out as a member of the regiment and go to an operational squad was learn some infantry tactics, get through the battle camp at Brecon and the parachute course. All parachute training in the British forces is run by the RAF, and back in the late fifties the parachute school was at RAF Abingdon near Oxford. Coming after a week of being screamed at on P

Company, the parachuting was a bit like a holiday. Provided you turned up on time and were properly dressed, nobody gave you a hard time. You did the work and then off down the Naafi in the evening for a couple of pints followed by bed. The early part of the course went through all the various techniques for fitting and adjusting the parachutes and equipment, exiting from the aircraft, steering the parachute in the air, landing, rolling, and getting sorted out again. We also learned what happened when you got a serious malfunction in your parachute: you whistled in and hit the ground very hard.

I enjoyed the battle camp as well, even though it was, I think, the toughest training I'd ever done. The great thing about the Parachute Regiment was that it didn't muck around. It was a regiment that prided itself on being ready to go at any time and this meant you had to work hard, but we played hard as well and I had a great time. There are some funny ideas going around about what the Paras do. An old colleague of mine, in a book he wrote, describes them as 'shock troops', as if that was a special role that they've been given, but I think he's wrong. Although the original Paras were descended from the wartime army commandos, by the time they'd earned their battle honours in Tunisia, at D-day and at Arnhem, their role had changed and they were essentially a light infantry force capable of being delivered by parachute. So when I passed out of the Airborne Forces Depot at Aldershot, proudly wearing my maroon beret with the Parachute Regiment badge and cloth wings of a qualified military parachutist, I was proud to be a member not of some kamikaze shock squad, but the best airborne infantry regiment the world has ever seen.

There are three regular battalions in the Parachute Regiment: 1 Para never seem to go anywhere, and they're known as the 'Home Guard'; 3 Para were the drinking battalion; I was posted to 2 Para, the drill pigs (instructors). A couple of days after passing out of the depot, I joined the troopship TT *Dunera* and sailed for Cyprus, for my first overseas posting.

Between 1954 and 1959 Cyprus was the scene of a fierce guerrilla war between Greek Cypriot EOKA terrorists and the British colonial authorities. The Greeks wanted Cyprus to be unified with mainland Greece, and as they made up 80 per cent of the population you could see they had a point, but oddly enough the 20 per cent Turkish population didn't agree. Instead the Turkish Cypriots wanted reunification with Turkey, which had ruled the island before the British takeover at the turn of the century. As it happened, us Brits had been keen to hang on to the place for ourselves, seeing it as a key strategic base for our operations in the Middle East.

The upshot of all this was that the Greeks had imported Colonel George Grivas, a Greek Nationalist extremist, and he had set up EOKA, which had spent several years bumping off Turks and Brits in roughly equal numbers. Fortunately, all this was quietening down by the time I arrived to join A Company of 2 Para and reported to their camp just outside Limassol.

Cyprus has changed a lot in the forty years since I first arrived there. Although it was in the process of becoming independent, it remained undivided at that time and in many ways retained a kind of British veneer, despite the splendid Mediterranean backdrop. I wasn't exactly a fresh-faced squaddie when I turned up – I'd been in the army for five years after all – but I knew enough to work out that the best way to settle in would be to keep my head down for the first few months and play the grey man, even though I knew, with my sense of humour, that this was not going to be easy.

The first problem arose when I was given the job of rounding up and shooting the stray dogs that infested the camp. I've always liked animals, but these things were horrible: scabby, mangy, often half blind and riddled with all sorts of diseases, they hung around the open-sided cookhouse marquee, stealing food and scraps, fighting and making a nuisance of themselves. I was sent out with a pair of thick gauntlets, some rope to tie them up, a 9mm Browning pistol and a box of rounds to thin them out. After a hard morning chasing the buggers around, I'd got a bunch of them in a gully outside the camp, which we used as a tip, and went through the grim business of shooting them with a round to the back of their heads, between their ears which, if nothing else, is the quickest way to do it.

Having shot the dogs we then set about burning the bodies in a big heap, after soaking them with petrol. With this done, we were making our way back to the camp when we saw another one, a great big fucker this time, and with some trepidation we enticed it down to the tip where I did the necessary – and threw it on the fire.

The company was on guards and duties this week so I had various other tasks to do before I headed back to the guardroom to hand in the pistol. When I arrived there, the provost sergeant was waiting.

'Scholey, you need to get your arse up to the RSM's office right now!'

'Okay, Sar'nt, but why?'

'Just get up there, at the double!'

I doubled over to the RSM's, wondering what the hell I'd done. Arriving outside, I reported to the clerk then heard a big voice booming: 'Is that Scholey? Get in here.'

I formed up in front of the RSM's desk.

'Scholey, you realize you're in the shit? We've had to send for Pierrepoint.'

Pierrepoint was the hangman who'd just retired after topping the best part of 500 victims.

'Why, sir, what have I done?'

'It's murder, Scholey. You've shot the Devon and Dorsets' mascot!'

'Fuck me!'

'Don't tempt me, sonny! It's a corporal and they're holding a regimental funeral for it this afternoon.'

The Devon and Dorsets were in the camp below us and, as it happened, their mascot was an English bull mastiff which they allowed to wander round their patch. A series of complicated phone calls managed to persuade the D and D's hierarchy that it was an honest mistake and no action was taken.

But battalion-level diplomacy failed to convince the D and D's soldiery that they weren't the victims of Para brutality and revenge was planned. A three-man fighting patrol of Devon and Dorsets was despatched the next night on a mission to assassinate our mascot, Bruneval, a Shetland pony.

Most people think of Shetland ponies as sweet little things that children can happily learn to ride on and which wouldn't say boo to a goose. Wrong. Bruneval was a vicious little bastard – Para trained – who was notorious for dealing out savage bites to his handlers if they made a false move. The first we knew of the assassination attempt was the thumping of little hooves against the wooden sides of his stable, and the shrieks of pain from the three would-be hit-men trapped inside. The net result was that Bruneval remained undamaged whilst two of the killers suffered broken ribs and the third had a broken nose and concussion.

Not every senior NCO in the Parachute Regiment in 1960 fitted the stereotype of ruthless efficiency that the Paras have since acquired from Northern Ireland and the

Falklands. My platoon sergeant in A Company was eccentric, to say the least. He was a little Irishman with an unusual way of going about his business. We were moving out on exercise for a fairly long period so all bedding had to be handed in to the company stores. Our sergeant was Acting Company Quartermaster Sergeant, and he was determined to create a good impression in the hope that he might make the promotion permanent.

It was Friday and we were moving out on Monday morning at about 0930. Because most people left camp over the weekend, he wanted us all to hand in our bedding before we dispersed. But not everyone was going away, of course, so he then decided that we could keep our mattresses, hand the other bedding in, and use our sleeping-bags. Meanwhile, he decided to put a notice into the company routine orders that he wanted all outstanding mattresses returned to the store by 0800 on Monday morning. Unfortunately, while he was writing the orders, the company commander phoned him to discuss some other stores matters and when he got down to finishing them, the mattress problem had gone clean out of his thoughts.

Monday morning arrived and our sergeant is running about organizing stores, rations, weapons and all the other details that come up on a big move. Suddenly he realizes that he's forgotten to ask for the mattresses back. Bugger! But there's no time to type up a notice now, nobody will spot it, and, anyway, he's not entirely sure how to spell mattress, and doesn't want to look like an idiot in front of the company commander. Instead, he uses his 'airborne initiative' and come about 0700 hours he runs down to the stores, gets a hammer and a six-inch nail, nails a six-foot mattress to the notice board, and writes on it in blue chalk 'These will be handed in by 0800 this morning'.

He had no sense of proportion whatsoever, and you only had to make the slightest mistake to get extra guards and duties which he would never rescind. I'd managed to fall foul of him one day for no particularly good reason and collected three extra guard duties as a result. Pissed off by this and with nothing to lose I was determined to get my revenge on him. As it happened, we were doing a parachute jump that day, and our sergeant incautiously asked me to sort out his container for him and get it loaded on the aircraft, as he hadn't time to do it himself. No problem. Once I'd got my hands on his container, it was easy enough to acquire a two-hundredweight block of concrete of the right size, load that in, and then to bend back the retaining pin so that he couldn't easily open it.

We fitted our 'chutes, got in the aircraft and took off, heading for the DZ (drop zone) at Ladies Mile Beach. As the jump approached, we got up to sort out our equipment and it was then that our sergeant noticed something was wrong. Realizing that his container weighed at least twice what it should have done, he demanded, 'What the hell have you done, Scholey?'

By now the red light was on and we were hooked on, ready to jump. The doors were opened, the green light came on and out we went. Although our sergeant was only just ahead of me in the stick, he hit the ground some time before me, probably towed in by the weight of his container.

'Scholey, you bastard! You're on guard tonight!'

'You've already put me on guard tonight, Sergeant.'

Even better, because he couldn't undo the container, the silly sod actually picked it up and carried it on his shoulder the two miles to the RV (rendezvous), rather than simply leaving it where it was.

As a trained driver, I was given quite a lot of driving

details soon after I joined the battalion, ranging from transporting the company to the Troodos mountains for training to moving equipment to various locations around the island. On one occasion I was detailed to go to Nicosia in a 3-ton Bedford R.L. to collect a horse which the battalion had acquired for adventurous training purposes.

I got the horse, which was called Brandy, onto the back of the truck and the vet, who was accompanying it, helped me secure it to the frame that normally held the canopy. The weather was hot, so when we set off, the horse was actually enjoying the cool breeze of the vehicle, which was travelling at a reasonable speed.

Nowadays Cyprus is a very modern and sophisticated place with motorways and dual carriageways crisscrossing the Greek side of the island, but at that time most of the roads were little more than dirt tracks. About halfway back to Limassol, we suddenly came face to face with three large, black American-style Fords travelling at high speed. The track was pretty narrow and there was nowhere for me to go so I brought the truck to a halt, but the driver of the leading Ford decided to try to sweep round me. He didn't make it. As the two cars behind screeched to a halt, the front one slid some twenty metres down the embankment at the side of the road. Fortunately it didn't roll, and the passengers all got out, shaken but uninjured.

While the vet kept Brandy calm I went over to the Cypriots and offered them a hand. After a little pushing and pulling, we managed to haul the car back onto the road using my truck's winch, at a place where all three cars could get past. I hadn't taken much notice of the passengers who'd got out of the car but as they were about to set off, one of them walked over to me, shook my hand and said: '*Endaxi, endaxi.**'

* Thank you, thank you.

And I found myself looking at Archbishop Makarios who had just become the President of Cyprus.

Being in Cyprus also allowed me to get to work on my piss-up technique. The great joy of overseas service in the British army has always been the widespread availability of alcohol at kamikaze prices and warm weather is always conducive to a bit of a drink-up. Although the emergency in Cyprus had ended, it was still not advisable to go out of camp in groups of less than four, so Jock Thompson, Brummie Hassall, Lippy Lipton and I went down to Limassol together for a big night on the Bacardi and Cokes. Around about 2 o'clock in the morning, Jock and I found ourselves on our own, so we decided to get a taxi back to camp. Being half cut we poured ourselves into a grotty and dilapidated Greek-Cypriot taxi. After about fifteen minutes going through the back streets of Limassol – and in those days it was somewhat less charming than it is now – Jock and I began to get suspicious, imagining we were being Shanghaied to a hideous death at the hands of EOKA.

The driver claimed not to speak a word of English, and as we got more agitated, we began a big argument with him in sign language and loud shouts, but no matter what we said and mimed, he would not stop to let us out. By now we had convinced ourselves that we were in for a duffing up at the very least and were desperate to escape.

Then Jock had a brainwave. As a good Scot, he often wore a kilt when out and about, and he happened to have it on that night. He stood up as close to the driver as he could in the back of a cab and dropped his kilt over the poor man's head. The driver let out a muffled scream and slammed on the brakes, the car skidded round then rolled slowly onto its side.

We got out, uninjured, and as we ran from the irate Cypriot, Jock shouted back, 'Just remember, matey, it's Arabs and Scots that wear skirts. The difference is that Arabs wear underpants as well!'

As we turned the corner, the poor taxi driver was still spitting bits of unidentified fluff from his mouth.

Jock Thompson could be something of a monster. At one point he had just received his Post Office savings book back from the UK where he had sent it to get it updated and decided to treat himself to a big night out in Heroes Square in Limassol.

Around five the next morning he arrived back at camp looking completely poleaxed, complaining that he'd been rolled by some bird in a brothel who'd pinched the best part of his two hundred notes. By Naafi break at ten, he had sobered up a bit and was seething with righteous indignation at being the victim of a heinous crime, even though, by all accounts, he'd got pissed and spent most of the money buying drinks for the girls at the bar. Nevertheless, he was not going to let it pass and after work he got another two hundred quid from the Post Office and recruited a couple of mates to go with him to smash up the brothel on the promise of free drinks. They got dressed up in their jeans and bovver boots, and off downtown they went.

Nothing was heard of the punitive raid until the next morning, when a taxi pulled up outside the main gates of the camp and out poured Jock and his two mates. When we enquired whether they had done the place over, the response was: 'No. After drinking ten pints Jock fell in love with one of the girls and blew another £200.'

But all play and no work makes Paras dull boys and in 1961 my first operational deployment duly came along.

On 19 June 1961, a new treaty came into force under

which the government of the oil-rich statelet of Kuwait assumed full responsibility for its foreign affairs, after many years in which the British Empire had effectively controlled it, without ever having full legal responsibility. On 25 June 1961, the Iraqi government, under the dictator General Qasim, announced its intention to annexe Kuwait and began massing troops on the border. Sounds familiar? I thought so.

In fact, the new treaty specified that Britain would continue to be responsible for the defence of Kuwait and the nearest available unit able to get out to the Gulf and put in a block was 2 Para from Cyprus.

The original plan was for a para drop but the winds were too fierce and instead we flew by British Eagle Airways from RAF Akrotiri to Kuwait and were then bussed to the Mutla Ridge, north of Kuwait city, to await whichever came first: British reinforcements or Iraqi invasion.

On the ridge itself, the ground was too rocky to dig in so we moved back to the reverse slope, leaving pickets out to give us advance warning of any Iraqi move, and then we waited.

Now I don't want to sound like a smart-arse, but when I read *Bravo Two-Zero* and the other books about the Gulf War, and saw the lads' descriptions of how they'd been screwed by the weather, I thought to myself: they should have asked me! Because, much to my surprise, even though it was steaming hot during the day it got bloody freezing cold at night, and this was in July. We were lucky enough to have quite a few Second World War veterans in the battalion, and they knew enough about desert conditions to ensure that we were issued with big greatcoats you could snuggle up in after the sun went down.

We'd been there on our own for a couple of days when the Commando carrier – in fact a converted aircraft carrier –

HMS *Bulwark* arrived, carrying with it 42 Commando, Royal Marines.

If the Parachute Regiment is the finest airborne infantry in the world – and it is – the Royal Marines are the best amphibious soldiers. This was the first time I'd really come across them, and I have to say I was impressed. They were smart, fit, keen and skilled, just like us. What's more, although I didn't know it then, they included amongst their number a certain Second Lieutenant Paddy Ashdown, serving as a troop commander: one of those all too rare politicians with operational military service.

So there we were: a battalion of Marines on the right flank, a battalion of Paras on the left, and assorted support elements dragged in from Kenya, Cyprus and Aden to our rear. On paper, not much of a force to hold off the Iraqi army with their tanks and air support. But the paper equation isn't always accurate. The reality was that we were itching for them to come over, because we would have given them a hell of a thumping.

With the arrival of the Marines, A Company was pushed forward about ten miles as a screen, sitting on the Kuwait to Basra road whilst the diplomats and politicians played chicken with each other.

After a couple of months, we were relieved in the line by 3 Para, our sister battalion, who were then based in Bahrain, and in fact we continued to swap with them until the crisis came to an end when the Iraqis backed down in October. With that, we returned to Cyprus, the Marines went wherever Marines go, and General Qasim was brutally murdered by other members of his government.

Back in Cyprus we returned to the usual round of training and duties. Two or three times every week we would go parachuting before breakfast at the DZ on the salt flats next to Ladies Mile Beach, between Akrotiri and Episkopi, and we would regularly visit the training area at Akamus in the west of the island for field training exercises, often against a live enemy.

On one such exercise, our enemy was the Black Watch, the famous Scottish infantry battalion. About midnight one night, I was part of a patrol that went out to recce the Jock position. We came back, reported the info and were then sent out in platoon strength as a fighting patrol to attack them. We hit their position, there was a bit of a kick up, they gave us a bit of a bashing, but all in all we got out okay.

So now they decided they must send a fighting patrol against us. We had met some of them on a social occasion, so we knew that they had a big rugby player, a kind of man-mountain known as 'Big Angus'. They sent out their patrol, but we managed to ambush it and duffed them up. In the dark, we heard the order go down the line: 'Get Big Angus. Get Big Angus, he'll sort them out.'

A couple of hours later, they came back and we ambushed them again. There was much firing of blanks and thunder-flash flares lit up the sky. Then it went quiet until a little Scottish voice called: 'Get a stretcher. The Paras have clobbered Big Angus!'

After six more months in Cyprus, the battalion returned to the UK, taking up temporary residence in Guillemont Barracks, at Cove near Aldershot, before returning to the Middle East to relieve 3 Para as the garrison in Bahrain. We also lost our very popular CO, Lieutenant Colonel Frank King (who went on to become General Sir Frank King), and this was accompanied by a perceptible rise in the bullshit level as the battalion got into the round of parades, duties and demonstrations that accompanied the Bahrain posting.

By mid 1962, I'd regained my second stripe and I was still enjoying myself, but I had begun to look around for something else to do in order to maintain my motivation and enthusiasm for the job.

In the early 1960s, the SAS wasn't the super-glamorous organization that it has since become – in the eyes of the rest of the army, that is. In fact, at that time, 22 SAS was very small – just two under-strength operational squadrons – run on a shoestring and very poorly paid because you had to give up your previous rank when you joined. Nevertheless, I'd heard enough about it to know that the selection course was a challenge I wanted to attempt, and after chatting it through with a few of the lads, I began to work on my fitness with a view to doing selection when we got back to the UK.

After a year in Bahrain we came home and settled back into life at Guillemont Barracks. Bullshit and discipline were, if anything, even more strictly enforced than in Bahrain and if we weren't out on exercise, we were back in the block polishing the soles of our spare pair of gym shoes, or some equally fascinating task. To make sure that we did actually 'screw the nut', we were always being inspected by somebody or other, ranging from our platoon sergeant up to the commanding officer and, of course, everything had to be pretty well immaculate.

On one weekly inspection, our company sergeant major was carrying out a pre-inspection to make sure that everything was okay prior to the arrival of the CO and the RSM. We were standing by our beds, rigidly to attention, as the CSM cruised through the billet, checking this and that, making sure that everything was spick and span.

Having completed one side of the room, we seemed to be doing well, with only two men charged: one for dirty boots, one for long hair. By now he had reached my mate John

Wriles and went to his big green metal locker, standing as they do in uniform line against the wall. Everything looked in good order so far, but when he eased the locker out from the wall to see if it had been dusted at the back, a big black spider ran across the back of his locker and scuttled inside. The sergeant major put him on a charge and he was given seven days confined to Barracks.

When he returned, looking glum-faced and miserable, we asked him what he had been charged with.

'Keeping a pet without authority.'

No question, the army has always had a strange sense of fun. When I eventually put in my request to be allowed to do SAS selection, I found myself waiting outside the CO's office with an old corporal called Fergie. Now, Fergie had been in the army commandos during the war and had a distinguished record, but latterly he had been working in the officers' mess as a steward. Now he was approaching his last six months in the army and had decided that he wanted to serve it out as a proper soldier in a rifle company.

As Fergie and I stood outside the CO's office, the drill sergeant came up and asked, 'Corporals Ferguson and Scholey . . . what do youse two want?'

We explained and he laughed.

'SAS selection, you must be fucking joking! And, Fergie, you're on a charge: you're improperly dressed.'

'What do you mean, improperly dressed? This is my best uniform.'

'You haven't got your false teeth in.'

'Look, sir, I want to talk to the Colonel, not eat him.'

I burst out laughing and we both got three days jankers (confined to barracks). Thanks for that.

CHAPTER THREE

There were three of us from 2 Para going up to Hereford
for our shot at SAS selection in August 1963: me,
Brummie Hassall and Alan Lonney. We'd all been training
hard and I was certainly as fit as I'd ever been in my life, but
what was bothering me was the uncertainty and mystery
that surrounded the whole process. In the battalion we had a
couple of lads who'd done a tour with the SAS and come back,
and a good handful who'd failed selection at one time or
another, so we'd been pumping them for information and we
knew that we were in for a rough few weeks as we were
beasted about the Welsh countryside.

But what was less clear was what the SAS was looking for
apart from physical fitness – and everyone I'd spoken to reckoned that fitness on its own wasn't enough. From what I'd
heard, the SAS looked for a certain 'X-factor' in its soldiers: a
combination of intelligence, initiative and imagination, and if
you didn't have it you might as well not turn up. Having
acquired a reputation in the battalion as a bit of a clown,
everyone I'd spoken to was convinced I didn't have *it*. Word on
the street was: 'SAS selection? Scholey's got no fucking
chance.' But I thought they were wrong.

Just before we left, we got a little chat from Drum Major
Williams. He told me, 'Corporal Scholey, tomorrow you're

going from the 2nd Battalion of the Parachute Regiment –
the finest regiment in the British Army – to the Special Air
Service, another fine regiment. I don't want to see you back
here unless you've earned the beret and badge that they
wear.' He didn't have to say that – what did he care about the
SAS? – but I was determined not to let him down. So I continued to clown around as usual, but underneath there was a bit
of steel: I wasn't going to fail!

Still, you do have to be fit and Brummie and I had taken
some leave to do hill training out in Wales. We booked
ourselves accommodation at the training camp at Dering
Lines in Brecon, which is handy for the Beacons, and headed
on up for ten days' hard work. Unfortunately, we'd had an
even harder time from one of the camp staff, a sergeant major
with an attitude problem who wanted to pick on us, so eventually we'd decided to stay out in the hills the whole time,
bivvying at night in one of the forestry blocks.

On our first morning in Brecon, Brummie and I had gone
to the toilets, where they had a set of scales, to weigh our
Bergens. I'd packed mine to about thirty-five pounds, which
was about the weight we carried in Para training, but
Brummie immediately told me, 'No, mate, that's not enough.'

I was a bit surprised by this, because thirty-five pounds
was heavy enough for me.

'What do you mean? How much do they want?' I asked.

'You've got to have fifty-five pounds in your pack, and don't
forget you're carrying a rifle as well. That's another fourteen . . .'

'That's bollocks, Brummie, nobody can carry that much . . .'
But he was right, and we spent the next ten days humping
these huge rucksacks over the hills, marching from point to
point as we tried to accustom ourselves to the monstrous
loads and tricky terrain.

So as we arrived at Hereford on that summer afternoon, and we unloaded our kit-bags and suitcases onto platform two, I would have to admit that I was more than a little anxious about what was going to happen next, and from the looks on their faces, I could tell that the same was true for the others as well. As we walked out of the station into the car park, the first thing to confront us was a green Bedford 3-ton truck with a small blue square painted with the winged-dagger badge on the bonnet: our transport into Bradbury Lines.

Brummie walked over to see whether the driver was in it and came back to report that there was nobody about but the keys were in the ignition. This started an immediate debate: was it an initiative test? Were we already being observed to see how we would react to this unexpected situation? There were a few other squaddies from different units who had been on the same train as us and they came over to join in the argument. The question was this: should we wait for a driver to appear to take us to the camp, should we ignore the truck and make our own way there, or should we take the truck and drive ourselves there? We were still arguing over this a couple of minutes later when I heard a friendly voice behind us: 'All right, lads? Sorry I'm late, chuck your kit in the back and climb aboard . . .'

I turned round to see a scruffy-looking ginger-haired soldier wearing a sandy-coloured beret with a cloth winged-dagger badge, a faded camouflaged windproof smock with a hood, and a *Daily Mirror* tucked under his arm. 'I've just been over the road for a cup of tea and I didn't hear the train come in.'

We piled in the back and as the truck started up, Brummie leaned over and nudged me: 'That was lucky.'

This was the first time that I had been to Hereford (you

might say I've never really left it since) and on the short drive through I was able to see what a lovely little town it is. The main features are the river Wye, which winds through the middle, and the cathedral, which sits just on the edge of the town centre. In those days, before developers began to get their hands on it, most of the buildings were old and original, and the whole place had a kind of unspoiled charm that you don't really see nowadays.

Bradbury Lines was a Second World War wooden-hutted camp on the outskirts of the town, just beginning to get a bit shabby, but ideally suited for a small regiment that didn't have a lot of vehicles or heavy kit, and did most of its training elsewhere. It had the usual fixtures and fittings of an army camp: a parade square, drill sheds and neatly tended flower beds, but there was something odd about it as well, and it took me a while to realize what it was. Unlike every other army base I'd ever been on – and having been a truckie, a Gunner and a Para, I'd been on a few by now – it was quiet.

Now I don't mean that it was silent like a monastery or anything daft like that, but there was nobody shouting or yelling at us, nobody doing drill, nobody doubling about. There was an air of quiet professionalism if you like – completely unlike the usual noise, bustle and bullshit of a regular army unit. Mind you, a big part of the reason was simply numbers: in 1963 the Regiment only had two squadrons, and they were on operations most of the time, so there was hardly anyone there!

When we arrived, we were taken down to Selection Troop to book in. As I waited in the corridor outside the office, I had a chance to look at the various notices stuck to the wall. Alongside the standard military-issue training posters were a lot of photographs of SAS soldiers on operations and training in various exotic locations, and some framed proverbs and sayings. I'd seen or heard most of them before, but they weren't the sort of thing you normally found pinned on the walls in regimental training wings:

Many are called, few are chosen.
A Guerilla is a Fish that Swims in a Friendly Sea.
Recruit to Sergeant: 'Sergeant, if I don't classify on the range, will it stop me going abroad?'
Sergeant: 'No, son, but it's likely to stop you coming back.'

Pretty corny, but different. The other surprise was that the whole permanent selection set up consisted of a captain, a squadron quartermaster sergeant and a clerk. There were other instructors, of course, but they were busy doing other things, and not hanging around waiting to give us a hard time, which is what would have happened in the rest of the army. Instead, the captain told us that we had to parade the next morning at 0800 hours and sent us down to the stores to collect our kit.

Now, I had half an idea that we would end up with armfuls of specialist kit, which would fit in with the slightly mysterious reputation that the SAS had, but I was soon put right. We got a bolt-action Lee-Enfield No. 4 rifle with no sling, a dog-eared old Bergen rucksack, a prismatic compass, a couple of maps, a belt and a pair of water-bottles, and that was it. No x-ray spectacles, no exploding cigars, no James Bond kit at all. Oh, well, that'll come later, I thought.

The accommodation was pretty basic – a bed and a locker in a twelve-man room in a wooden hut – so getting settled in didn't take too long, and then Alan, Brummie and I wandered off down town for a pint and some fish and chips to prepare for the action tomorrow.

The whole selection course was at muster parade at 0800 hours. Alongside the three of us from 2 Para there were a few more from other battalions of the Parachute Regiment, a handful from other parts of 16 Para Brigade, distinctive in their maroon berets, and a great mass from all parts of the army, not to mention the Marines, RAF, RAF Regiment and the Navy, coming to 130 candidates in all. The instructors called the roll and came up one short: 'Edwards? Where's Edwards?'

A voice answered up: 'He was late into breakfast, Staff, he's on his way.'

A couple of minutes passed and then Edwards trotted up and reported to the instructor. 'Sorry I'm late, Staff, permission to fall in?'

'Just go in the office a second, will you, they've got something for you.'

They did: a rail warrant back to his unit. He hadn't even made it to the first event. These guys were serious. After this, we got a quick pep talk from Captain Wilson, then it was onto the trucks and off up to Dinedor Hill, which overlooks Hereford, for lessons in map reading.

No question, after the dismissal of Edwards the first day of selection was a bit of an anticlimax. We sat on top of Dinedor with our maps and compasses as the Training Wing staff ensured that everybody there had sufficient navigating ability to get through the early part of the course. Map reading shouldn't have been too much of a problem for us infantry soldiers, of course, but the idea was to make sure that nobody would suffer just because their military background didn't require them to have certain skills. In any case, there was still a feeling in the army at that time that maps and map reading were for officers, and I can't say I was completely familiar with all the precepts. This was followed in the afternoon by a couple of lectures in first aid and basic survival, and then we knocked off, in good time for me, Alan and Brummie to get down for more beer and fish and chips after first getting our kit together and having the evening meal in the cookhouse.

The second day was when the fun started. The main activity, after we'd mustered at 0800, was to get on the trucks for a short drive out to the Malvern Hills, twenty miles or so to the east of Hereford. Once we'd disembarked and formed up in threes, we were detailed off with our instructors and sent off on a fourteen-mile speed march over the hills, carrying our rifles and Bergens weighted at 55 pounds (thanks, Brummie!).

Well, not too difficult, apart from the weight, but this was when reality hit home for the lads who hadn't prepared themselves properly, and it wasn't long before people started dropping out. It was seven miles out, a quick stop for a rest and a brew, then seven back; but as we formed up in threes at this big car park – called 'British Camp' – a little sickener was thrown in by Captain Wilson.

'Right, lads, well done. Now I want you to take five minutes to grab a breather and sort your kit out, then we'll be running back to Hereford.'

For the first split second after this announcement, I nearly fainted. Bloody hell! Hereford was twenty miles away, I was carrying fifty-five pounds on my back, and I was shagged out after doing fourteen hard miles on the Malverns. But then reality kicked in. Brummie was next to me, and as we bent down, taking swigs from our water-bottles, tightening straps on our belt order and Bergens, and getting ourselves sorted, I said to him, 'Don't worry, mate, it's a con.'

'What do you mean?'

'There's no way they're going to run us all the way back to Hereford. Look at them. They've all been on operations till a couple of weeks back, they're married with families waiting for them, and they've got to take us out again tomorrow. If they run back with us, they'll be completely fucked as well. I reckon they've got the trucks parked up a couple of miles down the road.'

Brummie took a look at the rest of the course, half of them dressed in weird and wonderful 'magic' gear.

'Scholey, you're right. They're just getting rid of the Walter Mittys.'

We'd just got ourselves sorted out when the order came from one of the Training Wing staff sergeants: 'Course! Course, 'shun!'

We braced up into the position of attention.

'Course will move to the left in threes. Left TURN!'

We dutifully obliged.

'By the right, double MARCH!'

And off we set. By now, the murmurs of disquiet at the idea of running back to Hereford were growing, and it wasn't long before the first few lads started to drop out with 'muscle strains' and 'twisted ankles'.

Well, fair enough, but on SAS selection there are no second chances, and anyone who jacked now was off the course for good. Sure enough, we jogged on down the road for a mile or so, rounded a corner and there were the trucks, lined up to take us back to camp. We'd lost about fifteen off the course already.

It's always been the same on selection courses. A lot of the people there have come for the wrong reasons: they're bored with conventional soldiering; they've spent too long in Germany; they don't get on with the other guys in their units; they're looking for a change. There's nothing wrong with that, but if you don't have sufficient motivation, you simply won't pass. It's too hard.

But you also get the Walter Mittys. These are the guys who turn up with all the extra kit: special foods; go-faster boots;

weird and wonderful combat kit, and so on. There's nothing particularly wrong with that, if the gear is useful, but the point about selection is that you don't need it. If you can do the course comfortably in the clothing and equipment you've been issued, then why bother bringing all the other stuff? Wearing flash kit won't help you get over the hills any quicker, but it will attract the attention of the training staff, and that's the last thing you want. A good example of this happened a few years ago.

A young parachute-trained officer was going through the special officers'-week section of the course, part of which involves standing in front of an audience of experienced SAS officers, NCOs and troopers to give presentations and talks, under hostile questioning. As it happened, this officer was wearing a set of jungle combats onto which he had sewn his British Parachute wings, as per regulations, on his right sleeve, and a set of American Para wings on his left breast above his pocket. Now this is quite a common practice in the airborne brigade, but in the SAS, where you rarely see anybody wearing badges other than on their beret, it attracts attention. One of the questions the young officer was inevitably asked was, 'Why have you sewn American Para wings on your shirt? Are you trying to impress us?' Well, there's no answer to that, and of course the extra stress certainly didn't help him. This was compounded the next day because he removed the wings and was inevitably asked, 'Why have you taken those American Para wings off? Do you always do what NCOs tell you?'

The moral of this tale is that once you get noticed, you can't win. Of course, officers' week is something I've never been through – thank God! It's a constant moan with some of my old mates that nearly all the officers we have in the Regiment are rubbish, but I think they're wrong. You do get some rotten apples, of course, but by and large they're good soldiers who are keen to learn, and when they've spent a few years in the Regiment, they often end up making a bigger contribution than some of the non-commissioned ranks who've been in much longer. And anyone who's been through officers' week successfully has my respect!

In the seventies, a retired member of the Regiment, known as 'Drag', was employed as range warden for the SAS training areas. Although he was in his late fifties, Drag was a keen marathon runner long before it became a mass-participation sport and was super-fit, as well as possessing a wicked, dry sense of humour.

During one officers' week, when Lofty Wiseman was the Training Wing sergeant major, all the hopeful young Ruperts had been at a lecture given by the second in command which was supposed to be followed by 'fitness training'. Lofty had the officers standing outside Training Wing as he called the roll when Drag happened to walk past, carrying a couple of shredded targets off to the target shed to be repaired.

Now Drag was dressed in a donkey jacket, a threadbare checked shirt, old corduroys held up with baler twine and grotty wellies, and combined with his bald head and grubbiness (he had just been cleaning up the pistol range), he looked every inch the village idiot, rather than the experienced, if retired, SAS veteran he actually was. This gave Lofty, who was supposed to be leading the officers on a road run, an idea.

'Mr Rowbottom! Wait a moment, I've got a job for you.'

Somehow, Drag sensed that a gag was coming up and played along, tugging at his forelock. 'Yes, Mr Wiseman, sir!'

'I'm a bit busy at the moment. Would you mind taking these gentlemen for a run?'

'Right-oh, sir!'

Drag dropped the two targets on the verge outside training wing, and carefully laid his donkey jacket on top of them. Standing in front of the squad of officers in cords and wellies: 'Right, gents, left turn, by the front, double march . . .'

And off they went, a scruffy civilian leading a squad of bewildered officers. An hour and a half later they returned, Drag still leading despite his wellies. The only one of the officers to stay with him slumped on the grass in disbelief.

'That little bastard just took us on a twelve-mile run!'

I suspect the best advice I could give to anyone attempting selection is this: expect the unexpected!

After the first run on my selection, we got back to camp and were paraded outside Training Wing. Captain Wilson stood in front of us.

'Okay, gentlemen, that was an easy introduction. From now on, the marches get longer, harder and faster.'

He wasn't joking.

The next three weeks were hard work. Every morning we would parade at the crack of sparrowfart, with our Bergens, webbing and rifle, and pile onto the three-tonners for the drive to the Beacons. As we got close to the mountains, the trucks would separate and eventually they would begin dropping us off, one at a time. We were called out of the back, given the grid reference where we were, the grid reference for the place we had to get to, and that was it, the truck would bugger off. Even so, you couldn't just stand there in the road looking at your map, you had to stay switched on and semi-tactical. This meant that as soon as we got our instructions, we had to scuttle into the hedge to start working out the navigation, and then get moving quickly.

The first march was ten or twelve miles and there were about five truckloads of recruits, but as the distances lengthened, the course thinned out so that by the end there was just one truckload when we began the final endurance march: and this the monster!

But even before the endurance march, I'd had my own frightener. Out on the Beacons, I made a stupid mistake. I wasn't too confident in my map reading at the time, and I decided to follow a bunch of soldiers who were walking down a ridgeline about half a mile ahead of me. Trouble was, when I got close I realized that they were from the battle school at Brecon: nothing to do with the SAS at all! Cobblers! By then I was miles out of my way, and I knew I wasn't going to make it to the last RV in time. Still, I wasn't about to give up. I eventually got there, in pouring rain, at about one in the morning and discovered, with no great surprise, that there was nobody about. I found a phone box and called in. Whoever was on duty made me describe my surroundings, so he could be sure I'd actually got there, then told me to make my way back to the small training camp that was serving as our base.

I got there two hours later, wet, cold and shattered. The instructor on duty in the office showed me into a large room, littered with wet, snoring bodies: 'Get your head down in there, son.'

I took off my boots and smock, unrolled my sleeping bag and lay down. It seemed as if I'd blinked, then it was morning. An hour or so later, we were parading for the next march and the Training Wing sergeant major asked, 'Where's the lad who came in at three in the morning?'

'Sir.' I put my hand up.

'You'll want to drop out, then, I expect.' It almost sounded like an instruction.

'No, thank you, sir. I'd like to carry on.'

'Okay, that's fine.' It was a lucky escape. If I hadn't made it to the last RV, they would have binned me from the course.

Not surprisingly, the final march was the longest of the course and covered all of forty-five miles through six RV points, starting at the Talybont reservoir and heading out over the top of Pen-y-Fan, past the Storey Arms, over the Black Mountain and back, starting at 0830 on the Thursday morning, and finishing before 1230 on Friday. No easy task at any time, but by this stage, three weeks of humping over the mountains with a heavy rucksack had taken its toll on all of us. We all had little injuries like blisters and Bergen burns, and some of the lads were carrying more serious problems that they'd picked up out on the hills: twisted ankles and knees, bruises, sprains, the whole lot.

Having said that, the weather conditions were fair and I made good time after we set off, getting through the first four checkpoints before nightfall. Not that anyone told me I was doing well or anything nice like that! When you got to the RVs they simply checked that you were physically all right then gave you the grid reference for the next RV. Thanks, lads. Still, I have to admit it was a system I got to quite like: a good soldier – a good anything, come to that – shouldn't need someone to tell him how clever he is every time he does something well.

By the time I got to the last leg, every bone and muscle in my body was aching. At 1000 I reached the last RV, back at the reservoir, and checked in. Nobody said much, except that we couldn't go back to camp until everyone was in, so I walked off a little way, took off my Bergen and settled down to make a brew. It was the strangest sensation: taking off the Bergen was like putting on a jet-pack: I thought I was going to lift off at any moment and float away. Once I'd brewed up, I sat down with my back resting against it to drink my tea and wait for the others. I tell you, my eyelids ached I was so tired.

But it wasn't really till the next day that the pain hit home. By then even my aches were aching, and although we'd been debriefed and I'd found out – along with Brummie and Alan – that I was one of the nine who'd passed (out of 130), all I could think of was getting my head down for some rest before the next phase of the course started.

Well, that wasn't too far off. Next step was jungle training out in Borneo, and for this we were marrying up with the previous course who'd been doing their continuation training in and around the camp. The reason for this was simple: with only two squadrons, both of which were committed to operational theatres, there weren't enough experienced instructors around to run separate jungle courses, and there were so few people getting through selection that it wasn't economic to set up a whole jungle course for a handful of students.

I enjoyed my first experience of the jungle, and I enjoyed working with the instructors, who were incredibly professional. If you'd asked most civilians at that time what the SAS was, the few who could have given you an answer would probably have told you about David Stirling and desert operations in the Second World War, but the real home of the SAS, at that time anyway, was the jungle.

Back in the late 1940s, Communist guerrillas in Malaya, who had fought against the Japanese with our help during the Second World War, had decided to turn on us, even though we were in the process of handing over the government of Malaya to the Malays. The Communists had then started a terrorist and guerrilla campaign, basing themselves in the jungle, which they could use as a safe haven, and coming out to strike at military and civilian targets, more or less at will. Britain and the rest of the Commonwealth decided to resist this and sent in the army.

But there were problems: the British Army's main task

then was in Europe and most of the training was geared towards that; and British Army units themselves had a large proportion of National Service soldiers and officers who lacked the experience and know-how you need for internal security and counter-insurgency tasks in the jungle environment. The upshot of this was that, although things improved in some parts of Malaya, the security forces lost control of the jungle to the guerrillas.

The man who was brought in to sort the situation out was a Second World War veteran called Mike Calvert. He had been one of the earliest volunteers for the Commandos when they were formed in 1940, and had gone on to serve in the Chindits in Burma and at the very end of the war he became commander of the SAS Brigade, which was then made up of two British regiments, 1 and 2 SAS, two French regiments (the 1st and 2nd RCP), and a Belgian squadron, together with various attached arms and whatnot. After the war Calvert, like most regular soldiers, had had to drop down in rank to carry on in the forces, in his case from brigadier down to major, but he'd soldiered on as a staff officer until the call came to go out to Malaya.

Calvert spent about six months studying the problem then sat down to write a report that covered most of the major faults in the campaign so far. The biggest problem was caused by bickering and in-fighting amongst the high command, but he also identified a need to take the war into the jungle, and to get the jungle people on our side so that they wouldn't provide support for the guerrillas. He also reckoned that a special unit should be formed for deep patrolling and 'hearts and minds' operations and, after his report had been accepted, he was handed the job of raising and training the unit, which was given the name 'The Malayan Scouts'.

The Malayan Scouts had a bumpy start, but after a couple of years' hard work it began to be a real success, not only in running its own operations, but in showing the rest of the army in Malaya that they could stay in the jungle for much longer than they imagined possible. It wasn't too long before the unit was made a permanent part of the army as 22 SAS Regiment. At that time, there were three British SAS squadrons: A, B and D; a Rhodesian squadron, C; a New Zealand SAS squadron; and a squadron of volunteers from the Parachute Regiment.

So, in 1963 when I turned up, almost all the instructors were Malaya veterans, while some of them had been in Korea and a few had seen service in the Second World War (one lad, Bert Perkins in D Squadron, had been at the Anzio landings in 1943, fought with the Glosters at the battle of the Imjin river in 1951, spent two years as a prisoner of the Chinese and joined the Regiment almost as soon as he got back!). If these guys told you something, you listened, because they had been there, seen it and done it: they knew what worked and what didn't; and they knew when one of their students was bluffing.

The first part of the jungle training was pretty basic. We learned the rudiments of living in the jungle: putting up A-frame shelters; first aid; survival techniques, and so on. From there we moved on to the basics of patrolling: movement which left as little sign as possible; navigation in an environment where you can rarely see good landmarks; maintaining good communications. Then it was tactics: contact drills; ambush drills; anti-ambush drills; close target reconnaissance; all done thoroughly, efficiently and using live ammunition. Finally, we began to put it all together in a series of exercises under the watchful eyes of the instructors, working together as a team.

Of course, the main purpose of the jungle training was just that, teaching us jungle warfare, but not far behind came the selection aspect as well. To succeed in the SAS, where you're often working alone or in very small groups, you need to be an individualist, but you also have to be able to fit in with a team and work well together for extended periods. If you're so horrible that the rest of the patrol want to kill you after two days of operations, you're actually going to be an impediment, and there's no better place to find out who doesn't fit in than the jungle, where everyday life puts you under more than enough pressure.

With the jungle course finished, it was back to Hereford for continuation training in the skills required for an SAS soldier. Apart from the obvious ones – advanced weapons training in Nato and foreign weaponry, communications with various sorts of radio, sabotage and demolitions, first aid and all the rest of it – we also had language aptitude tests, mortar and artillery control, an introduction to air controlling, combat survival, resistance to interrogation and a range of other subjects that wouldn't necessarily spring to mind as part and parcel of the individual skills a soldier might need.

The end of the training came after the combat survival course. The lads who weren't from airborne units were sent off to Abingdon to do their para course with the RAF and the rest of us paraded in one of the lecture rooms.

At that time, the CO was Lieutenant Colonel John Woodhouse, who'd been with the Regiment more or less since Calvert had reformed it. More than anyone else he was responsible for turning the Regiment into what it later became: he had devised the selection course and insisted on the highest imaginable standards for anyone coming into the Regiment; and he had been at the forefront of developing

The Scholey family at home – wife Carolyn, daughter Amy and son David who gave me their unwavering support at all times.

My mother Violet, taken outside our home in Brighton during the war. She brought up six of us while my father was serving in the RAF.

My dad George, taken in the 1950s. He never missed a chance to 'perform', a trait he passed on to me.

My grandad George Stephen Haslen, with his dog Biddy. He served in both the Boer and First World Wars.

Just after passing out parade in the Royal Regiment of Artillery 1957. Gunner Scholey is on the far right.

3 Platoon, A Company, Paras. Two sticks of fifteen waiting at RAF Akrotiri, Cyprus to board Hastings aircraft for an exercise in Libya, early 1960s.

Sgt Major Andy Morrison briefing A Company before our quick move to Kuwait, which was threatened with invasion by Iraq, 1961.

A Company disembarking from Royal Marines landing craft after a day's intensive training in beach assaults, Kuwait 1961.

Myself and Len Walby having a 'Naafi break' during an exercise in the Troodos mountains, Cyprus, 1960s.

On a hill overlooking Caen, Major Graham gives A Company a brief history of the events that took place there on D Day, 6 June 1944.

The Rt Hon. Harold Watkinson, Minister of Defence, inspects A Company, 2 Para Guard of Honour at the 'Army of the Sixties' display in Aldershot.

Heavy drop of Land Rover and trailer using three 60-foot diameter parachutes which cut away on impact. Paras de-rig it ready to drive away.

Kevin Walsh (right) seen here with his pal in 1 Para. Later we were to serve together on many ops with 18 Troop.

Myself with Ken Gillott and Mick Hughes sailing home from Cyprus on the
T.T. Nevasa after 2 Para's three year tour.

A Squadron inside a Belvedere helicopter. First left is John 'Lofty' Wiseman, author of *The SAS Survival Handbook*.

D Squadron 1964. Front row, on attachment, Capt Akehurst and Sgt Major Konor, US Special Forces.

many of the techniques that we used in operations and training. As an officer and a leader, he had the absolute respect of every man in the Regiment. We were called to attention as the colonel entered. He stood in front of us and smiled.

'Well done, gentlemen. You've passed selection and continuation training, and you have what it takes to begin a career with the SAS. Before you do, there are several things I want you to think about.

'First, no one here is indispensable: you are now beginning a year on probation and if we find you aren't up to the mark after a year, you will be returned to your unit. Having said that, the same will be true throughout the rest of your time with the Regiment.

'Second: rank. If you join the Regiment, you will immediately lose any rank you have and revert to the rank of trooper. You will certainly not be promoted to lance corporal until you can convince us that you are capable of commanding a four man patrol on operations.

'Third: pay. We are an operational regiment. We do not have time to waste pursuing expenses claims and special allowances or queuing at the Pay Office. The only queues I ever want to see will be outside the Operations Room door.

'Fourth: medals. Don't expect medals, you are SAS and much more is expected from you.'

There was no sound. The RSM had a cardboard box containing our sand-coloured SAS berets and parachute wings and he now stepped forward so that the colonel could present them to us. It was one of the proudest moments of my life so far.

So here I was, a probationary member of 22 SAS, all fired up and ready to join D Squadron's Amphibious Troop and to begin the learning process all over again. Since the return to Europe after the Malayan campaign (and the short operation in northern Oman that the Regiment had carried out in 1959), a lot of hard thinking had been carried out.

The upshot of this was a complete reorganization of 22 SAS. The foreign squadrons had been sent home, the Parachute squadron had gone back to the Parachute Regiment and B Squadron had been disbanded and absorbed into A and D Squadrons. The SAS moved back to Britain for the first time, being based in Malvern and then in Hereford.

It had become fairly obvious that the sort of operations the Regiment would be likely to be called upon to carry out needed a much more flexible organization than a regular infantry battalion. In fact, it was decided to abandon regimental level operations and fix deployments at squadron level and below for everything short of all-out war. By the time I joined the Regiment, this had already happened, and although the system had only been running for a year or two, it had proved to be a success and still forms the organizational basis of 22 SAS.

Basing deployment at the squadron level meant that each squadron needed to possess the full range of available talents, so each was established to consist of four sixteen-man troops, with a different specialized 'entry' skill. The four troops were the 'Free Fall' troop, specializing in parachute operations; the 'Rover' troop who would be operating from specially adapted 'Pink Panther' Land Rovers; Amphibious Troop, using canoes and diving techniques; and Mountain Troop.

Within these specializations, each troop had various tasks and standards which had to be achieved in order to give the squadron its required capability, so that, for example, Mountain Troop had to be able to guide a company or squadron-sized unit safely, effectively and tactically on climbs rated at up to 'Very Difficult' standard* and to be able to train a certain number of partisan or irregular troops in mountain warfare; Air Troop were required to be able to parachute from various types of aircraft at high altitude, to mark drop zones and heli-landing sites; and all the myriad special tasks associated with air operations.

My first posting was to D Squadron's Boat Troop, which meant various courses in canoeing, scuba diving and other strange aquatic pastimes. I did these, and hated them, but after a very short period I was shifted to the Rover Troop, 18 Troop, where I was to encounter two big, ugly, complicated things, which were to take on a major significance in my life over the next few years. The first of these was the specially modified, long-range, SAS Pink Panther Land Rover, the second was the Troop Sergeant, Don 'Lofty' Large.

Once you've met Lofty, it's unlikely that you'll ever forget him. Six foot five inches in his socks and built like a brick shithouse, his facial features make him look like Frankenstein's younger brother. But his terrifying appearance was completely deceptive, because Lofty's biggest secret was that he was one of the most laid-back men in the history of the British Army. The reason for this was pretty straightforward. Lofty came from a small village in the Cotswolds, just outside Cheltenham in Gloucestershire, but for some reason he had joined up as a bandsman in the Wiltshires when he was fifteen. Five years later a call came round for volunteers to go to Korea with the Glosters as infantrymen.

Very soon after arriving in Korea, he took part in the battle of the Imjin River when the Glosters were effectively sacrificed to buy time for the rest of the British brigade to

* This is internationally recognized standard of difficulty for climbing.

withdraw in the face of 25,000 or so Chinese soldiers. Lofty had taken two machine-gun bullets in the shoulder and been captured by the Chinese, and along with most of the rest of his battalion, he'd spent the next two years or so in a POW camp, without any real treatment for his wounds and on an inadequate diet that caused him to lose about six stone in weight. Every now and then he was taken out to face pointless, frightening interrogations and, like his comrades he was subjected to continuous propaganda and indoctrination from the Chinese Communists.

Lofty was eventually given early release from the POW camp along with a few others who were judged by the Chinese to be unfit for further military service, and he'd returned to Britain with little prospect of soldiering on. Somehow, through constant effort and determination, he had not only regained his health but got fit enough to take and pass selection for the Regiment. When you've been through a series of experiences like that, you can afford to be pretty relaxed about life!

Lofty had joined D Squadron in Malaya in 1957, gone on to fight with them during the Jebel Akhdar operation and had recently returned to the squadron after spending a couple of years as an instructor with 23 SAS (part of the Territorial Army) in Birmingham.

So it was for Lofty and the other members of the troop to introduce me to one of the Regiment's latest acquisitions: the Pink Panther. The inspiration for these beasties came from the vehicles that had been adapted for use by the Long Range Desert Group and the original SAS during the Second World War. These had been Jeeps and Chevrolet trucks modified with new suspension, special tyres, extra fuel tanks and extra gun-mountings, to give mobility, speed and flexibility to small units working out in the desert. Our version was based on the long wheelbase Land Rover, and carried a huge selection of added equipment and firepower: our personal rifles; two GPMGs on stabilized mountings; an 84mm Carl Gustav anti-tank launcher; front and rear smoke grenade dischargers; a theodolite and sun-compass for desert navigation; a powerful spotlight; different radios for communications with base, ground to air and vehicle to vehicle; sand channels; a motorized winch; cooking equipment; rations; water; extra built-in fuel tanks; patrol kit for dismounted work; in fact, pretty much everything short of the kitchen sink. It always struck me that this was a slightly more civilized way of going about operations than in the other three troop specializations where you were effectively limited – in the field – to the kit you could carry on your back. The only drawback was that the engine was a bit underpowered for all the extra weight that the vehicle was carrying about, and the turning circle was enormous, which made these early Pinkies pretty much useless for operations in North-west Europe. In the desert, though, they were fine.

But the thing everyone noticed about them, and the reason for their name, was the colour we painted them for desert operations: pink. A couple of years later, Lofty and I got sent down to Sandhurst with a Pinkie for some sort of equipment demonstration which was being visited by Field Marshal Montgomery. We'd set up our little stand, with our nicely polished vehicle and various bits and pieces arranged around it, when Monty turned up with his entourage. He must have been well into his seventies by then, but he looked dapper and fit, and he was obviously intrigued by the Land Rover. He walked over to us, and as we saluted said, 'Ah, SAS I see! And who are you?'

'Sergeant Large and Trooper Scholey, sir,' replied Lofty.

'Large, eh? How appwopwiate. Now, tell me, why have you painted this vehicle pink?'

'Well, sir, we have found on operations that this colour actually affords us the best camouflage in the desert. It stems from the Second World War when some tanks had to be put into action before they had been camouflaged. They were painted with a pink-coloured primer, but it seems they were even better camouflaged than vehicles painted a sand colour,' Lofty explained.

'Weally?' said Monty. 'How fascinating. Thank you vewwy much, Sergeant. Cawwy on.' We saluted and Monty moved off, but as he was walking away, he turned to one of his aides and said, in a stage whisper, 'Bollocks!'

Well, I don't know if the story is true or not, but that's what I'd been told as well, and the camouflage certainly did work. On an exercise in the Libyan desert before Colonel Gaddaffi took over the country we were operating against ground and air forces who were trying to locate us. At one stage, we were listening in on the ground-to-air net when we heard a reconnaissance aircraft reporting that he had spotted our position. As he went round for another pass, we moved about 400 metres and that was it. He reported that he'd lost contact and never re-established it: SAS 1; RAF nil.

Apart from getting to grips with the troop vehicles, the other important qualification I needed was my 'patrol skill'. Within each four-man SAS team, it's important that there are a wide range of basic skills, and before you are operationally deployed, you need to qualify in one of them. The key specializations are: communications, demolitions, medic and languages; and, of course, you need a commander as well. Continuation training before you join the squadron gives you a basic grounding in all of them, but I was lucky enough to be selected to do the patrol medic course.

There's a lot of rubbish talked about some aspects of SAS training, and the medic course is one of them. What it doesn't do is turn you into a super surgeon or fully qualified paramedic. The course itself was twelve weeks long, when I did it, and consisted of six weeks in the classroom in Hereford, followed by a six-week attachment in the casualty department of a major hospital, putting the theory of first aid and trauma management into practice under the supervision of qualified doctors and nurses. Together with the first aid, we were being taught how to keep an operational patrol healthy when in the field for extended periods, and a certain amount of general health and hygiene practice that might enable us to assist a doctor or field surgical team if necessary.

Once you qualify as a patrol medic, you have to attend regular refresher training and hospital attachments to keep the qualification, and while this is hard work, it can also be great fun. One time, Taff Springles, a couple of other lads from the squadron and I were doing an attachment at the John Radcliffe Infirmary in Oxford. Taff and I were on shift when a huge, burly man was brought in after falling off a ladder while cleaning his windows. He'd managed to land on his greenhouse, so in addition to his bruises and sprains, he had some nasty lacerations as well. I cleaned and dressed his minor injuries and then, under the supervision of the ward sister, Taff prepared to suture a large cut across his chest. Up until this point, the atmosphere had been light-hearted and jolly but as Taff was getting the gear ready, he asked the sister whether he should use '30' or '50' thread for the stitches. 'Are you sure you're doctors?' our patient asked jokingly. We reassured him and he seemed happy until, after Taff had put a couple of stitches in, he asked the nurse some other question. At this point, the patient narrowed his eyes suspiciously: 'Here, you *are* doctors, aren't you?'

'That's right,' replied Taff.

'Well, if you're doctors, how come you keep having to ask the sister here what to do?'

Taff launched into our prepared cover story. 'Well, we're attached here from a different hospital and we have a different way of working.'

The patient thought about this for a couple of seconds, then jumped up off the trolley: 'Hey, fuck off, man! Listen, I'm a plumber and I can fix pipes in London, Birmingham or Glasgow, 'cos they're all the fucking same!' and with that, he took off through the ward and out into the waiting room, trailing odd bits of swab and bandages behind him. As he passed the other patients in the waiting room, he warned them: 'Hey, you don't want to go in there, they're all fucking amateurs!'

I chased after him and managed to coax him back, so we were able to retrieve the needle and thread from his chest and, eventually, give him the treatment he needed. Later on, at the end of our shift, Taff and I headed down to the local pub for a pie and a pint and who should we see but our patient, drinking with some of his mates. He beckoned us over and bought us a drink and we spent a very pleasant evening with him.

Someone once asked me whether I would be in a position to, say, take out an appendix if a member of my patrol went down with acute appendicitis on an operation and I suppose, yes, in theory I probably could. I certainly knew enough to make a reasonably confident diagnosis of appendicitis; I knew enough anatomy to be able to find it; and enough minor surgical technique to be able to cut it out and close up the incision afterwards. But the fact is that I wouldn't. We also learned that any kind of surgical procedure carried out under operational conditions would be likely to lead to massive infection, whilst my knowledge of surgical technique was not

sufficiently comprehensive to deal with any unusual complications, which an experienced surgeon would normally be
able to take in his stride. In this – and similar – theoretical
circumstances, my response would be to dose the patient with
antibiotics until it was possible to evacuate him to trained
help. For what it is, the SAS medics course is pretty comprehensive, but basic training for a doctor lasts six years and for
a paramedic three, so you do have to keep it in proportion.
When I did my original hospital attachment at St Mary's in
Paddington, one of my colleagues did get over enthusiastic
and stitched a patient's mouth shut when treating a gash to
his top lip, so we aren't necessarily of *ER* standard at all
times.

But even with my medical training under my belt, I wasn't
going to be an effective member of the troop until I'd got some
operational experience and that wasn't too long in coming.
We had a training deployment to Aden, which passed off
without incident, but my first big test as an SAS soldier was
to begin in February 1965 with the squadron's deployment on
operations in Borneo.

CHAPTER FOUR

The Borneo confrontation kicked off way back in December 1962 with a revolt in Brunei against the rule of the hereditary Sultan. Brunei, Sabah and Sarawak were three old British colonies that made up the northern third of the island of Borneo, while the rest of the island (under the name Kalimantan) was ruled by Indonesia. At this time, Indonesia was ruled by President Sukarno, a nasty piece of work who had been in charge since the end of Dutch colonial rule without ever quite managing to introduce the democratic reforms he was always promising. With the British handing over power in Borneo, the three colonies were due to join the federation of Malaysia, along with Malaya and Singapore, but Sukarno rather fancied the idea of taking over himself, and was prepared to use any excuse to do so.

In fact, the trouble in 1962 was caused by local Bruneians and stemmed from all the usual reasons: more democracy; more money; and so on. But Sukarno was quite happy to give it a bit of support in order to try to up the ante. The upshot of this was that British troops who'd been brought in from Singapore to help stabilize things ended up staying in place, and this gave Sukarno an excuse to do the usual and start shouting on about anti-imperialism as a neat way of diverting attention from his problems at home.

Sukarno's next move was to send small incursions of Indonesian troops across the border to stir up trouble and discontent, to raid small villages, and to frighten the locals. This was a provocation that the British general in charge of operations in Borneo, Major General Walter Walker, couldn't ignore. Walker's problem was that he had a 900-mile jungle frontier to guard, as well as the prospect of an internal uprising and terrorist activity from a group called the 'Clandestine Communist Organization'. One of the options he was given was the use of an SAS squadron, and the result was that A Squadron went out to Borneo for the first time in January 1963.

Walker's original plan was to use A Squadron as a quick reaction force, parachuting them into the jungle to intercept Indonesian incursions inside friendly territory. Colonel Woodhouse quickly persuaded him that this wasn't such a tremendous use of their talents and instead they were deployed into remote jungle areas to befriend the local tribes and keep an eye on the border. The reasoning for this was sound: a four-man SAS patrol can only cover a certain amount of ground – and can only stay eyes down on a tiny patch of border – but once you get the locals on your side, you can get them working for you and they do a lot of the border surveillance for you. The other big benefit was that members of the jungle tribes were routinely crossing the border on hunting trips and visits to friends and relations, and they were ideal sources of intelligence on what the 'Indos' were up to.

Of course, at the beginning of operations in Borneo, 22 SAS consisted of just two operational squadrons, A and D, and this meant things became very tight in the Regiment because, along with training, the squadron that wasn't in Borneo was increasingly being called on to mount operations in Aden. The physical and mental strain of extended patrolling in the Borneo jungle was such that squadrons were restricted to four- or five-month tours and this meant very little rest time. To everybody's delight, the decision was made in early 1964, when I was still going through continuation training, to re-form B Squadron.

In effect, what happened was that the Regiment plucked some experienced NCOs out of the other two squadrons then ran some extra-large selection courses through the spring and summer of 1964. This meant that they were able to put together the nucleus of an operational squadron without compromising the standards that all the rest of us had been forced to meet. So no complaints there. While this was going on, our Aussie cousins were also building up their own SAS unit, with a view to deploying it in Borneo, and the Kiwis were doing much the same thing. So as 1964 continued, things were on the up for the Special Air Service.

It was also during 1964 that our role began to evolve from straightforward information reporting within 'British' Borneo to offensive intelligence gathering, attacks and ambushes across the border. Patrols were now tasked to cross the border covertly, investigating reports of Indonesian terrorist and special forces camps, in order to target them for larger, more conventional attacks. When we arrived in January 1965 things had moved on a bit, and the old hands in the squadron, now beginning their second tour in Borneo, were looking forward to some interesting operations. On the other hand, I had the tense, anxious excitement of someone about to lose his combat virginity.

The first thing that hits you when you arrive in a tropical area is the heat and damp: a wall of humidity that you walk into as you leave the air-conditioned interior of the plane. Then there's the smell: the rich, ripe, loamy scent of the jungle. The smell soon fades into the background but the humidity is always there, doubling the discomfort of everything you do, invading everything you have, rotting your clothing and rusting your equipment.

For the next four months we were to be based, when not in the jungle, in various places in and around the town of Kuching in the west of Sarawak. There were three locations: the old Palm Grove hotel, which was being rented by the army from a Chinese family and which accommodated various odds and sods as well as the SAS; some space in a hutted camp on the edge of town; and a place on 'Pea Green Road', which also housed our Ops set-up. Of course, being the SAS, we didn't have our own bed-space: in effect we operated on a 'hot-bunking' system – when we returned from a patrol or operation, we simply moved into the space vacated by someone who was going out on one.

At this point, the squadron was commanded by a major from the Devon and Dorsets called Roger Woodiwiss, a nice man with a very pukka accent and the right attitude for our kind of operations, but the squadron sergeant major, Bob Turnbull, was a legend in the Regiment. He had waited in the jungle, in the pouring rain, for days before successfully trapping a band of Communists and had won the Military Medal for gallantry. Anyway, for various reasons, there has always been a certain amount of informality in the SAS: the soldiers tend to be older and more experienced; we always work in very small groups where a formal hierarchy is superfluous; and, above all, part of the SAS philosophy is that discipline comes from within – officers and NCOs shouldn't have to impose it. This means that you often find troopers and junior NCOs calling senior ranks and sergeant majors by their Christian names or nicknames. But not Bob, or not in my case anyway, because I found that I instinctively called him

'Sir'. As for my patrol: there was Don Large in command, unflappable as ever; Nobby, a Scots lad; and Paddy Millikin, from southern Ireland via the Royal Signals, who was patrol signaller.

The first week or so after we arrived in Borneo was spent getting back into the swing of jungle operations: getting a feel for the ground and practising our immediate action drills, that sort of thing. This was the first time on operations in Borneo for me, Lofty and Paddy, but Nobby had been there before on D Squadron's last tour and he'd had a bit of a rough time. He'd been on patrol with Lofty Allen, Smoky Richardson and a young Irish lad called Paddy Condon when they'd accidentally crossed the border and stumbled into an Indo camp. Inevitably there was a bit of a kick-up as they tried to extricate themselves, and while they were breaking contact poor Paddy Condon got separated, wounded and captured. This was a disaster for him, because the Indos tortured then murdered him, but it dropped the rest of the patrol in the shit as well because Paddy had the radio.

Well, this had left Smoky, Lofty and Nobby in a bad situation. They knew they were caught up in a complex of Indo camps – and from what they'd seen, it could have held anything up to 150 or so soldiers and terrorists – and because they were lost, the only sure way they had of getting out was to retrace their steps, which would have been madness now because they were compromised. In the end, after several days, creeping about in the thick jungle, during which they also searched for Paddy but failed to find him, they made it to a heli-landing site and were lifted out. The stress and exhaustion of this situation had been enough to put Nobby in hospital for a couple of weeks to recover and there was no question that he was still a bit twitchy.

During the next few months, the Indos had also killed Billy

White from D Squadron and Buddha Bexton from A Squadron in separate incidents, so we were under no illusions that operations were going to be easy. With his usual thoroughness, Lofty was damned certain we were going to be properly prepared. So when our first tasking came up – my first real live operation with the Regiment – I was pretty much confident I was ready for it.

We had a standard routine for operations. Lofty would get his briefing and prepare his orders whilst the rest of us got the basics sorted out: kit preparation, checking the radio worked, that kind of thing. Then Lofty gave his orders, and afterwards we could crack on with specific things that we would need for this operation, get our rations broken down, test-fire weapons, and rehearse patrol drills ready for the off.

The first operation turned out to be a recce of the area between the Koemba and Sekayan rivers, looking for routes and tracks that might be useful for future cross-border operations, and nosing around a village called Kapoet where there was meant to be some kind of Indonesian special forces patrol base. Our patrol was teamed with Alec Spence and Joe Lock's patrols so that we could cover more ground, and maybe support each other if the shit hit the fan. The idea was that we'd cross the border mob-handed, establish a patrol base of sorts, which would be manned by Joe's boys, while Alec's and our team went off to do our tasks. The plan was that we were going to stay there for fourteen days, then we'd reunite and re-cross the border as a big gang ready for our pick-up. Before we left, the OC took Lofty to one side and briefed him.

'You've got one new boy; you've got one nervous wreck; and you've got Millikin. If anything starts to go wrong, don't hang around, just bring 'em straight out . . .'

Well, that was understandable, in my case anyway. I was

very much the untested member of the patrol having never served on operations with the Regiment; and it would be hard not to be a bit anxious if you'd been through an experience like Nobby's, but to know why the Boss was worried about Paddy you really had to see him. I don't go in for all this cobblers about the Irish but Paddy Millikin *did* look like a pantomime Irishman. Five foot nine inches tall, black-haired, brown-toothed and thin, he was perpetually scruffy and dirty – in uniform anyway – making a shirt last three days where we'd all change after one. He spoke with an Irish brogue as thick as porridge, and in the field he bumbled about apparently oblivious to any kind of danger, with his personal kit jumbled about in a mess we referred to as 'Bergen pie'.

But appearances can be deceptive: Paddy had actually been with the Regiment since before the Jebel Akhdar campaign in 1958, having originally come in as a member of 264 SAS Signals Squadron, and although he'd only done selection fairly recently, he had a good deal of experience under his belt. Even better, those of us who worked with him knew him to be the most talented signaller in the Regiment, capable of getting through in conditions where many in his position wouldn't have bothered trying.

With everything ready, we flew into a border LZ in a helicopter and, after shaking out, crossed the border and began heading south-west at a steady patrol pace. As soon as we left the clearing, the jungle canopy folded around us and we were absorbed into the strange twilight of the ancient rainforest.

Most people are surprised the first time they go into the jungle at how dark it is and how noisy it can be. When the first lads from the Regiment had travelled out in 1963, the local commander had insisted that they stop off for a few days in Singapore to try to develop a bit of a tan so they wouldn't stand out amongst other troops: what he didn't realize was that soldiers who spend any length of time in the jungle invariably turn as white as ghosts because of the complete absence of direct sunlight. Now, as we headed into Indonesian territory, I was trying to remember the lessons of the jungle warfare course: trying to stay alert; trying to look through the trees rather than at them; trying to spot any movement or sign that shouldn't have been there.

Most soldiers find the jungle a very hostile environment. You move very slowly because it isn't safe to use ridges, rivers, tracks and paths; you're constantly wet from sweat, rain and humidity, and this means that your skin chafes and your feet rot; and you're under constant attacks from insects, leeches and even the occasional snake. We even had to strain our tea though our teeth to avoid swallowing all the insects swimming in it. Around 1900 hours, when the sun goes down, you stop entirely because it's pitch black. Underneath the thick jungle canopy, you can hardly see your hand in front of your face, but you can hear all kinds of strange noises – insects, monkeys and birds, squeaking, hooting, jabbering and crashing around amongst the trees – which can terrify the uninitiated. Even during the day it's dark and gloomy most of the time, except when occasional shafts of sunlight pierce through the leaves and branches above, casting impenetrable shadows. We basked in these rare rays of sunshine, drying out our clothes as best we could. Paddy would open the radio and try to dry it out. The thick vegetation on the ground means it's rare you can see more than fifteen or twenty metres at best: you can never be sure that you aren't being watched by an enemy lying in ambush.

Worst of all though were the loads we had to carry. We weren't at war with Indonesia, it was a 'confrontation', and that meant that British forces could not overtly cross the border. When we went in to Indonesia, we went on our own, carrying everything with us.

Of course, it helps to have someone like Lofty leading the patrol when you're on your first time out. Unlike a lot of patrol commanders, Lofty also acted as the lead scout with me as his number two, covering his back. I reckoned this was a small advantage because if we did bump into any enemy, chances were that Lofty was so big and frightening they'd try to nail him first rather than go for me. But it also meant we operated at Lofty's speed, and that was a tremendous advantage.

The thing about Lofty – the secret of his success – is his laid-back attitude. He's not lazy – that's the last thing you could accuse him of – but he's not bothered about doing things quickly for quickly's sake. He knew that in the jungle you have to go slowly. For instance, walking alone you'd easily get caught up by these atap thorns – wait-a-whiles we called them. Struggle and they'd dig deeper in. Stop and carefully disentangle yourself and you'd be all right.

The Borneo jungle is good jungle in many ways, clean and reasonably easy to move through, but it has its own hazards. One of these is that the ground tends to be very broken: beneath the canopy there are a lot of ravines, gullies, cliffs and ridges; and like most jungle areas I've been to, there was a lot of crap on the ground, ranging from tangles of creeper and leaf litter up to massive dead tree trunks. Lofty was brought up in the country – as a boy he practically lived in the woods – and while the Forest of Dean isn't the Borneo jungle, he had the woodsman's knack of spotting tracks and paths that most of us wouldn't see. He also had experience in Korea, Malaya, Oman and everywhere else he'd been, and he knew how quickly operations go tits-up if you don't operate in a cool and professional manner. So we went along at a steady pace, stopping when we needed to and getting the job done without hassle or mock heroics. All the time we'd be constantly monitoring our surroundings, pointing out emergency RVs and good landing spots. One of the reasons the SAS is so professional is that they fully understand the need for good intelligence.

The first night we followed a long, gently rising spur up on to a high ridge from which we set up the RV Joe Lock's patrol would operate, and the next day, the three patrols did clearance recces to make sure the entire area was free of the enemy, which it was. Then, after spending the night at the RV, we set off the next morning to complete our task.

But we didn't get very far. A couple of thousand metres past the limit of our clearance patrols the previous day, we had found ourselves at the top of a cliff-face some 250 to 300 metres high, a cliff-face that wasn't marked on any of our maps. We recced about 1,000 metres in either direction but couldn't find a way down and so, with evening drawing on, we basha'd* up for the night.

Next morning Lofty and I left our Bergens with Nobby and Paddy and headed off along the cliff top in our belt order† in the hope of finding a route down. We'd covered about a mile when I saw Lofty pause then signal to me to get down. I slowly sank to the ground, wondering what he'd seen, and then I noticed it too: a hundred metres or so in front of us there was a great crashing and commotion going on in the trees, as something large and presumably unpleasant made its way towards us at high speed. I was wondering if it was an elephant or even a buffalo when I saw Lofty point upwards, and we watched as two huge ginger orang-utans chased each

* *Basha*: shelter (Malay).
† Belt order: escape belts containing water-bottles, an emergency medical pack, rations, ammunition, compass and parang. We slept with them on.

other through the treetops, swinging from branch to branch and hooting raucously.

Well, not something you see every day, even if you are patrolling in deep jungle. In fact, by this time the squadron had already adopted a pet monkey (called 'Scholey' for some strange reason!) but it was only small; the big apes were a rare sight. One other encounter took place on a later operation when the patrol were being winched out of the jungle. I was coming up through the canopy when a problem developed with the winch and the crewman indicated that I should unhook myself and step onto a thick branch about 200 feet above the ground while it was fixed. As I was sitting there, I noticed a large irate-looking orang-utan staring at me, and as I watched he began to become more and more agitated, obviously pissed off that some SAS trooper had invaded his personal living space. After a few minutes of hard staring, the huge ape suddenly came straight at me, scuttling very nimbly along the branches. Perched precariously 200 feet up and faced with 400 pounds of orange-furred muscle power, I did the only thing I could: I shot it.

Even though I was carrying a Sterling SMG fitted with a silencer, the sound of a shot caused consternation down below, and this was compounded when the rest of the patrol heard the crashing of a body tumbling down through the branches. Catching a fleeting glimpse of an apparently human form dropping from the trees, Kevin, one of the guys in the patrol, got underneath it to catch it – or at least to break its fall. Instead he wound up lying underneath a quarter of a ton of warm, dead ape. The usual near silent patrol routine went for a ball of chalk.

'Jesus Christ! Get this fuckin' thing off me!'

The rest of the team grabbed the orang-utan to haul it off and found they had to walk a few metres just to straighten its arms out.

Once everything was sorted out, we decided to take the orang-utan down to the local aboriginal kampong to see if they wanted to eat it. This also proved to be a mistake: to the locals, the orang-utans were pretty much regarded as sacred, and they certainly wouldn't dream of scoffing one. It took a load of chocolate and meat blocks from the patrol's ration packs to straighten them out. A good lesson learned for the whole Regiment.

Not that Lofty and I had any plans to shoot the orang-utans that we'd seen on this occasion but it is good to be aware of the consequences of that kind of act, not the least of which is a great big dead ginger-haired monkey dropping on you from a considerable height.

Scholey the monkey became quite a popular member of the squadron, so much so that it was eventually decided to take him parachuting and award him his 'wings', which is where disaster eventually struck. The first few jumps went okay – he didn't seem to mind the experience at all – but it all went wrong on his last descent when he heard me coughing. Unfortunately, we used to communicate with him by making these sort of coughing, grunting noises so the sound obviously confused him. The upshot was that he started to climb the rigging lines of his chute, partially collapsed it, plopped into a river next to the DZ, unravelled himself from the harness, swam ashore and made off into the jungle, jabbering frantically. RTU* one monkey.

We finished our exploration for that day and headed back to our RV with Nobby and Paddy. Lofty found a decent basha site and we began to get settled in for the night. The army has a saying, 'Any fool can be uncomfortable', and that's just as true for the SAS as it is for some rear-echelon desk driver.

* Return to Unit.

The rations we carried were the standard army compo of the time: meat blocks, packets of rice, boiled sweets, brew kit, that kind of thing; but because we were going to be out for fourteen days, there was no possible way we could carry the contents of fourteen full ration packs and keep our Bergens under fifty-five pounds, which was the squadron limit at that time. So we'd break the rations down, select the bits we liked, bin the bits we didn't, and fill the gaps with little extras to make what we took taste better. Everyone carried curry powder to add to their rice and meat, but lots of the lads might take a few small onions, or even some *ikon billis* which were small dried fish much favoured by the locals and the old Malaya hands from the regiment. They stank like old manure before you cooked them, but when you boiled them up with your curry they were rather pleasant, and certainly made a change from compo.

The patrolling we did was physically and mentally demanding so when we stopped for the day, although we couldn't switch off, we always made an effort to relax as much as the operational situation allowed. We would put up our bashas, cook our scoff and send off our sitrep (situation report) while it was still light, which meant we could get into the night-time routine, alternating sleeping with keeping a watch, as smoothly as possible. It also meant that everything was squared away when night fell. In equatorial regions you don't get much twilight. It's dark very soon after the sun sets and down under the canopy it's absolutely pitch black.

Basha'ing up at this time was fairly easy, because Lofty had got hold of a great big piece of polythene from Dick Cooper, one of the other patrol commanders. This was about the size of my living room and Dick had painted leaves and streaks all over it to camouflage it, creating a nice big water proof cover for the whole patrol that we could string up in the trees to protect us for the night. This left all of us happy, with the exception of Nobby who had insisted on doing his own clearance patrol round the area and reckoned we might as well have put up a lighthouse to advertise our presence. Despite his jitters, we overruled him and while Paddy and I got the scoff going, he went to escort Lofty while he was having his evening dump.

We were getting the curry under way when Paddy noticed a huge pig-fly settling on the underside of the polythene, just near where he was peeling an onion with his fighting knife. Without thinking he flicked at the fly with the sharp end. Disaster! He missed the fly and cut a two-foot slit through Lofty's prized 'super-basha'.

'Oh, Jesus Christ! Quick, Pete, pass me some masking tape and for God's sake don't tell Lofty!'

I passed a roll of tape over and he made a quick repair before Lofty returned with Nobby. It was getting dark now and we were lying under the basha eating our curry while Lofty wrote out the patrol sitrep for Paddy to send out. It was also pissing down with rain outside, but we were all secure and dry under the polythene. Well, temporarily: as the rain continued, Nobby, Paddy and I watched a bulge growing in the polythene just where the masking tape was placed, which happened to be above where Lofty was lying down, having a last fag before turning in. Suddenly *splosh*! The masking tape gave way and the water emptied all over Lofty. In a flash, Lofty was up, brushing water off himself, effing and blinding, and cursing the polythene sheet. Almost as quickly, Paddy was there helping him, rapidly seizing the opportunity to remove the evidence of the masking tape.

'Bloody thing must have split,' moaned Lofty.

'I'm sure you're right, Loft,' agreed Paddy, making frantic

hand signals to me. We sorted ourselves out and settled down again.

Next day we continued with our recces along the cliff-top – and the next, and the next – until we ran out of time. Then we began the trek back to our step-up RV and the other two patrols. It had been very frustrating: we'd followed hundreds of animal tracks which seemed likely to lead us to a route down the cliff, but each one had petered out after a few metres. Quite often, we could see rain glinting on the hut roofs of our target, Kapoet, a few kilometres from where we stood, but there was no way for us to reach it.

We made it back to the RV and met up with the other patrols without any bother, and began preparations for the trip back over the border. By now, at the end of the patrol, we were getting pretty short on food. This wasn't a problem for most of us – we had enough to keep going for the last day or so – but poor old Lofty was getting a bit desperate. The fifty-five pound weight limit was being rigorously enforced, but being a man mountain he needed more food than most to keep going, and he'd also had the experience of two years' starvation rations in his POW camp. So Lofty was not entirely happy at running out of scoff.

But he did have plenty of fags, and this gave him an idea. Alec Spence is only a little bloke so he still had a fair amount of scoff in his Bergen, but he was trying to pack in smoking, and hadn't taken any cigarettes with him, while Lofty – a chain smoker – still had a fair few left. Lofty got a little way upwind of Alec and lit up, and in no time flat Alec was gagging for a smoke. Very soon, a deal was done and Lofty was filling his face while Alec filled his lungs.

We crossed the border without incident and lifted out to our base at Kuching for a couple of days' relaxation before being retasked. To nobody's great surprise, we were to be sent back to the same area, once again trying to find a route to the supposed special forces camp at Kapoet. This time, we had the benefit of experience from our previous patrol – as well as Alec's, which had found a route down from the plateau where we'd found ourselves – and the approach phase of the patrol was no big problem. When we got close to Kapoet Lofty decided that the best way to handle the target phase would be for us to cache our Bergens and get the whole recce over with quickly, rather than spend several days hanging around an area that was likely to be relatively thickly populated.

Well, this struck me as sensible, but Nobby was none too happy. On his previous tour he'd been compromised in just this kind of area, and he was very wary of repeating the experience. Nevertheless, he eventually agreed to go along with it and off we set.

We cached our Bergens and approached the village from the north, moving quickly with all our senses on maximum alert. We reached the river and found a crossing a few yards up from an old disused fish-trap, then moved into thick secondary jungle to the east of the village through which we could travel quickly and without too much risk of compromise. After a quarter of an hour or so we came to the edge of the jungle on some slightly higher ground from where we were able to see straight into the village, about half a kilometre away. We sat quietly for half an hour or so, scanning for any sign of movement or life, but as far as any of us could tell, the whole place was dead.

We moved off as rain began to fall, carefully making our way closer to the village through new secondary jungle. If this was the site of a special forces base, we could be damned sure that this kind of area would be mined or booby-trapped at least, and our nerves were now stretched to breaking point. However, we got through without incident and arrived at the riverbank opposite the village itself. Lofty made his way into a position where he could do a binocular recce of the village while the rest of us deployed to cover him.

And then Nobby cracked.

On his last tour he'd found himself accidentally on the wrong side of the border, being hunted down by Indo special forces, with one member of his patrol missing and probably dead. Now he was deliberately crossing the border to try to find the same enemy and I guess the tension was just too much for him. All he wanted to do was to get away from the danger. Unfortunately, there was nowhere for him to go.

By now, we had a good idea that there was nobody about but Lofty needed to be sure, so the next move was to try to calm Nobby down while he went off to check. He was away on his own for forty minutes or so, poking around as the rain got steadily heavier, while we tried to maintain a watch on what was going on around us and talk Nobby out of his state of terror. By the time Lofty returned, Nobby had calmed down enough that we didn't need to hold him down, but he was still in no state to operate effectively. It wasn't that he was paralysed with fright so much as that he'd just decided enough was enough. 'They're all around us,' he kept saying, 'we're surrounded.'

When he got back, Lofty briefed us that he still hadn't seen any movement or sign of life in the village, but that he hadn't covered all the ground because he'd been on his own with no back-up. Then he proposed that he would patrol along the riverbank, in full view of the village, in the hope of drawing fire, while we covered him from the jungle. This may sound foolhardy, but it wasn't completely mad because it was pissing down with rain, visibility was fairly poor and troops operating in the jungle rarely have their weapons zeroed for long ranges: most engagements take place at around twenty to thirty metres range and weapons are generally fired instinctively. Lofty was hoping that any enemy in the village would see him, but he knew that at the 400 or so metres range, they weren't going to hit him unless they got very lucky. Well, we all thought it was a reasonable enough plan, except for Nobby. The idea of deliberately trying to attract the enemy's attention wasn't his current idea of a good day out. His past experiences had made him apprehensive and now he was arguing that Lofty's plan made no tactical sense.

Eventually Lofty lost patience. 'If you don't get a move on I'll stuff this barrel up your nose and blow your brains out!'

Not surprisingly, Nobby gave in.

We carried on with the patrol, but nothing stirred and, after Lofty had walked several hundred metres in full view of the village, we headed back into the jungle, making our way towards the Bergen cache. Or so we thought. Lofty was a brilliant jungle navigator, but somehow or other he managed to get us lost this time. We farted around for nearly an hour, with Lofty hacking away at a big stand of *ladang* – tall thick bulrushes – before we stopped, sat down, and Lofty had a fag, got his map out and methodically worked out what had gone wrong.

It seemed that he had mistaken a fish trap in the river for the one we had seen on the way into the village. Lofty did a few calculations, found where we actually were and led off again into the relative safety of the primary jungle. Unfortunately, night was falling and there was no chance of getting to the Bergen cache before it became too dark to operate. Instead, we stopped in a suitable bit of cover, and tried to get what sleep we could in the freezing rain with nothing but leaves to shelter us.

Next morning, at first light, Lofty led us straight to the Bergen cache but before we could settle down, he took me off to do a clearance patrol round the area, leaving the other two with the packs. We didn't find anything untoward but somehow, probably the result of exhaustion, we got lost again, even though we knew we were no real distance from the cache. Patrol standard operating procedure (SOP) in this case was straightforward: hoot like an owl and home in on the reply. We stood still and Lofty clearly but softly called, 'Woo-hoo.'

There was no response. A little louder this time, 'Woo-hoo!'

Still no response. Even louder, 'Woo-hoo!!'

Nothing. What we didn't realize was that the other two had heard us perfectly well but that Nobby wouldn't let Paddy answer in case 'they' heard them. Now Lofty was pissed off.

'WOO-fucking-HOO!!!'

At the sound of this tremendous shout, all the birds in hearing range took off in fright.

The response came from close by and we rejoined them.

As we arrived at the basha, Nobby looked up and said, 'Oh, good, it's you. Let's have a quick brew and get out of here then.' And certainly the SOP now should have been to press on back to the border in order to evade any follow-up that might have started, but we were shagged out and Lofty made a judgement call, deciding that we would lie up that day to rest and eat, get back in shape and make sure that when we did the exfiltration we'd be firing on all cylinders. We moved a little way from where we'd left the Bergens, sorted ourselves out, sent off the patrol sitrep and settled down.

Next morning we were in much better condition, and the move back to the border was accomplished in good time. The plan was that we should RV with the other two patrols at the LZ, but it was our task to make sure that the LZ itself was clear. We'd been told in the sitrep from base that the area was free of British troops but we hadn't been at the RV long when

Lofty spotted movement and saw two small local tribesmen dressed in jungle greens and carrying pump-action shotguns. They were wearing the recognition sign of the Border Scouts – a white strip sewn round their hats – and they were immediately followed by a platoon of Scots Guards. Almost at the moment they emerged into the clearing, Tak – Joe Lock's fearsome looking Fijian lead scout – appeared from the opposite direction. Fortunately, both sides spotted Lofty and no harm was done, but it was a sticky moment for everybody.

Alec and his boys turned up a little later and we lifted out for debrief back in Kuching. By now Nobby was much calmer, but it was obvious that there was no point in his carrying on with the Regiment, or the army for that matter. There were two ways forward: a formal report from Lofty followed by official action to expel him, or a quiet word here and there to enable him to get out without a cloud hanging over him. Not surprisingly, Nobby went for the second option, using an old injury to show that he was medically unfit for further operations. It was a shame, really, because he was a nice bloke, but he'd had to face more than he could take and the stress became too much. He wasn't the first SAS man to break down under those circumstances, and he wasn't the last.

Back in Kuching, the lads were having a laugh at the expense of one of the young officers who'd recently joined the squadron, a guy called Robin Letts. He'd gone off on a patrol with Taff Springles and they'd called in at a tribal kampong on the way back to make sure that everyone was OK and do a bit of 'hearts and minds' work. These kampongs consisted of a wooden longhouse on stilts – where the tribe all lived, cooked, ate and slept – with an interesting method of waste disposal. The floor of the longhouse had big gaps in it and all the left-over food and rubbish was dropped down through the holes where it was devoured by a herd of wild pigs below. Just before the patrol left the kampong, Robin asked Taff if he had any bog-paper left in his ration pack. Taff gave him a few sheets but told him, 'You won't need it.'

'Why not?'

'You'll see.'

Robin sloped off into the undergrowth, dropped his kecks and got down to business. A few moments later there was an anguished shout: 'Get away from me, you filthy beasts!'

Seconds afterwards, Robin emerged from the bushes with his trousers round his ankles pursued by a selection of kampong pigs, one of whom had started to eat Robin's turd as it emerged. When they'd finished laughing, Taff graciously offered to demonstrate how it should be done. He climbed a tree, hung his arse over a branch and let fly. As it happened, Taff's turd dropped into a thick patch of undergrowth and although the pigs could smell it, they couldn't find it. Taff helped them out as they rootled amongst the leaf-mould: 'Warm . . . you're getting warmer . . .'

The next tasking we had was a little unusual. An Australian infantry battalion was coming out to relieve one of the Gurkha battalions as part of the Commonwealth effort and would be moving into a notoriously hot sector of the front. As a result, the whole squadron was to be deployed over the border as a screen to give the Aussies early warning in the event that the Indos decided to make a move while they were still settling in. With Nobby gone, we needed a replacement in the patrol and somehow or other the system coughed up Bert Perkins, one of my instructors in jungle training. This ex-Gloster had been captured with Lofty in Korea. Shortly before we were due to go into the jungle, Paddy's appendix flared up and he got hauled off to hospital for an appendectomy at somewhat short notice, so he was replaced temporarily by Jock Griffin.

In fact, with one exception, it was a very quiet and almost restful operation. We didn't have anything much to do except sit and wait for the Indos – and they didn't show up, except for one brief moment literally a few minutes after we'd crossed the border. I don't know why, but for some reason the headshed, the bloke in charge, had specified that on this job we had to send off a signal as soon as we were over the border, which, where we crossed it, was marked by a river. We got ourselves across and found a suitable place to stop while Jock, the signaller, got set up and did his stuff. While we were waiting, Bert and I had to keep a look-out because the other two would be busy and, having tried a couple of positions which weren't really suitable, I was just shifting into a good spot when I sensed something wrong behind me.

I slowly turned round and immediately noticed that the others had frozen: Jock Griffin was sitting with his back to a tree and the Morse key on his lap, his face white as a sheet; Bert was poised in a crouch with his rifle in the aim; Lofty, just in front of me, was staring intently into the undergrowth a few feet away. Then I saw it. Not more than five metres away, through the foliage, I could see the boots and lower legs of soldiers walking slowly past. A platoon of Indos doing a border patrol.

We stayed as quiet as we could as they passed us, hardly daring to breathe let alone move until they were well clear, then we let out loud sighs of relief. Lofty was the first to speak. 'Pete, what the bloody hell are you doing standing there? You should've been covering your bloody arcs.'

I couldn't resist it. 'Your orders Lofty.'

'What do you mean?'

'You've always said, "If the shit ever hits the fan, get behind something thick," so I got behind you.'

'You cheeky bugger!'

The biggest benefit I got from that patrol was spending time with Bert Perkins. Although I'd done the patrol medic course, Bert had been doing the job for years and really knew his stuff. We spent a lot of our time going through the medical pack with him showing me various tricks of the trade, so much so that at the end of the two week deployment I felt as if I'd done a postgraduate medical cadre.

Back in Kuching we got a permanent replacement for Jock in the distinctly misshapen form of another ex-member of the Parachute Regiment, Kevin Walsh, a man with a face like the last date in an Arab's knapsack, widely known as the airborne wart. Now Kevin has had a bit of a mixed press in the Regiment over the years, mainly because his sense of humour rarely coincided with that of the hierarchy. On one occasion we were doing a classroom map exercise in Hereford and Willy Fyfe, our young and impressionable troop commander, came up with the following scenario. 'Corporal Walsh, we're on an operation, doing an evasion, and you fall and break your leg. There's no way you can keep up with us and we're short on ammunition and rations. I decide that the rest of the patrol must continue onwards so we leave you with two rounds of ammunition and enough food and water for forty-eight hours. What would you do?'

Kev thought about this for a moment and then replied, 'Sir, as you walked away from me, I'd put both rounds right between your fuckin' shoulder-blades.'

He'd been on the selection course before mine but there had been a delay on his joining the squadron because at the end of his jungle training he'd nearly managed to chop his own leg off with a parang. He'd been kicking his heels in hospital then recovering in Hereford while we were training in Aden and had only come to join us a few weeks into the Borneo deployment. He'd taken part in several patrols with different teams, all of which had gone slightly wrong and wound up with them being chased out by the Indos. By the time he got to us, as well as being short, ugly and northern – I forgot to mention he was a Yorkshire lad* – he also had the reputation of being a Jonah.

Rumour had it that the only time anyone had been pleased to see him was a few weeks before when a patrol led by Geordie Lillico had walked into a platoon of Indos. Geordie got hit through the thigh, which blew a big hole in his back, while Jock Thompson, his lead scout, got one in the leg, breaking his femur and severing his femoral artery. Geordie and Jock had put down enough fire to blunt any immediate threat and get themselves – just about – clear of the area, but they were in deep shit: severely wounded, separated from the rest of the patrol who'd followed the Regiment's 'shoot and scoot' drill and made it back to their previous RV, and cut off behind enemy lines.

A search was mounted, more in hope than expectation, involving helicopters, the local Gurkha battalion and several nearby SAS patrols (we were on patrol at the time and Lofty had offered our services when Geordie's patrol had disappeared off the net, but we were too far away to be any help). It was Kevin who'd found Jock, stoned out of his mind on morphine he'd pinched from the dispensary and half dead from loss of blood after he'd crawled nearly a mile with his leg hanging off. Jock's a tough little bugger, though: the shock of seeing Kevin's face after an ordeal like that would have

---

* Any speech by Kevin should be immediately translated into a strong Yorkshire whine.

been enough to finish most people off. Thankfully, Geordie also made it. It would have been a terrible thing to have deprived the Regiment of his fun-loving, laid-back, easy-going approach to life.

So, as it happened, the first time that the newly formed team of Large, Scholey, Millikin and Walsh had the opportunity to test their collective abilities was on yet another recce in the direction of Kapoet and the rumoured special forces camp. Once again we went through all the preparations over several days, and although it was a familiar routine by now, we didn't cut any corners.

Over my twenty-odd years in the Regiment, a lot of people have asked me, 'So what makes the SAS so special, then?' (with varying amounts of scepticism and aggression, normally relating to how much they've had to drink). My answer has usually been something along the lines of: 'The SAS is no better or worse than any other part of the army. It simply has a particular role that not every soldier is suitable for, blah, blah, blah.' (Scholey, ever the diplomat!) But that isn't really true. The thing that marks the SAS out from the rest of the army is the meticulousness of its approach to everything it does. There's no point in mounting operations that don't work: it's a waste of time, money and, above all, lives, and the SAS has never had enough of any of those commodities to throw them away. Every time we went out to do the job, we made damn sure we were prepared and ready for it.

Which is not to say that we were fanatics. While we were getting ready for this operation, Alec Spence was chatting with Lofty and told him, 'I wouldn't go out with any one of the three blokes in your patrol, mate, let alone all fucking three of them!' Lofty told me later that he'd thought about this and come to the conclusion that the only thing likely to happen was that we'd all die laughing at some cock-up or other. This was true enough. I only have three memories of that particular patrol: when we arrived at the border LZ prior to crossing, we found that it was a company patrol base manned by a Guards unit. As we were sorting ourselves out, Lofty was ushered away by some character, and we were taken off to a little 12 x 12 tent and given a meal. Well that was very nice, but it later transpired that Lofty had been to the sergeants' mess for the full works: a three course lunch with coffee afterwards! You can imagine the hard time we gave him after that. Throughout the patrol we made him eat separately, labelling his part of the basha as the 'sergeants' mess' revenge.

Once we got ourselves over to the Indo side of the border, the hilarity level dropped a little bit, but even so it was never far from the surface. At the bottom of the border ridge, right in the area which was usually heavily patrolled by the Indonesians and which required maximum stealth, there was a stream about eighteen inches deep and six or seven feet across. At six foot five Lofty could leap across it with ease; at five foot ten it wasn't too hard for me to follow him; at five nine Paddy made short work of it; but as Lofty and I made our way forward to see what was going on up ahead, all we heard was the splash of the airborne wart hitting the water, followed by the unmistakable sound of poorly suppressed hysterical laughter. We returned to find Paddy curled up laughing while Kevin, effing and blinding at him, was covered from head to toe in water and stinking mud. As he'd made the jump, his feet had caught in a tree root and he'd fallen flat on his face into the stream, then found that his ankles were so caught up that the only way he could get his face out was by doing press-ups.

Later on in the patrol, he was the victim of another unfor-

tunate incident after Paddy had gone off to lay his evening
'egg'. After he had finished he was rabbiting away in his
usual fashion: 'Ah, now, that's better, I've been a bit blocked
up but I'm all clear now. . .' et cetera, et cetera, as he busied
himself round the basha. Suddenly, Kevin spoke up: 'What's
that fuckin' 'orrible smell?'

He sniffed around a bit, then groaned: 'You fuckin' dirty
Irish bastard! I'm all covered in your shit!' Poor old Kevin.
When Paddy had finished his dump he'd managed to step in
it and then trodden it all over Kevin's part of the basha;
Kevin had then sat down in it and managed to get it all over
himself.

Something about Kevin seemed to attract these incidents.
Later in the year when we were back in the UK we were exercising round mid-Wales in the Pinkies. The weather was
awful and, because the Pinkies are completely open to the
elements, we were wearing big, thick, quilted 'tank suits' to
keep out the cold. Kevin had been on the piss the night before
and was suffering a bit, and after we'd been driving for an
hour or so he piped up: 'Lofty, we've got to stop so's I can have
a dump or I'll shit myself.' We pulled over and Kev hopped out
into the bushes, rapidly undoing the fasteners to get the tank
suit off. There was a bit of rustling and the odd satisfied
remark, 'Thank God for that', and that sort of thing.

After a few minutes, Lofty called out, 'Come on, Kevin,
aren't you finished yet?'

'Keep your hair on, Lofty, I'm just coming . . .' There was a
pause and a loud moan. 'FOR FUCK'S SAKE! . . . I don't fucking believe it!'

'What's the matter, Kev?'

'I've shat in me hood.'

Three weeks before the end of the Borneo tour, a new job
came up for the patrol. This time the idea was to cross the

border into Kalimantan then try to locate the river Koemba near a village called Poeri. This had been attempted by at least five previous patrols from both D and A Squadrons and none of them had made it, mainly because the area seemed to be largely surrounded by swamps. Major Woodiwiss, the squadron commander, had had to return to Hereford because his wife was having complications having a baby, but he had briefed Lofty that this was a high priority, and Lofty was determined to see it through.

There was a fair amount of excitement in the headshed about the operation because Intelligence was sure that the special forces base, which we'd looked for but never found near Kapoet, was getting its resupply by river. Brigade command's view was that if we could maintain a covert observation post on the river we would be able to confirm this, and that if we subsequently put in an ambush, we would certainly disrupt – and maybe even close down – their operations in this sector of the border.

Preparation was intense: we read the previous patrols' reports, studied aerial photographs, and looked at all the mapping. Then, as usual, we carried out thorough rehearsals of the physical side of the operation, our patrol drills and standard operating procedures: making sure we were all practised in RV and bug-out drills (where you need to break contact with the enemy and fire while moving back); obstacle crossing; and all the other little details that mean the difference between success and failure. Communications were going to be the usual high-speed Morse code using an HF '128' set – a great heavy thing when you included all the batteries and other bits and pieces – and while Paddy Millikin got on with sorting that out we carried out our own preparations. As the patrol medic I had to be prepared to deal with any combat injuries we experienced, as well as treating the various illnesses and problems that can set in very quickly in that harsh environment. But we all double-checked each other's preparations as well. If we'd lost Paddy, for example, another of us would have to take over the radio, so we all needed to be confident that it worked; if I was wounded, I'd have a job treating myself, so the other boys needed to know what goodies were in the medical kit and what to do with them. This may seem pedantic, but it's the only way to operate successfully in the long term, and it's worth remembering that the real problem with the Bravo Two Zero patrol in the Gulf was that when they reached Iraq, they found that their radios didn't work and they had no way of getting back or calling for help. Proper checks by every member of the patrol might well have prevented this happening.

On this operation, I was carrying sixteen days' rations for myself, as well as the patrol medical pack, a SARBE* and my own kit, plus two days' worth of rations for Paddy Millikin who had to carry the heavy radio. Not a lot of room for personal kit as you can see, which meant that the dinner jacket had to stay home.

Spending a lot of time on this kind of operation puts you under a huge amount of pressure – stress, we'd call it now – and before we set off, Lofty took me to one side and asked me if I wanted to drop out. I'd done a lot of patrolling in the past few months and, apparently, Major Woodiwiss thought I'd spent enough time in the jungle for one tour. I told Lofty 'Bollocks!' and it was left at that, though actually Paddy was more of a worry than I was, because he'd had his appendix taken out fairly recently and hadn't had a great deal of time to recuperate.

* Search and Rescue Beacon.

With our kit packed and squared away, we just had to wait for the vehicle that was bringing our weapons from the armoury and taking us on to the airfield where we were due to get a Twin Pioneer helicopter flight up to our forward mounting base, and it was now I hit a snag. For some reason the clowns at the armoury had sent the wrong rifle. The rest of the lads had their normal weapons, but I got one that I hadn't had a chance to zero-in or even test-fire. This was really annoying, and also a little worrying: you need to have confidence in your weapon because your life may depend on it, and my usual rifle had never let me down in months of training and operations. As the number-two man in the patrol, my job involved protecting the leader, who would be busy with navigation and route-finding, and he needed to know that he could depend on me to engage any enemy he hadn't seen. I spent the whole twenty-minute flight stripping, cleaning and reassembling the rifle, and although Don told me that I'd get a chance to test-fire it at the forward mounting base, I still wasn't happy.

Sure enough, when we arrived there twenty minutes later, there was already a helicopter 'burning and turning', waiting to take us off to the LZ from where we were to cross the border. Cursing, I ran to it holding on to my Bergen and the suspect rifle, and from there we were whisked off to the border where we were met by a platoon of Argyll and Sutherland Highlanders.

The Jocks' job was to escort us a short distance over the border then head back to friendly territory, and this they did, leaving us on our own, and me very unhappy about this potentially duff rifle. We moved off at a wary pace, heading west of our true objective for the rest of that day. When we'd put a bit of space between us and the border, we basha'd up. This gave the rest of the patrol the opportunity to give my rifle the once-over and try to reassure me and, to be fair, I couldn't see anything wrong with it myself, but I was still uneasy, and I set the regulator to zero so there was no chance of a gas stoppage.

The next day we continued on the same route. We didn't want to head straight for our objective for one simple reason: tracks. No matter how good you are in the jungle, you inevitably leave tracks that can be followed and we didn't want to give away our target by making a beeline straight for it. Instead, we would aim off until we reached a recognizable point, then close in from there. Not only did this preserve our operational security, but it would also make navigation easier in the final stages of our approach.

It was during the second day that we came across our first sign of the enemy. As we slowly pushed through the undergrowth, Lofty suddenly signalled us to stop. We froze initially, then slowly moved into all-round defence, waiting for him to brief us on what was going on. A few moments later he was back with us, talking in a whisper. 'There's someone up ahead. Paddy and Kev, you stay here with the kit; Pete, drop your Bergen and come forward with me for a shufti.'

Without the heavy rucksack it was much easier to move quietly through the thick jungle, and it wasn't long before I could also hear something, or rather someone, a short distance in front of us. As we closed on the noise, I recognized the faint sound of somebody chopping wood. Lofty signalled to me to stop and slowly sank down into a position from where he could observe whatever it was that was in front of us. Frustratingly, I couldn't see a thing, but I knew better than to move. Lofty squatted down for several minutes then slowly made his way back to me.

'There's about a platoon's worth of Indonesians about forty

metres that way,' he told me, pointing through the foliage. 'They're not moving and a couple of them are cutting branches, but it's too early for them to be making camp so I don't know what they're doing. We'll head back to the others and make a detour.'

We made our way back to our RV with Kev and Paddy, backtracked a little, boxed around to the east then carried on, none the wiser as to what the Indos had been doing, but knowing, because we hadn't found their tracks, that they'd come from west of our route and that they might continue in the same direction and find our tracks instead.

We carried on through that day and the next, making slow but steady progress through the thick primary jungle, but then we began to hit the swamp that the other patrols had reported. It wasn't so bad at first, because round the edges it was only small pools with banks and raised mounds where it was possible to stay dry, but after a little while we started to get into deeper and deeper water, round our knees and sometimes up to our waists.

The thing about this kind of swamp is that the jungle carries on beneath water level. You still have the same tangle of creepers, tree-roots, fallen branches and whatnot that you get on dry land, but all complicated by the fact that you can't see it. This means that progress is slower than ever, that you can't avoid making even more noise and commotion as you move and that you're very visible to any enemy watching the swamp. There's no question that this is really hard graft, physically and mentally, and the frustration of staggering through the tangle of unseen obstructions can be increased by a feeling of powerlessness when you're a follower in the patrol rather than the leader. It can be difficult to remember that your main job at this point is scanning for the enemy and protecting the lead scout, but professionalism demands that you must. Mind you, the responsibility of leadership in this kind of situation isn't all beer and skittles either. Don told me that he developed this nasty suspicion that some Indonesian with a machine-gun was sitting there quietly laughing at us, waiting for him to get us into the perfect position to finish us off. Luckily for us he was wrong.

What was also worrying was that there was a fairly obvious 'high-tide' mark on the trees around where we were – and it was several metres above us! The danger wasn't so much from drowning, though that isn't impossible, but that in a heavy storm we might quickly find ourselves cut off by the water a long way behind enemy lines. It also meant that all kinds of jungle rubbish was sticking out of trees and bushes at a height where you wouldn't expect to see it, adding to the difficulty of moving.

We spent the next three days probing gently south trying to find a way through to the elusive river – and bloody knackering it was too! At one point, I'd gone with Don to check out a potential route, leaving Paddy and Kevin behind. As I waited twenty metres back from Don, watching him standing waist deep, pondering our next move, I suddenly had a flashback to the cowboy films we used to see at the pictures on a Saturday morning.

'Hey, Don,' I whispered, 'I hope we're the goodies.' He was lost in thought and it took him a few seconds to respond.

'What? What do you mean?' I shuffled over to where he was standing.

'I hope we're the goodies, because they always win. If we're the baddies, chances are we'll finish up with our hats floating on top of this lot.' Don started laughing, very quietly.

In all, we spent four days splashing around the swamp, trying to find a way through to the river. We knew we were close to our objective: sometimes we could hear diesel engines as launches ploughed up and down the open water. Once or twice, we even felt the wash of the boats going past.

When we actually found the river, it was almost an accident. We reached a low ridge of dry ground and made our way up onto it. From the top it opened up into what was obviously a disused and fairly overgrown rubber plantation, but through the more widely spaced trees we could see open water.

This took us into phase two of the operation. Our job now was to find a suitable position to establish an observation post that would allow us to watch the river without ourselves being visible from any angle. Don did a quick recce down to the riverbank and soon found a perfect position for us: a dried-up ditch surrounded by bushes, which offered a commanding view over a bend in the river, giving us the opportunity to see up- and downstream. The only danger of being observed was from a position back the way we had come; and that would only be when we took up our ambush positions. All in all, we were well set up.

We settled ourselves in and began the normal routine of watching and sleeping, waiting for some customers to turn up. We didn't have to wait long – the river was obviously a major thoroughfare – and there was evidently a military camp within a kilometre of us, given the number of transports that chugged past us. There were also a few fish-traps staked out in the water not far from us, and this was a little worrying because it was quite likely that someone would turn up to empty them from time to time. Despite this, Don was keen to make sure that we were ready for our 'bug-out' and, on his instructions, we brewed up tea every few hours, smoked, and made good hot meals each evening while we waited there. This was a far cry from the 'hard routine' that you learn during SAS jungle training but it actually worked: our morale was sky high; we were well fed and physically content; and we were fettled for the firefight and evasion that we knew was coming.

We spent four days sitting on the riverbank, watching oblivious Indonesians go past, reporting everything that moved on the river and waiting for the inevitable contact. The only really tense moment came when a couple of fishermen turned up to check the traps, unfortunately while Kevin was lurking close to the water's edge filling his water bottle. He was in decent cover but the bottle – on a length of paracord – was clearly visible to anyone looking in the right direction.

As it turned out, the two fishermen were concentrating too hard on the more important task of feeding their families to scope for enemy soldiers and their equipment, and they moved off without spotting him.

When Don decided that we'd been there long enough, he sent a signal back to Kuching requesting permission to move to our secondary task: the ambush. At this point there was a bit of a fumble. This was 1965 and the biggest thing in films was Sean Connery as James Bond. Lofty decided to cut short the usual cumbersome retasking request and got Paddy to send 'Request 00 licence'. In other words, a 'licence to kill'. Now this might seem a bit childish but, in reality, it was perfectly straightforward and comprehensible. Apart from sitreps and sighting reports, the only message that the Ops Room were expecting from us was one asking permission to mount our ambush and bug-out. Well, this was what we thought, and this was what everyone in the Ops Room thought as well. Everyone, that is, except the ops officer himself. Instead of a succinct 'yes' or 'no', what we got was a long-winded request for clarification, which meant wasted time as this was decoded and our reply encoded and sent off.

For patrols in the field, the farting about they did in the Ops Room could become a real pain in the arse. Operational security and integrity is very important to SAS-type operations, but you also have to be efficient, flexible and helpful with the troops on the ground, otherwise they lose confidence in you. One ops officer, who shall remain nameless, took operational security so seriously that he, quite rightly, never allowed anyone to see the operations map he maintained in his office in case it compromised the locations of patrols. Whenever anyone knocked on his door there was much elaborate folding and tucking of the heavy blue curtain that covered his map so that you never saw anything other than what you were supposed to see. All very well and good, until he took the map with him for a helicopter border recce, leaned out of the window to get a shufti and dropped the map, fully marked and on the wrong side of the border. Whoops-a-daisy!

In the end, though, clearance for the ambush came through and we began preparations for phase three.

The ambush was very simple. Lofty's plan was that he would take over the observation position whilst we waited in the OP (observation post). When a suitable target came along, he would initiate the ambush by opening fire and we would dash a couple of yards out of concealment and join in. As soon as the target was neutralized, we would make our way back into the jungle and extract back to a helicopter landing site on the border, which we should be able to reach the next day.

The next step was to pack our gear ready to leave. The ambush was going to be fairly easy – the Indos obviously had no idea we were there – but the problem lay with the getaway. During our approach to the river, we had come across several newly cut paths in the jungle that looked very much like rapid deployment lanes for the Indonesian base nearby. As soon as we shot up a boat on the river, the Indos were likely to come piling out of their camp in hot pursuit, and that was when things could turn nasty. Don set a time limit for our ambush: no later than an hour before dusk. If we hadn't got a target by then we would have to wait for the next day. This would give us the time to get out of the immediate area before darkness brought a halt to the Indo follow-up.

So there we sat, waiting for a target with tension steadily mounting. On the last four days there had been plenty of military traffic on the river for us to choose from, but on this one afternoon? Bugger all. Around 1500 hours it began to rain, gently at first but soon we could hear thunder in the distance, and we all began to wonder about our escape route. Would it still be there when the time came to bug-out?

But the sound of the rain had masked something else: the approach of a large motor launch. The first I knew about it was a hiss from Don, who was poised in an alert crouch just behind me. As we watched, this gleaming fifteen-metre boat slowly slid past us, flying the Indonesian flag and a number of military pennants, and we were all simply waiting for Lofty to squeeze off the first rounds and set the ball rolling. But he didn't.

Behind me I heard Kev muttering, 'What are we waiting for? The fucking *Ark Royal*?'

Lofty settled quietly down again. 'Sorry, lads, there were women on that boat. Might have been kids as well.'

There was no argument. No British soldier will willingly open fire on women and children, even if they are in a 'military target'.

We carried on waiting as the rain increased, lightning

flashed and thunder rolled around us. The intensity of a tropical downpour is difficult to explain to someone who hasn't
been in one: the noise is amazing; the crash of water pouring
through the jungle canopy and the hiss of rain hitting the
river drown out almost everything. We could have been
shouting to each other and no one on the river would have
heard us. As it was, I can now reveal that this was the first –
and possibly only – SAS ambush conducted with musical
accompaniment. Paddy had been doing something with the
radio and came across a music station broadcasting a dance
band. So he'd put the radio earpiece in a tin mug, which just
about amplified it enough for us all to hear it, and we were
happily listening to this as we waited for a target.

Just as we reached the deadline for that day, another
boat came into view. Another big one, but much more functional in appearance, with a green canvas cover running
most of the length of it, and a built-in diesel engine. As it
passed us heading upstream, Don could see that its cargo
consisted of soldiers in green jungle fatigues and some
forty-gallon fuel containers. As it chugged out into
midstream, he gave the signal and all hell was immediately
let loose.

Lofty fired off the first shots, taking out two Indos sitting
at the back of the launch, and then we were all in position,
keeping up a steady rate of fire into the passenger area. In
those days, the 7.62mm SLR was still pretty much standard
in the Regiment, although there were couple of lighter, fully
automatic Armalites around for the squadron. Unfortunately,
one of these was in use by another patrol whilst the second
was being touted around as a piece of male jewellery by a
certain officer whose job at that time kept him well away
from the action. Even so, we weren't that bothered because
the big 7.62 rounds from our SLRs had awesome stopping

power: when you hit someone, you flattened them, and they could easily punch through several bodies, as well as a wooden bench or two, before they even began to slow down. Not surprisingly, no fire came back. In between the crashes of our rifles, all we could hear were the shouts and screams of the terrified Indos as our bullets tore through the flimsy boat.

Bugger! Sure enough, after firing four rounds my dodgy rifle got a stoppage. I knew it wasn't a gas problem because the regulator was set at zero but I didn't have time to set up an inquiry. Instead I had to cock it by hand after each round: not a big difficulty for someone who'd done his basic training with the old, bolt-actioned Lee-Enfield number 4 rifle, but a stupid situation nonetheless, and one that should never have happened.

Only a few seconds after Lofty fired the first round, it was all over. The noise of the ambush had temporarily frightened the jungle into silence, broken only by the hiss of rain on the river. No sound came from the boat as it drifted in the current, smoke pouring from beneath the canvas tarpaulin. As we changed magazines for the bug-out, a body rolled heavily into the water, then there was the *thud* of a fuel explosion from the rear of the boat.

Now it was time to move.

The drill was that Paddy and Kevin would pull back first, taking a position where they could cover me and Don as we scooted back through the rubber plantation to the comparative safety of the jungle. There was a slim chance that the ambush hadn't been heard because of the ferocity of the storm, but we couldn't count on it, and we had to accept that the Indo follow-up could be on us very quickly.

Kevin and Paddy were back in cover and now it was time for me and Don to get a shift on. We started running when, to my horror, Don did a fast about-turn and ran back towards the ambush position. My first thought was that we were cut off, but then I saw Don was getting his handy collapsible water-bag, which he'd left behind. He emptied it, rolled it up, and stuffed it down his shirt. He ran back past me saying, 'They ain't getting that!'

I'd nearly shat myself. 'Lofty, you bastard!'

We made good time bugging out from the ambush because the rain continued to crash down, which masked the sound of our movement. The only delay occurred when we came to the cut-off lane, which lay across our route back at the closest point to the Indo camp. Lofty, in the lead scout position, caught a sudden movement directly in front of him. I stopped and he carefully moved forward to the fallen tree where he'd seen the movement. As he got there, a great big cobra reared up at him, hissed then disappeared off into the undergrowth. He gave me the signal for 'snake', stepped over the log and carried on. I, in turn, passed the signal to Paddy who was behind me.

A little bit later, we stopped for a quick breather and Kev, the last man in the patrol, asked Don what the interruption had been. When Don told him, he went ballistic. Paddy hadn't passed on the message and Kev had a bit of a thing about snakes. 'You fuckin' Irish bastard! I might've been scoffed.'

Kevin hated snakes. On one long operation we were due to be resupplied by airdrop but, through simple bad luck, the resupply bundle with all our fresh rations got hooked up in the trees. This left us with a problem because we were going to have to attempt to survive off the jungle for several days whilst still attempting to fulfil our task: no easy job. Even worse, the mail package contained a thirty-pound tax refund I was due! In the end we went down to a local kampong where we knew the aboriginals. They looked after us very well and we joined them in a big cook-up in their longhouse that evening. One dish was a spicy meat stew, which tasted great, and we all got heavily stuck in, particularly Kevin. At the end of the evening we asked what it had been made from. The answer? Python.

Just before last light, well pleased with our progress, we looped off our route and back-ambushed the way we'd come. As we lay amongst some fallen trees we heard the *whoosh!* of mortar bombs being launched. Mortars are terrifying in the jungle because the bombs usually explode when they hit the canopy, rather than the ground, creating an effect like an airburst and showering a much wider area with lethal shrapnel. Fortunately, we could hear that the explosions were some way off and Kev, who'd been a mortar instructor in the Paras, said, 'We're OK, they're firing to the east.'

I felt relieved at this news, but this was punctured by Don, the veteran of Korea and Malaya. 'Why do you think they're not firing here?' The answer was obvious: because this was where their troops were looking for us.

'Shit!'

Despite this, Don told us to get a brew on and a good meal inside us ready for the next day, and we got our heads down for the night, safe enough because only an idiot will try to patrol in the jungle at night.

Next morning we were up before first light and ready for the off. We made good time and soon got into primary jungle – relatively easy going because there's very little undergrowth beneath the thick canopy – and by mid-afternoon we were within striking distance of the border. Now things began to get more complicated. Paddy was beginning to feel the effects of his appendix operation and was dehydrating fast, but we had to assume that the Indonesian follow-up was fairly close behind us.

The choice that faced Don was whether to push on, staying ahead of the follow-up but risking Paddy getting into a bad way, or to stop and call for a helicopter to lift us out, but risking the Indos catching up while we waited. He called a quick 'Chinese parliament' and we went for the second option.

Against the odds, Don's request was granted almost immediately, and shortly afterwards, after we'd gone a little further, an RAF chopper appeared, hovering over the trees directly to our front. Don switched on his SARBE and a few moments later the helicopter was directly over us.

We had no voice communication in those days, so we couldn't talk to the crew, but they dropped a can with a message to say they were going to winch us up. Don told me to go first, but because of the height of the trees the winch line couldn't reach us, so the crewman attached some parachute strap, making a large loop in place of the usual two slings. The winch was lowered, the two slings rotating slowly. Don put the four rucksacks on one sling and I got into the other. This was a bit dicey, as the pilot had to juggle with the helicopter to clear me of the trees, and as he did so, the rucksacks fell off. It could just as easily have been me.

The helicopter carried me the two hundred metres or so to our LZ and lowered me down to be met by the platoon who'd escorted us over the border in the first place. As my feet touched the ground and I unhooked myself from the strap, their company sergeant major handed me a mug of tea, which was very nice of him, and the chopper roared off to pick up the rest of the lads.

It wasn't too long before we were back in Kuching and headed for the Ops Room for a debrief. After we'd cleaned our weapons and had handed them in to the armoury, I grabbed a yard or so of flannelette, the cloth strip we pulled through our rifle barrels and, after a whispered briefing, got the rest of the lads to tie them round their arms. We went through the whole patrol in detail with the ops officer, the intelligence collator and 'Punchy' Williams, the new OC who'd just taken over from Roger Woodiwiss. Once we'd finished what we had to say, and got up to head off for some scoff, Punchy stopped us.

'I don't want to sound stupid, but why are you wearing white armbands?'

'Sorry, sir, we forgot to take them off. It's the reason we've got away with it so long. We've been dressing as umpires.'

It's a tradition that at the end of every operational tour, we hold a party to thank everyone who has helped us and to let off as much steam as possible before we head for home (we also have one when we get home for the wives and families, to thank them for their support), and this occasion was no different. Of course, it's also a chance for the squadron naughty boys to get up to some spectacularly bad behaviour and we were rarely disappointed in that either. This time, the early part of the festivities was enlivened by Kevin, who'd got himself so pissed that Bob Turnbull had had him tied to a fence near where some Kiwi SAS lads had a pig tethered for that night's barbecue. Mostly this was to prevent him injuring himself, of course, but there was some speculation about the possibility of mistaken identity when it came to killing the pig.

The chief guest was the brigade commander who turned up with his wife and teenage daughter, all looking very spruce in their civvy finery. Despite Punchy Williams' and Bob Turnbull's efforts, he inevitably managed to spot Kevin who was effing and blinding at the top of his voice: 'Fuckin' let me go, you Kiwi bastards!'

They moved on to the immaculately manicured lawn and the hierarchy began making polite small talk, with Punchy making use of his most *refained* accent. Now we had a sort of love-hate relationship with Punchy, who'd previously been the adjutant and who was, in SAS terms, a big fat pest. When the party kicked off, I was just as pissed as Kevin was, though I'd been somewhat more successful at staying out of trouble, but it hadn't taken much for two of the other lads, Ken Connor and Dick Tubman, to persuade me that it would be a good idea to empty one of the fire buckets over Punchy when they gave the signal. Consequently, I was lurking round one corner of the house whilst Punchy, the brigadier and company made their way slowly towards me.

They were just round the corner when Ken gave the thumbs down and I stepped out and let fly with the bucket. Whoops! I missed Punchy but got the brigadier's daughter, who was now covered in a rather unpleasant mixture of water, piss, spit, dog-ends, dead insects and all the other detritus that collects in the fire buckets at SAS parties. Punchy forced a grin as I ducked away: 'Oh dear, I am sorry. It looks like the lads are getting a little boisterous. If you'll excuse me, I'll just go and see what's happening.'

Still grinning stupidly, he edged towards the corner and then nipped round it, breaking into full speed (not too fast in his case, the fat git) as he spotted me haring off. The accent slipped a bit as he chased after me.

'Come back here, Scholey, you cunt! I'll fucking RTU you when I catch you, you bastard!'

He didn't have a hope, and soon made his way back to the party where the brigadier's daughter had now been more or less cleaned up.

'I'm so sorry, Brigadier, they're good boys really but they do get a little exuberant . . .' he told them, laughing weakly.

By now, I was on the balcony with the second bucket, lurking just above him. Dick Tubman gave the signal again and I let go with the second bucket: a direct hit! Punchy momentarily forgot himself: 'Scholey, you fuckin' arsehole! . . . Oh sorry, Brigadier!'

The party carried on as we all got drunker and drunker, the Brigadier and his family watching with fixed grins as we did the 'Dance of the Zulu Warrior' as a kind of prelude to the *hangi*.* After we'd eaten, some of the boys decided that we should start ripping each other's shirts off. I was standing watching when Taff Brown, who was one of the squadron's slightly more pukka members, crept up behind me and tore off my shirt, ripping away all the buttons with a roar of drunken laughter. I was sober enough to remember that he had about ten more shirts hanging in his locker upstairs, so I went and got one of those and put it on. Sure enough, ten minutes later, Taff had torn this off as well. I repeated the procedure and so did he, getting through six of his shirts in the process. Then someone tore his shirt off and he went up to get another.

All in all, I spent the best part of that party on the run.

Being back home gave me the chance to get to know Hereford a little better and to resume some of my hobbies, which in those days centred around beer-drinking, betting on the horses and the better class of young lady living in the Hereford area.

It was around now that I met my future wife Carolyn. Thinking to demonstrate my more sensitive side, I took her

* *Hangi*: pig-roast.

to see *Snow White and the Seven Dwarfs*. Everything was going smoothly until Grumpy appeared.

'Look, it's Kevin,' I exclaimed, struck by the uncanny resemblance.

'Shut up, Scholey,' an indignant voice bellowed from the darkness.

The audience, composed mostly of SAS members it seemed, erupted.

Soon after this incident, we got a long weekend's leave and I invited Kevin to come back to Brighton with me. I had a longer time off than Kev, who had to be back on the Monday whilst I had until Thursday morning but, nothing daunted, we went out for a few beers on Sunday evening, and eventually rolled back at about four thirty on Monday morning.

Kev got his head down for a couple of hours and at ten to eight, I woke him, we got dressed and had a cup of tea. Then I took him down to Brighton station about twenty minutes' walk away.

By the time we arrived at the station it was twenty-five past eight and Kev's train was due to leave at 0830. He heard an announcement over the tannoy, rushed to his platform and leaped on the train just as it was pulling out. Meanwhile, I headed for home.

At about eleven o'clock there was a ring at the doorbell: Kevin.

'What happened?' I asked.

'I'm in the shit now. They'll post me AWOL.'

'But what happened?'

'It wasn't the right train. As it pulled out, I realized there was no one else on it. It went four hundred yards up the line and stopped. Then these big brushes started to wash the bloody thing down. I sat in that train for an hour before it moved back to the station.'

I went into the other room to laugh. He phoned the Regiment and fortunately everything was okay, except of course that everyone knew about it in seconds.

My second tour of Borneo, which kicked off in June 1967, was an entirely different kettle of fish. By then, an outbreak of peace was in the offing. Sukarno was gone, replaced by General Suharto in a bloody coup, while the pragmatists of the Indonesian military were in the ascendancy and keen to bring the confrontation to as quick an end as possible, without giving the impression that they'd had their arses kicked – which, of course, they had. In previous months, entire infantry companies, and even complete SAS squadrons, had been crossing the border to hit Indonesian targets and the Indos had lost their stomach for the fight completely.

Which meant that when we arrived there wasn't all that much to do. We sent out patrols to monitor the border but we stayed on our side and, in reality, they were training as much as operations. We also did a fair bit of straightforward training as well, and before too long, when negotiations had reached a crucial stage, we were sent away from mainland Borneo, as a goodwill gesture to the Indos, to the island of Santubong down the river and off the coast of Sarawak.

Santubong was a beautiful place: a small island with a white sandy beach and a bit of jungle. We were given a pile of fresh rations and, for some strange reason, a vast quantity of Merrydown cider. We travelled there in a small flotilla of flat-bottomed assault boats and, once we'd got our tents set up, we named it 'Merrydown Camp'.

But, being the SAS, we couldn't just have a straightforward holiday could we? No, we had to do some training, or at least pretend to, to justify our lotus eating existence. Fortunately, nobody took this too seriously.

First up it was decided that Willie Mundell would teach us how to do assault landings. So I and a few others from 18 Troop were detailed off to have first go while the rest of the lads got on with their sunbathing and swimming. We set off out to sea for a kilometre or so, turned round and then came screaming in towards the beach with the two forty-horse-power engines going at full tilt. In theory, the next move would be to cut the engines at a certain distance from the beach then sweep in all silent and deadly.

Anyway, Alfie Tasker was at the controls and when Willie gave him the signal . . . er, nothing happened. The engines continued to roar and we were still skewering towards the beach at high speed. By now we were in a bit of a panic. Taff Springles was standing in the front, waving his shirt to try to warn the swimmers, and we could see Clancy Bean splashing about in front of us, desperately trying to get out of the way. Fortunately, we shot past everyone in the water and now the only obstacle was the beach. Alfie was still trying to cut the engines but nothing doing, and we piled in at high speed. I was standing near the front and as we hit, I was heaved out into the surf. As I got up, undamaged, I looked round to see the boat half way out of the water with the engines still churning away like mad, and Alfie Tasker jumping out onto what he thought was the beach and disappearing under the water.

So that was the end of beach landings. Next came fishing.

Ray Allen, a big Yorkshire lad, fixed up an ammunition box full of plastic explosive and he, Alan Lonney and a couple of others took the boat out to where they thought the fish were. First they dropped Ray on a little island and then couldn't get him off because the tide had gone out; then an hour or so later when they had retrieved him, they took the great bomb out to where they thought the fish were, lit the blue touch-paper, dropped it in . . . and stalled the boat. They calmly tried to get it going again, then they panickingly tried to start it up, then one of them dived over the side and started swimming. With a few seconds to go, the engine started and the boat almost stood on its tail as they pulled away from the danger zone, slowing down to pick up the swimmer. Alas, it was too late. With a huge roar the depth charge went off and a vast column of water rose up and flipped them all into the sea. They all swam back to the beach clutching on to the upturned boat. No fish were caught.

So no more fishing. Time for water-skiing.

Willie said, 'Who fancies a drag on the planks?' and I thought, Yeah, why not? So I got the kit on and zoomed out about a mile or so, then I fell off. I wasn't the world's greatest swimmer then and as I was splashing about in the water, I realized I couldn't feel the bottom. This started me thinking, What if there's sharks?

Anyway, Brummie Hassall saw me floundering around and started swimming out to me, and he'd been going about fifteen minutes when he got cramp so the boat, which by now was coming to get me, had to stop to pick him up and take him back to the beach so they could massage his legs and get him going again. Meanwhile, I'd now got myself close enough to the beach that I could put my feet on the sand and I was able to walk in.

Next up was Pickett, who got in the boat, started it up, then fell out and wound up with the boat circling round and round him like some demented shark. And he was followed by Nick who started the boat up, but got the propeller stuck in the sand. When he went to free it he managed to lacerate the insides of his thighs. This probably wasn't as bad as it looked but led the five assembled patrol medics to start fighting over who got to suture him. Nick was followed by the cook, who managed exactly the same thing.

The only option now was to start drinking heavily. We settled down with some Merrydown and I spent the next hour or so doing my 'turn', taking the piss out of each member of the squadron in turn. Then there was a dull thud.

'What was that?'

'The camp's on fire.'

Someone had chucked a cigarette end into the shit-pit and ignited it all. We rushed around like headless chickens for a few minutes before someone got a big tarpaulin and threw it over the burning crapper. That put it out and we carried on. Then Ron Barker went out to see if it was okay, lifted the tarpaulin and it went up again.

'Leave it alone, Barker, you twat!'

Then someone said, 'Let's get the Army Air Corps up here for a party!' Someone got on the radio and gave them a call and an hour or so later, three or four choppers turned up with all these Army Air Corps lads on board, come to spend the night with us. We were all very friendly, giving it loads of glad-handing and smiles until, around half past one, a big fight broke out: SAS versus AAC. We all got stuck in and gave them a good thumping.

Next morning we all got up with our black eyes and thick lips, and helped the Air Corps boys into their choppers: 'Great party, lads, thanks . . .'

Finally it was time to return to Kuching in the two assault boats. We had a bit of a problem now because the shear-pins from the engines kept breaking and we only had one left. This meant that one boat would have to tow the other all the way back down the river. As we were loading the boats, Alfie Tasker handed me the pin. I dropped it, and watched with my heart in my mouth, as it spiralled out of sight into the blue water. Oh, shit.

Alfie Tasker grabbed the front of my shirt. 'Scholey, when we get back, you are fucking dead. You understand that, don't you?'

Two hours of hard rowing later, we were back in Kuching only to find that Captain Mackay-Lewis was missing. He'd taken Punchy's little sailing boat upriver and somehow managed to get lost. He showed up eight or nine hours later, sunburned and dishevelled. We weren't impressed.

'Typical fucking officer. How can you get lost on a river? You go up it, then all you've got to do is come back down again.'

A few days later, we flew out, heading for Singapore. We were in an RAF Britannia, I think, and I wound up sitting near the front. We were bored and tired, but for some reason, I couldn't sleep. I'd read everything on the aircraft, including the emergency card, about four times. By now the cabin lights were dimmed and everyone had more or less settled down.

But I was still restless (the lads used to say I walked to our destinations, moving up and down the cabin) and as I sat there, twitching away, I bent over and pulled a life-jacket out from under my seat. I tried it on and found that it fitted rather well, so I sat there in the life-jacket with a can of soft drink left over from my 'haversack rations'.

After a few minutes of this, the life-jacket was getting a little sweaty and I decided to take it off. But on the cramped aircraft, this meant standing up. I did this and was wrestling my way out of the rubbery yellow embrace of my RAF 'Mae West' when some of my drink splashed on the regimental second-in-command who was asleep in the row of seats behind me. This woke him up, and his first sight was Scholey, stood there with his life-jacket on.

'Bloody hell, Scholey! What on earth's happening?'

I couldn't resist it. 'Sir, we're ditching in about thirty seconds!'

This took a couple of seconds to sink in.

'Fucking hell!'

There was about five minutes of complete panic as the flower of the Special Air Service struggled into their life-jackets, followed by a period of anger and sullen resentment as revenge was plotted. My reward was a £20 fine, two weeks extra duties and an involuntary dunking in the standing water reservoir at Changi Field, Singapore. Oh, well. I did think, though: Scream and shout in a library, and everyone thinks you're a loony, but do it in a plane and they all join in.

The stop off in Singapore gave us a chance to unwind a bit more, as well as allowing the Malayan lags to revisit their old haunts. One visit we made was to an ordnance depot where Kevin spotted a big pile of interesting-looking boots.

' 'Ere, what are those, mate?'

'They are experimental jungle boots.'

We looked at these boots which were a sensible concoction of canvas, leather and rubber, apparently ideally suited to our purposes.

'Do you mind if we blag a few pairs then, matey?'

'Sorry, pal, I'd love to help but those have got to be destroyed.'

It turned out that these boots had failed the trial and no amount of pleading, even with Lofty adding his weight, could get them to give them to us, even though they looked, at least, as though they were ideally suited to our needs. Our problem was that the army issue jungle boots, which in those days were knee-high canvas and rubber lace-ups, used to fall apart after a couple of weeks' hard use, which effectively meant that we were getting through two or three pairs on every patrol. Standard army ankle boots were really too heavy for jungle use, so we wound up using a range of civvy boots, or modifying the issue ones, which was a pain the arse. In fact we didn't resolve the problem until we were given the excellent US issue boots a few years later.

We had a few days in Singapore and naturally decided to have a bit of a drink one evening in the transit accommodation we were occupying. After a couple of bottles of Tiger, we began to run short of booze until somebody spotted Kevin's duty frees lying on his bed. A single man at this stage, Kevin hadn't bothered to waste any money on scent or anything poncy like that, but instead had opted for six bottles of vodka, reasoning that the import duty wouldn't be too severe. It didn't take us long to get through it but we were sober enough at the end to top up the bottles with water.

Somehow I'd imagined that he wouldn't spot the switch until after we'd got back to camp, but I suppose that going through customs and having to fork out several quid in import duty had reminded him that he was carrying dangerous cargo. Anyway, he opened a bottle in the coach just after we left Lyneham. It's hard to imagine the shock he must have received, taking a swig of what he thought was going to be export strength vodka and finding it was Singaporean tap water.

'FUCKING HELL! YOU FUCKING BASTARDS!'

Just south of Hereford, on the A49 Ross Road, there's a hill called the Callow. As you come over the top of it you can see Hereford in front of you, and Dinedor hill off to the left. In those days in the sixties, when we were alternating between tough operational tours, where our lads were being killed and wounded, every time we came back over the Callow, the bus broke out in cheers. We'd made it; we'd survived; and, above all, we were home.

BORNEO CAMPAIGN – D SQUADRON TOUR 1965

Myself and patrol with local border scouts (used as jungle trackers) awaiting resupply by helicopter. Landing zone secured by other personnel.

Taken by Lofty (patrol commander) en route to a forward base for infiltration in to enemy territory on fourteen day operation.

17 Troop test-firing weapons ready for ops the following day. Nothing is left to chance.

Landing zone secure, patrol wait for lift-out.

Back to base HQ for debrief. I'm waiting for 'thumbs-up' from pilot – the last man to emplane.

Fast extraction winch-out, used when patrol are in immediate danger.

Base signallers being moved to a forward base.

Myself with Tony Ball and Pete Hogg enjoying three days R&R in Kuching.

The parachuting monkey, nicknamed 'Scholey'– cheek! After seven jumps he was appointed freefall troop mascot.

ADEN CAMPAIGN – D SQUADRON

18 Troop await heli-lift to support 16 Troop who are engaged in firefight with enemy.

Five-minute breather en route to secure the high ground in Radfan mountains while Royal Marines do low ground sweep to flush out enemy.

18 Troop preparing to move to intercept enemy who are advancing to attack forward base. 16, 17 and 19 Troops already en route – no problem!

Jungle training with D Squadron in Malaysia. No risk of booby traps or ambushes.

Myself accepting presentation of regimental shield to D Squadron from R.C.T. who covertly transported patrols to operational drop-off points in Aden.

Myself, with George as cover man, visual tracking in Malaysia, 1970s.

CHAPTER FIVE

My first trip out to Aden with the SAS came a little while after I'd joined the D Squadron Mobility Troop. We'd gone out there for a training exercise, getting to know the Pink Panthers, getting to know desert conditions and practising cooperation with the RAF, but although there was a certain amount of tension in the area at the time and A Squadron had lost a couple of guys in a kick-up in the Radfan mountains, we weren't out there to start mixing it.

Even so, it was tough going. I was the new boy in the troop, so I was on a steep learning curve and trying to keep up with all the information being fired at me by the old lags as I was assimilated into the troop and the squadron. Of course, I wasn't a new boy in Arabia – I'd seen operations in Kuwait and garrison duties in Bahrain when I was with 2 Para – but now I was SAS and it was all change.

We'd no more dipped our toe into Aden than we were back in Hereford and preparing for the squadron deployment to Borneo, which of course meant getting our minds round the concepts and techniques essential for jungle warfare and putting the desert stuff on the back-burner.

Even so, events in Aden were clearly building up a head

of steam and it didn't take the brains of an archbishop to understand that there was every likelihood of us becoming further involved. Oddly enough, though, it wasn't until 1966 that D Squadron got there in an operational capacity whilst the problems had actually started years before. In fact things had been pretty uncomfortable for the British in the Middle East for a long time, going back even to the First World War and Lawrence of Arabia. Way back then, most of the Middle East, Arabia and the Persian Gulf had been ruled by the Ottoman Empire from Turkey. But Turkey had been coming apart at the seams for years and the First World War – Turkey joined in on Germany's side – changed everything. In 1916, with British help, the Arabs, led by King Hussein of Jordan's great-grandfather, had revolted against the Turks and begun the process of pushing them out of the Arabian peninsula. This was where Lawrence of Arabia came in: he was military adviser to one of the main Arab commanders and led the Arab army when they captured the key objectives of Aqabah, the port at the top of the Red Sea, and Damascus.

When the war came to an end, though, the Arabs didn't get half of what we'd promised them at the start of the revolt. Instead, the usual series of dirty deals was played out, and a good chunk of the Middle East was carved up between Britain and France. So – surprise, surprise – it was hard to find a huge number of Arabs with anything nice to say about us.

Britain stuck it out through the twenties and thirties, with garrisons in Egypt, Palestine, Aden, Iraq and in some of the Gulf States: but even back then these states were troublesome, and after the Second World War, when Britain was on its uppers, the writing was on the wall and we had to start to pull out.

So by the beginning of the 1960s, everything had pretty much changed. We had a garrison in Bahrain on the Persian Gulf, a garrison in Aden at the southern end of the Arabian peninsula, which was well positioned for stop-offs for aircraft and ships going further east to Hong Kong and Singapore, as well as a scattering of airbases in friendly countries like Oman, where there was often a small British presence in the form of advisers and so on. Aden, which was the location for the Headquarters British Forces Middle East, was a strange enough place. The port and city – which was bustling and cosmopolitan – had been under British control for more than a hundred years because of its role as a staging post for India and the Far East, but the interior of the country, sometimes called south Yemen, was very different. Partly desert and partly mountain, real power was in the hands of tribal chiefs and minor warlords, who were paid by the British to keep their areas in order. If the cash was late, or they were feeling stroppy, they kicked up a fuss; otherwise, they were our best mates.

By and large this policy had worked until the early sixties but with General Nasser making a row in Egypt, and with our old mates from the KGB active in the area, it was only a matter of time before something went wrong. As it turned out, this was a coup by the army in Yemen, which got rid of the hereditary Imam and set up the usual left-wing government instead. Soon after, with Egyptian and Soviet backing, they started moving arms and guerrillas over the Radfan mountains into Adeni territory.

Nobody took a lot of notice of this at first. I don't suppose anyone really knew it was happening, and by the time they did, it had really taken hold. Grenades were being thrown about, district officers were being shot at and everything had turned totally pear-shaped. A state of emergency was declared at the end of 1963 and shortly after that the UK government announced that they were planning to give Aden independence, though keeping hold of the British bases.

This was meant to pacify the rebels, but it had no real effect, so the next big plan was to use military force. We'd put together a small colonial army in Aden, the Federal Regular Army (or FRA), and they cobbled together a task force and sent it up into the hills. Seeing this lot coming, the rebels hightailed it for the safety of the Yemen and all went quiet.

Unfortunately, having occupied their positions in the mountains, the FRA didn't have much idea of what they were supposed to do next. They didn't collect any intelligence, they didn't do any 'hearts and minds' work and they didn't catch any baddies. When they eventually sloped off to their barracks, the rebels came straight back over the border.

After this first cock-up it was time for a second approach. The headshed in Aden had a rethink and decided that they would use British forces as well as the FRA, and this, by a complicated string of coincidences, was how the SAS got involved.

At this time in 1964, the officer commanding A Squadron was Peter de la Billière (known generally as DLB – which is short for 'Dead Letter Box' – or to me as 'ta-ra-ra boom-de-ay', a nickname that, strangely, hadn't much amused him). He'd previously had a staff job in Aden and when the Radfan operation was being set up happened to be out there setting up a training exercise for A Squadron. The plan involved using two battalions of the FRA together with 45 Commando Royal Marines (with B Company of 3 Para, then based in Bahrain, attached to them) to secure two hill objectives in rebel-held areas, one of which would be taken in an airborne assault by the Paras. DLB thought that his lads might be used to secure the Paras' DZ (Drop Zone).

By all accounts it was rather a rushed job. A Squadron arrived in Aden in April 1964 and after a couple of days moved up to a forward base in the mountains. Then they set about patrolling to get the lie of the land and acclimatize themselves to the harsh conditions. This meant trying to operate in extreme heat – it could easily reach 120° Fahrenheit during the day – with just the water you could carry: a couple of two pint bottles on your belt, maybe, and another container in your Bergen. This, of course, restricted the scope of the operations they could mount.

After less than a week of patrolling, DLB was given orders for his main operation: sending an eight man patrol to secure 3 Para's DZ at the head of the Wadi Taym, which was well inside rebel-held territory. They were going to lie up for a period, observing enemy activity, before emerging to clear and mark their target.

The operation started at last light on 29 April 1963 with a heli drop-off of the patrol 5000 metres inside rebel-held territory. They began to move forwards towards their LUP (lying up point) when they hit their first problem: Nick Warburton, the patrol signaller, fell ill with suspected food poisoning. Although he managed to keep going, he slowed the patrol down and it became evident that they couldn't reach their objective before daybreak.

This meant that they were up shit creek without a paddle in sight. If they were spotted, it was likely that they would be outnumbered and quite possibly overwhelmed by the rebels – referred to by the press as the 'Red Wolves' – who were known to be in the area. They were well out of range of artillery support and probably not strong enough to secure an LZ for helicopter extraction: all in all, a poor situation to find themselves in. After a quick Chinese parliament, they decided to try to find an emergency lie-up and wait it out.

Disaster struck during the late morning when an armed man wandered up to where they were hiding. Almost inevitably he saw them and did a runner, and with a split second to make the decision, Geordie shot him.

The killing of the man started an immediate reaction from the locals who, not surprisingly, were keen to find out what was going on in their area. As they approached, a firefight developed and the patrol was soon trapped by an increasing number of angry rebels. For the rest of the day there was a stalemate. Once the shooting had started the patrol had called for air support and there was a steady shuttle of RAF jets coming in to strafe and rocket the guerrillas, but the rebels' firepower was sufficient to keep the SAS pinned down.

Darkness meant the end of close air support but it also gave the patrol the opportunity to make a break for it. By now the enemy snipers were closing on the SAS position, and as the patrol prepared to move, Warburton, the signaller, was shot in the head and killed. A few minutes later, as they left their shelter, the patrol commander, a young captain called Robin Edwards, was also killed.

Leaving the two bodies, the patrol skirmished towards a wadi that would cover their retreat to safety. During the remainder of the night, they fought their way back along the wadi, occasionally 'back-ambushing' their track to deter follow-up by the rebels. By morning, the survivors were safely back in friendly territory. So, not a great start to operations in Aden, but at least it forced the rest of us to remember that it wasn't going to be easy.

But before we went out to Aden, we found ourselves getting a bit of a warm-up in Libya, of all places. In fact, before Colonel Gaddaffi took power in 1969, British troops exercised there quite regularly, going over a lot of the same ground that had been fought over during the Second World

War when the SAS had first been formed. The idea of this particular deployment was to test the Pinkies in true desert conditions, and to get us all up to speed with desert navigation, astral navigation and so on.

One interesting aspect of this exercise was the army's attempt to teach us how to ride camels (better than smoking them). I can't quite remember why – maybe it was one of Lofty's gags – but Kevin was selected to go off with a couple of Arabs to learn the basics so that he could then impart his new-found skills to the rest of us. It was coming up to noon, the hottest time of day in the desert, and it was a tad warm at about 130° Fahrenheit in the shade as we all lined up to watch the demo.

By now Kevin and the camel had decided that they really didn't like each other. Every time he tried to get it to do something it didn't want to, it spat on him, and each gob of camel spit was about the size of a lumpy, stinking dinner plate. After ten minutes of argy-bargy, the camel finally hauled itself to its feet, nearly catapulting Kev off as it rose. Now, following the instructions of his Arab teachers, he walloped it on the arse with a cane. This should have put it into a steady jog-trot but instead the camel bolted, accelerating to about 30 m.p.h. as Kev clung on for dear life. It got about five kilometres into the wilderness before slumping down and refusing to move. Kevin came up on the walkie-talkie to ask the Arab how to get it moving again. The response was none too helpful. 'I don't know. It's never done that before.'

An hour went by as we watched the distant black blob through our binoculars, desperately trying to get the camel back 'on the road'. Poor Kevin was in a bit of a state by now, having left his water-bottle behind, and occasionally came up on the walkie-talkie effing and blinding about this and that: camels, Arabs and the army mostly. Then, suddenly, we saw the camel set off again at high speed in our direction, dragging Kevin behind it. Not long afterwards, he returned, knackered, battered and thirsty.

'Hello, Kev, back with us?'

'I am never going on a fuckin' camel again. Anyone who wants me to can fuck off!'

'How did you get it moving?'

'The bastard. I shouted at it, pleaded with it . . . in the end I stuck a hexi-block under it and lit it, that got the fucker going!'

Which was the last time we experimented with camels on that trip.

Much of the training in Libya involved driving out into the sand sea, navigating from point to point, and learning the technique for keeping the vehicles from bogging into the sand. Experience showed us that the areas around the top of the dunes tended to be very soft and if we weren't going fast enough, we would almost inevitably bog in up to the axles, whereas a fast approach gave us enough momentum to get over the top and start down the other side. This usually worked except, of course, for the one occasion when the crest of the dune turned out to be rock-hard and the Pinkie took off like Evel Knievel. So far so good, but then the tail hit the sand on the way down and damn nearly flipped the whole thing through 180 degrees. Kev was thrown forwards and would have fallen over the front had Lofty not grabbed him by his belt and pulled him in. We reached the bottom and Paddy slammed on the brakes, at which point Kevin really did get flung out, landing in a small cursing heap on the sand in front of us. Lofty and I got out to check that the vehicle was OK and the next thing we saw was Kevin and Paddy, locked together as they attempted to batter the living crap out of each other, rolling the remainder of the way down the sand dune. By the time they reached the bottom, they were so knackered they'd decided to call it a draw and they returned to the Rover with no harm done. We paused for a brew to calm down and then Lofty announced, 'Right, I'll drive. Pete, you sit in the front; you two can stay in the back,' and off we went again.

Lofty wanted to prove a point now. He started up, got the Rover in gear and set it off at the next dune, foot hard down. As we hit the crest, I decided enough was enough: I bailed out the side and jogged down the dune as Lofty took the heavy Rover through a terrifying slide towards the bottom.

'What are you doing, Pete? Get back in, you fucking coward!'

I couldn't disagree with him, but I can't help noticing from my military service that there are a lot of dead heroes in cemeteries around the world, and a lot of live cowards sitting in front of the television with their slippers on and a cup of tea at their elbow, looking at their pension statements. It's worth thinking about.

Once we'd finished in the sand sea we returned to a slightly more solid area where we worked closely with a squadron of RAF Hunters out of El Adem airfield. This was to give us practice in avoiding fighter ground-attack and added up to fairly useful training: whenever aircraft noise was heard, we went through various drills to disperse the troop, as well as slinging high-priority equipment off the vehicles so that if they got hit, the key stores and equipment would survive. (It was perfectly logical when you think about it – the Pinkies were the biggest targets.) The Hunters took gun camera film rather than actually shooting, and these were passed on to us so that we could make our own tactical appreciations.

Normally we stopped at midday when it became too hot to

train, but we would always take a shot of the sun to determine our position and then laager up (as opposed to lagering-up, which we generally did after operations), positioning the vehicles facing outwards for easy dispersal. When it had cooled, we would continue, making our way from RV to RV, relying on astral navigation to fix our position.

When evening came the temperature was quite pleasant and at night it was actually icy. This brought on a problem that Kevin was having with his back. He'd injured it parachuting some time before and his various exploits with camels and Rovers had made it worse, so much so that he was having difficulty sleeping. One morning, Don asked me if I could give him something to help him. I broke out the medical pack, pulled out a bottle of tablets and passed four to Kev.

'Here you go, mate, get these down your neck.'

He shovelled the tablets into his mouth and as I put the bottle back in the medical kit I glanced at the label. Bollocks!

'Kev, spit 'em out *now*!'

'Why?'

'Because you'll be dead in an hour if you don't.' He would have been too. I'd given him the wrong pills.

'You fucking prat, Scholey!'

He spat them out and I gave him two different ones, which he swallowed.

'What were those, then, Scholey?'

'Piriton.'

'What are they for?' he asked suspiciously.

'Bites and stings,' I said, tongue-in-cheek.

'What the fuck do I want those for?'

'Lofty said your back's been bit.'

'You arsehole, he said my back's in shit.'

'Well,' I said jokingly, 'you might have swallowed a bee.'

At night, we buried our water-bottles in the sand and, by morning, the water would be almost ice cold. As he crawled back to his vehicle Don said, 'I'll fix your back, Kev.'

'How?'

'Like this,' and he chucked a mug of water over him. Kev's back straightened up stiff as a board. He let fly a fusillade of swearing as the whole troop collapsed into fits of laughter.

This wasn't the last time that Kev faced a problem with medication. A few years later, stricken with constipation, he'd gone to the MO for help. The doctor gave him some enormous suppositories to ease things along. A couple of days later, Kev returned.

'How are the guts, Kevin?'

'Still the same. For all the good them pills have done, I might as well have shoved 'em up me arse!'

That evening, as night fell again in the open desert, the perennial problem of officers evacuating their bowels in the presence of the common soldiery reared its ugly head, so to speak. Willy Fyfe, our twenty-year-old troop commander, took himself quietly off into the privacy of the desert for his evening constitutional and was straining hard when evil Corporal Springles nailed him with one of the vehicle search-lights.

We set off early next morning and, around ten o'clock, stopped for a brew. *Whooooooosh!* A pair of Hawker Hunters appeared from nowhere and screamed over us before pulling up into a steep climb. The pilot came up on the radio. 'Gotcha that time, Don!'

They certainly had. As they circled he called us again: 'Line up your vehicles and I'll take a photo.'

We lined them up and he came over again, so low that the picture shows me covering my ears against the noise.

Taff Springles, still pleased with himself for catching Willy with his pants down, now ostentatiously went for a dump. He casually dropped his kecks and squatted down, giving it full steam ahead, but then leaped to his feet.

'AAAARGH! FUCKING HELL!'

Alas, poor Taff: being notably well hung, his enormous cobblers had made contact with a sizzling rock, raising a blister half as large again.

After three weeks or so, the fun and games came to an end and we drove to El Adem to prepare for our return to the UK. Checking on a map I saw that we were only twenty miles or so from Tobruk, so I borrowed one of the Pinkies and a few of us headed on down to the military cemetery there, a relic of the Second World War.

I'm not sure why, maybe just sentimentality or superstition, but wherever we were in the world, we always made an effort to visit any British military cemeteries nearby. And there always seemed to be one.

Lucky D Squadron, we were back in Hereford for Christmas and the New Year, but soon afterwards we started receiving briefings and updates on the situation in Aden in the expectation that we would soon be out there. Of course, normal training had to continue at the same time, and as the troop medic I was put on the annual update and refresher course run out of Training Wing. This period of individual training was always a chance to unwind, not because the training was easy, but because you got most evenings and weekends free. This gave a chance for 'normality' to reassert itself in our lives, although actually, of course, our normality usually meant flogging around some jungle or desert: the domestic routine of life in Hereford was something we only occasionally got to experience.

So it came to pass one evening that Kevin and I had adjourned to the Imperial after work and were just getting around the outside of our second pint on a chilly February evening when Lofty Wiseman – a corporal in A Squadron – came in. He was still in uniform and grinning all over his face as he walked over to us.

'All right lads? There's free beer for D Squadron back at the camp. Want a lift?' He made off towards another group of D Squadron lads leaving us to consider his invitation.

'For fuck's sake . . .' Kev's reaction was no big surprise, but it was an offer we couldn't refuse. We both took a last big gulp of bitter and headed outside where Lofty had left the duty short-wheelbase Land Rover with the engine ticking over. I climbed in the front seat and Kevin – the airborne wart – clambered over the tailgate into the back, still chuntering and swearing.

Lofty jumped back into the driving seat, crunched the Rover into first gear, floored the accelerator and we took off into Hereford, cornering on two wheels as we hurtled through the narrow streets, stopping off at pubs, restaurants and houses, giving D Squadron the good news. In the front I was able to grab hold of the dashboard as Lofty threw the vehicle around, but in the back, Kev was being bounced around like a rubber ball. 'Fuckin' 'ell, Loft, at this rate you'll kill us before we fuckin' get there!'

By the time we reached camp, the party was in full swing in D Squadron basha which had become a hive of purposeful activity. As I headed for the locker room, one of the lads told me: 'On the square, ready to be on the buses at 2000 hours, Pete.' Looking at my watch I saw that we had just over an hour to be ready. No problem. Like everyone else in the squadron, I kept a complete duplicate set of operational kit ready to go in my locker. All I had to do was get my civvies off and squared away, pack a few extra bits and pieces into a holdall and I was ready to go.

Free beer: not a piss-up this time but the codeword for a rapid deployment by the designated 'quick-move' squadron of 22 SAS. Operation Flashbulb.

So at 2000, there we all were, ready to pile into the three old army charabancs which had drawn up on the parade ground in Bradbury Lines. Dressed in our lightweight jungle green uniforms, we had our windproofs and para smocks thrown on over the top to keep us warm on the trip down to the RAF airfield at Lyneham in Wiltshire. By now, the three-tonners with the squadron kit were already on their way, taking weapons, ammunition, radios and rations out to the airfield for onward transport to our final destination.

One of the things about the SAS is that the soldiers are generally older than you find in the rest of the army. In my troop, 18 Troop, the average age at this time was around thirty-two and this means more of the lads are married and settled down. So although there was a buzz of adrenaline in the air, there was also the sadness of separation from wives and young children. For most of the trip to Lyneham many of the lads were sitting quietly, smoking and thinking about home.

At Lyneham, we piled aboard an RAF Britannia and within two hours of the codeword being passed we were airborne, racing from the icy cold of February in the Welsh border country towards the southernmost tip of Arabia.

Engine trouble in the Britannia aircraft meant it took us three days to reach Aden, but gave us time to sort ourselves out into our nondescript operational uniforms, and when we arrived at the airport we expected to be able to deploy quickly up country, without the locals realizing who we were. Our briefing had been that the deployment was covert, 'Top Secret' even, but things didn't quite work out as planned. Somewhat to our surprise, Joe Schofield, the quartermaster, turned up to greet us at RAF Khormaksar dressed in his SAS 'pea greens', complete with SAS beret, wings, stable belt and shoulder titles. As this was sinking in, an announcement came over the airport tannoy, welcoming the 'new arrivals from the SAS Regiment'.

I happened to be standing next to Lofty Large, and heard him chuntering away: 'Fucking thanks for that, Joe, you prat...' To be honest, it's often unrealistic to keep a deployment of that sort completely secret, but even so, we did feel that they might have made a bit of an effort . . .

The next day we flew up country in an RAF Beverley to Al Milah, a small village on the road from Aden to Dalah. This was a camp for the Royal Engineers unit that maintained the road, a graded track rather than a motorway. It was based a few hundred metres from the village, which consisted of mud and rock-built buildings and a small fort occupied by the local police force. The camp itself was literally just that: tents, a vehicle and plant park for the Sappers' equipment and a helicopter pad, all surrounded by a barbed-wire entanglement to keep out any unwanted visitors. Our job was to mount a series of day observation posts and night ambushes in the hope of pinning down and then, with luck, finishing off a gaggle of Arab terrorists who were operating in the area: sniping at soldiers and police, rocketing and mortaring military bases, and laying mines on the roads.

Of course, this was not the first time that D Squadron had been to Aden, but since then we'd been on jungle operations in Borneo, followed by winter in Hereford, and we all looked as white as sheets, whilst the Sappers who shared our camp were tanned a deep brown from working outside during the day wearing just their shorts and boots. As we lined up for our first meal in the cookhouse after we arrived, one of the Catering Corps cooks remarked to Don Large: 'Just got here, mate? Wait until you get up the sharp end.' Don looked down at his own pale skin and replied, 'Son, you ought to see it from the inside.' The cook got the message.

We settled in for the night in our accommodation, which turned out to be marquee tents with a ditch at the end for us all to get into in the event of any unpleasantness. This wasn't long in coming. We'd been in bed a few hours when we heard the metallic cough of mortars being launched. No big surprise, we were all awake instantaneously. Kevin, our resident mortar expert, gave us the verdict from his scratcher.

'Don't worry, lads, I'm an instructor. They're not coming this way.'

His pronouncement was followed by the eerie whistle of the bombs coming down.

'Fuckin' 'ell!'

There was a scrambling sound as we dived for the trench. In the middle of the pitch black tent I crashed into the airborne wart.

'Thanks for your advice there, Kevin.'

'Don't fuckin' mention it.'

Not too far away, the first bombs exploded, and we heard the patter of dirt and spent shrapnel hitting the canvas.

It was a feature of operations in the Aden Protectorate, as it has been in other terrorist campaigns involving the British Army like Northern Ireland, that the enemy, in themselves, don't present much of a problem. Once we were in contact with them, their training, tactics and equipment were so poor that we would almost always come off better than they would, except on occasions where British troops were greatly outnumbered. Militarily poor as they were, they weren't stupid. And, as a result, the biggest problem we faced was finding them. Over the two or three years of trouble that had preceded our deployment, the terrorists had developed a fairly good knowledge of British Army techniques – good enough, anyway, to recognize when trouble was brewing – and as soon as they sensed that anything was up, they got out of the way sharpish. That's terrorists for you, though: it isn't in their interests or capabilities to take on regular troops if they can avoid them, and as far as they're concerned, why should they?

So the key to successful operations was surprise. If we could get in amongst them before they'd cottoned on to the fact that we were there, then we could sort them out, but it required forethought and subtlety.

One of the benefits of the SAS's multi-skilled approach to squadron organization is that there is a wide variety of ways in which the soldiers can be inserted into the operational area. Mountain Troop can lead the squadron up sheer slopes; Air Troop can insert by freefall parachute to mark a DZ for subsequent parachute or helicopter insertion; Boat Troop can bring us in in their Zodiac or Gemini assault craft. Alternatively, as we did for this operation, we can all get in the backs of the RCT's Stalwart trucks as they're moving off in a convoy, then leap out when they're close enough to the area we're trying to get to.

On the day after we arrived we found ourselves quietly climbing into the backs of the Stalwarts in the late afternoon, ready to deploy for an eight-day operation into the hills once darkness fell. What we knew about the enemy was this: there were two gangs of between twenty and thirty terrorists operating between us at Al Milah, Habilayn further to the north, and the Darla road. They were armed with small-arms and light support weapons, like mortars and rocket launchers, and their task was to keep the security forces' heads down whilst they covered the movement of weapons and explosives into Aden city. Our job was to stop them.

We sat quietly waiting in the backs of the Stalwarts until after last light when the convoy formed up and we moved off. Our area of operations had been picked from the map: we were to be dropped at a bend in the road where the convoy would have to slow down anyway, but which opened onto the mouth of a wadi up which the squadron would move before making for an RV, splitting up and occupying daytime OP positions, which had also been selected from the map.

There's a saying in the army, 'Time spent on reconnaissance is seldom wasted,' and that's true, particularly in special forces operations, but by the same token, careless recce can give away your intentions to a vigilant enemy. It was safe to select the RV and OP sites from the map because the headshed trusted us to change them if we arrived there and found they weren't suitable.

From the Stalwarts, we made our way into cover as best we could, staggering under the weight of upwards of a hundred pounds of kit. The idea was that we were going to be on the ground for six to eight days, in half-troop (eight men) strength, and clearly this meant carrying a good deal of gear. The terrorists' standard operating procedure was that their lead scout would carry a hand-held rocket launcher to give them firepower if they got bumped, and to counteract this, our leading scout, in this case me, carried a light machine-gun (the old .303 Bren gun, converted to Nato 7.62 calibre). The weapon itself was nineteen and a half pounds, and with it went ten fully loaded magazines, carried in a vest, but there was the rest of my kit as well: two one-gallon plastic water containers at ten pounds weight each; my two water bottles; six to ten days' rations; a selection of grenades (fragmentation, smoke and white phosphorus); batteries for the A41 radio; and finally, of course, the troop medical pack. We also had to carry Paddy's kit; weighed down by the bulky radio he had little room for his own gear.

We began the approach march to the squadron RV in a long column, led by 16 Troop, D Squadron's free-fallers. The troop commander was Robin Letts who, apart from being blind as a bat, had never operated in these desert/mountain conditions before. His previous operational experience was entirely in Borneo and, as a consequence, he set off extremely slowly, moving at jungle pace and checking his navigation all the time, all of which was entirely unnecessary. With the huge loads we were carrying, we didn't want to wait around. Eventually the 16 Troop sergeant, Mick Reeves, got on to him on the short-range walkie-talkie.

'Come on, sir, you've got to get your arse in gear. We're not in the bleedin' jungle now.'

'Oh, I'm frightfully sorry, Sergeant Reeves!'

Mick took over as 'column leader' and the pace began to pick up, but something was bothering Robin, now at the back of 16 Troop. A reedy whisper came over the walkie-talkie on Mick's chest.

'Sergeant Reeves, Sergeant Reeves.'

Mick was busy concentrating on the route ahead and ignored him.

'Sergeant Reeves, Sergeant Reeves!' It was a little more insistent this time, but Mick continued to ignore it as he tried to sort out some problem with the troop, though he began to mutter something about 'stupid fucking officers'.

'Sergeant Reeves, Sergeant Reeves!' Robin's voice was now coming dangerously loudly through everyone's walkie-talkies.

Mick finally lost his rag: 'WHAT?'

As Mick's bellow echoed amongst the boulders, the entire squadron took cover, with everyone thinking, What the hell was that, then?

With order restored, we reached the RV and broke down into our half-troops, making off at speed for our prearranged OP positions on the mountain tops. It was crucial that we got there before first light so that our positions weren't compromised and we did need time to build protective sangars.* At the same time, a blind rush might have got us killed. In the jungle, visibility is such that members of a patrol are rarely more than five or ten metres apart – any more and they lose sight of each other – but in these conditions, the lead scout needed to be right out in front so that if he came across an ambush, the rest of the patrol had a chance of surviving it, and hopefully of rescuing the scout as well!

The problem was that the ground lent itself very well to ambushes. The only places where it was relatively easy to move were in the beds of wadis, but the sides of the wadis consisted of a range of broken boulders, cliff-faces, scree slopes, ledges, fissures and even smaller wadis, any of which could conceal an ambush party. Fortunately, a successful ambush requires some preparation, and throughout our first tour we got away with it.

By pushing ourselves we reached our position with time to spare and began the hard slog of building sangars from the loose rocks and boulders that were lying around. The purpose of the sangars wasn't just to conceal us but also to give us a measure of protection against small arms fire and mortar fragments. On TV and films, you see this and that weapon being described as 'high velocity' or 'high-powered', and you see the heroes in gun battles dodging behind dustbins and car doors when they come under fire. The truth is that real high-velocity rounds – the sort you fire from rifles and machine-guns – will go through an obstacle such as a

---

* A defensive position constructed above ground.

car door like a hot knife through butter. With a GPMG or a Bren gun and a couple of hundred rounds of ammunition – not very much really – you could demolish a decent-sized semi-detached house in a couple of minutes. Consequently, our sangars weren't going to be much use to us with walls less than about a metre thick and it took some effort to get them built when we arrived at our site.

But thanks to Lofty's inspired leadership, we did make it to our designated OP site in good time, and this despite the presence of our troop commander, Willy Fyfe, who'd arrived during our build-up training.

One of the things you find in the SAS is that a significant minority of the lads have little time for officers, or the junior ones anyway. The reasons for this vary, but it's basically down to the fact that a young guy with a couple of years' experience of regular operations comes into the troop, supposedly as its 'commander', over people who have been there much longer and who have a vastly greater range of skills. The army's the army, and you do what you're told, provided it isn't completely barking, but some of the officers who've come into the Regiment were definitely not up to the job. But, having said that, officers who didn't have much experience of hard soldiering had other attributes that made up for it: a university education, for example. Willy Fyfe was all of twenty years old when he joined the squadron and was placed in command of a troop that included men who'd been in combat in Malaya when he was still in short trousers, but he was fit, intelligent and keen to learn – and, by and large, he was prepared to listen to the advice of people like Lofty and not interfere too much.

But all we learned on that first job was how hot it could get. During the day we sat there, two men to a sangar, hidden under a camouflage net made from six 'face veils' sewn together, observing the low ground, valleys and wadi beds through our binos and being gently roasted as the temperature climbed to around 130° Fahrenheit. We were looking for any movement: men, mules and camel trains. At night we cached our heavy equipment in the sangars and scrambled down into the valleys and wadis to place ambushes on likely enemy routes. Again, even with just our belt order, this was no easy task, because the ground was so broken and boulder-strewn. But that first time out, none of the enemy showed up and we returned to Al Milah empty-handed.

In between operations the form was much the same as in Borneo. A couple of days to rest and recuperate before beginning the battle procedure for the next op. The big difference lay in how we spent our relaxation time. In Borneo we were based in Kuching, a relatively large and safe town with bars and restaurants where we could get into our civvies, go out for a meal and some beers, and wind down away from the military environment. In Aden, when we were up country at any rate, we were effectively confined to tented military camps whenever we weren't on operations, which was a little more constricting. Still, we made the best of it, drinking and eating together in makeshift messes and, in the evenings, watching film shows projected onto a big screen outside the cookhouse tent.

The film shows were popular, not only with us but with the locals as well: they would congregate outside the wire to watch the proceedings from a distance. The big favourites for them were Westerns, during which they would inevitably be cheering for the Indians, but woe betide us if the action was too one-sided. During one scene of slaughter, as the US cavalry dealt with a particularly fierce Indian band, one of the lads went round the back of the screen for a piss and noticed that small holes were appearing in the fabric. He ran back to order the projectionist to switch it off and, sure enough, in the absence of the film soundtrack we could hear the crack and thump of terrorist sniper fire ranging in on us. So that was the end of the show for that night.

But the terrorists were much more than a mere irritant. At 0600 the next morning we were lying on our camp-beds when we heard some small-arms fire off in the distance. It wasn't until our briefing two hours later that we discovered what had happened. Two of the young Sappers from the camp had gone down to the village to fill the water bowser from the well that the Engineers had dug. It was something they did every morning and, from the purist's point of view, it was a mistake because they were setting a pattern the terrorist could learn from. On this particular morning, the terrorists had set a simple ambush, and as the soldiers went about their work, they were machine-gunned at close range. One died, the other was severely wounded. As they lay there, the terrorists had calmly taken their weapons and made off. It was a repulsive murder – not least because the Sappers had dug the well for the benefit of the villagers – but in one respect it helped us: we now knew that there was a terrorist group in our area.

For the next operation we were fairly quick off the mark, insofar as we were following up on the two murders. The format of the op was much the same: we deployed out at night and occupied hilltop OPs in half-troop strength, then waited to see what we could see. This time it wasn't long in coming. Some time in the late afternoon we heard a loud outbreak of firing from one of the other half-troop locations and Paddy, listening in on the set, told us: '16 Troop's got a contact!'

What had happened was that one of the OPs had spotted a group of enemy on the move and half of 16 Troop, the free-fall boys, had been scooped up in a helicopter to intercept them. Unfortunately, as the result of some kind of cock-up, they'd been put in too close and Swede Smith, a sergeant in the troop, had collected an explosive round through his shoulder.

As it happened, the rest of Swede's half-troop were all ex-Parachute Regiment soldiers, infantrymen well drilled in the basics of ground warfare, and with Swede down, they executed a perfect section attack, killing two of the terrorists and taking the position from them.

Whilst this was going on, Lofty was calmly getting the troop ready for the inevitable lift out to go and help 16 Troop. This was what you got with Lofty: he didn't wait for orders, he anticipated them, so when the chopper appeared a few minutes later, we were already down at the LZ with kit packed, weapons ready and everything in order.

Thirty seconds or so later, we'd been dropped off on a ridge-line much closer to the action, and now we were really in amongst it as the scattered terrorists attempted to use their firepower to dig themselves out of trouble. This was little Willy Fyfe's first action and he was a bit overawed by what was happening, but Lofty quickly asserted control, offering to take his half of the troop forward to engage the enemy. Leaving Willy to the rear in support we moved off – Lofty, me, Big Ron Adey, Johnny Partridge and Hughie, our token American (a Good Ole Boy from the deep South on attachment from the Green Berets, who'd come on operations with us against the strict orders of the Pentagon).

We trotted towards the little peak closest to where the fighting was taking place and Lofty went forward to check it was clear. When he'd done that, he signalled to the rest of us to come on forward, with me, carrying the Bren, giving cover from the rear. As Ron and I got closer, we were suddenly enveloped in a hail of dust, rock splinters and noise as a long burst of machine-gun fire hit around us.

'JESUS CHRIST!' We started running like the clappers and got down amongst the rocks where Lofty was waiting, looking slightly apologetic.

'Sorry about that, lads, I could've sworn there was none of 'em down there. Still,' he consoled himself, 'you can't be right all the time.'

Ron started laughing, much to Lofty's puzzlement.

'What's the matter? Why's he laughing?'

'Because he's still alive, Lofty.'

There was still a lot of shooting going on but, frustratingly, we couldn't see precisely where the enemy were so Lofty wanted the rest of the troop to come up and reinforce our position. Unfortunately, Willy decided to put his foot down. Punchy, the squadron commander, was busy bringing up more support for 16 Troop and didn't have time to micro-manage our troop commander who, rather helpfully, came up on the net saying, 'I'm twenty-one today, and someone's shooting at me for the first time in my life!'

Despite this interesting information, he wouldn't let Lofty bring the rest of the troop up to where we were, simply because Punchy hadn't told him to. Lofty's idea was for us to get closer in to the firefight and then, maybe, put in an attack on the enemy's flank, but with just the five of us, it was a non-starter.

Poor old Willy. He wasn't Lofty's favourite officer that day and it was a while before Lofty could bring himself to refer to him without using an adjective beginning with the letter 'F'.

So, with our flanking assault ruled out, Lofty now decided to try to find some targets for us to engage. The machine-gun that had fired on me and Ron had been quite close, but it hadn't fired again and our assumption was that it had been somebody trying to do what we'd done – get to the high ground – and that he'd buggered off when he saw we'd beaten him to it. Then we saw a little group of them about 500 metres away, part of the gang who were shooting it out with 16 Troop. Lofty gave me a target indication and I put in a few bursts but they were too far away to be good targets and I don't think I hit more than two of them at the most.

It's an interesting thing, but one of the questions you get asked by people who haven't been soldiers is, 'Have you ever killed anybody?' That may seem straightforward, but the truth is that very few soldiers can put their hands on their hearts and say, 'Yes, I have killed *x* number of people.' The reason for this is simple: most of the time you're too far away to know. Certainly I've shot at people who have then gone down, but you can rarely tell if that's because they've been killed, wounded, fallen over in shock or simply dived for cover. Even on the Koemba ambush in Borneo, at a range of less than fifty metres, I couldn't say for sure if I hit anybody. I probably did – that's all I can say – and they probably died.

But whether I hit them or not, a couple of bursts was enough to get the terrorists moving into cover sharpish and we now needed another means of getting at them. This wasn't long in coming. One of the Wessex helicopters had brought in a mortar crew and Lofty began to bring fire down on the enemy. Once the mortar crew had got the range, Lofty gave the targets a real stonking, and when the smoke and dust cleared we were surprised to see one of the terrorists staggering about dizzily in the impact area, apparently unhurt. He made a fairly straightforward target and I offered to knock him over with the Bren, but Lofty, who'd been on the wrong end of similar bombardments in Korea, was obviously feeling charitable.

'If he can survive that he deserves a break. Let him go.'

Around now, the chopper carrying Swede went past close enough for us to see splashes of blood on the windows but the firefight didn't seem to be going terribly well, mainly because of the problem we were having locating the enemy. Lofty decided that desperate measures called for desperate solutions: he decided to offer himself as a target in the hope of getting one of the enemy snipers to reveal his position. He pulled the camouflage cover off his walkie-talkie antenna, stood up on a rock and waved it in the sunlight, while we watched and listened. There was a loud *crack!* and an explosive bullet hit the ground a few inches from Lofty's feet, and not all that far from Hughie the Yank's head.

'Jesus, Lofty, do you have to do that?' was Hughie's reaction.

'Don't worry, they're lousy shots, they'll never get me.'

'Yeah, but what if they miss you and get me?' came the pained response. Lofty thought about this for a few seconds then hopped down from the rock, back into cover. Hughie looked over at me and said, 'Scholey, I've never come across so many complete fucking lunatics in one place at the same time.'

Well, with one thing and another, it had been a tough day.

By now we had word from the radio that a pair of RAF Hunter fighter-bombers were on their way to give us a bit of close air support. Lofty got back on the net to call them in while the rest of us watched from cover. In the crystal-clear mountain air we could see them coming from miles away, silhouetted against the azure sky. Watching, Johnny Partridge remarked, 'Don't they look amazing ... Jesus! They're coming straight for us!'

I managed to fumble out my air-marker panel and hold it up to show them where we were and Lofty gave them a target indication. After a bit of chit-chat, they came screeching in to strafe the terrorists, and the last thing the pilot said was, 'You'd better keep your heads down, my shell cases will give you a nasty bump.'

The two planes roared in at us and opened fire with their 30mm cannons a little way short of where we were, before screeching overhead and pulling up. The sound of aircraft was suddenly replaced by the noise of the empty brass shell-cases clanging on the rocks around us. They were heavy enough to kill you if they landed on you so we found what cover we could. After several more passes at the enemy position, the Hunters roared off back towards Khormaksar.

By now the quick reaction force of Royal Marines had deployed from Habilayn, and the SAS half-troops were ordered to pull back onto the ridge lines to act as a picket, ready to hit any terrorists who were flushed out by the boot-necks. One of the 16 Troop picket teams saw movement way off in the distance.

Les was first off the mark. 'Look, lads, it's a terrorist.'

We strained to see what he was pointing at and, sure enough, about 600 yards away we could make out a small khaki-clad figure. Brian Dodd had got hold of one of the new Armalite AR15 rifles before the op – a 5.56mm lightweight weapon with the capability of firing fully automatic, but not really suitable for long-range work – and he now eased it into the aim, even though his target was about 300 metres beyond what was thought to be the normal effective range.

'You'll never get him.'

'No problem, mate!'

Bri gently squeezed off a shot and, sure enough, the terrorist went down.

'Great shot, mate, well done!'

We were pretty chuffed with Brian, but it wasn't long before word came back that the 'terrorist' was actually a

Marine who'd strayed into our area, and had collected a flesh wound in his thigh for his trouble. Oh, shit.

As dusk began to fall, the squadron got the order to pull out. By now we'd cleared through the location and retrieved the bodies of the dead terrorists, as well as scraps of information from documents they'd been carrying and a selection of weapons, including the rifles taken from the two Sappers. One problem that had arisen in Aden was that the terrorists had occasionally mutilated the bodies of their own dead then claimed that we'd done it as propaganda. This meant that if we did get a kill, we had to get the bodies back to HQ and out of the way a.s.a.p. As we were shaking out for our return to camp, a Scout helicopter flew in to collect the dead, and Punchy told Derek Gorman to escort them back.

Unfortunately, once the bodies were piled on the helicopter it became clear that there was no room for the escort, much to Derek's relief.

'Ah, sorry, boss, looks like the pilot'll just have to run 'em back on his own, then.'

'I don't think so, Derek. They're not going to mind if you sit on top of them.'

'Fucking hell, you don't just have to chase them halfway round Arabia, you've got to turn the bastards into furniture as well!'

Well, it was a result but certainly only a partial one, and this became a kind of pattern for operations in the next three months. When we did get to grips with the enemy, we overwhelmed them, but they had very little interest in taking us on on an even basis. As far as they were concerned, the slightest success – a dead or wounded British soldier, or an attack carried out without serious loss – was a major propaganda coup. Whenever we made contact, the terrorists' first inclination was to get the hell out of it as quickly as possible.

We flew out to Habilayn and went to the Naafi for a few beers to wind down. While we were sitting there, replaying the events of the day, members of the Marines' Quick Reaction Force came in and, naturally, we called them over to join us. Brian Dodd was mortified that he'd shot the Marine, even though it wasn't his fault in any real sense, but when we raised the subject with the young booties, they weren't too bothered.

'Actually, mate, you done us a favour.'

'Why was that?'

'The bloke you shot is the drill sergeant.'

This certainly explained their blasé attitude. The Marine thought for a few moments and then added, '. . . and actually, it was a pretty good shot, at that range.'

Brian wasn't having this. 'No, mate, it was crap.'

'Why?'

'I was aiming for his other leg.'

Brian was actually a tremendous soldier and he earned the Military Medal for his actions that day, but he didn't always manage to maintain his sense of humour. Back in Hereford he'd bought himself an old Austin Seven, which he completely renovated over a period of about eight months, spending all his spare time and money on it. Having finished the bloody thing, he was enormously proud of it and made sure everyone in the squadron knew what he'd achieved.

One afternoon, around the time when he was finally finishing his great project, Jock Thompson and I were walking down to Hereford for a pint when we heard a sound like a foghorn going off behind us. We looked around and saw Brian, pleased as punch, sitting in his car and letting off the klaxon.

'Want a lift, lads?'

'That's very kind of you, mate.'

We piled in and he set off, extolling the virtues of his pet car. As we reached the Wye Bridge he said, 'Okay, lads, where shall I drop you? The city centre?'

'No thanks, Bri, the back of Woolies will do.'

'Why there?' asked Brian.

'It's secluded and we don't want to be seen getting out of this fucking jalopy.'

With this Brian slammed on the brakes. 'You bastards, get out and fucking walk!'

Like many officers, Willie Fyfe didn't stay with the troop very long, not because he wasn't up to it but because the Regiment moved him on to other tasks. Later in that Aden tour, though, his time with the troop was cut short in a highly dramatic way. We were acting as the 'Crash Rescue Team' on standby when a signal came in from an infantry call sign in an area called Cap Badge Ridge. The message was that a group of the enemy had been seen going into a large cave.

Two choppers were ready, 18 Troop – us – with light weapons were to fly into the area, drop off and investigate and, in the meantime 19 Troop – the Mountain Troop – were to go on to Cap Badge Ridge itself and ready themselves to give us support using machine-guns and a 'Carl Gustav' anti-tank weapon.

We had a good look around, but couldn't find the cave at first. Eventually, some distance below us, we saw what might be a cave entrance. Willy decided to go down and investigate.

'Scholey,' he called, because, like a prat, I was standing closest to him, 'you and I will climb down and if it is a cave we'll go in and shout to them to surrender. If they don't obey, I'll throw in an M26 hand grenade.'

This struck me as a very bad idea, but that wasn't all: he then told me to get my bright orange air marker panel and drape it around my neck. I could see the rest of the troop laughing and taking the piss out of me, but I wasn't going to take this lying down.

'Why do you want me to do that, Willy?'

'So that 19 Troop can see from their position that we're not the enemy and won't fire on us down there,' he replied.

'But any enemy in the area will spot me a mile away. I'll have more shit fired at me than they did at Dunkirk, so if you don't mind, piss off!' I said.

'That's an order.'

'I don't give a shit. It might be an order, but it's not a lawful command.'

'You're a coward,' he said.

I said just two words to him: 'YOU'RE CORRECT!'

By this time the troop were having fits of laughter behind his back. He then said, 'Okay, no panel.'

Now I had a suggestion.

'Instead of a hand grenade let's get the anti-tank weapon over from 19 Troop. Put that into the cave and it'll certainly get their back teeth rattling.'

'No,' said Willy, fiercely. 'It's my job to go in.'

With that, he pulled out the grenade and half withdrew the pin, ready for rapid use.

Unfortunately, it had been raining very heavily for a few days and the rocks were still very wet. We were wearing Clark's desert boots, which were fine when the ground was dry, but highly dangerous in slippery conditions. There was a ledge in the rock which we had to manoeuvre across before we could descend to the so-called cave. Willy said, 'I'll go first, you follow.'

As he began to scramble across I could see how slippery it was. I started to say to him, 'You're going to fall.'

He'd just said, 'No, I'm not,' when he fell, sliding about three hundred metres down a sloping scree field towards the lip of a cliff. He managed to grab hold of a small bush, which saved him from going over.

One of the lads shouted, 'The bastard's dead!'

A thin, indignant voice from below shouted up, 'No, I'm not!'

Taff Springles called over, 'Come on, Pete, we'd better get down there and get him.'

'Hang on five seconds,' shouted Kev. 'He's got a grenade with the pin half out and it has a five-second fuse.'

As this was going on 19 Troop Command came up on the radio.

'We've seen movement through the binos. What's happening?'

'Our Sunray's just fallen off the cliff,' Taff answered.

'Is he okay?'

'We don't know, he ain't reached the bottom yet,' said Taff.

Eventually Taff and I got him and, with some difficulty, brought him back up. As well as the cuts and bruises you'd expect, he clearly had a broken collar-bone. As we watched the helicopter take him to hospital Kev broke the silence.

'Now,' he said, 'the troop can get back to normal.'

In between operations, we occasionally got to go down to Aden town for some R and R, which gave us plenty of opportunities for serious misbehaviour. One time, after we'd cleaned and stowed our kit, Kev and I decided to take ourselves off on a crawl round the officers' and sergeants' mess bars of all the garrison units. We were chancing it a bit because we were both still troopers in the SAS, but we reckoned what the hell, and went for it, and we found that we were welcomed in some, got slung out of others and generally had a good old time. The last place we went to was the sergeants' mess of the Royal Anglians where, it turned out, they were having a smart function for members and their wives, with everyone dolled up in tropical mess kit and evening dresses. Unfortunately, Kev and I were just wearing shorts, and as we made our way to the bar, the duty sergeant ran up to us.

'Oy, you two! Where are you from?'

We told him the name of our camp and he realized we were SAS. 'Well, you can't come in here with those shorts on!' he continued. I think as he said it he realized he was making a mistake, because as all attention switched to us, Kev and I had the same idea.

'Fair enough,' Kev replied, and we both whipped our shorts down – we weren't wearing underpants – and did a runner. This got us hauled in front of Punchy the next day and we were both fined ten shillings, though he did tell us that the wives were hoping we'd go back the next day for an encore.

Aden was also the first time that the Regiment had really dipped its toes into urban counter-terrorist operations. The commanding officer at that time was John Slim – son of the Second World War Field Marshal Sir William Slim and a soldier with real vision. He had seen the potential for small and flexible special forces units and had encouraged members of the Regiment to acquire a range of special skills which could be passed on within the SAS, thus expanding the number of tasks we could fulfil and guaranteeing our continued usefulness in an ever-changing world.

One of these skills was close quarter battle with the 9mm Browning pistol, which was standard issue for staff officers, military policemen and so forth, but had never really been considered as anything other than a joke in the rest of the army because of its supposed short range and inaccuracy. In fact, encouraged by John Slim and led by Alec Spence, the Regiment had adopted a system which turned the Browning into a real aggressive weapon, combining a rapid draw technique, instinctive aiming and the 'double-tap' (squeezing the trigger twice) as well as various kicks and punches to keep the opposition clear of the weapon itself. This formed the basis of SAS armed undercover and bodyguard skills, which have subsequently been used in Northern Ireland and elsewhere. In Aden, it gave members of the Regiment the ability, when suitably disguised as Arabs, to lurk around the streets and alleyways of the city in the hope of nailing the urban bomb-throwers and assassins who were prosecuting the campaign there. Although I was never personally involved in this side of our operations in Aden, by all accounts they were notably effective, even though one of the more dangerous threats the lads faced was from undercover squads of the various infantry battalions who were attempting to do the same thing over the same ground.

While we waited for our flights home, we were living in flats, four to a room, in downtown Aden. We spent our spare time shopping locally and doing a bit of socializing, winding down after the tensions of the tour with friends we had made while we were out there.

I was sharing a room with Kev, Taff Brown and Paddy Millikin. Poor old Taff had terrible piles and was waiting to have an operation when we got home, but in the meantime was using some ointment to keep the pain at bay. He administered it by inserting the tube into his arse and giving it a good squirt. We also shared lockers, two to each locker. I shared with Paddy, Kev with Taff.

Taff had just finished with the tube of cream when the lights failed. Meanwhile, Kev was having a shower ready to go out to dinner with some friends. He had his shower and shave, but forgot his toothpaste. Rushing back into the darkened room, he put his hand into his locker and got his toothpaste, as he thought.

He came back in spitting and spluttering. Before he could say anything, Taff said, 'Kev, why have you pinched my pile cream?'

Kev said, 'Pinched it? I've eaten half the fucking tube!'

He used half a bottle of whisky to wash his mouth out.

Our first operational tour in Aden culminated, as usual, in a somewhat raucous party which was held, for some reason, in the Irish Guards' Naafi two days before we were due to fly home. It was some time after midnight when in walked the Guards' battalion orderly sergeant: a huge creaking mass of bullshit in his highly polished boots, tropical number two dress with razor creases on trousers that came to just above his ankles, a red sash, a cheese-cutter cap with a peak so slashed it was resting on the bridge of his nose, and, of all things, a swagger stick. He came over to where we were happily partying and, instead of accepting the various jovial offers of drinks, and not realizing that our squadron commander was there, poked Jock Thompson in the back with his swagger stick and screamed, in true Guards NCO style, 'What are you lot doing in 'ere? The Naafi should have closed an hour ago!'

As he drew himself up to his full height and prepared his second volley, Jock snatched the swagger stick from under his arm and snapped it over his knee. The Guardsman stood there, his mouth hanging open like a goldfish on Mogadon, as someone else whipped his cap off and poured a pint of beer into it – at which point it was suggested that he might like to fuck off. He ran from the Naafi and we carried on partying.

Unfortunately, ten minutes later he was back, this time

with some members of the barrack guard in tow, screaming and raving as they stood laughing at him behind his back. Our RSM got up and ushered us out and we went quietly as the bullshit king continued his rant. It didn't end there, however. The Irish Guards' hierarchy worked themselves up into a stew about the whole situation and demanded court-martials and sackings, but our headshed quietly told them to get stuffed and nothing came of it.

Our second operational tour of Aden, which began in April 1967, was, if anything, even more frustrating than the first. When we'd deployed on Operation Flashbulb, the political situation was confused but comprehensible: Aden and the Protectorate would become independent, but Britain would retain her bases there and continue to use it as the Headquarters Middle East. In effect, this meant that Britain guaranteed the defence of Aden against any outside aggressor and gave local politicians a stake in maintaining British friendship, trust and support, and in assisting the British against the Yemeni-sponsored guerrillas of the National Liberation Front and the People's Front for the Liberation of South Yemen. But in the spring of 1966, Harold Wilson's Labour government announced that, for financial reasons, Britain would be leaving Aden completely after independence. As the implications of this sank in, it became every man for himself and the security situation began to spiral out of control. The reasons for this were straightforward: if the British weren't going to be there after independence, nobody had any stake in supporting us, so why bother?

The pattern of up-country operations was much the same as before. Deploying to high ground to maintain observation on the valley floors and wadis then moving in to ambush by night. One operation, out of Habilayn, involved us in cordoning off a village near the border which was suspected of harbouring terrorists. I was paired with Taff Brown, often known as Bent-legs because of his bandy legs. As we approached the village, there was a sudden burst of fire from in front of us and we hit the deck as rounds started pinging from the rocks all around us. I was carrying a GPMG, and as we ducked for cover I shouted to Taff, 'Quick, you get down there. I'll get behind this rock with the gympy.'

I settled down behind a big, comfortable, solid, bullet-proof rock as Taff gingerly made his way forward towards slightly more dubious cover. There was another burst all round us and Taff looked back to ask, 'Scholey, are you going to return their fire or what?'

'Why would I want to do that? It'll only annoy them.'

'Scholey, you are lower than a rattlesnake's belly!'

On the same operation we had another funny experience when we stopped a minibus near the village. The occupants were being a bit stroppy and one of our guys fired a warning burst close enough to their heads to gain their instant attention, at which point one of the Arabs started complaining in a strong Brummie accent. He turned out to be a worker from the car factory at Longbridge who'd come home for a holiday with his relatives.

But there was also a grim side to the operations in Aden. We'd got orders for another ambush north of Habilayn. This would follow the same general pattern as previous jobs – we'd infiltrate into a position by night, lie-up, and then 19 Troop would put in an ambush on a track while we gave them top-cover from the ridge line. Fairly straightforward.

We got a drop-off from the Stalwarts and began the march in. It was the usual hard bash along narrow tracks strewn with fist- and head-sized rocks as we climbed slowly in the dark, laden with heavy rucksacks, radios and weapons. When we reached the ridge line, we shook out into our positions almost unconsciously, seeking the widest possible view over the ambush area below.

It's a strange feature of the SAS that even though the soldiers are trained to the highest possible level of skill, they come from all kinds of different military backgrounds, and someone from, say, the Royal Electrical and Mechanical Engineers isn't necessarily going to have the same degree of tactical know-how as someone who's been in the Paras for five years. In this case the troop commander down below – who was a Para – made the odd decision to split his ambush. This meant that some of the guys in the killer groups couldn't see what was happening in the other part of the ambush: a risky situation.

It so happened that Yogi in 19 Troop was an ex-Gunner who'd never been in the infantry. Lying in his position on the right of the ambush he felt the need for a piss, but instead of crawling back to the rear of the position to do it – which is what he would have done if he'd come from an infantry background and had had a hard-arse sergeant to bash him round the head for being stupid – he went forward to the edge of the killing zone.

Yogi was kneeling up taking his piss when the enemy turned up. The boys on the left side of the position, not being able to see Yogi, initiated the ambush while he was still in the killing zone, and a devastating crossfire developed as the guerrillas returned fire in greater numbers than anyone expected.

From above we could see that all hell was let loose, but the situation was too confused for us to join in and we could only watch in frustration as the firefight developed. Inevitably, word came over the VHF set that 19 Troop had a man down, Yogi, and needed a medic fast.

The first to get to him was one of 19 Troop's medics, Ray Allam. Yogi was soaked in his own blood, lying in a semi-foetal position amongst the rocks, as if trying to hug himself. He'd been hit maybe five or six times but he was still conscious, and in dreadful pain.

Ray gently began to examine him, taking in the big exit wounds from the high-velocity bullets that had ripped through his body.

'Where does it hurt, mate?'

'Jesus! My arms are killing me . . .' Yogi could just about manage a whisper. This was bad: it meant that his lungs had been lacerated by the bullets passing through his torso.

'Don't worry, mate, this'll sort you out.' Yogi had two army-issue syrettes of morphine on a cord round his neck, along with his dog-tags. The medic carefully cut them free and injected the first one into Yogi's thigh. In theory you should never use morphine for wounds to the head and torso – it depresses the respiratory system at a time when your body needs all the help it can get – but it was obvious that Yogi wasn't going to make it, and the decision was taken that he should go as quickly and in as little pain as possible.

As the drug took effect, Yogi sighed and began to breathe slightly easier. 'Thanks, mate . . . thanks.'

We'd called for a helicopter Casevac, but there was no way it would make it in time, so for twenty minutes the big tough SAS medic held his friend's hand and stroked his forehead as he died.

Then a message came to leave the body and make for the emergency RV.

'It's not a body, it's Yogi,' the troop signaller replied, 'and we're bringing him out with us.'

The troop put together a makeshift stretcher and carried him for the two hours it took to reach the emergency RV.

Not long after that 16 Troop, the free-fallers, got a break from operations and went parachuting from Scout helicopters for a few days. At the end of the training, the pilot asked whether anyone fancied going on an internal nighttime security patrol with him. The idea was that the helicopter would fly over dodgy areas at altitude, drop powerful parachute flares then fly around underneath them, seeing if they could spot any baddies. A couple of the lads fancied a 'cabby' around in the helicopter but there was only space for one and Taff Iles won.

Later that evening 16 Troop were sitting around having a couple of beers with some of the other aircrew when a message came through: the helicopter had crashed in a nearby wadi.

A Wessex was quickly organized to fly 16 Troop out to the scene of the crash, but when they saw it, they immediately feared the worst. It seemed that the rotors had touched the walls of the wadi and the helicopter had smashed into the rockface about half way down, where the wreckage was still precariously poised. The Wessex pilot immediately agreed to take a group up to the wreck to check for any survivors, and he held his helicopter in a steady hover, the rotors just eighteen inches away from the rockface, whilst a team from the troop roped down. As they feared, the pilot and the crewman, a REME fitter, were both dead, and so was Taff.

A few days later, a funeral was held in the cemetery at Silent Valley for all three, and Taff's elderly father was flown out from Wales to attend. As his son's coffin was lowered into his grave, he stood proud and still, his black civilian suit a striking contrast to our khaki drills. A piper played a lament, and then Taff's dad produced an ordinary jam jar from his pocket. In the silence we could hear him unscrewing the tin lid. The jar was filled with rich, dark soil, and he poured it over the wooden coffin.

'I've brought some of home for you, son,' he said.

Our second tour lasted about three months in all. Mobility Troop hung around in Aden for several weeks after the main body of the squadron had gone, in the hope of carrying out a Land Rover-based task between Aden and the mountains, but nothing came of it because most of the troop had been poached to bodyguard Foreign Office personnel and other political types. Soon after we left, the Federal National Guard mutinied, killing and wounding a number of British troops before they were suppressed, and in the last months of the British presence, the whole place became almost ungovernable as the various local factions fought it out with each other. For my part, I was happy to leave, and with the benefit of hindsight, I can only wonder why on earth we expended so much effort and so many lives on a place that we were abandoning anyway. It makes no sense to me.

CHAPTER SIX

About a year after we returned from Aden, things started to change. I'd been in the Regiment for five years now, I'd earned my first stripe and I was accepted by the hierarchy, even if they didn't necessarily share my sense of humour. In some ways I felt it was time to move on within the regimental system. In part this was prompted by the departure of Lofty from the troop. He'd reached that 'up or out' stage of his career and went off to 23 SAS – the TA Regiment – as a sergeant major. Lofty's successor as 18 Troop staff sergeant was someone that I didn't get on with at all – an ex-REME mechanic, as it happens – so I made the decision to move sideways into 16 Troop and become a free-faller.

I'm not going to dwell on free-fall. I did it for a couple of years and even made it on to the Regimental free-fall team which, astonishingly enough in the ultra-secret SAS, used to do the occasional display at local fêtes and fairs. But the only reason I was able to do it was because I was near comatose with fright. It is a tremendous thrill to leap out into the slipstream of an aircraft at 20,000 feet and free-fall down to 3,000 feet or so at 120 miles per hour, but you've only got to see the mess when something goes badly wrong to realize how dangerous it is. During the second part of my free-fall

training, which was conducted down at the French parachute
school at Pau near the Pyrenees, I bought myself a pair of
special jump-boots, which had extra thick, spongy, padded
soles. Some time later, 16 Troop were doing a jump on
Salisbury Plain for the BBC *Tomorrow's World* programme
and one of the lads – Pat Martin – asked to borrow the boots.
I lent them to him and off he went.

It was a routine jump and shouldn't have been a problem,
but for some reason Pat's main canopy didn't open properly
and when he deployed his reserve, it caught up on his oxygen
bottle then tangled up with the remains of his main 'chute.
Someone gave me the boots back but I never wore them again.

There were other deaths at this time. Alan Lonney, who'd
come from 2 Para with me, was killed when a Pink Panther
rolled over on a training rally in the Hereford area; and Ron
Adey died of cerebral malaria during Christmas leave,
having gone home thinking he'd got a touch of flu.

These sad events, and a quiet year or so of training in 16
Troop – it was a relatively quiet time for the Regiment as a
whole – were followed by a real change as I moved out of D
Squadron. The biggest problem that the Regiment had was
that it was always under strength. When I'd joined there
were just two squadrons, adding up to about a hundred operational SAS men in total, but as I was finishing my training
B Squadron was being established, which brought the
numbers up.

In the mid-1960s we'd had two operational theatres
running simultaneously, Aden and Borneo, and the stress
had begun to tell. For one thing, there was relatively little
time to unwind between operational tours because you'd no
sooner got back from one than you had to start build-up
training for the next. Taken in combination with the fact that
we weren't very well paid, and that we were always being

dragged away from home to do something or other, it wasn't surprising that we were all under a certain amount of stress.

One attempt to solve this had been the creation, in 1967, of G Squadron. The experience of establishing B Squadron had shown that to get an operational squadron up and running from scratch was hard work and took a long time. G Squadron was an attempt to circumvent this. Out in Borneo, we'd had various organizations working for us under the command of the SAS 'theatre' headquarters. These had included the Australian and New Zealand SAS contingents, the Border Scouts, who were locally raised and trained tribesmen, the Parachute Regiment squadron and the Guards Independent Parachute Company. The Aussies and the Kiwis had done pretty much the same job as us, the Border Scouts were doing their own thing anyway, but the Para and Guards squadrons had a sort of hybrid role. They did long patrols in the jungle, but their operations weren't mounted on quite the same basis as ours.

Nevertheless, when it was decided to found a new squadron for 22 SAS we looked to people who had worked with us in the past, and the nucleus of the squadron was created by simply taking fifteen volunteers from the Guards Parachute Company, giving them nice new berets with winged dagger badges, and telling them that they were now members of G Squadron, 22 SAS. It's fair to say that there was a certain amount of outrage in the Regiment over this decision. It wasn't that they weren't good soldiers – almost all of them were – but so were a lot of lads who'd failed selection over the years. It was the principle rather than the people.

But the formation of G Squadron still wasn't enough to keep pace with the demands that were placed on the

Regiment by operations and by our other commitments, so it was therefore decided to set up an additional squadron of territorials and reservists who could be called upon in time of war to supplement the regular squadrons: R Squadron.*

The idea was that we'd recruit a combination of ex-members of the Regiment who wanted to carry on doing some training after they'd left the Army, ex-members of other army units, as well as local Hereford lads who fancied training with what, after all, was their local regiment. They would then do the proper selection course, followed by continuation, combat survival and parachute training as and when they could fit it in (obviously, the people who'd already been in the Regiment didn't have to bother with this). At the end of this they would be badged and would then do most of their training with regular squadrons on exercises.

The regular staff for R Squadron was small: an OC, a sergeant major, a storeman, a clerk and me, the PSI or permanent staff instructor, and temporarily promoted to sergeant. My job was to ensure that the volunteers were fit enough to turn up for selection, to organize courses for them and instruct them in the basics, making sure that they weren't going to let the squadrons down, and keep an eye on them all on a day-to-day basis.

R Squadron shouldn't be confused with the two territorial SAS regiments, 21 and 23. 21 SAS was set up after the Second World War and is the direct successor to the wartime SAS of David Stirling and Co. Their original role was the classic jeep-mounted long-range reconnaissance and behind-the-lines raiding that had evolved as the SAS task in the western desert and northern Europe, before eventually becoming

---

* Now renamed, somewhat pretentiously, 'L Detachment', in honour of the original SAS unit set up in 1941 by David Stirling.

the Corps Patrol Unit for 1st British Corps in Germany. 23 SAS had also started life as a successor unit to a Second World War organization, in their case MI9, which fixed evasion lines for downed aircrew and stranded soldiers. Like 21 SAS they had also slowly evolved into a part of the CPU. Both regiments wore the SAS badge and were part of the SAS family, but they had their own job and their own selection and training procedures. R Squadron was a part of 22 SAS and had to cut the mustard.

But despite this, it wasn't a job that I was hugely enthusiastic about. After a couple of years off operations I was feeling the call of the wild: I wanted to get a Bergen on my back, get overseas and do my job. Too much sitting around in Hereford makes Pete a dull boy. And so it came to pass, at the beginning of 1971, that I swapped jobs with Jimmy Collins.

Jimmy was in 6 Troop, B Squadron: Boats. When I'd first joined the Regiment I'd been in Boats. I'd done the course – diving, canoeing, rigid raiders and so on – and I'd hated it. But B Squadron were off to Malaya for Operation Pensnet. Hmmm, at the end of the day there was no choice: I wanted to get out and about again, and if that meant going to a Boat Troop, I was prepared to do it.

Malaya was pretty straightforward. We did three weeks' training before moving into Brinchang in the Cameron Highland for a jungle survival and patrolling exercise/operation. Even then, ten years after the end of the Malayan Emergency, there were still tiny groups of Communist terrorists hanging around in remote parts of the country and our presence was partly, at least, to act as a deterrent against any renewed activity on their part, particularly as the Vietnam War was now at its height.

But we were only a few weeks into the exercise when we received a signal: training was cancelled and we were to return to Hereford to begin build-up training for a new operational deployment. We were to be sent to the province of Dhofar in the south of the Sultanate of Muscat and Oman, directly adjoining, as it happens, the former Aden Protectorate, now renamed the People's Democratic Republic of Yemen. The task was named Operation Storm.

Oddly enough, it wasn't the first time that the Regiment had operated in Oman (as the country is usually called). In 1958 when the Malayan Emergency had been winding down and the Regiment was preparing to leave to come to Britain for the first time – and was facing an uncertain future – a job had come up in Oman that had saved 22 SAS's bacon.

Oman is a thinly populated country, which occupies about 1300 miles of the eastern coastline of the Arabian peninsula, and features a coastal strip, mountainous inland regions and part of the desert known as the Empty Quarter. Most of the people live in the towns and ports of the coastal strip. The traditionalist tribes live in the mountainous inland areas, notably the plateau of Jebel Akhdar in the north and in the mountains of Dhofar to the south.

Historically Oman, which also at times controlled the island of Zanzibar and parts of the coast of East Africa, was ruled by a religious imam who combined spiritual with secular authority – a bit like the ayatollahs in Iran – but in the eighteenth century the two roles were split and the country came under the authority of a sultan based in the port of Muscat. In the early nineteenth century Britain began to develop a relationship with the Sultan of Oman, mainly because it was anxious to bring an end to the slave trade in the Arabian peninsula, but also because of the country's relative closeness to British India.

The relationship was developed in the second part of the nineteenth century when the Sultan was forced to call on the

British to help him put down a rebellion by angry fundamentalist tribesmen from the interior of the country. This created a pattern for, effectively, the next seventy-five years: the coastal-based Sultan ruled with the backing of British military force and control of the ports. The relationship was formalized in 1920 with a treaty between the inland tribes and the Sultan, which kept the peace until 1954.

The cause of the rebellion that ultimately led to the deployment of 22 SAS in the Oman was the death in 1954 of the Imam who had negotiated the 1920 treaty. Leaders of the influential Bani Riyam and Bani Hinya tribes conspired to have a young Bani Hinya man, Ghalib ibn Ali, elected as his successor. Having achieved this, the new Imam's brother, Talib, used his authority to attack a group of oil prospectors working in a neighbouring tribe's area. This in turn provoked a reaction from the Sultan's army, which forced the new Imam and his Bani Riyam allies to take refuge in their tribal villages, and which led Talib to leave for Saudi Arabia where he hoped to raise and arm a force of expatriate Omanis.

The rebellion began at an interesting time in Arab history. In Egypt Gamel Abdul Nasser had seized power and was attempting to reassert Egyptian control over the country, which had been virtually occupied by Britain for many years. At the same time the huge wealth created by oil deposits in the Gulf states was giving the Arabs a level of influence they had not enjoyed since the time of the Crusades. As a result it was a good opportunity for Talib to seek help to get rid of a sultan he could smear as a puppet of the British. When he returned to the Jebel Akhdar in June 1957 with considerable quantities of weapons, some Saudi-trained Omanis and the support of the two tribes, he quickly seized control of the central part of Oman and declared its independence from the Sultan.

Although Talib's rebellion was not widely supported outside the Bani Riyam and Bani Hinya tribes, he was in a strong military position because of his control of the Jebel Akhdar. The massive plateau effectively controlled the land routes inland from Muscat and was supposedly impregnable to attack by land forces. Once again, the Sultan called on the British for assistance.

In reality, the military problem presented by the rebellion was not that great. Talib's force of Saudi-trained soldiers numbered no more than five hundred and would be no match for a British infantry battalion, for example, provided one could be got on to the plateau. The real problem was political: by the time that Britain came to consider committing regular forces to resolve the situation we'd had the Suez fiasco and British prestige was at an all-time low amongst the Arab states. Sending in regular British Army units or formations for long-term operations in any part of Arabia which wasn't actually a part of the British Empire (unlike Aden) would be met with enormous hostility and suspicion and probably denounced in the UN. Instead, in 1957 an infantry brigade was briefly deployed from Kenya to seize low-lying areas held by the rebels, and a number of British officers and NCOs were attached to the Sultan's forces to 'stiffen' them with experienced leadership and more up-to-date tactics as they attempted to enforce a blockade of the Jebel Akhdar, where Talib's forces had scuttled after the arrival of the British brigade. At the same time RAF squadrons based in the region began a campaign of bombing against suspected rebel bases.

In the meantime, Major Frank Kitson, a staff officer working in the Military Operations branch of the Ministry of Defence, was sent to study the problem with a view to finding a long-term solution and had come to the conclusion that a fairly small-scale special operation could be mounted with a reasonable chance of success. He wanted to use bribery to discover when groups of rebels were coming off the plateau, and to mount ambushes to capture as many as possible. He then reckoned that sufficient of these people could be 'turned' to form a pseudo-rebel team that might be able to bluff the pickets at the pass onto the Jebel, or at least to get close enough to overpower them, which would allow a larger infantry force to get up there and hunt down the rebels.

This idea was accepted by the powers-that-be and a trawl began for personnel suitable to carry out Kitson's plan. While this was going on, some bright spark suggested that the ideal solution was to send an SAS squadron and the call went out to Malaya for one.

Not long after the initial recces, D Squadron flew out from Malaya on a roundabout trip that took them via Ceylon and Aden as a deception, and after a week to acclimatize to the conditions, began a campaign of aggressive patrolling around the foot of the Jebel, in an attempt to find a way up. Not long after this, they found one – an unguarded and long-forgotten track – and soon after this the first SAS patrols – including a young, fresh-faced and cherubic Lofty Large, rosy-cheeked with excitement – had established themselves on the plateau.

This unforeseen success led the headshed to bring out A Squadron as well, and not more than six weeks later it was all over: the rebels had fled or been killed, their weapons captured, and the Jebel Akhdar was firmly under the control of the Sultan's government.

The most important effect of the Jebel Akhdar campaign, which made no impression in the UK at all, was that it ensured the survival of the Regiment by showing that 22 SAS was more than just a specialist jungle warfare unit, but it also gave the Regiment a track record in Arabia, which was to stand us in good stead in later years.

The roots of the second rebellion that we got involved in lay in several different areas of Omani life. The Sultan was an old guy called Sai'id bin Taimur (the same man who was ruling the country during the Jebel Akhdar revolt) and to describe him as a feudal and autocratic despot would be somewhat mild. Although he was apparently a charming and kindly individual, he had little understanding of the modern world and was fearful of its intrusion into his kingdom. Oil had been discovered in Oman in the early 1960s, making it potentially very wealthy, but Sultan Sai'id was unwilling to borrow money to modernize the country and most of it was like something out of the Middle Ages. This situation was compounded by Sai'id's belief that in preventing modernization he would be able to maintain control of the country. Fearful that modern education – even modern techniques of agriculture – might serve as a focus for dissent, he ruthlessly used his armed forces, which were still largely composed of British officers on loan and 'contract' service (mercenaries, in other words), and Baluchis from Pakistan, to suppress any signs of development, even going to the extent of concreting over newly dug wells and destroying crops.

Not unnaturally this pissed the people off. They were perfectly capable of discovering how the world was changing outside their own borders, and anyway they were now being subjected to a stream of propaganda from the Communist People's Democratic Republic of Yemen, as well as from Cairo, Baghdad and other centres of Arab nationalism. In any case, although the Sultan was, theoretically, an absolute monarch, in practice his freedom of action had always been partly circumscribed by the tribal chiefs of the interior, who traditionally regarded him as an effete plainsman. Not surprising, then, that rebellion was breaking out throughout Oman within two years of our victory on the Jebel Akhdar and that, despite the best efforts of the Sultan's Armed Forces (SAF), it was growing stronger all the time.

But, having said that, the discontent of a gaggle of traditionally rebellious mountain tribesmen in a feudal backwater on the Arabian peninsula would have been of little interest, were it not for the strategically vital position of Oman at the mouth of the Persian Gulf. Oil from Kuwait, Iraq, Iran and Saudi Arabia was transported in vast quantities through the narrow Straits of Hormuz, which divide Oman from Iran, and an unfriendly government would theoretically possess a stranglehold on a considerable proportion of the world's oil supply. Not surprisingly, a number of parties had a strong interest in the outcome of the Dhofari rebellion and both Soviet and Chinese aid was making its way to the rebel factions in the mountains.

We began to get involved again when Johnny Watts, the commanding officer, made a covert tour of the Gulf travelling as Mr Smith. From his visit to Oman and from his previous knowledge of the country (he had commanded D Squadron during the Jebel Akhdar campaign), he recognized that a number of urgent measures needed to be taken in order for the increasingly beleaguered Sultan's armed forces to get a grip on the situation. Principal amongst these was a need to begin to win over the 'hearts and minds' of the Dhofaris rather than just punishing them, but the Sultan proved impervious to persuasion on this front. Johnny came marching home again, knowing that it was likely we were going to have to get involved, but not knowing when.

Just four months after his quiet visit to Oman – and possibly partly as a result of it – the situation changed drastically. On 23 July 1970 Sultan Sai'id was deposed in a *coup d'état*, almost certainly engineered by MI6, and replaced by his son Qaboos, who had been partly educated in Britain, had trained at Sandhurst, and had served in a British Army regiment. He had been under virtual house arrest after returning to Oman. The way was now clear for a radical policy change.

One of the first things the Regiment did was to send in a bodyguard team to look after Qaboos and to make sure that nobody did to him what he'd done to his dear old dad. Then it was on to proper operations. The first people in were G Squadron, who did an operation right up in the north of the country, on the Musandam Peninsula where Iraqi special forces were supposedly subverting the local tribes. This information turned out to be complete cobblers, but this was only discovered after Paul Reddy, from G Squadron Air Troop, had whistled in from 12,000 feet on an operational free-fall. Meanwhile, Keith Farnes, who was B Squadron's commander, had led a recce to assess the prospects for a counter-insurgency campaign in Dhofar and Johnny Watts himself had set to work on what he hoped was going to be a winning strategy.

To a very large extent the main cause of Dhofari unrest had been removed when Qaboos took power from his father. A lot of the rebels, who were simply traditionalists who didn't like being oppressed by the Sultan and his armed forces, began to drift back to areas under the new Sultan's control in the months which followed. This actually served to highlight a division amongst the rebels between a hard core of Communists and the more traditionally minded tribesmen who had simply baulked at the Sultan's repressive regime. Some Dhofaris were now beginning to suffer at the hands of the anti-Islamic Communists who behaved with typical arrogance in the areas under their control. Nevertheless there were many areas of policy in which rapid changes had to be made if the whole of Dhofar wasn't going to fall under Communist domination. Johnny Watts came up with a five-point plan to bring the situation under control. He argued that the Regiment should provide or facilitate:

1. An intelligence cell.
2. An information team.
3. A medical officer supported by SAS medics.
4. A veterinary officer.
5. When possible, the raising of Dhofari soldiers to fight for the Sultan.

These five fronts, as they were called, became the basis for most SAS operations conducted as part of Operation Storm.

But the big problem in the early days of the campaign was getting out on the Jebel where it mattered. The Sultan's armed forces had spent so long getting their arses kicked by the Adoo* that they'd developed what we called *jebelitis* – they spent as little time as possible out on the Jebel, often staying for only twenty-four hours or less – and this was having serious negative effects on the campaign. One factor in warfare – psychological warfare particularly – which is often overlooked by us westerners is 'face'. In many cultures, it's almost as bad to suffer loss of face as it is to be physically defeated. Even after the Sultan's armed forces had changed their *modus operandi* and switched to attempting to win the hearts and minds of the Dhofaris, every time they left the Jebel with their tails between their legs, they lost face in the eyes of the people they were trying to win over. Our job was to get on to the Jebel and stay there.

* The rebels.

So Operation Pensnet came to an end and we hurried back to Hereford to begin our pre-deployment training for Oman. The annoyance of this rapid change of plan – a fast-ball, as it's referred to in the army – was lessened somewhat by the twenty flagons of army-issue rum that Arthur Eggleston, the squadron quartermaster sergeant, had smuggled back with us. As we started the round of weapon training, navigation and so on, a small team under Ken Borthwick and Mal Parry headed straight out to the SAS base at Um al Gwarif, close to the Dhofari capital at Salalah, to act as advance party for the squadron.

With our work-up complete, and under the command of a new boss, Major 'Duke' Pirie, we boarded C-130s at Lyneham for the flight out to Oman. We flew directly into Salalah, and after a couple of hours' stretching our legs and unloading the Hercules, we all piled aboard two SAF Caribou short take-off and landing transports, with a motley selection of Arabs and their goats and chickens, for the hop to a small airfield at the foot of the Jebel codenamed 'Midway'.

At Midway, we had an overnight stop, sleeping out in the open. Then we piled aboard a convoy of open-backed three-ton trucks and began a laborious eight-hour drive up a wadi bed to an RV. There we met up with our advance party and the other elements who were taking part in the operation – now named Operation Jaguar. Apart from ourselves, we also had G Squadron, who had been out in Oman for some time, conducting recces, two companies of SAF Baluchis, and five Firqat units all under the command of Johnny Watts.

Now the 'Firks' were an interesting bunch because almost all of them were former members of the Adoo who had changed sides. They were one of the first elements of Watts's five fronts that got going and they were largely trained and led by the SAS, under the cover of the 'British Army Training Team'.

When they had surrendered, they were welcomed back into the fold, they weren't mistreated, they were paid for turning in their weapons, and they were gently debriefed about their experiences with the Adoo. Although their job was supposedly to defend their tribal areas, their mere existence was a potent weapon in the intelligence and psychological war against the Communists, because it gave the lie to the propaganda that prisoners were routinely abused and killed and that the Dhofaris could not trust the government. They were also a force in which Islam was tolerated and even encouraged.

What the Firqats weren't so good at was fighting. They were certainly brave and they knew the terrain very well but, at the end of the day, they lacked the discipline of a well-drilled military force, which put them at a disadvantage in the kind of broken-up running battle we were preparing to fight.

We spent about two days getting ourselves acclimatized to the heat and conditions, sending out patrols to look over our anticipated routes onto the Jebel and getting briefed on the plan. This was pretty straightforward: the force was to be broken down into two groups, West and East, which would then climb up to the plateau and, in effect, advance to contact, hitting the Adoo with everything we had. The difference between this and previous operations was that this time we were going to stay for good.

The briefing from the G Squadron recce was that we would be on the Jebel in approximately four hours, but that we would reach a waterhole in two. It occurred to me that this was probably optimistic: I'd heard similar things in Aden. Even though it would add a considerable weight to my Bergen, I went off and filled a gallon can to take with me. Ted Stafford saw me doing this and started to take the piss, but I shrugged it off.

'Ted, don't forget that when G Squadron did their recces, they were in light-order four-man patrols. There's nearly a battalion of us, speaking at least three languages. It's going to take us four hours to leave here, let alone get on the Jebel.'

'Bollocks, Scholey.'

Well, it didn't bother me and I was the one with the extra weight after all.

At about 1830, in the cool of the evening, we set off on one of the hardest marches I've ever done. I was a member of one of the mortar teams with West group, but at that stage we didn't have the mortars with us because they were too heavy to manpack over long distances, so I was with the guys, just plodding along at the back. After about six hours' climbing, we halted for a rest on an open area while Mal Parry went forward with Cappy to recce the next phase of our route. By this time everyone was so chin-strapped that they just flopped to the deck and lay there. I had to go round telling them to get themselves shaken out into all-round defence while we waited for Mal to return. Funnily enough, and it's a point worth making, nobody resented me telling them to do this. In some units I'd have got an earful if I'd started making this sort of suggestion when everyone was shagged out, but in that situation I was correct and every-one accepted it, even if it did mean a certain amount of inconvenience.

Mal and Cappy got back from their recce looking completely shattered, having run out of water. I passed them a full bottle and told them to share it.

'We can't take this, Pete. What about you?'

'I brought a gallon with me from Aden.'

Cappy had been in Aden with me and managed a laugh, and then we got the lads up and began to trudge onwards.

We hadn't got very far when word came up the column. 'Slow down, slow down! Ginge Rees has dropped dead!'

'WHAT?'

'Doc McLuskey's giving him the suck of life . . .'

Poor old Ginge was carrying well over a hundred pounds of kit and combined with the heat, the humidity and the climb, he'd keeled over and appeared, to all intents and purposes, to have died. In fact it was a severe case of heat exhaustion and after treatment, his kit was distributed amongst the squadron and he carried on. Talk about guts!

We kept climbing, and just over fifteen hours after leaving the drop-off point, made it to the plateau, though by now the entire force was strung out down the mountain in a great long line. From the top of the escarpment, our B Squadron positions were about a thousand metres across an area of flat open ground and I soon made it over there, dropping off my Bergen and watching as the rest of the squadron trudged into the position.

I was talking to two of the young troop commanders, Mike Kealy, a captain from the Royal Fusiliers and Derek Dale, a flight lieutenant from the RAF Regiment, who was in command of my mortar team. As we stood there, I saw Ted Stafford limping slowly along in the distance, bowed under the weight of his gear, so I nipped out and took his Bergen off him and brought it in. When I got back, Boss Kealy blinked at me through his little gold-rimmed glasses and said, 'That was very nice of you, Peter.'

'I was taught that in the Gunners, boss. It's called team spirit.'

By now the rest of my mortar group had arrived and were slumped down, poleaxed by exhaustion and dehydration. I got the gallon can out and made a brew of tea and we sat there and drank it as we tried to recover enough energy to get on with our tasks. Apart from me and Derek, there were four of us in the team: Topper Brown, Charlie Cook, Jakey Ovendon and Frenchy Williams; they were all surprised I had any water left.

'Where'd you get that, Pete?'

'Like I said, I brought it from Aden.'

We secured the flat ground, an old SAF airstrip codenamed 'Lympne', and soon after the helicopters began to arrive, bringing in food, water and ammunition. First go at this went to the Firks who tended to need a bit of jollying along (and also because a lot of them had thrown away their rations rather than carry them up the hill) and we didn't get ours before about four in the afternoon.

By now we were in a position to make an assessment of the kind of shape the squadron was in. Ted Stafford's knee was completely fucked up, and he went back down the Jebel, never to be seen again (on this operation at least) and Pete Spicer – 'the Toad' – had gone down with heat exhaustion and needed a day or so's treatment before returning to the operation. With the area secured, B Squadron were then told to concentrate at a nearby waterhole for the night.

We got to the waterhole and I immediately thought, 'Whoa! No way!' The problem was that it was a kind of steep-sided rocky crater with water in the bottom, and if we were all inside it wouldn't take much more than a couple of mortar bombs or an artillery round to really screw us up. It was at this point that the shooting started up above us, and no messing about, it was serious shit.

We were all looking about us, waiting for someone to take a lead when a round came in, pinged off some rocks, then slapped into Jakey Ovendon's leg, without breaking the skin. I reached down and picked up the twisted, spent Kalashnikov round, gave it to Jake, and said, 'Here you go mate, a souvenir for you.'

But, despite the jokes, I was worried that we hadn't reacted sensibly to the fire that was coming in and that we were still skulking down in the waterhole. Adrenaline took a hold of me and I shouted, in my best John Wayne accent, 'Come on, guys, we've gotta get to the high ground!'

There was general agreement to this suggestion and as the volume of fire began to decrease, Cappy led the squadron into a more sensible defensive position and we began to dig in for the night, not without feeling a certain amount of tension.

We'd sorted ourselves out with shallow shell-scrapes (the ground was too hard for anything deeper than a few inches) and were standing around having a brew and a chat when there was a sudden burst of fire right in amongst us. Luckily nobody was hit but the scene looked like *Bambi* when the gunshot goes off and all the little animals scamper hippity-lippity back to their holes, in our case leaving a trail of spilt tea and compo biscuits. We stood to, but the contact soon died down, leaving us in a state of uneasy peace for the rest of the night.

Next morning, Johnny Watts was with us as we formed up to begin the advance to contact in our little teams. We'd split down into action groups and support groups and the plan was to skirmish forwards through this undulating scrubland towards a place called Jibjat until we ran into the enemy, and then to take them on. As we were shaking out, Duke Perry walked over to Johnny Watts and said, 'Colonel, we've spotted some movement. What shall we do?'

'We'll go and fucking kill them!'

And we were off.

The first patrols out of Lympne were some of the most intense soldiering I've done. Apart from the fact that it was extremely hot and tiring and that we were, as usual, carrying a great deal of kit about with us, we were running into heavy contacts every time out. On the first day, as I carefully patrolled forwards with Derek, we suddenly came under intense sustained fire from an Adoo machine-gun. We both dived for cover, but I noticed that Derek had got himself into the illusory safety of a bush, as opposed to the rather more substantial rock recommended by most training manuals.

With the *crack!* of high-velocity bullets smacking all around us I peeped out to look at Derek, and using my best officer's voice told him, 'Derek, cover from view is not cover from fire.'

He gave this proposition a couple of seconds' thought – 'Fuck!' – and he scrabbled into cover with me.

But we weren't out of the woods yet. The Adoo machine-gunner was dropping bullets all round us and it was clearly time to move. A little way away, Jakey Ovenden was crouching behind a rock with a sniper's rifle, and I told him I'd cover him as he headed for a ridge a couple of hundred metres away.

Jakey set off, and as he ran, I fired a few double-taps in the direction of the enemy from my SLR. When Jakey reached cover at a little knoll near the ridgeline, I set off in the same direction jogging as fast as I could under the weight of my Bergen, belt kit and weapon, with Derek Dale close behind. As I got close to Jakey, I shouted that I would cover him on the final stretch, but as I was saying this, he shouted back, 'Scholey, don't stop, don't stop!'

I looked around ... JESUS CHRIST! The machine-gunner was tracking me and the bullets were hitting the ground just behind my feet. If I'd stopped, he'd have taken my legs off.

I shrugged off the Bergen and sprinted the last few metres past Jakey and over the ridge line where I found about ten members of G Squadron, pissing themselves laughing at me.

I had a momentary sense-of-humour failure. 'You cunts! They nearly fucking got me!'

I sank down to the ground feeling completely drained as the adrenaline left my system. As I lay there, a message came over to say that Jim Vakatalia had been hit further over, and they needed volunteers to go and help him. Old Joe Little jumped up to go and I watched as he darted out of the position.

I was still lying there recovering myself a few minutes later when I heard the sound of the Casevac chopper taking Jim out to the FST,* and I distinctly remember thinking: I really don't want to do any more of this: it's fucking dangerous!

The contact died down a bit and Jakey and Derek made it up to the ridge. Then Ned Kelly, one of the G Squadron boys, called over, in his thick Scottish accent, 'Scholey, yer gannae have tae get yer Bergen.'

I looked down to where I'd dropped it, about 150 metres away and thought, Bollocks! But it was true, I did have to go and get it. I slowly got up then wearily walked down to where it was lying and pulled it onto my shoulders. I turned about and began to trudge back to the position when *BAM-BAM-BAM-BAM-BAM-BAM!* A long burst of tracer whipped over my head. I dived to the ground, crawled a few yards and then dashed as fast as I could back up to the ridge. When I got there, the G Squadron boys were literally crying with laughter, and I looked down to see smoke coming off the barrel of Ned's gympy.

'You bastard, Kelly! Never forget, I am going to get you for that.'

* Field Surgical Team.

'Sorry, Pete, we could have sworn we saw a suspicious movement . . .'

We continued the advance until the evening, arriving at a hill with a couple of small trees at the top of it which we called, with typical imagination, Twin Trees. We dug in round here, as best we could because, being SAS, we cleverly hadn't brought our digging tools, had we? And we sat out the night as the Adoo let all hell loose at us.

While all this was going on, the East group were also in the thick of it. Steve Moores, a G Squadron sergeant, was badly wounded in an Adoo ambush and died whilst being evacuated. Steve was one of the original fifteen G Squadron members but was an excellent soldier, well-liked in the Regiment. Even Kevin Walsh, the airborne wart, got hit. He was in a position that was suddenly swept by machine-gun fire and, because he couldn't get into a sangar (because, he used to claim, they'd all filled up with officers) he took cover behind a stack of jerrycans. Unknown to him, they were all empty and he took a round up the arse fired, so Lofty Wiseman alleged, by a fat Arab TA cook on a weekend exercise.

There was something poetic, if that's the right word, about the location of Kevin's wound. As he was carried through the position to the Casevac chopper, he was telling the doctor, 'It hurts, it hurts.'

The doctor responded briskly, 'Of course it hurts: you've been shot.'

'Not that, you prat, you've left the needle from the morphine sticking in my arse.'

They got him away to the FST at Salalah where he was in a ward with a number of other wounded men, lying face down on a nice crisp hospital bed. Unfortunately, there was something really pissing him off, and it all came to a head when the Brigadier paid him a visit.

PARACHUTING WITH 16 TROOP, D SQUADRON

16 Troop D Squadron at the Norwegian Army Parachute School, Trondheim, late 1960s.

Myself and 'Spider' Martin at Trondheim.

Myself, Colin and Jock at British Army Parachute School in Germany, 1970s.

Back to paratrooping. Continuation static line training jump at Brize Norton.

Familiarization with new weapons in the 1960s.

17 Troop (amphibious) offshore patrolling in Middle East.

3 Platoon A Company on the Jebel Akhdar, northern Oman, early 1960s.

My turn for three days R&R in Salalah after eight weeks ops on the Jebel. Now in B Squadron on our first tour with G Squadron in the Regiment's 'secret war' in Dhofar, southern Oman.

Baroness Thatcher (then Prime Minister) on a visit to the Regiment in the early 1980s.

Demonstration of Viet-cong bunker system to members of D Squadron.

Iranian Embassy siege, 1980. B Squadron assault the rear of the building.

The soldier without a hood is Tommy Palmer. He was forced to rip it off when it caught fire, but he pressed on with the attack while inhaling gas and smoke. For this he was rightly awarded the Queen's Gallantry Medal.

HRH the Prince of Wales after a live firing demonstration by the anti-terrorist team. He was somewhat bemused by the fury and aggression of the experience, though he seemed to enjoy it. Seen here with Major General Sir Michael Rose, then the C.O. of the Regiment.

My wife Carolyn and myself chat with Prince Charles during an informal visit to the Sergeants' Mess, December 1981.

'Kevin, I'm so sorry to hear that you've been shot in the arse . . .'

'Brigadier, I've told everyone else, and now I'm going to tell you: IT IS NOT MY ARSE, IT'S MY UPPER THIGH!'

The brigadier was a bit taken aback by this, but an SAS NCO who was there visiting another of the wounded, chipped in, 'Sir, you have to remember that Kevin's arse starts at the back of his neck and ends up at his ankles.'

In the end, he got so fed up with all the jokes that he discharged himself and returned to duty.

We spent a little time at Jibjat and then pushed on to a position known as White City which was to become our firm base for the time being and where we set about establishing a proper airstrip, as well as reinforced sangars, mortar pits and all the other mod cons.

From there we began to go out on patrols every day in order to dominate and then secure the area, while those who weren't out on patrol concentrated on strengthening the position, clearing the airstrip and securing the base against persistent fierce Adoo attacks.

Construction of the airstrip was being supervised by a miserable old contract officer in the Sultan's Air Force, known as Chalky White. After we'd been at White City a few days, I heard some of the lads call him Rent-a-trench, but I couldn't think why until a couple of days later when we were unloading ammunition from a helicopter that had just flown in. As the chopper was idling, we started taking machine-gun fire from outside our perimeter and we scattered for cover. I spotted a trench out of the corner of my eye and ran to jump in it, only to be stopped by Chalky.

'How many cigarettes have you got?'

'None, I don't smoke . . .'

'Well, if you want to come in here you've got to give me two fags.'

The miserable old sod wouldn't let me get in, and despite being under heavy fire, I had to find another trench to clamber into.

The Adoo were determined not to let us walk over them and almost every patrol got into a heavy contact. Soon after we'd arrived I was sitting in a trench sharing a brew with Ken Borthwick when a patrol went out on an area clearance task. No more than a few minutes after they left they came under heavy fire, and Ken and I listened as our outlying defensive positions joined in, using GPMGs set up on fixed lines. As we sat there, listening to almost continuous fire, I said to Ken, 'They'll be getting a bit short of ammunition by now . . .'

Ken's response was, 'You're right, let's run a couple of boxes up to them.'

We each grabbed a box of 7.62mm link for the gympies and scuttled up a reverse slope towards the sound of firing. Nearing the top, a lad called Griff was crouched down over a radio set, trying to make some sense of what was happening. He radioed to Sean Scanlon, who was running the gympies, to see if he needed any help and now called over to us, 'Don't go over yet, they've still got incoming fire.'

By now the contact was slackening off and Ken decided that he wasn't too fussed by the enemy fire and carried on. I, on the other hand, decided to let discretion be the better part of valour, and opted to wait with Griff until everything had quietened down.

The contact finished but word came back: 'Ken Borthwick's been shot.'

I went up to see what had happened and found Joe Little

piggy-backing him back down the hill. Ken had taken a nearly spent round in his foot and was in a lot of pain, but wasn't actually too severely injured. He got a Casevac but there was an amusing sequel to this when the padre back in Hereford was sent to see Ken's wife to tell her what had happened. One of those grim rituals that the army has is that when a soldier becomes a casualty, an officer is sent off, in full service dress, to tell his family. Usually it would be the families officer or the adjutant, but padres also get to do their share of this work, depending on the regiment. Poor Gwen Borthwick answered the door to find the padre standing there and immediately feared the worst.

'I'm sorry, Mrs Borthwick, I'm afraid I have some bad news for you.'

'Oh, my God!'

'I'm afraid that your husband has been shot.'

'Oh, no!'

'Yes, I'm afraid that he has been shot in the right foot, but he is going to be all right.'

'Thank God for that!'

But a couple of days later the padre appeared again. 'I'm sorry, Mrs Borthwick, but I'm afraid I made a terrible mistake . . .'

'Oh, no! He's dead, isn't he?'

'No, Mrs Borthwick, but it was actually his left foot.'

'Padre.'

'Yes, Mrs Borthwick?'

'Will you just piss off?'

The Green Slime (also known as the Intelligence Corps) had now worked out that the terrorists were holed up in the Wadi Darbat, a big valley about ten kilometres from White City, and that they were filtering out to hit us virtually at will. To bring this to an end, a great scheme was hatched.

The plan involved advancing to Darbat, putting in a defensive position on the high ground and then using artillery, mortars and aircraft to push the Adoo out. We had a platoon of Firqat attached to us for the operation, and as we were approaching the top of one of the wadis, a Firqa stepped on what is known as a butterfly mine.

These horrible little things are made of plastic, which means they are difficult to detect, and are about the size of the petrol cap from your car. This means that they're easy to scatter about but hard to spot, and they have become a real menace in combat zones. This particular type of mine operates on a release switch – it doesn't go off until you step *off* it, but when it does go, it will take most of your foot and ankle with it. Fortunately, our lad noticed what it was he was standing on and had the presence of mind to keep his foot firmly down. Lucky for him, but it left him and us with a problem: how were we going to get him off it?

We gathered round him to discuss what to do next as he stood there stock still, his face pale and his eyes bugging out like organ stops. This was the first time I'd seen a Jebeli sweat. Once we'd made the decision, we watched his reactions as the Arabic linguist translated the plan to him. As the explanation continued, his eyes got wider and wider: no surprise there. With each sentence, he responded in a sort of Peter Sellers accent: 'What? Again what?'

And here's what we did. We filled four sandbags and placed them around the foot that was on the mine. We then got about 150 feet of parachute cord, tied a loop round his waist, and retreated back into cover. He was staring at us over his shoulder. It seemed to go on for ever: we explained to him that we would count from ten down to one (in Arabic of course), and on the count of 'one' a team of ten of us would haul on the cord as hard and fast as we could to pull him clear. We hoped that we would be able to jerk him off the mine quickly enough for his foot to be out of the way so that the explosion was absorbed by the sandbags.

It more or less worked. We pulled him off, he lifted in the air, the mine exploded and instead of losing a foot or leg, he lost two toes. He was relieved to be still alive.

He forgot his toes and went round thanking each one of us. Brave man.

Notwithstanding this, the operation wasn't a resounding success. As we approached the wadi, the enemy met us in strength, and we were chased most of the way back to White City in a fire and movement running battle that, almost miraculously, left us with no further casualties.

But despite the occasional setback, word was beginning to get around amongst the Dhofaris that we were on the Jebel to stay, and slowly but surely, the Jebeli people began to arrive at White City to seek our help and protection. One of the first things we did was to establish a medical centre, originally in a tent and later, as the area became more secure, in a hut. When this was done, we put the word about that medical help was available and waited to see what happened.

After a while, local Jebeli tribesmen began to drift in to see our doctor – Phil McLuskey from the Royal Army Medical Corps – and the other medically trained SAS men, including me, who would act as his assistants when we weren't patrolling. As their confidence grew, they would bring in their kinsmen who were Adoo, who would surrender their weapons, join the Firqat and take part in operations, under our leadership, against their former comrades.

Everyone who arrived at the medical centre would get a good old-fashioned army FFI (Free From Infection) inspection. The men would strip off and hold their arms above

their heads whilst the doc checked for lice and other external parasites, taking a few seconds per person. On average
we might attract anything from ten to twenty people each
day.

One morning fifteen turned up. The first thirteen went
through quite happily but the doc was unhappy with the last
two. Although he had checked them over and told them that
they were okay, they had refused to leave and had stood
gibbering at him in Arabic, which he couldn't understand.
After they had stood naked with their hands up for about five
minutes, he called me in. 'Pete, what's wrong with them? I
finished with them ages ago.'

'I think they want to surrender to you.'

Looking amazed he asked, 'What makes you think that?'

'I asked them when they were outside, but I thought you
might have had a clue from the fact that they've got their
hands up and they're both offering you their AK47s.'

'You learn something new every day out here.'

We had another laugh a couple of weeks later when a
tribeswoman brought in her husband. She told the doc,
through one of the lads who was an Arabic speaker, that her
husband had had a headache for a day or two. After the doc
had examined him, he gave the woman three aspirins and
told her to bring him back if they didn't work.

Six hours later the wife returned. 'The medicine has not
worked, he still has the head pains.'

'Where is your husband now?'

'He's sitting outside the tent,' she replied.

'Bring him in,' said the doc, who was only a very young
chap.

In came the old Jebeli with the three tablets carefully
Sellotaped to his forehead.

Along with their medical problems, the Dhofaris also

began to bring their animals to White City. Somehow or other, the system had managed to burp up an army vet who was soon installed providing routine inoculations to the cattle and goats. But what they really wanted, apart from physical protection for their animals, was the chance to get them off the Jebel so they could sell them.

By the end of October, there were more than 1400 goats at Jibjat and White City, and around 600 head of scabby old cattle, and a plan was formed for us, the SAF and one of the Firqats, the Khalid bin Walid, to escort them down to the coastal town of Taqa where they could be sold. This, of course, was easier said than done.

The cattle drive was not too much of a problem in itself, because there were enough herdsmen amongst the Firks to sort out that side of it, but what was going to be hard was protecting them from the Adoo who would suffer a major loss of face if we succeeded. The vital ground of the operation – codenamed Taurus – was a canyon through which the cattle would have to pass as they descended from the Jebel. It was ideal ambush country and if we didn't secure it, the operation would rapidly turn into a complete disaster.

The solution was for teams of Firks, Baluchis and SAS to picket the high ground, and we moved out to do so some four hours before the cattle started moving. For obvious reasons, the move would be taking place at night, so we set off at last light to give the cattle time to get sorted out and make the distance before daybreak.

We started off with Cappy in the lead, steering with the aid of an IWS, a kind of first-generation image-intensifying night-sight that sat on top of your rifle like a big telescope. In relatively easy going, we were moving quite fast and the tail-end of the convoy started to get strung out. Soon word was whispered up the column: 'Tell Bob Lawson to fuckin' slow down, we're going too fast. Pass it on.' This went all the way along the line of sweating soldiers, always double-checked to make sure it wasn't turning into some gobbledegook, until the message came back: 'Bob Lawson's at the fucking back.' This caused a moment's pause for thought: 'Well, fucking slow down anyway!'

We reached the beginning of the high ground and decided that we would send a platoon of Firks up to pioneer the route, together with Mal Parry's action group. They set off, and before too long, all hell was let loose as they walked straight into a group of Adoo. There were bullets flying everywhere as Mal's gang returned fire, and the rest of us took cover against the risk of being hit by stray rounds and ricochets.

I now found myself amongst Jimmy Joint's action group as he started to give a briefing.

'Listen, lads, if we follow up behind Mal and there's Adoo on the other side of the canyon, we are going to get shat on. So I want us to go up onto the high ground on the other side and clear that as well while Mal sorts out this lot.'

I said to Jimmy, 'I don't know where my lot are. I'll come up with you if you don't mind.'

'Sure, Pete, the more the merrier.'

We moved off in single file until we reached the brow of the hill, then Jimmy told us: 'Right, lads, we'll move into extended line, like we do in the Paras. If we hit an enemy position, we'll assault straight through, okay?'

We all nodded and made fierce noises, but in the back of my mind there was a nagging thought: There's only about ten of us, we could get into some serious shit here!

We set off, patrolling purposefully forwards, but as we crested the high ground, Jimmy passed the word: 'Stop, stop!' We gathered in for an update and he told us that we were to return and rejoin Mal's group as there were no enemy on our side of the wadi and they had several casualties to deal with. We made our way quickly back, but stalled as we approached Mal because the Firk who was acting as our lead scout wouldn't go into the position because he was scared of being shot. We swapped him over and rejoined Mal to find that 'Connie' Francis and two or three Firks had been hit during their contact.

Poor Connie, he'd taken a machine-gun round in the back that had made a hell of a mess, and Mal had already used up eight or nine field dressings in an attempt to staunch the bleeding. I treated the Firks, who had relatively minor injuries, and then got on with Connie. We didn't have a stretcher with us, but I had a sleeping-bag in my Bergen and I jogged back to where I'd dropped it so that we could use it to carry Connie back to cover. We gently moved him onto the sleeping-bag and then six of us carried him back to a sort of dry stone-walled corral where we could keep him sheltered until the morning.

He was incredibly brave. He lay there the rest of the night with Bob Lawson stroking his forehead and holding his hand, hardly uttering a sound even though he must have been in a good deal of pain. In the early light of dawn, we got a message to say that the Casevac chopper was coming in but Connie was going into shock, and was convinced he was about to die.

'Bob, I'm going now, I'm going . . .'

'Aye, you're right. You're going in this fucking chopper down to Salalah.'

Which he did, and where the FST were almost miraculously able to save his life.

With all the excitement surrounding the contact and Connie, I somehow managed to miss all the cows going through, but go through they did, and safely on to Taqa where they were sold to the great profit of the Dhofaris and the intense annoyance of the rebels.

We got back to White City and resumed work on the position as the Adoo continued to probe our defences. By now we had the mortars properly set up, together with all the world's supply of ammunition, and this gave us the opportunity to conduct a few unconventional shoots. One regular event was the dawn chorus of Adoo mortars, which fired into the base at around the same time every morning. It occurred to me that it might be possible to disrupt this if we set up for a pre-emptive shoot into the enemy's firing areas at the same time. We got everything ready, with the ranges worked out, bearings taken and ammunition prepared, and I dropped the first bomb down the tube of the mortar.

There was the usual metallic sliding sound, followed by the cough of the propellant igniting. Then a strange, dreamlike sensation came over me. Everything went quiet and for a few seconds I couldn't think what had happened – then I realized that the mortar bomb had detonated as it left the barrel.

It was a high-explosive bomb with a lethal fragmentation radius of sixty metres. My head was maybe two metres from the centre of the explosion. I thought: That's it then, I'm dead and I'm a ghost. Then I could hear someone shouting 'Medic! Medic!' and it began to dawn on me, I'm still alive! I felt over myself with mounting disbelief: I'm not even wounded. I can't explain it to this day.

But both Jim Penny and Jock Phillips had been hit by shrapnel from the blast and, groggy as I was, I went over to assist Doc McLuskey as he treated them. Jock had taken a big chunk of shrapnel in the leg and a helicopter had been called up to take him to the FST. As we carried him on a stretcher across to the HLS, we began to receive incoming mortar fire and as shrapnel began to spatter around us, I told the lads, 'Right, we'll put the stretcher down there by those burmails* and get into cover.'

Jock wasn't too happy about this. 'What are ye talking about? You cannae leave a wounded man.'

'Don't worry, Jock, you'll be perfectly all right.'

'What are ye saying, you bastard? Don't fuckin' leave me here! Those burmails are full of avgas.† What if they get hit?'

'Well, then, I'll treat you for burns.'

'Scholey, you cunt!'

He was perfectly safe, of course, from pretty well everything but a direct hit so we left him there until the firing stopped and we could load him aboard the Jet Ranger, which flew him on out to the FST.

We continued to consolidate our position on the Jebel for the next four months. We averaged about two or three contacts a day and the Adoo continued to hit us whenever they could. In one mortar shoot I conducted, with Steve Fraser out spotting from high ground, we managed to get a direct hit with our second round on a small gang of Adoo, causing several secondary explosions. Word later filtered back via the Firks that we'd actually taken out a complete Adoo section of eight men, which wasn't bad for a day's work. On the other hand, one patrol ran into an ambush, and in the course of a section attack, led by the CO, but also including the second-in-command and the RSM, Chris Loid took a round in the head and died the next day after evacuation to the FST.

We continued to have a few laughs as well, though, if only

---

* *Burmail* is the local word for large gasoline canisters, derived from 'Burmah Oil' which was painted on many of them.
† Aviation fuel.

to keep sane. We'd done a two-day patrol, which had entailed us building a small defensive position, and when we were leaving to return to White City, the drill was to blow it up so that it couldn't be used by the enemy. One of my lads, Topper Brown, was mad keen to get involved in everything and he volunteered to place the charges and do the demolition on our sangars. He did his stuff while we retired to a safe distance. He soon came scampering up saying that the charges would blow in about three minutes.

Three minutes passed and nothing happened, then four, then five. Kevin was back with us after his 'upper thigh' wound and he started quipping, 'Looks like you've fucked up, Top. Let's have a look.'

We raised our heads to see what was going on and spotted a tall skinny Arab herdsman, complete with flock of goats, poking around the sangars with his long shepherd's crook. We were trying to win the Jebelis' hearts and minds, not blow them apart.

'Top, if that lot goes up, you'll be for the high jump,' I told him.

'Not half as much as the fuckin' Arab,' observed Kev.

We started waving and shouting at the goatherd, who looked at us in puzzlement.

Suddenly there was a bright orange flash followed by a loud *THUD!* and a huge cloud of smoke and dust obscured our view of what was happening. Topper went white as a sheet as his career flashed before his eyes.

'Oh, fuckin' 'ell.'

Then, in a scene reminiscent of the Keystone Cops, the Arab emerged from the cloud of smoke, apparently unhurt, but shaking his fist in extreme annoyance.

Topper and I approached him and handed over rations and chocolates to try and appease him. As the goats milled round

I couldn't resist. 'So,' I said to the shepherd, 'how are the kids?'

Topper started laughing and the Arab's fist started shaking again. Definitely time to leave.

The end of the first tour saw us back in Hereford for a period of recovery before we began build-up training for our second go round. Before we'd left, we'd been talking to D Squadron's advance party, who had found it hard to believe that the intensity of the conflict had rocketed up so high in the short period between their first tour, which took place about six months before Op Jaguar, and now. Over a brew, one of them said to Kevin, 'I thought this was meant to be like the Second World War? When are we going to get our first contact, then?'

Kevin's response was straightforward. 'What time do you fuckin' fancy one? You've only got to go outside the perimeter and you'll get all the contacts you want.'

I didn't make it out on B Squadron's second tour because I'd been nominated to go off on the Infantry Jungle Warfare course in Malaya. This might seem a little strange because, first, the SAS use different jungle tactics from the infantry, and second, I guess I'd spent as much time patrolling in the jungle as any of the instructors there. A number of SAS NCOs had been sent out on the course over the years, but few had done well, not because they weren't good in the jungle, but simply because they were used to doing things differently and were unwilling to change to conform with the course requirement.

Well, that struck me as a short sighted view, to be honest. We were doing a lot of 'team tasks' by now, going overseas to train friendly armies in varying types of tactics and techniques, but one of the principal rules of this sort of work was that we taught them infantry tactics to a high standard, not SAS tactics. But if you hadn't done an infantry jungle warfare course, how could you teach infantry tactics? I put a lot of effort into the course and was rewarded with an 'A' grading and the best student award, which I was rather pleased about.

In fact, the SAS was going through one of its periodic looks at itself at about this time, with the arrival of Peter de la Billière as CO (replacing Johnny Watts). He decided that all sergeants had to go off to do the infantry 'Senior Brecon' course as a qualification for promotion. Apart from that, though, and the creation of the anti-terrorist team, some of DLB's innovations weren't quite so welcome.

One of the most outrageous was the weekly muster parade at Bradbury Lines on a Monday morning. When this was announced, there was more than a little consternation. Drill? DRILL!? The last time I'd done any serious drilling was at a Regimental funeral in the late 1960s. Lofty Large was put in charge of the burial party, which was a mistake because the last time he'd done any rifle drill was in 1957 when the army was still issued with the Lee-Enfield No. 4. The rest of us had either learnt arms drill with the SLR or the Sterling SMG, so when Lofty started giving commands like 'Slope Arms' (which weren't drill movements with the modern weapons) a certain amount of confusion ensued. Once we got that sorted out, it became a little easier and because it was the funeral of one of our comrades, we knuckled down and got it right. But a weekly parade: no thanks!

Together with drill came edicts on dress and saluting as well. By and large, most of us wore the old Second World War camouflage windproof smock when we were in the field, with olive green cotton trousers, but these too were banned in favour of the new army DPM camouflage. In barracks, we suddenly found ourselves wearing rank badges for the first time. I was determined not to let these changes go by without a protest, and having been pulled up by Keith Farnes for not saluting him, I made a point of always saluting him with my left hand. Much good it did me; he didn't notice until I told him.

One consequence of missing B Squadron's second Op Storm tour was that I wasn't around for the battle of Mirbat, one of the turning points in the Dhofar campaign. At first light on 19 July, more than 250 Adoo guerrillas of the Dhofar Liberation Front began to move towards the coastal town of Mirbat, covered by fire from both mortars and recoilless artillery. Their opposition consisted of approximately thirty Askars armed with .303 Lee-Enfield rifles, twenty-five members of the Dhofar Gendarmerie (DG) armed with Belgian FN rifles, a light machine-gun and nine members of the Regiment under Boss Kealy – eight from B Squadron, one from G Squadron, who was only there to do a stores check before his squadron took over responsibility for the town later that day. The three groups of defenders were all occupying different locations: the Askars (local soldiers) were in the town Wali's fort; the Gendarmes were in their own fort; the SAS were in their two storey BATT*-house.

Alerted by the incoming mortar fire, the SAS team stood to, expecting that it was no more than the usual 'dawn chorus' of harassing fire from the Jebel. Instead, they soon realized that they were being subjected to a sustained attack. After sending a contact report, the lads began responding using their own support weapons: an 81mm mortar and a .50

* British Army Training Team.

Browning heavy machine-gun; whilst Laba, a Fijian SAS corporal, made his way across 500 metres of open ground to the DG fort to operate a 25-pounder field gun which happened to be there.

The rebel attack was concentrated on the DG fort, probably with the aim of capturing the field gun. After Laba reported that he had been 'chinned' by a bullet he was joined by Tak, another Fijian, who helped him for a short period before he too was hit. By now the rebels were very close to the gun-pit and Laba was using the artillery piece as a direct fire weapon, aiming over open sights at the enemy only a few hundred metres away.

At this point Laba decided to give up on the field gun and use a 66mm mortar which was nearby. As he made his way towards it, he was shot in the neck. He died almost immediately. Tak was now on his own, wounded, and firing his SLR one-handed from the gun-pit at Adoo less than a hundred metres away.

In the BATT-house, Mike Kealy decided to take the team medic, Tommy Tobin, to the DG fort. They covered each other across the open ground but as they arrived at the gun-pit, Tobin was mortally wounded by shots to the face. Taking cover in a nearby trench, Kealy was now able to talk to Tak, but they appeared to be in an impossible situation, virtually overrun by the guerrillas attacking the fort. It was now that salvation arrived in the form of Strikemaster ground-attack aircraft of the Sultan's Air Force, which made repeated bombing and strafing runs at the guerrillas. As the momentum of the rebel attack faltered, members of G Squadron, under Alistair Morrison, arrived to reinforce the position.

It was a complete coincidence that there were two SAS squadrons in Dhofar at the time of the Mirbat battle, and even more fortunate that one of them had just completed its build-up training and was literally about to take over from the first, providing an extremely effective quick-reaction force. In the face of the stiff resistance of the Mirbat garrison, close air support and unexpected reinforcements, the Adoo had no option but to withdraw, leaving behind thirty-eight bodies. In contrast the defenders suffered nine dead, including Laba and Tobin.

As well as being a stiff military defeat, the battle of Mirbat was a major symbolic blow to the rebels, demonstrating that even in strength they were unable to overwhelm a well-organized garrison of the Sultan's forces. Although it would be incorrect to ascribe the victory entirely to the BATT, the action of Laba, Tak and Kealy at the gun-pit, supported by the mortar and machine-guns at the BATT-house, delayed the Adoo enough to ensure that they had not achieved their objectives by the time that air support (delayed by low cloud) arrived. Both the DG and the Askars in the Wali's fort fought well and deserve their share of the credit for resisting the attack but it was, in essence, an SAS victory.

The great shame was that for political reasons, only a few decorations could be awarded. Boss Kealy got a DSO, Bob Bennett an MM and Laba a posthumous Mention in Despatches. It was thought that Laba should have got the VC. Tak got the DCM. Tommy Tobin did not receive anything for his valiant action. Neither did Fuzz Hussey who was firing his 81mm mortar on the lowest charge to bring the bombs down as the enemy were so close to his own position. Nor did Roger Cole receive anything. He stood out in the open under heavy fire to put down a red smoke grenade to warn off the helicopter pilot who would surely have been shot down if he'd approached. Pete Warne was on the wall of the fort firing the Browning machine gun under heavy fire. By the end of the battle the gun had a number of hits on it – but Pete was uninjured. He got nothing for his actions. Compare them to, say, the Bravo Two-Zero lads (which is not to say that they didn't deserve their decorations) and you will see how times have changed.

By the time of B Squadron's third tour in Oman in 1974, things were somewhat quieter. By this stage of the campaign a lot of the work was being done by Civil Action Teams and hard-core soldiering had taken a back seat – in comparison to Op Jaguar at any rate. The Adoo were feeling the squeeze by now, although they weren't beaten by a long chalk but, in any case, in recognition of my advancing years and distinguished service, I was given the role of squadron quartermaster sergeant at the SAS Headquarters at Um al Gwarif for part of it at least.

This wasn't a full-time post: when a big threat material-ized against Salalah, we all took turns manning picket posi-tions in the Jebel overlooking the coastal plain and the airfield; and they were getting hit on a regular basis (I still have a spent bullet somewhere that hit a sandbag just behind my head on one of these jobs) but it did mean that for a lot of the time I was out of the direct firing line.

There were still plenty of laughs to be had. On one occa-sion, a group of senior Firqa personnel showed up to collect some kit from Kevin Walsh. Kev had asked me to get every-thing set up for them but there was a little flurry of confusion and the squadron commander, Arish Turle, got involved. He was under the impression that we didn't have sufficient stores to give them what they needed and very apologetically told them, 'I'm very sorry, gentlemen, but we don't have the equipment you need right now. If you can come back next week, it will all be ready for you.'

Unfortunately, none of them spoke English.

'I say, Sergeant Walsh, would you mind translating that for me please.'

Kevin had just finished an Arabic course, so this shouldn't

have been too difficult for him. As Arish, Lofty Wiseman (the squadron sergeant major) and I watched benevolently, Kevin gathered them together in a half-circle. 'Come 'ere, gather round.' He now had their full attention. 'Listen: *ma'fee buckshees*.* Now fuck off!'

But being back at HQ meant that I was given the unpleasant task of escorting a mate of mine, Joe, to Colchester, the military prison in Essex. Joe had been sentenced to fifty-six days' detention for, let's say, showing a lack of judgement.

It was a very odd process. I had to get dressed up in full No. 2 dress, complete with beret and wings, and go from Hereford to Worcester where he was being held at the Light Infantry Barracks pending confirmation of sentence. Then I was handcuffed to him and we travelled by train, across country, to Colchester where we were picked up by a Land Rover at the station. We'd managed to have a bit of a laugh as we travelled down, but not surprisingly, as we got closer to Colchester, Joe's mood got a bit more sombre.

When we arrived at the guardroom, the first thing we heard was a bollocking being screamed at someone, followed by the stomp of hobnailed boots as a huge provost sergeant major emerged to see who we were. They were expecting Joe, of course, but I was a bit taken aback when having unlocked the handcuffs from Joe's wrist, the sergeant major marched me outside and began cobwebbing me round the square at high velocity.

'LEFT, RIGHT, LEFT, RIGHT, LEFT, RIGHT. LEFT...MARK TIME...LEFT, RIGHT, LEFT, RIGHT, LEFT, RIGHT, LEFT ... QUICK MARCH. ...!'

Initially I assumed I was being taken to his office to fill out some paperwork. However, after about ten minutes of

---

* No freebies.

marching at triple time, I realized a mistake had been made.

I tried to interrupt. 'Sir, I . . .'

'SHADDAP! LEFT, RIGHT, LEFT, RIGHT, LEFT, RIGHT, LEFT . . .'

'Sir, I . . .'

'I SAID SHADDAP! MARK TIME! LEFT, RIGHT, LEFT, RIGHT, LEFT, RIGHT, LEFT . . .'

'SIR! I'M THE ESCORT!'

'HALT! What did you say?'

'Sir, I'm the escort, the other one's Corporal C——, the prisoner.'

'Why didn't you tell me, Corporal?'

'I tried, sir, but . . .'

'Never mind, come with me.'

We went back to the guardroom, where Joe was having a cup of coffee with some of the other provost staff.

'Are you Corporal C——?'

'Sir!'

'GET OUTSIDE AT THE DOUBLE! LEFT, RIGHT, LEFT, RIGHT, LEFT, RIGHT, LEFT . . .'

Poor Joe's arse didn't touch the ground. The sergeant major came back a few minutes later, while I was having a cup of coffee.

'I'm sorry about that, Corporal. Still, I expect you enjoyed the experience, didn't you?'

The reason he'd made the mistake was straightforward. At well over six feet himself, the sergeant major had looked at Joe, who was considerably taller than me and had G Squadron's red and blue Household Division backing behind his beret badge, and decided he couldn't possibly be the bad guy!

All I can say is, I might not be tall but at least I don't have the IQ of a flip-flop – and a left one at that.

CHAPTER SEVEN

As I said, the first time we dipped our toe into counter-terrorism was in Aden with Operation Nina, the so-called Keeni-meeni work in the town, when squads were sent in covertly with decoys to bring out terrorists and bring them to book, using the pistol and close-combat techniques developed by Alec Spence during the 1960s. But the role of the SAS in combating terrorism in Britain had yet to be defined. In that year, the new commanding officer, DLB, got one of the young officers, Captain Andy Massey, to make a study of possible SAS roles in counter-terrorism. Massey came up with the concept of the 'team', a self-contained assault force on permanent short-notice standby for deployment in case of hijackings, hostage takings and so forth, and this idea was 'staffed' through to the Ministry of Defence where it was shelved because of fears about using the army in police tasks.

It was a source of considerable concern at that time, when strikes and other industrial upheavals were commonplace, that the military should not be seen to be taking on any of the functions normally reserved for the police. 22 SAS had a clear role to play in fighting counter-insurgency campaigns but it was much less obvious that there was a need for some form of domestic assault force and, at that time, mainland

Britain had remained largely free from the kind of violence that might be countered by a military anti-terrorist force.

But Massey's ideas were soon revived. In September 1972 a group of Palestinian terrorists, from the so-called Black September group, attacked the Israeli team in their accommodation in the Olympic village in Munich, killing two and taking nine others hostage. The German authorities, utterly unprepared for such a situation, attempted to negotiate and then launched an ambush at Furstenwald airport, from which the terrorists and their hostages were about to be flown. In the chaos that followed, four Arab terrorists, one German policeman and all the Israeli hostages were killed. The operation was a complete fuck-up.

The shockwaves from Munich reverberated around the entire Western world. It was evident that very few, if any, domestic police forces were equipped, trained or psychologically prepared to deal with groups of well-organized terrorists armed with military weapons. In Britain, which already had a domestic counter-insurgency situation in Northern Ireland, Prime Minister Edward Heath's government turned to the Director of Military Operations for a solution. The DMO was immediately able to produce Massey's paper and authorization was granted to form a counter-terrorist team.

Well, this had to come from somewhere and in fact it turned out to be us in B Squadron. Starting from scratch, under the leadership of Lofty Wiseman, we began to put together what has since become 'the Team': the best-trained counter-terrorist force in the world.

But it wasn't all plain sailing. At the start all we had were pistols and SLRs as weapons – in other words, standard infantry equipment – while our vehicles were a selection of half and three-quarter ton Land Rovers, along with a couple of ropy old civilian Humbers, which we'd somehow acquired.

None of this was very satisfactory, and in the few weeks that we had available to acquire an operational anti-terrorist capability we made strenuous efforts to beef up our capability.

We were helped in the modernization and upgrading process by the airy promise of unlimited funds, given when the Regiment was first authorized to set up the team, under the codename 'Operation Snowdrop', and also by the arrival of Alec Spence, the close-quarter battle specialist, as the training guru. The money enabled us to buy some Range Rovers, then just coming on to the market, as our basic civilian type vehicle; while Alec made an assessment of our training requirements and weapons needs.

In the short term we got hold of a consignment of Ingram MAC-10 machine pistols, a compact but basic 9mm design which has since become popular amongst US-based drugs gangs, and which fulfilled our basic requirement at the time; and in the longer term this led to the testing and acquisition of a much wider range of weaponry as Alec and his newly created counter-revolutionary warfare cell defined the problems we would face in the course of counter-terrorist operations and then set about solving them. These included the Heckler and Koch family of sub-machine guns and rifles, Remington shotguns, stun grenades, the Arwen riot gun and an array of other weapons for specific tasks, ranging from low-profile 'bodyguarding' up to full-blown hostage rescue assaults. But, and it's a fairly big but, the techniques that were developed then are sensitive and remain secret for a good reason: the more they are discussed, the more terrorists can develop counter-measures. These things are so secret, that if I told you what they were, I'd have to come and kill you all afterwards; and at my age, with my dicky knee and back, that could take for ever.

But what we did do was swap techniques with allied teams that were set up at the same time. The Germans, after the Munich fiasco, were quick off the mark in setting up GSG-9 to prevent any further incidents, while the French came in with the GIGN, and the Americans, after a certain amount of um-ing and ah-ing, also created 'Delta Force' (Special Forces Operational Detachment Delta) in direct and conscious imitation of us, under Colonel Charlie Beckwith, a hugely experienced Vietnam veteran who had served in 22 SAS on attachment in the 1960s.

It is an acknowledged fact that counter-terrorist techniques are willingly shared between the democracies in order to maximize their chances of defeating this menace, and the Western world has become an enormously hostile environment for terrorists since 1972. This doesn't mean we don't get to laugh at each other. Snapper from B Squadron, one of the team that subsequently stormed the Iranian Embassy, was given the job of escorting a bunch of GSG-9 (the German anti-terrorist boys) to the 'Killing House' at the training area near Hereford. They trundled down there in a big charabanc, but as they arrived at the camp gates, the front tyre on the bus blew out and the whole thing lurched over in a kind of automotive stupor.

Snapper stood up at the front and told them, 'Sorry, lads, everybody off the bus. I'm afraid we'll have to walk from here.'

One of the Brussels* stood up and asked, 'How far iss ze range?'

'I'm afraid it's about three kilometres.'

'Vot about all ze assault eqvipment und veapons und ammunition?'

'I'm afraid we'll have to carry it.'

* Brussels sprouts = Krauts.

There was a certain amount of understandable moaning and griping as the Germans debussed, followed by the classic line as one blond stormtrooper disconsolately picked up his heavy body armour. 'How did zey vin ze var?'

The 'Killing House' was an actual house that we used to practise in - though being the SAS our role-playing was taken very seriously. The point, after all, is to learn how to deal with real terrorist situations and this can't be done if you're pussy-footing around.

Playing a terrorist was my least favourite role in these exercises. Even though I was fairly sure no one was going to stick a bullet in me, my adrenaline would start pumping at the sound of the team breaking in and clearing the house, room by room ... I knew I was in for a certain amount of manhandling when they finally caught me and the sight of those big men dressed in black, faces hidden by gasmasks, was pretty intimidating. I couldn't see them smile as they recognized me but to show that they knew who I was, I'd often get a reassuring squeeze of the bollocks. They're a friendly lot, the SAS.

One time I took realism too far, though. On this particular exercise I had been appointed the role of chief terrorist, with a high-ranking army official as my hostage. He had been told to wear a gas mask for protection – but no one had told me this. So when the team threw the lot at us – gas, stun grenades – I did what any self-respecting ruthless terrorist would do. I grabbed the gas mask off my hostage and made my escape.

The team dragged him out of the house, red-faced with streaming eyes, and he calmed down eventually. I got a rocketing while G Squadron, safely round the corner, were collapsed with laughter.

Suffice to say that some of the skills we learnt were fairly strange and were not always used in the cause for which they were taught. I got back early from leave one Sunday evening and bumped into Jock from 16 Troop in the locker room as I was unpacking my gear. The Naafi was closed so we started to chat as he began to empty his suitcase into his locker, but we hadn't been there long when he made a kind of 'Ah hah!' sound, and produced a set of tools that he'd recently acquired whilst doing a Covert Methods of Entry course with the Intelligence Corps. He was showing me the contents when he suddenly said, 'Are you thinking what I'm thinking, Pete?'

'Almost certainly,' I told him.

So he started systematically going round the room, swapping the locks around. He got to the last one and stood back to survey his handiwork.

'That won't be enough, Jock, we've also got to change the name-cards.'

These are the little bits of cardboard that slip into a slot on the locker. We swapped them all.

Jock turned to me. 'That's still not enough, Pete.'

So we changed over all the rucksacks, webbing and other bits of kit that were stowed away on top of the lockers. Still not satisfied, we then physically moved all of the lockers around, so that even if they could still remember where it had been, the lads wouldn't be able to identify their own locker. By now we were knackered, but we were also in hysterics, waiting to see the lads' reaction when they returned.

As the boys began to arrive back on camp, Jock and I set up a discreet observation post at a window and waited for the fun. Sure enough, the whole billet was soon a mess of swearing, raging SAS troopers, surrounded by piles of other people's kit as they attempted to sort out the mess. At this point, it started to turn nasty. From our vantage-point, I heard big Brian Dodd saying, 'I bet fucking Scholey's behind this.'

There was general agreement. I reckoned I now had two choices: I could write out my will, or I could try to wriggle out of it. A thought occurred to me.

'Wait here, Jock, I'm going to the other window,' I whispered.

'Okay.'

I'd done some amateur theatricals and I reckoned it was time to collect my Oscar. I walked into the locker room and, before anyone could say anything, announced, 'Has someone been fucking around with your lockers? Mine's the same.'

Big Brian looked surprised. 'We thought you'd done it.'

'Not me, mate, it was fucking Jock. Look at him there, laughing at us through the window!'

I didn't need to be able to hear Jock to know what he was saying. 'You bastard, Scholey!'

He bolted, a fraction ahead of four members of his own troop.

In 1976 my twenty-two years regular service came up and I was faced with a choice: leave and try my hand at something new; or soldier on a little bit longer on continuance. Carolyn and I discussed it for some time, but in the end I decided to carry on. I was a bit over forty now, but I didn't feel ready for the knackers yet, and I still felt that I had something to offer the Regiment, even if I was no longer quite the lean, mean fighting machine I'd been when I'd first joined.

I now moved to operational research, the small team within the Regiment responsible for testing and assessing new equipment, and for developing our own stuff when we couldn't get hold of a commercial alternative. This was a cracking job, because it meant working with all the squadrons and departments within the Regiment, as well as a lot of outside agencies, including the police, the intelligence services and the various research and development departments belonging to the government.

It also meant a lot of liaison work with the Team and now, being effectively non-operational, us old lags in ops research did occasionally get roped in to help out with various forms of training. On one occasion I got detailed off to act as a hostage in one counter-terrorist team exercise. The scenario was that a group of terrorists – a regular army infantry platoon – had captured a group of hostages, including a VIP (me), and were holding us all in an old Victorian building.

These exercises always involve maximum realism: the commander is the actual chief constable of the area involved, they use a real negotiating team, and so on. This time, the terrorists' demands were not being met, so they decided that their VIP hostage was going to be executed to jolly things along a little. They gagged me, tied me up, 'shot' me and then shoved me out of a window. I rolled down a long, grassy bank, and finished up lying face down in the grass in the pouring rain for an hour and a half, whilst the team, from G Squadron, went through the drills and procedures before their assault.

I was lying there, looking forward to being untied and taken back to the holding area for a nice cup of tea, when four members of the team ran forward in their black assault gear. They lifted me shoulder high but instead of taking me back to 'safety' and the tea urn, they carried me up the grass bank and threw me back into the building, shouting at the terrorist inside, 'Have him back, he's a fucking creep!'

My boss in ops research was Lofty Wiseman, one of the great

characters of the SAS and also one of the key people who helped transform the Regiment into what it is today. Had his career prospects not been slightly dimmed when he had a set-to as squadron sergeant major with his squadron commander (I happened to be standing in the next door office and was surprised to see Lofty's huge fist come crashing through the wall as he took a wild swing at the officer in question), Lofty would almost certainly have ended up as quite a senior officer himself. In his time he helped reorganize the selection and training of SAS recruits, as well as putting in place the combat survival training for which he's since become well known, but he was an inspirational soldier and a really nice guy as well.

Some winters, heavy rains in Hereford would cause the Wye to break its banks and parts of the city would flood. On these occasions, the police would often ask for assistance from the Regiment and we would be found ferrying folk across a flooded area, using our amphibious craft.

On one occasion one street was completely cut off by the floods. It was a dark, cold miserable night with continuous rain. We got news of some old folk who were cut off and had been unable to get out to buy food for about two days or so. Lofty and his troop set out with rations and two large urns of tea on board an assault craft. Having given mugs of tea and sandwiches to a number of folk, he noticed an old lady about two storeys up looking out of the window. He somehow climbed from the craft up to her window with a big mug of tea. He went to hand it to her.

'Here you are, love,' he said to her, 'here's a nice warm mug of tea.'

'Has it got sugar in it?' she asked.

'Yes, it's lovely and sweet, do you the world of good.'

She looked at him hanging up there by the skin of his teeth and said, 'I don't take sugar.'

Lofty's philosophy of life was refreshingly straightforward. He was checking his passport in the orderly room one day when Angela Rose, the wife of Mike Rose, the CO, came in. Seeing Jakey, one of the troop corporals, doing some photocopying, she asked whether he would be prepared to help put up a marquee at the weekend at one of the local schools for some public-relations event or other, and Jakey agreed. Then she spotted Lofty.

'Lofty, why doesn't your wife ever turn up to the Wives' Club events?'

Lofty gave it to her straight, tongue firmly in cheek. 'The thing is Angela, in my family, I'm the warrior. I go out and fight the wars, and my wife stays home and looks after my house and my seven kids.'

'Lofty, that's the most disgracefully chauvinistic thing I've ever heard! A woman can do anything a man can do and a lot more besides.'

Jakey was just leaving the office. 'You can put up your own bloody tent, then!'

It was also while I was in ops research that the Regiment was put on the map in a very big way. On 30 April 1980, a group of six Iraqi-sponsored terrorists arrived outside the Iranian Embassy building in Princes Gate in Knightsbridge, London. The six were ethnic Arabs from the oil-rich Iranian province of Khuzestan (also called Arabistan) which had been annexed by Iran in 1926; and the mainly Arabic population were undoubtedly the victims of persecution by the ethnically Persian authorities put in place above them. Nevertheless, it is most likely that the terrorists were agents of Iraqi intelligence, intent on causing trouble for the unstable Islamic government of Iran.

After a brief struggle, the terrorist overpowered the Metropolitan Police guard, PC Trevor Lock, and took control of the building, seizing twenty-six hostages in the process. We initially got involved because 'Dusty' Gray, an ex-corporal from the Regiment, who had left to become a police dog-handler, phoned the ops room at Hereford and the Team actually began its move to London before a formal request had been made for SAS assistance. After a brief stopover at the army's language school in Beaconsfield, Red Team were deployed into a building close by the embassy in the early hours of 1 May and set to work on an Immediate Action option, a rough and ready plan for use in the event that the terrorists started killing their hostages before a deliberate assault plan could be developed.

As the siege dragged on Red Team were relieved by Blue at the embassy and headed for Regent's Park Barracks, where a mock-up of the embassy had been constructed by the Irish Guards pioneer section and they were able to work out their plans for a deliberate assault. In the meantime, Steve Callan and I were sent up from ops research to the embassy to set up various forms of covert surveillance gear that we were then experimenting with, including fibreoptic lenses which could be pushed through into the embassy itself to monitor what was going on. It was a tense and busy situation, and when we'd finished what we were doing, we packed up and went back to Hereford in order to keep out of B Squadron's way.

The crisis came to a head shortly after midday on 5 May. The terrorists had been assured by their controllers that they would be flying out of Britain with their hostages within twenty-four to forty-eight hours and were not psychologically prepared for a long siege. By day six they were extremely edgy and anxious: at 1240 their leader warned the police negotiators that he would start killing hostages in two hours' time but in fact the first shots were heard from inside just fifteen minutes later.

It seemed clear that someone had been shot, but a decision had been made at ministerial level that the SAS assault could only begin when *two* hostages had been killed because the first death might have been an accident. There was a delay whilst William Whitelaw, the Home Secretary, was briefed on the current military assessment by DLB, who had assumed control as Director SAS, and then the Team were brought up to immediate 'notice to move' (i. e., ready to go as soon as the order was given). This order was given (by the police commander at Princes Gate) at about 1550 and the assault team were declared ready at 1700, nearly an hour ahead of schedule. Thereafter, it was a question of waiting for developments. These were swift in coming.

At 1820, the police deployed a cleric from the Regent's Park mosque to talk to the terrorist leader, but whilst the conversation was in progress further shots were heard and shortly afterwards a body was dumped on the steps of the embassy. After permission had been given to remove it, a quick autopsy was carried out which swiftly established that the body (which was that of the embassy's press officer) had been dead for some hours. The logic of this discovery was that it was now possible, if not probable, that the required two hostages were dead. The police sought a decision from the home secretary, who in turn consulted Prime Minister Margaret Thatcher, and permission was given to send the SAS in on the orders of Assistant Commissioner John Dellow who was in command of the incident.

Once the decision had been made to use the military option, the aim of the negotiators shifted somewhat. At least part of their task now became to lull the terrorists into a false sense of security, and they sought to do this by agreeing to the terrorists' demand that they bring a bus to transport the terrorists and hostages to Heathrow Airport. In reality, as this was happening, the assault team was moving into position for the attack. The surviving recording of the negotiator talking to the terrorist leader culminates in the following sequence:

> Salim (terrorist leader): We are listening to some suspicion . . . er . . . movements.
> Negotiator: There are no suspicious movements.
> Salim: There is suspicion, okay. Just a minute . . . I'll come back again . . . I'm going to check.

The sounds that Salim had heard were members of Red Team on the roof, preparing to abseil down the rear of the building, and a 'pair' from Blue Team placing a frame charge – designed by ops research – on the front window prior to scurrying back into cover. As Salim left the phone, the assault commander, Hector Gullan, gave the order 'Go! Go! Go!', and a large 'stun charge' in the embassy's lightwell was detonated. The explosion was audible halfway across London. Even so, the tape clearly shows the negotiator repeating *after the detonation*: 'Salim, there are no suspicious movements'!

It is not technically difficult to storm a single building like the Iranian embassy, but it is enormously difficult to storm such a building *and* rescue all or most of the hostages, and it was here that the long months of training paid off. In the first few seconds of the assault, one of the terrorists opened fire on the hostages, killing one of them, but very shortly afterwards the assault force had killed four of the terrorists and a fifth was shot by a sniper stationed in Hyde Park.

The sixth survived because he had downed tools and was no longer presenting a threat. As a result the lads were unable to positively identify him within the building and he was brought outside for arrest by the police.

Only one of the hostages died in the assault.

Things changed quickly after that. Apart from the fact that the Regiment was thoroughly in the spotlight all round the world, we'd become flavour of the month with the government as well. One of the most noticeable things that improved was pay: before 1980, you basically got paid one rank above the rank you held, and received parachute pay in addition. This actually meant that people like me, who were already getting parachute pay and held a rank, in my case corporal, lost money when they joined the Regiment because we dropped down to trooper. The upshot of this was that a lot of people used to moonlight when they were back in Hereford, working night shifts at local companies. Now we began to get a new allowance of Special Forces pay, which nearly doubled the pay of the troopers, and gave a big boost to the rest of us.

But despite this, I was beginning to think that it was time for me to move on. I'd stayed with the Regiment for so long because I loved the operational side of it but I had to recognize now that, in my early forties, I was getting too old for active involvement in operations. If the truth be told, I wasn't enjoying the operations and training so much either: there's a nasty moment in every soldier's life when lying in a ditch full of muddy water becomes a pain in the arse rather than a challenge, and as 1981 drew to a close, I decided that it was time to get out and make a fresh start.

EPILOGUE

I was in the process of becoming a sub-postmaster of all things, in Cheshire, when my nerve failed me. Driving up from Hereford with Carolyn in the early spring of 1982, I suddenly thought: I can't leave this town, and I can't leave this Regiment. It was almost as if I'd suddenly been stricken with homesickness. We had another long talk and agreed that I would stick with the army for the time being, and that she would go back to work, teaching special-needs children with behavioural disorders, when the children were older.

It was undoubtedly a difficult time for me: I'd been a soldier without a break since 1955, and I'd enjoyed almost every minute of those twenty-seven years. The time was coming when I would have to go, but faced with the immediate prospect of civilian life, I couldn't cut the cord that connected me to the army and the SAS.

And then, of all things, another war came along.

It was as much of a surprise to the SAS as it was to the rest of the British military and intelligence establishment when, on 1 April 1982, we discovered that Argentina was in the process of launching an invasion of the Falkland Islands, a rocky, windswept outpost of the former British Empire in the far South Atlantic.

In the confusion that followed, as the Task Force was hastily assembled, there was no clear thinking on how special forces might be employed and how many would be required, and it was at the initiative of the CO, Mike Rose, that D Squadron, under Cedric Delves, was despatched to the forward mounting base at Ascension Island, close to the Equator, on 4 April.

Rose went out the next day, taking a tactical SAS headquarters element, and soon linked up with Brigadier Julian Thompson, commander of 3 Commando Brigade, who was the land forces commander at the time. As a member of Thompson's planning staff, Rose was able to develop a special forces strategy which planned on using D Squadron in a raiding role, together with G Squadron in intelligence collection tasks.

The first difficulty to be overcome in the campaign stemmed from the unfamiliarity of the naval hierarchy with the potential scope and the type of support we needed for our operations. This was solved comparatively easily by establishing an SAS liaison cell within HQ Cincfleet in the bunker at Northwood, and by the personal intervention of DLB, who was still the Director SAS in 1982, and who ensured that the commander-in-chief, Admiral Fieldhouse, was fully briefed on SAS capabilities. The second difficulty was less tangible but, anecdotally at least, considerably more problematic: the chain of command and reporting. The full extent of the confusion over who was responsible for tasking special forces patrols at each stage in the campaign, and how the intelligence they acquired should be disseminated, wasn't ever completely resolved and the whole picture became crowded by inter-unit rivalries and jealousy based on a fear, I've always believed, that everyone thought this might be the last conventional war we'd ever fight.

The first operations in which we got involved were moves to recapture the island of South Georgia, 800 miles to the south-east of the Falklands group, which were held by a small force of Argentine commandos. South Georgia is a little over 105 miles long and approximately eighteen miles wide at its widest point, but its mountainous terrain and relative proximity to the Antarctic make it geographically and climatically a very different proposition from the Falklands, being icy and bleak, and scoured by severe winds carrying ice and snow particles at up to 100 miles an hour. For practical purposes, the island is uninhabited, apart from a small scientific team from the British Antarctic Survey, whose leader doubles as the island's magistrate and immigration chief.

It had been occupied by the Argentines on 3 April after a brief skirmish with a small party of about fifteen Royal Marines detached from the Falklands garrison at short notice, and landed from HMS *Endurance*.

The plan, developed in London, was to send a Royal Marines company (M Company of 42 Commando) together with an SBS section and a troop of SAS in a small Task Group consisting of the destroyer *Antrim*, the frigate *Plymouth*, and two auxiliaries, *Fort Austin* and *Tidespring*. The idea was that we would mount OPs providing information for the Marines who would then capture the enemy garrison with the assistance of naval gunfire support. The Argentine garrison was believed to be no more than about sixty strong, and to be based solely in the two tiny settlements of Grytviken and Leith (both former whaling stations), well out of range of land-based air cover, although a serious threat to the Task Group was present in the form of a submarine that was believed to be cruising the area.

The South Georgia Task Group left Ascension Island on 9 April for the voyage south with most of D Squadron embarked on the *Fort*, making intense preparations for their forthcoming operation.

The commander of the land element of the South Georgia Task Group was Major Guy Sheridan, the second-in-command of 42 Commando, but the SAS were placed under the command of the captain of *Antrim* who was the overall task Group commander. In reality, this meant that Cedric could act as his own boss – few naval officers would have sufficient experience or knowledge of special operations to question his decisions – but it led to D Squadron attempting an operation that came close to disaster: a helicopter insert onto a glacier.

Several people with experience of South Georgia thought that the heli-landing on the Fortuna glacier was a big mistake but, despite this, the SAS team, from 19 (Mountain) Troop under Captain John Hamilton, decided to go ahead. During the afternoon of 21 April, and after two abortive attempts, the troop bundled out of their helicopter and onto the glacier; the first British forces to return to the islands.

They soon realized that they had fucked up. The glacier was being buffeted by 50 m.p.h. winds that blew ice particles into their equipment and weapons and was criss-crossed by dangerous crevasses. They made about 500 metres in the first five hours' march, but then were obliged to seek shelter in a crevasse for the night. Having had a rethink they decided to request evacuation the next morning. This came in the form of three Wessex helicopters, of which two crashed in whiteout conditions without causing serious injury, before the last one got away, dangerously overloaded with the Mountain Troop boys.

A second attempt to land SAS soldiers was then made using the Boat Troop's Gemini inflatable motor-boats into Stromness Bay. This was similarly unsuccessful: three of the inflatables failed to start and had to be towed behind the two that did. Caught in a sudden squall, two of the unpowered boats broke free from their tows and were carried away. The crews of both were fortunate to be retrieved some time later after a few brown-trouser moments on the high seas.

As it turned out, the whole plan was somewhat over-elaborate. The end of the operation came when the Argentine submarine was spotted and rocketed by the *Endurance*'s helicopter, and D Squadron and the marines were then helicoptered ashore: the Argies bravely surrendered without firing a shot.

Meanwhile, back in Hereford, plans were afoot to mount a special operation on the Argentine mainland, and suddenly, Staff Sergeant Scholey found himself right back in the thick of it.

On 4 May the British destroyer HMS *Sheffield* was struck amidships by a French-built Exocet missile fired from a Super Étendard bomber of the Argentine naval air arm. In the ensuing explosion and fire, twenty members of the crew were killed and many more injured. The ship was abandoned and sank whilst under tow six days later.

The loss of the *Sheffield* had a huge impact on the Task Force and the war cabinet. The chiefs of staff had informed the cabinet that an amphibious landing, if it was to take place, needed to happen before 30 May, when the onset of the southern winter was likely to have made the weather too unpredictable, but the Super Étendard/Exocet threat appeared to be a potential war-loser even though the Argentines were known to have only a limited number of them. If an Exocet was to destroy one of the aircraft carriers or a troopship it might prevent the landings taking place at all. Some means, therefore, needed to be found to neutralize the Exocets. Various ideas were considered, and then rejected, before DLB managed to persuade Mrs Thatcher that he had the solution.

At the start of the Falklands campaign, B Squadron were put on standby as a strategic reserve for operations in the South Atlantic, under the command of John Moss, but there was a slight blip on the horizon in that Fred Marafono had just taken over from Jim Vakatalia as SQMS, but Fred had no experience of the 'Q' side of life. If B Squadron were deployed, they would certainly need an experienced hand in charge of the stores and resupply situation, so would Staff Sergeant Scholey mind lending a hand? He wouldn't mind at all.

But, to be fair, we didn't know what the plan was at that stage. We started doing a variety of different types of training: getting everybody up to speed on all the squadron weapons, working with helicopters and boats, practising signals procedures and all the hundred and one other things that need to be sorted out before we could deploy. I did some of the training but mostly I worked getting the squadron's equipment loaded and ready for the off.

But a few days after the *Sheffield* went down, we were summoned to the squadron interest room for a briefing. B Squadron was to launch an attack on an Argentinian airbase.

In essence, the concept was simple: two C-130 aircraft carrying B Squadron would take off from Ascension Island and fly, courtesy of air-to-air refuelling, across the South Atlantic ocean to Rio Grande where they would land and be abandoned. Once on the ground, B Squadron would fan out across the base, destroying as many Super Étendards and Exocet missiles as they could find and killing any Argentine aircrew that happened to be there. With the attack completed, B Squadron and their RAF aircrew would tactically evade across country, making for RVs.

We sat there gobsmacked. Then we started training. With a specific task in mind, I was now in a position to refine my stores loading, and we started to despatch material down to RAF Lyneham, pre-positioning it so that when we got the go-ahead, there would be no faffing about. Meanwhile, I was getting mildly concerned because, although the squadron were off doing mock attacks on airfields all round the country, I was still farting around with stores at Hereford. But if the squadron was going to do an attack then, as far as I was concerned, I was going to be part of it, and I needed to do the training as well. I tackled the SSM about this, and he told me that, as far as he was concerned, I was going, but that my first priority was to get the squadron's equipment sorted out, and I could join in with the specific operational training after that.

The guys had been training for ten days or so, and I was pretty much finished, when I got a call from the air movements people at Lyneham. There was a problem with our gear and could I help sort it out? I drove down in my old Maxi to see what the problem was and discovered that the two C-130s had been improperly loaded: the vehicles – Land Rovers and motorbikes – still had fuel on board; the explosives and ammunition were in the wrong places and the whole lot needed to be unloaded then reloaded safely. They were certainly in no state to fly and the RAF would refuse to try anyway.

About this time, a convoy with more kit on turned up from Hereford, together with eight drivers: six from the RCT and two civvies. When they'd finished unloading, I grabbed them all and said, 'Sorry, lads, you've got to stay here with me. If we don't sort out these C-130s, B Squadron aren't going anywhere.' To my surprise, there wasn't a murmur of protest, even though they were in for a huge amount of work. I turned to the two civvies and told them, 'You two had better head on back.'

'Don't worry, Pete, we can give you the rest of the day as well.' I was amazed. I phoned Dave Handley, the MTO, to clear it with him, and was told, 'Don't worry, Pete, you do what you've got to do.'

I sorted the drivers out with a meal in the cookhouse and accommodation and we got down to it, under the direction of an RAF air loadmaster. After two days of hard graft, we were finished and I phoned in to report that everything was ready.

'You'd better get back here, Pete, things are moving,' I was told. I finished a few final details and drove back to Hereford. It was strangely quiet. I went to the B Squadron office to find it empty. They'd gone and left me behind. A few phone calls confirmed that there was no chance I could catch them up: they were already on their way to Ascension Island.

Thus it was that I missed the last tumultuous days before B Squadron left. I knew that some people in the squadron weren't happy about the mission and, on the face of it, it looked very dicey, but I was surprised to learn what had happened. DLB had turned up at a squadron briefing (wearing his jumper the wrong way round, oddly enough) and, during the questions, had been asked why there was no air cover for the operation. His answer wasn't terribly reassuring.

'We wanted to take a couple of Phantoms, but we think they would probably be shot down by Argentine air defences.'

Boss Moss pulled a funny face at that. It was obvious what he was thinking: If they're going to take out Phantoms, what are they going to do to a pair of C-130s? Discussion became slightly heated, at which point DLB more or less ended the debate by stating, 'The bottom line is: B Squadron or the Fleet.'

DLB was pretty taken aback by the squadron's reaction to his plan and was even more surprised when one of the staff sergeants voluntarily resigned rather than take part in what he regarded as a suicide mission. During the night before they went, Boss Moss was replaced by Ian Crooke, so it was a pretty shell-shocked squadron that departed for Ascension Island without me.

Meanwhile, the war was continuing. G Squadron were inserted onto the Falklands to set up their OP matrix, whilst D Squadron launched a completely successful attack on an Argentine airfield at Pebble Island off West Falkland, where they'd dispersed a lot of their important Pucara ground-attack aircraft. Staff Sergeant Scholey, on the other hand, went home to wait and see what happened.

Two days after the squadron had left I had a feeling something was wrong and I decided to go onto camp to see what was going on. When I arrived, I could see that something was up: there were a lot of people bustling around, and I was told that there was a briefing for all personnel in the lecture room in thirty minutes. I knew then it was something awful. It was. A Sea King helicopter had gone down, taking twenty-two people with it, the majority of whom were members of D and G Squadrons, including both SSMs: Akker Atkinson from G Squadron, and Lawrence Gallagher from D . . .

The war came to an end three weeks later with only one further SAS casualty, John Hamilton, 19 Troop's commander. B Squadron never did get to launch their operation: the arrival of a radar guardship near to their target persuaded the powers-that-be that it was not going to work and instead they began to examine the options for a similar attack on Port Stanley airfield. In the end, that was binned as well, and elements of the squadron flew down to the islands just in time for the surrender.

It was also, finally, the end of the road for me. After we'd tidied up the squadron and brushed it down, I handed the stores over to Fred. I was forty-six now, and I'd been with the SAS for the best part of twenty years, and it was time to leave. I could have stayed, but it would have been doing a crap nothing-job like running the sergeants' mess bar, and that would have been a miserable way to end my career. I put my notice in, and I left.

But, of course, a career change at the age of forty-six is not the easiest thing to do. I had my pension but I also had two young children to support (Amy and David: born despite expert opinion that we'd never be able to have kids), and although my wife had her teaching job, we were accustomed to being a two-income family.

In the end, I started working on what is loosely called the circuit: bodyguarding a variety of VIPs of one sort or another, ranging from Mohammed al Fayed (briefly) to Cliff Richard, who is a very nice man. I also acquired the contract to run the security operation for the Miss World competition, the story of which would make a book in itself.

Whatever people like to claim, bread and butter bodyguard work isn't very interesting and isn't very well paid, and there are far too many people – some of whom have no conceivable qualifications for the job – chasing far too few contracts. When I first started out there were undoubtedly lean times but things improved over the years, and I've now reached a stage where I can work if I want to, but I'm secure enough not to have to.

As a sideline, my friend Mark Howarth and I also started to run leadership courses, under the name Black Knight, for schools, businesses and cadet forces units. I also work as a guest instructor for Colin Wallace's very successful Team Dynamics courses. So, all in all, things have worked out very well for me. I've survived, after all, to live in comfortable semi-retirement when many former comrades didn't: Paddy was killed in a car accident and Kevin succumbed to a tumour and so many other old friends have died young. They are never far from my thoughts. Whenever Lofty Wiseman, Don Large and I get together for a couple of beers we find ourselves chuckling over the exploits of Kev, the airborne wart, in particular.

There is no great moral to my life: I did the things I did because I enjoyed them; I liked the excitement; and I liked the people I worked with. The SAS was a tremendous organization to be part of, and I'm very proud to have been a member of it, but so was the Parachute Regiment, the Royal Artillery and the RASC. The British Army is far and away the most effective armed force, man for man, in the world; and we've achieved that without inflicting atrocities on civilians and non-combatants in campaign after campaign.

Throughout my military career, people saw me as a clown: well, I did muck about a bit, but when it mattered, I did the job and did it properly. In any case, no matter how you shuffle the cards, there's always a joker in the pack somewhere.

GLOSSARY

.303 The standard British Army rifle calibre from 1897 to 1958. A hugely powerful and accurate bullet, it is still encountered in some armies in the developing world.

44 pattern A type of canvas webbing equipment specially designed for jungle warfare and introduced in the British Army in 1944.

58 pattern The general issue webbing equipment in use by British forces since the early 1960s.

66 A light, portable, American-made, hand-held anti-tank rocket of 66mm nominal calibre and a maximum range of 200 metres. When fired accurately (no mean achievement), the 66 was found to have an impressive effect on static positions.

9mm The ammunition calibre used by British forces in pistols and sub-machine guns. '9mm' is also the generic term in the army for the Browning Hi-Power pistol issued to some personnel.

Adjutant An officer, normally of the rank of captain, who acts as the commanding officer's 'right-hand man' in peace and war, with special responsibility for personnel and discipline.

Advance to Contact A form of operation in which a unit, or sub-unit, travels along a set route until it meets an enemy position which it then engages. Normally used when the precise location of the enemy is unclear.

Armalite A 5.56mm light automatic rifle of American design used by the SAS since the mid-1960s, also known as the AR-15 and M16.

Bandolier A green plastic pouch issued to hold belts of 7.62mm machine-gun ammunition. An unpopular and fiddly item, the majority of soldiers prefer to carry belted ammunition slung around their bodies.

Basha An improvized shelter, normally constructed from the rainproof nylon poncho issued to all soldiers. In the SAS it is the generic term for all accommodation buildings.

Battalion A military unit typically composed of between 500 and 1000 soldiers commanded by a Lieutenant Colonel.

Belt-kit Webbing equipment adapted to be worn without a shoulder harness or yoke. In the British army it suggests membership of a Special Forces or specialist patrol unit.

Bergan The generic term in the British army for any military-type rucksack.

Beverley A British STOL transport aircraft of the 1950s and 1960s.

Brigade A military formation comprising two, or more, battalions and commanded by a . . .

Brigadier A 1-Star general of the British army or Royal Marines.

C-130 A 4-engined turbo-prop driven aircraft used as a general transport and Paratroop drop aircraft.

Captain Junior officer in the British army, typically employed on the battalion staff or as a company second-in-command. In 22 SAS, captains are employed as troop commanders.

Carl Gustav An 84mm anti-tank rocket launcher of Swedish design.

Chinook Large twin-rotor transport helicopter which can transport up to half a company of infantry.

CO Commanding officer. Normally a lieutenant colonel, a CO in the British army commands a unit of battalion-size or its equivalent.

Combats Generic army term for the heavy-duty camouflaged clothing worn in the field.

Company A sub-unit of an infantry battalion, normally comprising about 100 men commanded by a major. Equivalent-sized units of other arms are squadrons, batteries etc.

Compo Generic term for field rations issued by the British Army.

Corporal A junior non-commissioned officer, often to be found commanding a section of eight or ten men or a four-man patrol in the SAS.

CQMS (or SQMS) Company/squadron quartermaster sergeant. Appointment normally filled by a staff/colour sergeant, the CQMS is responsible for channelling stores from the quartermaster's department to his company, and for controlling their issue.

Crap-Hat (or 'hat') Any soldier who does not wear the maroon beret of airborne forces.

Crow A newly-joined, inexperienced soldier.

CSM (or SSM) Company/squadron sergeant major. A warrant officer class 2 who acts as right-hand man to a company or squadron commander. In battle, the CSM's task is to organise ammunition resupply for his fighting soldiers. In 22 SAS the SSMs are enormously influential figures and it is not unheard of for them to fulfil the squadron commander's appointment in the absence of a suitable officer.

D-day The specific day on which an operation takes place.

Det. Abbreviation of detonator.

DF A specific location onto which pre-arranged artillery fire can be brought.

Division A military formation comprising two, or more, brigades, and commanded by a Major General.

DMS Direct moulded sole, cheaply made, rubber-soled ankle boots issued by the British Army from the 1960s to the mid-1980s.

Dog-tags Metal discs worn by all soldiers in combat as a means of identifying their bodies afterwards. They bear the owner's name, number, religion and blood-group.

Doss-bag Military slang for sleeping-bag.

DPM Disruptive pattern material. British-pattern camouflaged cloth.

DZ Drop Zone

Endex 'End of Exercise'. Used on completion of virtually every task.

Exocet Effective French-built anti-ship missile used to devastating effect by the Argentine navy during the Falklands War.

Field Dressing Sterile pad with attached bandages issued to soldiers for emergency first aid in the field.

Firqat 'Company of men' (Arabic). Militia units raised and trained by 22 SAS during Operation Storm.

FOO Forward observation officer. Artillery officer, normally a lieutenant or captain, who accompanies infantry troops and brings in aimed artillery fire onto targets at their request or on his own initiative.

FPF Final protective fire. A high-priority DF used as a last resort very close to a friendly position if it appears likely to be overrun.

Gazelle A light reconnaissance helicopter.

Goon Troop Soldiers who have failed SAS selection by a narrow margin who remain at Hereford for a second attempt.

GPMG A belt-fed 7.62mm machine gun (also known as a gympy).

Green Slime Members of the Intelligence Corps attached to 22 SAS.

Headshed An SAS term for the commanding officer.

H Hour The specific time at which an operation starts.

HE High explosives.

Illum Starshells and flares used to light up a battlefield.

IO Intelligence officer. A member of the battalion staff - normally a captain or senior lieutenant - responsible for disseminating intelligence reports to the CO and company commanders, and reporting intelligence information to superior formations. In 22 SAS it is an officer from the Intelligence Corps.

IWS Individual weapon sight. A bulky nightsight that can be mounted on a rifle or machine gun, or used like a telescope.

Jebel Arabic for mountains.

Kevlar A fabric developed for the US space programme which has proved resistant to low-velocity bullets and shrapnel. Now used in body armour and helmets.

Lance Corporal The first rung on the promotion ladder for soldiers. Often carries with it the appointment of second-in-command of a section of eight men.

Larkspur Tactical VHF radio system superseded by the vastly superior 'Clansman'.

Lieutenant Junior officer with at least two years service (unless a university graduate). Will generally be commanding a platoon of 30 men.

Lieutenant Colonel A senior officer, normally commanding a regiment or battalion-sized unit or holding a senior staff appointment.

Lieutenant General A 3-star general under the British system, may command a Corps.

Major A 'field' grade officer, often commanding a squadron, company or equivalent-sized sub-unit.

Major General A 2-star general, often commanding a division.

Milan A wire-guided anti-tank missile with a range of up to 1950 metres.

Mirage A French-built fighter bomber used by the Argentines during the Falklands conflict.

MO Medical officer.

Morphine In combat, soldiers are issued with a dose of morphine-based painkiller to use on themselves if they are wounded. It comes in the form of a 'syrette', a small tube with attached hypodermic needle, for intramuscular injection.

MT Mechanical transport.

MTO Mechanical transport officer, an appointment usually held by an officer newly commissioned from the ranks.

ND Negligent discharge (of a weapon). An ND is a serious occurrence in the British Army; aside from being highly dangerous, it is indicative of sloppy drills and lack of professionalism.

NOD Night observation device.

O Group The O group is the means by which detailed operational orders are passed down the chain of command. It is, necessarily, a formal event which is usually carefully stage-managed and controlled by the commander giving the orders. The sequence of events is as follows: the commander describes the ground over which the operation he is outlining will take place and follows this with a briefing on the situation (the intelligence picture, what 'friendly forces' are doing, who is attached and detached for the operation, etc); once the situation has been described, the commander must then give a clear and simple mission statement (for example: 'to capture Mount Longdon'); at this point, the commander gives an outline of his plan and then goes on to describe in detail what he wants of each individual sub-unit under his command, this is followed by co-ordinating instructions explaining such crucial matters as timings; these are followed by a round up of essentially administrative points, and signals instructions. The formal structure and set format of an O group should mean that subordinate commanders will not miss any relevant orders or instructions.

OC Officer Commanding. The formal title of an officer in charge of a unit smaller than a battalion (i.e. a squadron, company, troop or platoon).

OP Observation post.

Ops Officer Operations officer. The battalion ops officer is responsible for the co-ordination and administration of the battalion's operational tasks and for assisting the CO in his planning process.

P Company P Company is a set of physical tests designed to assess an individual soldier's aptitude for serving with airborne forces. It occupies the most gruelling week of a Para recruit's basic training.

Padre All infantry battalions and most other major units have an attached chaplain known as the padre. Although padres are given officer's rank, they do not use it when dealing with soldiers to whom they are expected to provide spiritual leadership and moral guidance.

Patrol The four-man team which is the building block of SAS operations.

PC Platoon commander.

Platoon Sub-unit of an infantry company, normally comprising about thirty men commanded by a lieutenant or second lieutenant.

Pucara Argentine-built turbo-prop bomber designed for counter-insurgency and close air support applications.

QM Quartermaster. The officer, normally commissioned through the ranks, who is responsible for the battalion's logisitics.

R Group Reconnaissance group. A small team led by the CO, normally including the adjutant, a signaller and some bodyguards, which may leave the battalion tactical HQ in order to allow the CO to make a personal assessment of the battlefield situation.

RAP Regimental aid post. Battalion-level casualty clearing station where the wounded of both sides are assessed, stabilized and prepared for evacuation.

REMF Rear echelon mother fucker. A non-combatant soldier.

RSM Regimental sergeant major.

RSO Regimental signals officer.

RTU Returned to unit.

RV Rendevous.

Sangar A defensive position constructed above ground using sandbags, earth, peat or rocks, as opposed to a trench which is dug into the ground.

SAS Special Air Service. A multi-roled Special Forces unit of the British army. The majority of its members are recruited from the Parachute Regiment.

SBS Special Boat Squadron. A special forces unit recruited from the Royal Marine Commandos, with particular skills in amphibious and underwater infiltration of their targets. Now expanded, it is called the Special Boat Service.

Sea King Troop carrying helicopter in service with the Royal Navy.

Second Lieutenant The most junior officer's rank. A second lieutenant will normally be in command of a platoon.

Section A sub-unit of a platoon, normally comprising eight to ten men commanded by a corporal.

Sergeant Senior NCO, normally employed as second-in-command of a platoon or troop.

SLR Self Loading Rifle. Semi-automatic British variant of the fully-automatic 7.62mm FN FAL.

SMG Submachine-gun. A small fully-automatic weapon which normally fires pistol ammunition. In the British Army, this meant the 9mm Sterling-Patchett carbine.

SQMS see CQMS.

Staff Sergeant Also known as a 'colour sergeant' in the infantry. Senior NCO, usually employed as SQMS or sometimes as a troop commander.

Super Étendard French-made naval fighter-bomber. Capable of carrying the air-launched version of the Exocet missile.

Tab Tactical advance into battle. Paras slang for a forced march ('like yomping only faster and harder').

Team, the The SAS counter terrorist team.

Tom Any private soldier in the Paras.

Troop A 16 man sub-unit of 22 SAS nominally commanded by a Captain but in fact usually led by a staff sergeant.

Webbing The green canvas belt, harness and pouches used to carry ammunition water and other essentials into battle. Also known as 'fighting order', 'belt-kit' and 'belt order'.

Wetrep Weather report.

Windproof High-quality camouflaged combat jacket.

Wombat 120mm recoilless anti-tank gun issued at battalion level. Superseded by the Milan system.

Zulu time Greenwich Mean Time. Used in all military operations in order to avoid confusion.

INDEX

PENGUIN BOOKS

All Consuming

Neal Lawson is a political commentator. In between time spent shopping and thinking about shopping he writes regularly for the *Guardian*
and the *New Statesman*, and often appears on the radio and television.
He was formerly an advisor to Gordon Brown and before that was a
trade union researcher. He is chair of the fast-growing pressure group
Compass and managing editor of policy journal *Renewal*. In 2001 he
co-edited *The Progress Century* (Palgrave).

All Consuming

NEAL LAWSON

This book is dedicated to the work of Zygmunt Bauman

PENGUIN BOOKS

Published by the Penguin Group
Penguin Books Ltd, 80 Strand, London WC2R ORL, England
Penguin Group (USA) Inc., 375 Hudson Street, New York, New York 10014, USA
Penguin Group (Canada), 90 Eglinton Avenue East, Suite 700, Toronto, Ontario, Canada M4P 2Y3
(a division of Pearson Penguin Canada Inc.)
Penguin Ireland, 25 St Stephen's Green, Dublin 2, Ireland (a division of Penguin Books Ltd)
Penguin Group (Australia), 250 Camberwell Road,
Camberwell, Victoria 3124, Australia (a division of Pearson Australia Group Pty Ltd)
Penguin Books India Pvt Ltd, 11 Community Centre,
Panchsheel Park, New Delhi – 110 017, India
Penguin Group (NZ), 67 Apollo Drive, North Shore 0632,
New Zealand (a division of Pearson New Zealand Ltd)
Penguin Books (South Africa) (Pty) Ltd, 24 Sturdee Avenue,
Rosebank, Johannesburg 2196, South Africa

Penguin Books Ltd, Registered Offices: 80 Strand, London WC2R ORL, England

www.penguin.com

Published in Penguin Books 2009
2

Set in 11/13pt Bembo by Palimpsest Book Production Limited
Grangemouth, Stirlingshire
Printed in England by Clays Ltd, St Ives plc

ISBN 978-0-141-02941-2

www.greenpenguin.co.uk

Mixed Sources
Product group from well-managed
forests and other controlled sources
www.fsc.org Cert no. SA-COC-1592
© 1996 Forest Stewardship Council

Penguin Books is committed to a sustainable future
for our business, our readers and our planet.
The book in your hands is made from paper
certified by the Forest Stewardship Council.

Contents

Acknowledgements

We stand on the shoulders of giants. And no one stands so firmly on others than me. Are there original thoughts? I'm unsure. I read, hear or see something from someone else and an idea clicks in my mind – but this is just the process of putting together pre-existing ideas. As the dedication for the book implies, I am most indebted to the ideas of Zygmunt Bauman. His book *Work, Consumerism and the New Poor* (Open University Press, 2005) was instrumental in waking me from a political slumber and helped put me on the path to writing this book. His ideas, creative thoughts and sheer humanity have and continue to be a huge inspiration to me. But there are other shoulders. Not least Adam Curtis, whose BBC documentary *The Century of the Self* I found particularly inspiring. And Frank Trentman spoke kindly and wisely to me when I was starting this project. Everyone who is a member of and supports Compass, especially Gavin Hayes and Zoe Gannon, have helped support me in all sorts of ways. There is a talented and growing team of people involved in this organization, which I have been lucky enough to chair for the last five years; I owe all of them a massive debt for their ideas, enthusiasm and commitment.

A big thank-you goes to Madeleine Bunting, not just for her ideas and thoughts but because she generously introduced me to her agent, Natasha Fairweather. Natasha helped me write the book proposal and find a publisher in Venetia Butterfield at Penguin. In the book-writing process, the biggest acknowledgement goes to Jenny Dean at Penguin, who turned a rough script into something publishable. She worked extremely hard. Then Hazel Orme, who copy-edited the script, made it better still. Along the way I am, of course, grateful to everyone I interviewed and spoke to. In particular I would like to thank Susan Steed and

Michael Calderbank, who helped with much of the early research. Here my gratitude goes to the directors of the Joseph Rowntree Reform Trust, who provided a grant to help cover some of the research costs. But, of course, all the mistakes, omissions and faults are mine.

On a personal note I'd like to thank Buddy and Joe for putting up with a dad who too often was thinking about a book and not about them. I will strive for a better work–life balance in the future. Derek and Valerie have seemed to buy me everything I ever needed but crucially gave me the love and confidence to think that I could attempt to write a book. Sally has been the most wonderful thing I have ever taken home and her love and support I will cherish for ever. Finally I would like to thank Sarah and, in particular, Sharon. She was one of the key inspirations for the book and always wants me to get what I want – but she just hopes it doesn't mean she has to stop shopping. She wouldn't know what else to do.

Neal Lawson, March 2009

More!

'More?'[1]

the master of the workhouse, in Charles Dickens, *Oliver Twist*

I wake to the annoying electronic bleep of my BlackBerry Pearl
mobile and resist for as long as possible the demand to emerge
from Heal's organic cotton sheets and Habitat bed. My feet
eventually land on one of a thousand possible carpets from John
Lewis, then carry me to the bathroom. There, among wood,
stone and chrome, I ready myself for the day with bottles of Gillette this and Dove that from a cabinet filled with brands and
finally wrap myself in White Company towels. There is just time
to glance in the mirror to tell whether I'm thin enough or, more
realistically, too fat to look right in a world where a glance at
others tells me whether everyone else looks right too.

Then it's back to the bedroom to find the right clothing for
the day. Everything in the wardrobe was selected with as much
care as was everything that is in yours. I pick the outfit that suits
my mood, a combination I haven't worn for a while and can
face at least once more. As I dress I notice every mark, worn
thread and scuff. And as I put on each item I test my mood –
does this still make me feel good? I'm searching for reasons to
buy afresh and replace the tried and tired with new.

In the space of fifteen minutes, I experience and confront
hundreds of my purchasing decisions. My clothes and my flat, its
blinds, lights, furniture and mirrors, say everything I want said
about me. Welcome, in this small snapshot of my daily life, to the
consumer society.

I wasn't born to be like this. I didn't come into this world
determined to surround myself with bundles of clothes I can't

possibly hope to wear out and more gadgets than I could ever
understand, let alone use. It happened because I allowed it to
happen and even wanted it to. But it wasn't an accident and it's
not just me. It's most of us. And I wasn't really given a choice. We
consume so heavily by design.

From consumerism to turbo-consumerism

The first claim of this book is that we live not just in a consumer
society but in a turbo-consuming society. The second claim is
that this need not be the case in the future, especially now that
the hurtling train of consumerism has come off the rails.

Consumption once meant tuberculosis. Now it means 'to use
up'. A society defined by consumption 'uses up' on a systematic
and industrial scale. Indeed, while it isn't all we do, the culture,
institutions, laws and values of society are now organized primarily around consuming.

Throughout the book I will use the words 'shopping' and
'consumption' interchangeably to mean buying anything –
services as well as goods. Going to a restaurant is just as much an
act of consumption as buying a new shirt from Gap. Consuming
is applied to everything we buy: clothes, cars, holidays, escape,
sex, relaxation, support, care, health, education, even love. It is
the extent to which we shop and buying's hold on us that defines
society as being driven primarily by consumerism. Don't take
my word for it: take the word of the Prime Minister's best brains
in the Strategy Unit who, in 2007, declared that 'The UK is now
a consumer society.'

But it's more than that. Over the last three decades we shifted
from being consumers to being turbo-consumers. In that time
our consuming addiction raced away with us – gratification
could no longer be deferred: it had to be instant. We stopped
comparing ourselves with the Joneses and attempted instead to
match up to the Beckhams. The stream of new designer goods
just accelerated at a faster and faster pace, to such an extent that

throughout the 1980s and 1990s what we bought became solidly entwined with our identity. Now we are what we buy. Two homes and three cars became the reality for some and the aspiration for many; easy access to credit and new global supply chains meant there was more of everything for more of us. By 2008 there were 121 mobile phones for every 100 people in the UK. One commentator said that in the face of three-for-two book offers shopping wasn't just shopping but breathing. Shopping had become life. For some it has become death: boys will kill boys for possession of the right trainers.

In a turbo-consumer society they sold us anything. They sold us togetherness: 'Without others I am nothing' (Orange) and 'Life is better if lived together' (Volvo). They sold us individuality: 'True individuality is hard to find' (Jaguar). They sold us control: 'Imagine a phone you cannot manage without' (Samsung). They sold us identity: 'It's your watch that says the most about who you are' (Seiko). They sold us one-upmanship: 'Mediocrity is a sin' (Alfa-Romeo). They sold us exclusivity: 'Wealth – it's being able to tell the world to get lost' (Barclays). They sold us shopping: 'Shop. Don't Drop' (Peugeot). They even sold us ourselves: 'You buy a piece of yourself' (Seat Leon). As the wheels came off the extraordinary consumption vehicle that had entered every aspect of our lives, will they still be able to sell us anything?

The leap to an even faster and more furious using-up was the product of cheap imports from China, and new technology meant we could buy online 24/7. But this transformation of our lives had political roots. Days of rest became days to go shopping because of changes to the Sunday trading laws. Access to easy credit was a result of the deregulation of the banking industry. The opportunity to buy council houses and shares in the newly privatized industries encouraged more and more to think of themselves as mini-capitalists. A culture that said greed was good and that there was no such thing as society fuelled a possessive individualism. Planning laws favoured the building of more and more out-of-town stores. In areas like education and health we

were encouraged to behave more like consumers than citizens and make shopping-style choices about the services we received. Taxes were lowered so we could spend more, and in the last decade house prices were pushed up by allowing the restriction in supply of new homes so we could turn these rising assets into piggy banks for consuming more.

The centrality of consumerism in our lives was enshrined in the aftermath of the bombing in New York of the Twin Towers. In defiant mode, the liberal, secular West was supposedly returned to normality by the shopping expeditions of celebrities, who had caviar and champagne on Concorde and were greeted at Kennedy Airport by Mayor Giuliani's invitation to 'Spend! Spend! Spend!' National confidence was aligned to consumer confidence. As a signal of Western spiritual revival this seemed fairly bizarre, and its celebration of conspicuous consumption was hardly tactful in a global context, where living standards in the world's forty-nine least-developed countries were now lower than they had been thirty years before.

But living in a turbo-consumer society was about more than what we were sold and how. At its core, consumerism was a social phenomenon: the act of consumption had become our primary means of understanding ourselves and how we related to each other. It became the way in which society reproduced itself – not least because it marked a seismic shift in our identities: for centuries we had known ourselves and others through what we produced; now we identified ourselves and others by what we consumed. The age of production gave way to the age of consumption. Work still matters, but nowhere near as much as shopping.

Shopping matters so much because it now defines what it is to be normal. Normality was previously defined by having a job. Now it is defined by what we do with the money we earn from working. As a race we have always competed for status, but in the second half of the twentieth century it was no longer based on how much meat we brought home or how many sexual partners we had, but on what we bought.

We shopped because we were competitive. We shopped because we were seduced by the experience. But we also shopped out of fear. We kept up the pace on the hamster wheel of consumption, secretly knowing that it took us nowhere, but terrified above all else of falling off. Then we would stop being consumers and put ourselves beyond the pale, non-people who couldn't keep up. Despite all the pressures and the empty promise that buying more would make us happier, the only thing worse than turbo-consumerism was not being a turbo-consumer.

Until the financial crisis, the danger was in the emergence of a consumer monoculture that had two retail-driven purposes. First, it extended to the maximum the places in which profits could be made by selling the same things all round the globe. The world became a giant shopping mall of the same brands found on every high street from Shoreditch to Shanghai. Second, it reinforced the ruling-out of alternative ways for society to organize itself. For a consumer society to sustain itself, it must ensure that there is only time to shop; no distractions and no alternatives are permitted. We could no longer imagine anything else to do or any other way of being as we literally spent more and more of our lives on paid-for experiences. Now we can hardly remember a time when the shops weren't open on a Sunday, when high streets looked different , when we did something else in our spare time other than go shopping.

Just two decades ago television shopping was something to be laughed at. In programmes like *Are You Being Served?* and *Open All Hours*, the shoppers and shopkeepers were valued for their comic effect. Today the TV schedules are full of serious factual programmes about shopping and buying – from *Property Ladder* to *What Not to Wear* – because shopping is now a serious business.

A dangerous negative feedback loop has been in operation: the more a consumer society ruled out other ways of being free, other ways of being social, creative and happy, the more anxious and insecure we became. As such, shopping became a coping

mechanism for the problems it was creating. We shopped to forget, to distract ourselves, to have at least some fleeting power at the till and control over a small speck of our lives. We shopped to escape not just from our world but from ourselves as we constantly dumped our old identities in search of something new and better. 'Oh, reason not the need,' said William Shakespeare's King Lear. But it was a deeply flawed coping mechanism because it wasn't designed to help us cope but consume more. Consumer society sold us dissatisfaction, then sold us the cure.

Until very recently it seemed that modern consumer capitalism had discovered the art of perpetual motion, a cyclical process that offered enough to keep us hooked, ever anticipating the next buy, but never enough to quench our thirst. It was a process driven by what we can now identify as a consumer industrial complex of marketers, advertisers, media moguls, designers, retailers, psychologists, analysts, share traders, transporters, growers and producers with an insatiable appetite for more. Because all these people were locked into the same cycle of consumption as we were: they strove to sell us more, to win a greater share of the market, to grow their profits, boost their share price so that they earned more and bought more.

The mess we're in

But on 15 September 2008 shockwaves shuddered through the world of turbo-consumerism. On that day Hank Paulson, then US Treasury Secretary under George W. Bush, decided to pull the plug on Lehman Brothers Holdings, one of the biggest financial-services firms on the planet. The bank was forced to file for bankruptcy protection. The rest is history. From that point on confidence and trust in the global financial system drained away and world-wide recession ensued. Credit dried up, house prices plummeted and thousands of jobs were lost each day. All of a sudden overstretched mortgages and mounting credit- and store-card debts didn't seem such a good idea. No

one would lend so no one could borrow so no one could spend. We had shopped. Now it really was time to drop.

In the winter of 2008/9 prices in the shops were slashed to sell off unsold stock in a desperate attempt to get people back into the shops. One anonymous City analyst summed up the wave of retailer panic, saying, 'Desperate times call for desperate measures.' Credit insurers who protected suppliers from retailers' unpaid bills stopped providing cover: the risk had become too great. As established high-street names, like Woolworths, went under, they sold off stock at rock-bottom prices and therefore put their struggling competitors under even more strain.

But this was just the moment the bubble burst – a bubble that had been pumped full of more and more hot air for years. The credit crunch was the symptom, not the cause, of the great consumer crash of 2008. It was our obsession with shopping that was both creator and victim of the biggest global recession for more than eighty years. This recession, though, is unique in that its origins didn't lie in an external shock, such as rocketing oil prices or war, but in over-consumption and greed. Everyone wanted more. The final trigger was the US sub-prime housing market. After the unprecedented liberalization of financial services in the 1980s, mortgages were being sold to people with no secure employment who were highly likely to default on their loans. But no one wanted to believe the bubble would burst. Everyone wanted to live the home-ownership dream, and the lure of that dream meant more money could be made by reckless bankers and therefore more money spent. The system of acquisitive greed crashed itself.

But what was happening in the US was only a reflection of what was happening in the UK. Former building societies that had demutualized in the 1980s and 1990s were struggling to find their place in the competitive banking sector. New banks like Northern Rock began offering mortgages of more than 100 per cent on properties whose price would inevitably fall – leaving the owners deep in negative equity. The only issue was when. The aspiration to 'build society' had quickly been lost in the

greed of bankers to boost their pay, share options and, therefore, their propensity to spend. Everyone wanted their foot on the housing ladder, in part so that rising prices and repeated remortgaging would allow them to spend, spend, spend. What mattered was what you earned, what you could borrow, what your house was worth and what you could buy. Easy credit led to easy shopping and easyJet. Hedge funds and selling short, derivatives and default swaps, junk bonds and consolidated debts, securitization and share options – it was one giant pyramid-selling scam, built on a swamp of toxic debts, that sank overnight.

Who was to blame? Greedy bankers, of course, ineffectual regulators, over-eager salespeople and politicians who either did nothing or did the wrong thing to stoke the consumer bubble. But we bought the stuff. We wanted it. We defined ourselves by it. We allowed ourselves to drift into the comatose life of the turbo-consumer. We needed something to worship and something to believe in and had long since swapped God for Gucci. We had been living beyond our means, in debt beyond our ability to pay, in the naïve and hopeless belief that this would be the first bubble that would never burst. We tried to defy economic gravity so we could just keep buying. Because that was all there was to do.

Why there can be no going back

The crash of this mad and unsustainable system has caused seismic reactions across the planet, not least from our politicians. Leaders who had extolled the virtues of free markets for decades are now falling over themselves to nationalize banks and pump the economy back into action. The mission of all the mainstream party leaders is to get things back to 'normal', and no stone will be left unturned in the quest. In Britain VAT was cut by 2.5 per cent for thirteen months to urge shoppers back to the high street, and the Bank of England cut interest rates to their lowest ever level to entice them still further.

The system had crashed, but all the politicians could think to do was hit the rewind button of consumer capitalism. If everyone started shopping again it would all be all right. It's the political equivalent of keeping the family warm by burning down the house. But if it was shopping that got us into this mess, it won't be shopping that gets us out of it. This time, unlike with other recessions, there are compelling reasons why we can't go back to how things were before.

The first is that the past decades of turbo-consumerism have made us much wealthier but no happier. It doesn't mean that, given the chance, we won't opt for more wealth and more spending power. We may not become any happier, and the consequences of wanting more may be damaging to us, our society and the planet, but when that's all there is to do then it's all we do. However much 'stuff' we buy, we always want more because there's nothing else to have. But a society based on more can never be a happy place to live, and I believe people are beginning to recognize that they want more from life than competitive materialism.

The breakdown in the link between happiness and consumption is a very modern phenomenon because it only occurs when society goes beyond the point of survival to abundance. For most of us that happened in the last hundred years but has accelerated during the last thirty. As a species, humans were conditioned over hundreds of thousands of years to live with scarcity and the challenge of physical survival. We knew what to do when we were hungry or cold – we had to acquire enough to survive – but when those basic needs had been met, we developed a problem. The challenge of a post-material world has been emotional survival, how to live rich and fulfilling lives, which, until now, we have attempted to achieve through consumption. It hasn't worked. Now the recession is forcing us to rethink.

The myth that the more we have the happier we become is self-perpetuating: the more we consume, the less able we are to challenge the myth. The more we rely on shopping, the more other ways of being human are diminished because there is less

space for them to flourish. We've lost the ability to function without consumption. But the dramatic downturn in the economy is taking away even the distraction of shopping from a life in which we cannot truly be free.

And here is one of the central problems of a consumer society, which helps explain why we are wealthier but no happier. We've been competing with others, gaining and losing advantage, in a race that has no end, because there is no finishing line in a competition in which success and our happiness are defined by other people's unhappiness. We have out-consumed each other, so it's become an act of collective failure. When our neighbours acquired more, we wanted even more. They struck back and we tried endlessly to outdo each other. Ultimately no one had a lasting advantage and we all lost out. Now, when thousands are being fired, the credit is drying up, debts are looming and shops are going under, the majority will have to console themselves with window shopping or find something else to do in order to break the chain.

This is the real clincher about our unhappiness. A turbo-consumer society rests on the fact that our needs are never satisfied: if they were satisfied we would stop shopping – or, at least, stop shopping so much. A consumer society can't allow us to stop shopping and be happy because then the whole system would die – for good. Instead it has to sell us just enough to keep us going, but never enough that our wants are satisfied. Consumer society is based on the fine art of compensation, enough to reward us and keep our interest but not enough to stop us going back to the shops for more. Like all forms of compensation it offers rewards – but it is just that: compensation for a richer and fuller life. Turbo-consumerism is the heroin of human happiness. It's a quick and expensive high that soon fades, leaving us desperate for more. Now the credit crunch means that many can't even get the hit of compensation.

The second reason why we can't return to our old turbo-consumerist habits is because by buying more we have become increasingly empowered as consumers but increasingly disem-

powered as citizens, losing control over key aspects of our lives. The more we consume, the less space there is to be anything other than consumers. The space to be citizens and make decisions equally and collectively about the world around us is diminished. There are more individual choices to be made about the range of goods stacked on the shelves, but as we flex our solitary consumer muscles we have become weaker as citizens in command of our social, political, economic and natural environment – the big things in life. It is only as citizens that we can shape the world around us and the institutions that affect us. Laws, regulations, public investment, communities and society are the product of collective decision-making. It is only as citizens that we can choose *not* to choose, put boundaries around consumerism and decide where it can and can't go. We can decide what can and can't be sold and to whom. For instance, Sweden has decided to end the commercialization of childhood by banning all adverts to children under twelve. That country still has a civic culture that permits such a decision. Does Britain have such a culture? The crisis of consumption, brought on by the recession, gives us a chance to rebalance ourselves as consumers and citizens.

The third reason that we cannot return to turbo-consumerism is that the planet cannot sustain itself based on recent levels of consumption. If everyone in the world was to live as we do in the UK, it would take the resources of three planets to sustain us all. It is not just a question of slowing down the rate of increase in what we consume but of consuming less. Our lives are in conflict with our planet. Climate change beyond our ability to manage the consequences is a direct result of over-industrialization and over-consumption. We must relinquish our consumption habit or our habitat.

So, there can be no going back. We will always shop because we will always need to consume. Buying, trading and choosing are part of us. The issue is not whether we will stop shopping but whether we can rebalance our lives to do other things as well. Can we avoid permanently falling into the trap of an all-

consuming society? Or is it too late? Have we reached a tipping point into a form of turbo-consumerism that rules out the possibility of a different way of living? Will we bounce straight out of this recession and back into the bad old ways of turbo-consumption?

Though politicians beseech us to return to our normal shopping patterns, what happened before was not normal. What started in the latter decades of the twentieth century and came to a shuddering halt in 2008 was a blip. A blip between thousands of years of struggle for survival and the rapid arrival of super-abundance we did not know how to handle. If we return to a life of turbo-consumerism, we return not to normality but to abnormality. Of course, this remains an option, but if we take it, we will pay the price in unhappy lives that spiral even further out of control, and we will reap the whirlwind of climate change.

A time to decide

For the first time in a generation we stand at a crossroads. Events have polarized and focused the choices. The treadmill of turbo-consumerism has halted and most of us have been jolted off. Are we going to climb back on in the hopeless belief that the system has been cleansed? Or are we going to start afresh in a different way?

Politicians urge us to spend our way out of the financial meltdown. Once again we are called upon to shop till we drop to prop up the economy. Too many of our politicians, opinion-formers and journalists are still in the old paradigm that more means happiness. They want us to borrow money we can't afford to buy things we don't need to keep the treadmill in motion. Nowhere is this more apparent than in Shepherds Bush, West London, where the Westfield shopping centre opened as the markets and consumer confidence crashed. The site cost £1.7 billion, and houses 270 stores, 50 restaurants, 13 cinemas and

space for 4,500 cars over 40 acres. It was conceived in the age of abundance but opened in an age of austerity. Will Westfield be a monument to a consumer century, a relic, a folly or a taste of the future?

If we rescue the system without reforming it, it will be only a matter of time before the next bubble bursts. A nation driven by the urge to spend now and pay later will always have to pay later. Will today's recession be a diet before we return to the consumer binge? Of the £228 billion we spend every year in Britain, more than half is spent on non-essentials. We simply don't have to spend it.

Can we use the recession to break our shopping addiction? To do it, like all addicts, we must first admit we have a problem and recognize that we should expect more from our lives, that we should be happier, in more control, and allow the planet to sustain itself. We should aim for a good life in a good society in which we commit ourselves to strike a decent balance between ourselves as consumers and the richness of being citizens, family members, friends, colleagues and neighbours. We have always had the power to decide but the consumer crisis has given us an opportunity we can't ignore.

This is a book about shopping – why we shop and set so much store by it, how our consumer society came into being, the effects of it on ourselves, and how we might redress the balance so that our lives are less about consuming. When I told people I was writing a book that criticized shopping their reaction was often hostile. The subject seems to touch a nerve. People ask what is so wrong with a bit of shopping – the concern that we do too much is middle-class angst – or they become defensive: yes, they shop a lot but they do other things as well. The more robust will say that no one makes them go shopping, they do it of their own free will and will continue as they want to. Others admit that they shop but are quick to add that they hate it.

We have been trying to fool ourselves about our shopping addiction. It can never be just a bit of shopping. Consumption

has become the centre of our existence because it has been designed to do so by a complex web of interests and powers. And in criticizing consumer society I understand that it's easier for those who have more material possessions than others to do so. Of course it would better if we could consume more equally, but a better life, a good society and a sustainable planet won't come through everyone consuming more. Consumer societies always tend towards greater inequality – the US is more unequal than the UK, which in turn is more unequal than the Nordic nations – and the gap between rich and poor makes those at the bottom anxious and stressed to the extent that they live shorter and more brutish lives. Such hardship has been explored extensively by academics, including Richard Wilkinson and Michael Marmot. Poverty is a relative, not simply an absolute, blight that requires a reassessment of the good life and the way that consumer society creates emotional and social poverty, touching the lives of even the 'wealthiest' and causing environmental destruction.

Our relationship to consumption and our reliance on it has become unhealthy and dysfunctional. While it worked by providing compensation for the better life we hoped for, there was little chance of changing it. But the crash changes everything. I believe there is an alternative, and that it's worth fighting for. We can take action as individuals, collectively and through the state to tip the balance against lives that are all-consuming and define a new normality based on having the time and space to find genuine and lasting happiness.

'The great error of our nature,' wrote Edmund Burke in 1757, 'is not to know where to stop; not to be satisfied with any reasonable acquirement . . . but to lose all we have gained by an insatiable pursuit of more.' It is the 'insatiable pursuit of more' that must now be addressed.

We have lived in a turbo-consumer society and some want us to return to it as soon as possible. They want us to go back to just wanting more. I don't think we should buy it.

1. What went wrong?

Welcome to the British Aisles

Until very recently, Britain was a nation of shoppers. Low taxes, easy credit and soaring house prices stoked a buying boom that seemed unstoppable. But nothing lasts for ever and now we are a nation with a severe shopping hangover, mired in collapsing house prices, painful joblessness and the prospect of eventual tax hikes. As with all addicts when the source of their addiction is taken away, our desire to shop is still there but the means to do so isn't. People wander the shopping malls but their bags are fewer and lighter, window shopping their only cheap consumer thrill. We are going through the motions but it's a hollow experience, devoid of meaning because meaning can only be found in ownership of something new. The thrill can only be found at the till. Instead we are shopping zombies – neither dead nor alive.

This is because, in the long period of economic boom, our lives became all consuming. We are a nation that's forgotten how to entertain itself without throwing money at the problem. A nation that's become accustomed to defining itself by what it buys relative to everyone else, be it a house, a car, a wardrobe or a meal in a fancy restaurant. When you are what you buy, then buying nothing means you are nothing. And with these structures taken away, we're lost. So, how did we get to this miserable place that lacks meaning, purpose and direction?

Not so very long ago, on a Saturday morning in a big Victorian house in Whitstable on the Kent coast, two great friends, Sharon and Sarah, would get ready to go shopping. It was what they did every Saturday. Often they had no specific items in mind to buy – the goal was not necessarily to buy anything at

all, although invariably they did. Going shopping was all they wanted to do.

They had a rota. They went either to one of the main shopping centres of west Kent or to one of the smaller towns – Whitstable itself, Herne Bay or Canterbury. The first two meant charity shops, the last big stores or chains. And they had a routine. They would set off at ten or eleven to find an all-day parking spot, then off they'd go along a well-worn trail of shops. From then on, nothing could stop them.

They'd pass from shop to shop, perhaps pausing in WH Smith over a calendar they wouldn't have noticed had it not been reduced from £9.99 to 99p. It would be perfect for one of their mums. At that price it would be rude not to buy it. Especially with the counter offer of a half-price king-size bar of chocolate.

TK Maxx was their favourite. TK Maxx sells designer goods, everything from clothes to household items. In 1994 TK Maxx opened its first UK store in Bristol. In 2007 it had 210 stores across the country and annual sales of £688 million, up 161 per cent in the preceding five years.[2] It is one of the biggest players in the 'value sector', managing to seduce the middle class who would never confess to buying clothes from Tesco but are delighted to be able to discuss their latest TK Maxx designer bargain. Sharon and Sarah could spend all day in a TK Maxx store. Six hours in the same shop! But this is because TK Maxx is a discount store and discounts are the holy grail of shopping, guaranteed to get pulses racing. The bargain hunt is their biggest thrill – when they still find themselves parting with their cash. What kind of discount were they after? Seventy per cent was the magic figure. If they could get that, they'd hunted well.

The sales were a special time of year. Sharon and Sarah would head out early – sometimes as early as five a.m. – dressed in flat shoes for comfort and just a few layers for ease and speed of changing. They'd have done their research, working out the quickest route to the department they wanted, deciding whether the back stairs would be speedier than negotiating the escalators. They knew that shops always make mistakes when discounting

old stock so much of the day would be spent asking staff to check prices in the hope that they had found something that should have been marked down but had been missed. This was shopping gold dust. Most people, the two claimed, can't do the maths and don't know what the discounts are. It's said that half the population don't know what 50 per cent of the country is! But I wonder if they've ever stopped to think about the value of what was being discounted. If a skirt can be marked down by 50 per cent from £150 to £75, was it worth £150 in the first place?

I remember once hearing from the Woolworths' corporate-affairs office that they were 'surprised to hear high-street shopping was clocking up so many miles and helping to keep customers staying healthy'. So, this is how Britain's been fighting the obesity epidemic. Their research showed that the average British woman covers an estimated 133 miles a year by going to the shops. That's the equivalent of walking from London to Nottingham. They said that the average woman clocks up 2.77 miles every time she goes on a two-hour shopping trip. Well, we know Sharon and Sarah shopped for at least five hours per week – more than double the national average – so that's more like London to Newcastle.

I knew about Sharon and Sarah not because I read about or interviewed them but because Sharon is my sister and Sarah is her best friend. It was in part Sharon's fascination with shopping, her expertise and her dedication to the consumer cause, that led me to write this book. They are lovely, thoughtful, progressive women. But what they did was shop. They shopped more than most – but they were no longer the exception that proved the rule: they became the rule.

There is no identikit shopper. We are all different. Sharon and Sarah fitted lots of the stereotypes but they had their own shopping code. For instance, they had a one-in-one-out policy: if they bought a new pair of shoes, they had to throw an old pair out. A space issue, it also gave them licence to keep on buying – the perpetual motion of recycling stuff through their home

with no physical limitation. But for Sharon and Sarah shopping was primarily a social act, which fits with theories of shopping as essentially caring and loving. Academics such as Daniel Millar describe consumption as a form of gift relationship in which women in particular express their love for their family through what they buy them. Sharon and Sarah rarely hunted alone and would work the shops and racks as a team, finding sizes and styles for each other. And they were always looking out for items for other people – family, friends, work colleagues, for birthdays or Christmas or just because they knew someone who would like a particular bargain.

This side of the crash, Sharon and Sarah are much more sanguine about their shopping habits. They work in the state-education sector so are unlikely to lose their jobs. But money has been tight, not least because of the fuel-bill increases Britain experienced in 2008. They have a big house to heat, and drive a long way to work every day. They thought about trading down to a smaller house and ended up car-sharing. They now wait longer before they buy. But the up-side is that things are cheaper. A 20 per cent discount is nothing. They know the stores won't give stuff away but they expect them to go as close as possible. They were in on the last rites of Woolworths, the fire sale of goods just before Christmas 2008. They, like others, were out for a bargain but wanted also to pay their respects to a high-street institution that would be mourned if not really missed.

My sister got the shopping bug as a teenager but says that it was when she became a home-owner in her late twenties that it really took off. All of a sudden there were more reasons to buy. She knows she became a shopping obsessive but there was nothing better she could find to do with her time. And she was a good shopper. She and Sarah get a kick from hunting and gathering the bargains; from hunter gatherers to bargain hunters. They loved the thrill of the chase. Thousands of years on the Serengeti, the place from which we all derive, honed our instincts and our genetic make-up to seek and consume our prey. Shopping became Sharon and Sarah's modern version of the hunt,

ears pricked for the click of the gun marking down prices in a supermarket aisle, like the snap of a twig in the forest. But they bought food because it was cheap or exotic – not because they needed it. And that is the difference between consumption and turbo-consumption. It is the act of buying and having that matters, not whether you make use of what you acquire. But for Sharon and Sarah, shopping was a way to relax and let off steam. Where was the harm in that when no one was forcing them to do it?

The shopping society

Of course, it wasn't just Sharon and Sarah. It was all of us. As a nation we've become used to spending much more. In 2006 the British spent over £1 trillion. That was almost £40,000, on average, for every household in the country, and 10 per cent up on the year before. The insurers at the Prudential have calculated that on average we each spend £1.5 million during our lives, men spending more than women. That's almost 50 per cent more than a decade before. In ten years we almost doubled our consumption.

I remember 1996. It wasn't the year of the Irish potato famine and there was no Second World War-style rationing. It was the era of John Major, of 'back to basics' and the traffic-cones hotline. I don't recall thinking, I've bought sixteen shirts but I really need thirty-two. I seem to remember having enough. And it's funny but I don't remember making any conscious decision to buy twice as many shoes, socks or pants in the intervening years. Somehow it just happened. I graduated from five pairs of shoes to ten, from three weekend breaks a year to six, from a meal out once a week to twice – all without a thought or care. Does that sound familiar?

If we were happy once with fewer material goods, more free time and fewer office hours, can we go back? Can we suppress the urge not just to be consumers but the turbo-consumers that

we have become over the last decade or so? Perhaps the recession and the credit crunch, despite the real pain some people are feeling, are blessings in disguise because the option to shop is being taken away.

It won't be easy. In recent years we lived with an explosion of new styles, tastes and choices. We have been convinced that unless we keep up with the latest trends our lives are a failure. We are endlessly bombarded with ever-changing images of what is cool. The democratization of luxury means that there is no ceiling on our buying ambitions. Gucci, D&G and Mercedes-Benz are brands we can aspire to – even, at the lower end, own and enjoy. The pace of the treadmill has quickened to an alarming degree. The faster it goes, the harder the challenge of jumping off.

The industrial consumer complex has found new ways to persuade us that we need one product over another and favour one retailer more than another. The tried-and-tested means of adverts on TV, in print and on billboards was used to the full but new methods were deployed in the goals of turning wants into needs. Sponsorship, celebrity endorsement and product placement took off. But new technology drove the buying spree. As I typed this, a message popped into my email inbox from Amazon, the online bookseller: 'We've noticed that customers who have expressed interest in *Liquid Life* [it's about modernity, not drinking] by Zygmunt Bauman have also ordered *Global Culture Industry: The Mediation of Things* by Scott Lash. For this reason, you might like to know that this book is now available. You can order your copy for just £57.00 by following the link below.' It is impossible to escape the onslaught.

I have a large book collection. Shelves span one big wall and there are piles more books around the flat. They hang like intellectual trophies on the wall. As the moose head displays the hunter's skills, so the bookshelves display my shopping skills and through them the inner me. We all do it: we buy things as signals of what we want to be and how we want others to think of us. I've got rows of obscure political theory arranged, laughably, by colour and size, not by subject. It's an aesthetic thing. The books

are essentially expensive wallpaper. About a fifth of them have not been read – not properly – and probably never will be.

For a while I ponder the £57 price tag of a book I didn't know existed, let alone wanted, until that helpful email came along. And, of course, it doesn't stop there. Amazon are quick to tell me about six other titles I didn't know I wanted but do now. Suddenly it's easier to understand how I graduated from buying an average of twenty books a year to forty.

We've become used to buying twice as much because companies like Amazon make it so easy, because we define ourselves through what we buy, because we have the money, and because there is little else to do. It means our little island has been over-run with shops. With 250,000 staff in the UK, Tesco employs twice as many people as the British Army. Their turnover is bigger than the Gross Domestic Product (GDP) of Peru. One pound in every seven spent in Britain is handed over to Tesco. It made £2.8 billion profit in 2007, or £5,000 profit every minute of the year. The recession will hit it, but companies like Tesco turned the country into the British Aisles.

We have reached a point where almost anything can be sold to anyone – even our children. Indeed, the commercialization of childhood has become a big driver of our turbo-consuming world. Children are a major source of society's consumer impulse. In the last twenty years the quality and cost of children's toys have rocketed. Peer-group pressure, advertising and guilt-stricken parents combine with new electronic-games technology to ensure bedrooms are overflowing with consoles, gadgets and gizmos. The UK toy market is worth upwards of £3 billion a year, and by the time the average British child reaches sixteen, they will have owned £11,000 worth of playthings. It's a shame: the best present you can give a child is your time. But who can afford such a luxury when there is so much to earn because there is so much to buy to demonstrate that we're good enough parents? This was how one pressured mum reflected on her child's daily routine:

So far this morning I have brushed my son's teeth with a Buzz Lightyear toothbrush, using Mickey Mouse toothpaste, dressed him in Power Ranger underpants and a Superman vest before giving him Cheerios for breakfast – chosen not because they are his favourite cereal but because Cheerios were giving away a Finding Nemo toy. He wears a school uniform, which is where the branding ends, although I do sometimes wonder how long it will be before a company thinks of putting its logo on that too, and encouraging us to save empty packets of something or another to pay for it.[3]

At its recent height, competitive parenting spilled into the kind of birthday parties that put jelly and cake in the shade. The average spend on a child's birthday party is now £129; in some parts of London that rises to more like £500. One family in Gloucester spent £20,000 on a *Willy Wonka* party for thirty children, complete with 'real' Oompa-Loompas and chocolate fountains. Children are now taken *en masse* to Disneyland Paris or even to the Middle East. Concierge London has organized parties for £250,000. What was at stake was not the happiness of the child, but the status of the parents.

Children used to be happy going to school with a ham or cheese sandwich wrapped in tin foil. But parents started to send their children to school with sushi and smoked salmon because of pressure from other children to have the latest fashion foods. If their friends had posh sandwiches in ever-changing branded lunch boxes, they must too. Otherwise friends and self-esteem, at the tender age of eight, might disappear. But now everyone is cutting back. Not just on the small things like posh packed lunches but on the big things, like private education, which could only be afforded in the boom years. Now more and more want to get their child into the best state schools because the ability to spend privately has been lost. This will either be a temporary blip before any economic upturn simply means those who can afford it go back to consuming the best education or it will change attitudes more fundamentally by demonstrating that a good education can be secured through a mixed intake in a community school. This will have an impact on the emotional

drivers of our consuming habit. If we can scale back on the numbers in élite and segregated education, we start to unpick the basis for a competitive 'learn-to-earn', and therefore spend, culture.

If we are not trying to buy our children's happiness then we are regressing to our own childhood to find remnants of what once made us happy because turbo-consumption leaves us feeling empty. And the prime means of this regression has, of course, been buying back our youth. People in their forties and fifties are dressing like people half their age. It's not that there should be a fixed way for anyone to dress at any age – but the market exploits our anxieties and sells us solutions. Consumer society is a Neverland where we are seduced into a life of eternal youth. But the process of infantilization is encouraged by the retailers because only then will we buy with the means of an adult but the irresponsibility of a fifteen-year-old. Why make hard, grown-up choices about the world if you are fifty-five with a baseball cap turned back to front and money to burn? My kids borrow my clothes and we share CDs. Unlike Gordon Brown I do listen to the Arctic Monkeys. At one level it's a great point of connection. But at another it's deeply dispiriting that the post-punk alternative music of my youth has been translated into the corporate blandness of Coldplay. Where is the anger and rebellion of youth culture? Like everything else, it has been co-opted, corporatized and commoditized – turned into a saleable commodity. Alienated young kids living on miserable concrete estates stand on street corners with dummies in the mouths, both as a fashion statement and to symbolize their detachment and powerlessness in their world. Generational congestion is taking place and the driving force is the pressure to buy more. There is no generation gap, just Gap – where we can all look the same. Few of us, it would seem, can face the inauthenticity of modern consumer life so we regress and buy more in the hope that that will heal our emotional wounds. With no alternative, we succumb to the pleasure principle of shopping in its most foetal form.

If it is right to argue that we live in a consumer society and

our lives are primarily defined by our experiences as shoppers, there must be hundreds if not thousands of things that could be picked out to get under the skin of our consumer culture because they are all around us, filling up our homes, lives and time. I can't write about them all but what follows includes some of the more symbolic products, events and experiences to show the hold that consumer society has over us, a hold that is based on the fact that, increasingly, we are what we buy.

Who's driving whom?

Cars, like every other market, have crashed, but until recently the car was the highest-value status symbol that the consumer industry could offer us. Every time we chose a new one, we were succumbing to a status message that had been designed to hook us. So, who was driving whom? The manufacturers with their new designs or the consumers demanding the means to outdo their neighbours in the drive? For the manufacturers it's been a virtuous circle.

More money is spent on advertising cars than it is on advertising anything else because, since Henry Ford's day, they are for the mass market. Ford was a genius. He paid his workers just enough to live on and afford one of the cars they made. Mass production went hand in hand with mass consumption. But from being a vehicle to get you from A to B, the car has become a symbol of our personality. We are what we drive. Its shape, style and performance mirror our self-perception and send the message we want to project to the world.

Simon is a broker in the City. He has graduated from an Escort XR2, to a BMW, a convertible Audi and now a Mercedes. His cars are everything to him. He is his car. Me? I drive a 1969 Volkswagen called a Karmann Ghia. Why did I go for the car I did? What did it say about me? Like other old VWs, such as the camper vans and Beetles, to me the Karmann Ghia is a symbol of a certain type of chilled-out, laid-back, surfing cool. An

old VW like this says you are counter-culture and not fixed on the latest must-have design or technology. But we constantly kid ourselves that these mildly rebellious images have some meaning when anything that is remotely threatening to the perpetuation of the consumer society is co-opted by the market and turned into a money-making machine. Any hint of rebellion is semi-neutered, repackaged and sold back to us. It is the bee without the sting, the snake without the bite. From surf to punk, the market always wins.

And don't try claiming that your car says nothing about you. Just because you drive a Honda Accord or a Ford Focus you are not above car fashion. Some buy metal skins of fantasy rebellion, others safe conformity. Look at me, I'm sensible. By make, style and with an endless variety of 'personalized' extras and sporty accessories, we park our personalities in our cars.

Once our home was our castle but, for a while at least, our castle became our car when sports utility vehicles were the latest in a long line of motoring fads. Looking back, it is hard to imagine that four-wheel-drive SUVs were so popular. We managed to move ourselves, families and things before them and hardly ever drove them off road. But for a while they gave many a sense of comfort and, let's face it, control over others. SUVs, like the 2.5-ton Cadillac Escalade, imported direct from the US, were the chosen form of transport for everyone from Premier League footballers to rap stars. In four-by-fours, we bought on-the-road advantage in the guise of protection and safety. But, on aggregate, society doesn't get any safer through the use of SUVs. If my next-door neighbour buys a four-by-four then I have to buy a bigger one, or I'm less safe and less intimidating. So we ratchet up, and everyone's kids face greater danger as they walk to school. In a collision, pedestrians are 75 per cent more likely to be killed by an SUV than by a conventional vehicle. Even before the crash they had fallen from symbols of prestige to objects that people laughed about. Many people bought them because they were intimidating. In them they were the kings of the road. But a backlash started. Driven in part by high oil prices,

these gas guzzlers were tough on the pocket. They were also targeted by environmental campaigners and became a bit of an embarrassment. All of a sudden they were out of fashion. In Britain sales of SUVs didn't just drop, they disintegrated. Hummer sales dropped 88.9 per cent in December 2008. It meant they sold just one car. The Hummer could be joining the endangered-species list that it helped to lengthen. We don't yet know whether this is about cash and/or conscience. But whenever our tastes change the market tries to secure an advantage. Dual fuel and electric cars are becoming more popular. In part it's about ethics but better ethics are fashionable. Until, of course, the fashion changes.

Products like cars shape our aspirations through associated emotions such as lust and love. Only the right car will make us more desirable so we become passionate about cars, lustful for them, while the genuine target for our passions, other people, becomes an increasingly tiresome task full of too much commitment for the fleet-of-foot turbo-consumer. At the moment new cars are piling up at the end of the production line. No one is buying them. But powerful fuel-injected forces will try to persuade us that a new and faster car means a new and more fulfilling life. And they will try to persuade the government, in cases like Jaguar, to underwrite their survival with public money.

A poll in an *Observer* supplement called 'Pleasure – What it is and how to find it' declares that a salary of £100,000 is now necessary to sustain a pleasurable lifestyle. This was back in 2005. If a similar poll was conducted now the figure would be much higher. Such a salary is around four times the national average household income and relates to about the top four per cent income bracket. Which suggests that 96 per cent of the population isn't enjoying a pleasurable lifestyle. The 'Pleasure' supplement was produced in association with BMW, with lots of BMW features and copy that says things like 'It's only a car, but when you take a seat, start the engine – it's your ticket out of here.'

So close is the link between our cars and our identity that market researchers use cars to describe what kind of people we

think we are and what others are. What sort of person are you? An Aston Martin or an old 2CV? We are our cars and our cars are us. That's why we buy twice as many as we did a decade ago and it won't stop there. Our brains have an infinite ability to desire, and designers and marketers have an infinite ability to present us with new driving desires. The consumer society is a never-ending road on which freedom and fulfilment lie just round the next bend.

It's in the bag

Just like cars, bags have become an indicator of our social status and social style. A 2006 Mintel report found that British women spent £350 million a year on bags, with sales up 146 per cent on the previous five years alone. Women have been shown such a fast turnover in designs that businesses leasing rather than selling them have thrived. New designer handbags used to be carried by celebrities, but 'it' bags became celebrities in themselves, with waiting lists on limited editions to increase the buzz factor and *cachet* of ownership. Bags were even tipped as slimming devices – the bigger the bag the smaller you look. Of course, it helped if you could afford the £28,000 for the oversized Hermès Crocodile bag. Why did the handbag industry blossom?

Gail buys bags, lots of them. Around six years ago, on her reckoning, bags became status symbols. It was glossy magazines, like *Heat*, *Grazia* and *Glamour*, that did it. Paris Hilton, and others who became famous for being famous, started being seen with high-end, high-cost bags. When Kate Moss was 'spotted' carrying a quilted Marc Jacobs handbag in September 2005, its sales rose tenfold at Selfridges in two days.

Gail has recently bought a Mulberry. It's not an 'it' bag but it's good quality. She goes for quality. People in the know will know her bag. Gail is in the know and can spot a good bag as soon as she walks into a room or the bag walks into hers. Celebrity bags are instantly recognizable. She starts to talk about Jane Birkin

and Grace Kelly bags. She admits her Mulberry purchase was a moment of weakness. It had been a long, hard year and she needed a treat to pick herself up. She thinks a lot of people, especially women, use shopping as an anti-depressant. And it works. At least for a while. Buying the bag made Gail feel better. 'The problem' doesn't go away but it fades for a while in the warm glow of something new. Gail rationalizes the price away on a cost-per-day basis. It could be just a pound a day to feel good. It's not exactly that Gail really needed another bag. She has dozens of them.

Increasingly, manufacturers of luxury goods, like bags, are making entry-level products to attract consumers other than the very rich. Gucci and Armani attach their brands to sunglasses that are bought by people who could not normally afford to buy clothes or accessories by such prestigious labels. They do this to create new markets where none existed before and squeeze more money out of us. Accessories play a big part in driving the clothing market. If they can get us to change our belts, shoes and bags, we'll need to change the rest of our wardrobe to match them.

The goal is relentlessly to create new markets where before none existed. Nowhere is this more apparent than in the rise of the 'man bag'. Before 2000 there was no market and no demand for the man bag. This was not just a practical issue but there were deeply engrained emotional hostilities about having what is in effect a handbag. It was 'girly' or 'gay'. But by the summer of 2007 almost 14 million British men were sporting one. Why? A number of retailing trends and opportunities came together to create a new market. First, the designers and researchers at luxury brands like Prada wondered, if women could spend £500 on a bag then why not the other 50 per cent of the population? So, fashion shoots started to dress men with bags, and to help counter the non-macho image Mulberry called its £395 buffalo-leather and canvas-strapped man bag 'Alfie', apparently a real man's name. The gay community was the first to take up the man bag but the fashion soon spread.

It helped that celebrities, including Jared Leto and the solidly heterosexual Mick Jagger, were photographed clutching Mulberry's bags. Perhaps the defining moment was a 1999 episode of *Friends* in which the plot centred on Joey sporting a man bag.

This kind of product placement and the buzz it creates can help to make a new market. But other trends pushed sales upwards. Jeans became skinnier so there was nowhere to put your wallet, keys and phone. And, of course, there was more and more to carry. The contents of British men's bags are worth an astounding £4.4 billion. They are brimming with laptops, MP3 players, personal organizers and, often now, moisturizer and other cosmetics. All of this stuff defines who we are and how successful we are seen to be. All of it has to be stored in a bag that projects the right message. Even when the cost is £400.

Fifteen minutes of fame

But keeping up is hard when celebrities and the super-rich set the shopping standards to which we must all aspire. Paris Hilton, when asked why she is successful, responded, 'Because I'm a brand like no one else.' Paris Hilton™ is a registered trademark. Celebrities have become a brand. Where and how they live, their cars, holidays and, most of all, their clothes and accessories have come to define success and happiness in a consumer society. From celebrity television shows to magazines and catwalks, we are offered not a window into another world but the standard we must constantly strain to match. In a global and technical culture, there are no boundaries to what we can aspire to achieve. We are bombed with the same images and brands the world over. And with no one left to believe in, be they gods or politicians, celebrities have become the last of our heroes. The only hope, as predicted by Andy Warhol, is that we, too, can grab our own few minutes of fame.

Take, for example, the decadent lives of footballers' wives.

There is a designer shop in Liverpool called Cricket where some of the football WAGs of the North-west hang out. The shop's distinctive animal-print carrier bags have become a status symbol in their own right. One sold on eBay for twenty-five pounds. That means someone can have all the *cachet* of looking like they shop at Cricket without dishing out the cash. But twenty-five pounds for a paper bag gives us insight into the desperation of some to emulate the lives of their cash-rich heroes.

Even the footballers themselves aspire to grander things. Jamie Redknapp, once of Liverpool and England, explains the concept behind *Icon* magazine, which he helped found for professional footballers and their partners: 'We wanted the magazine to be aspirational – there are adverts for luxury brands and hotels . . . When I was playing for Bournemouth, I was always interested in the lifestyle of the top pros because theirs was the kind of life I wanted for myself. I was inspired by what they had achieved and how well they lived. I want our readers to be inspired as well.'

The bar of success is being set at a higher and higher level. According to Michael Winner, back in 2006, 'You cannot possibly lead a rich lifestyle on £2.6 million. A yacht is £100 million. A good house abroad is £70 million. A van Gogh is £50 million, and that's one painting. I spent £90,000 at Sandy Lane [a Barbados resort] on holiday last Christmas and that's nothing . . . To live like a proper millionaire, the minimum you need is £30 million, and that's tight.'[4] Lifestyles like his can't be afforded by everyone but, thanks to our worship of celebrity, they're always on our minds. And as celebrity lifestyles are pumped into our minds, luxury, at the lower end but certainly in terms of our aspirations, is becoming a commodity. The celebrated US economist J. K. Galbraith says that 'In the affluent society, no sharp distinction can be made between luxuries and necessities.'[5]

Is it any wonder then that the market survey company BMRB Access found that 60 per cent of Britons believe they can't afford to buy everything that they really need? £50,000 is what most people consider the annual income they require to be happy today, but even among those with incomes in excess of £50,000,

which is more than twice the national average, 40 per cent don't feel they are able to afford everything they really need. The poor suffering rich![6] And that delusion exists even though Britons today, despite the start of the recession, have incomes nearly three times higher, in real terms, than they did in 1950. The gap between Winner's £2.6 million and the losers on an average of £25,000 cannot in reality be bridged. But we keep trying.

Consuming 2.0

When people talk about shopping, they usually mean the physical process of buying things like cars, bags and watches. But that is Consuming 1.0. Just like its Web 2.0 equivalent, Consuming 2.0 is the new updated version, packed with extra features that put it in a qualitatively different place from Consuming 1.0. Consuming 2.0 is all about experience. In the world of Consuming 2.0 there is nothing tangible to put in your bag and drive home. It is all pure emotion. If there are at least some physical limits to what we can consume, then the competitive nature of shopping one-upmanship, fuelled by those seeking to profit from it, was bound to spill into the infinite emotion of experience. Here there is no limit to what we can purchase because our senses can be forever retantalized.

Celebrations have become as much of an industry as the manufacture of cars and accessories. As the age of abundance reached its height we wanted to demonstrate our spending prowess by what we did, not just by what we bought. Setpiece consumer events began to litter the calendar as carnivals of consumerism with little relation to their original purpose: Valentine's Day, Mother's Day, Easter, Father's Day, Hallowe'en, St Patrick's Day, St George's Day and, of course, Christmas have all become glorified excuses to buy more.

It is deeply ironic that Christmas is celebrated with an orgy of spending and overeating, because the nativity is essentially a story of going without. Over the last thirty years it has been

turned into a ritual binge of consumption. On average we spend £500 to £700 per household for one day of festive fun. And what do we now do, in our hordes, the day after Christmas? We go straight to the Boxing Day sales. One day without the option of shopping is now almost a day too much. Driven by ubiquitous advertising, all kids want the same must-have present, and parents anxiously hunt for the last remaining console games their children are desperate for. Christmas 2008 was rather different: spending was more muted as people worried about their jobs and debts. For most it was the fear of recession rather than actual job losses that restrained them. Without lines to easy credit and rising house prices to fall back on, people were, at least, not increasing their spending on the year before. But the same consumer rituals were observed. It was toned down but the fundamental urge to splurge our way to a happy Christmas remained. Despite the economic worries, one survey predicted we would buy £1 billion's worth of presents for children, which would be discarded just a month later. We still feel the need to buy our children's happiness with toys that don't hold their attention even until the first instalment on the credit-card bill has to be paid off.

We receive more and more presents we don't want and will never use. If you don't like what you've been given for Christmas or a birthday then go to www.stuffusell.co.uk, where they will help you get rid of unwanted presents on eBay. They collect the item, photograph it, put it on the site and deal with the sale. They charge a five-pound listing fee and take a third of the sale price. Thousands of people have given up their jobs to become full-time eBay sellers. They are a symbol of the turbo-consuming society.

But it's not just Christmas. In 2002 we spent £12 million on Hallowe'en paraphernalia. In 2006 that figure had risen to a scary £120 million. The shops are 'pumpkined' and, like Pavlovian dogs, we're taught to salivate at the anticipation of yet another special occasion.

But the biggest special spending occasion is the wedding. By

2005 the bridal business was worth £5 billion. On average, by 2007, getting hitched cost £17,000, with each wedding guest spending around £300 on the day. Some book the register office and put a hundred quid behind the bar for a few rounds. Others dig a bit deeper. Elizabeth Hurley had a seven-day party in February 2007: four days in an English country hotel in the Cotswolds, followed by three days in her new husband's native country, India. Estimated cost: £2 million. But Elizabeth Hurley is not someone to be mocked and ridiculed, instead she is admired, fêted and copied. As far as our credit cards and remortgaging will allow, we want a wedding like hers. In the pages of magazines like *Hello!* and *OK!* we have an open window into celebrity lifestyle and culture that encourages us to dream the same consumer dreams. We can be like them – we are them!

The less likely a marriage is to succeed, the more it costs. The average price of a wedding dress is now a staggering £826. That's just for a few hours' use! The importance of the wedding event has given birth to the pejorative term Bridezilla, applied to the increasingly deranged way in which the bride, groom and family members plan the day. It is fed by a wedding industry of websites, invitations, dresses, flowers, rings, photos, cakes, food, entertainment and honeymoons. It has led to brides having their teeth straightened, Botox injected and a regime of extreme dieting. There is a bridal boot camp you can go to in Wokingham for a ten-day intensive weight loss and beauty programme. Like everything else in the 1980s, weddings were deregulated to sell more effectively an expensive fantasy that increases the likelihood of divorce. The more marriages that fail, the more second, third and fourth marriages there are likely to be, and even more will be spent on the wedding industry.

After the wedding comes the baby shower, for which a hand-knitted cardigan will no longer do. Once again, inspired by parties for the likes of Jennifer Lopez and Gwyneth Paltrow, baby-shower gift lists, lodged at expensive stores like Tiffany and Harvey Nichols, became more extravagant and more popular. Requested presents included things like the £12,000 Silver

Cross pram. Often they were for parents – working hard until the last minute before the birth – who didn't have time to go out buying themselves. If there was no time for a shower then Baby Planners, at £2,500 a go, could help you buy the best buggies, hire the right nannies and advise on feeding patterns, saving 'time, money and hassle'. But even the best help won't mean you can avoid forking out to have the kids shrunk: for £150 an hour parents have their baby or toddler psychoanalysed in a bid to cure sleep or behavioural problems.

At the other end of life's spectrum Vic Fearn, a Nottingham coffin-maker, could make you a last resting-place fit for a pharaoh. Your coffin could be a personally designed car, boat, guitar or even a replica of the *Angel of the North*. And on your last big day you could have a pay-per-view funeral on the Internet for anyone who couldn't make the event.

But before we made our final journey in one of Vic's special coffins we wanted to travel. And not just to the Med. Even Cuba became 'so last-year'. Instead, destinations like Venezuela and Mongolia were what had to be consumed. Holidays became a prime concern of the new experience-seeking competitive consumer. On average, by 2007, we spent £790 per person each year going on holiday. But we no longer wanted to go 'on holiday', we wanted to 'go travelling' and be trophy tourists. The quest for authenticity took us to ever more far-flung spots in the search for the untainted and untouched. Travel became a lifestyle statement. Thirty-two per cent of British people rated luxury holidays as essential to the quality of their life. By 2007 nearly 30,000 were flocking to the Antarctic for their two-week break to help kill off the very tranquillity and remoteness that drew them there. And in a globalized world the tribes we wish to observe at first hand in the South American rainforests are about as authentic as flamenco dancers on the Costa Brava. But we love the bragging rights our trips confer.

Six-star hotels popped up when most of us had got nowhere near a five-star one. Exclusivity was what counted. Airtours offered a twenty-three-day, 32,000-mile, round-the-world pack-

age for £5,000. Richard Branson pioneered space tourism. The first members of Virgin's Galactic Club had to pay £100,000 for a ride taking them seventy miles into space and five minutes of floating weightlessness. Branson chose 100 people to be its founder members out of 13,000 who applied. They got what they wanted – exclusivity. But this was not the first company to take people into space. Space Adventures was already doing so but at an even heftier price. It was offering eight-day holidays on the International Space Station starting at £10 million.

In the *Observer* magazine, a special section on 'Ultimate Travel' offered everything from heli-skiing in Russia's remote eastern mountains to the perfect rum punch on a secluded Caribbean beach. Of course there are no 'ultimates' in a consumer society that has to keep offering new horizons to strive for. In another magazine next week there will be another series of 'ultimates' that put the previous ones in the shade. It's a race that never ends. Madonna is rumoured to have paid £13,000 a night for a stay in Miami. A new benchmark is set. The Portobello Hotel in London offered 'bed, breakfast and bath full of champagne' for £1,000 (Moët et Chandon) or £1,350 (Krug). In 1998 Johnny Depp and Kate Moss filled a tub with £750 worth of champagne. It is said that they popped out for a meal and returned to find, to their horror, that the maid had pulled out the plug. Lying in a bath of champagne would be the ultimate luxurious indulgence, but only until something better came along.

By 2007 the search for the most exotic and pretentious holiday destinations and the hippest hotels symbolized the consumer madness that had gripped the nation. The ability to boast about where you had been and where you had stayed became a feature of many dinner-table conversations. Now everyone is cutting back, staying in Britain and going camping. But the hangover hurts. How can we live happy and fulfilling lives without pushing the travel frontiers still further?

Time is money

We can't have it all and never could. Even at the height of the shopping frenzy before the crash something was missing. There was so much to want – and not just want but need. All the time we were working to spend, then shopping so assiduously to purchase the right things that we had little time for anything else. Every moment of every day had to be packed with more endeavour to buy paid-for pleasure.

Time has become the one luxury none can afford. Unless, of course, you're poor or one of the rising number being made redundant among all classes. When you're poor, you have all the time in the world to sit and contemplate what you can't do – because to do most things in a consumer society, by definition, costs money. The rest of us crave more time. It's not just that we shop more, but the routine of daily life and even the moments when we try to escape, like holidays, are mentally and physically exhausting.

It's another Saturday morning: a brief moment to enjoy the papers. For many of us, this is the best part of the week, our first and last chance to take it easy. I read the news before flicking through the supplements and magazines. One advert stands out. It's for Ikea. It's a picture of a father playing in the sun on the grass with his two sons. At the bottom there is a plush red kitchen with the strap-line 'If your kitchen costs less, you can work less.' There, in one full-colour-page nutshell, it is: the dilemma at the heart of our lives in the still affluent West. We want the kitchen, but we don't want to work every hour of every day for it and have no time for other things, like our children.

Ikea is not alone in knowing this. Hitachi offers the same deal. Their high-capacity data-storage technology will give you 'More time for the things you love' and a father holds his toddler high in the air. 'Being wealthy is having time,' claims an advert from a new division of Barclays Bank called Barclays Wealth. Again and again it's the same promise. We can consume more and have more time. It is a lie.

The adverts are clever – they know our minds better than we do. They speak to the essential truth and tension about our lives today, that buying things promises to make us happy but doesn't make us happy enough. Other things make us happier, like spending more time with our family and friends, but we can't buy them. So they must be ditched. At the bottom of the Ikea advert you are directed to www.lifeoutsidework.co.uk. There you can handily calculate time saved relative to the cost of different Ikea kitchens and the size of your salary. It's the tool by which you can have your cake and eat it. You can't. We are locking ourselves into a work-to-spend cycle, a consumer trap that relies on what we buy never being enough to stop us wanting more because what we buy is just compensation for our overstretched lives. They say that the definition of an idiot is someone who does the same thing again and again but expects a different outcome. Are we a nation of shopping idiots?

The economist Nicholas Georgescu-Roegen talks about 'the circumdrome of the shaving machine',[7] which involves us shaving faster so that we have more time to buy a machine that shaves faster so that we have more time to work to buy a machine that shaves still faster, and so on. Our problem is that we have no concept of how to spend our leisure time in a more intelligent way than buying extra blades on our razors. The Gillette Fusion six-blade razor represents the 'pinnacle of shaving technology'. We buy it because it's there. Why settle for five blades when six, despite being an already absurd number that costs more, are obviously better? The answer is that this is what we are conditioned to do. Six blades become the norm; to opt out and not be normal feels virtually impossible. Of course we don't all keep up all the time with all the latest fashionable gadget but the trend is inextricably towards more.

We used to buy labour-saving devices, like washing-machines and vacuum-cleaners. Now we buy things that take up more of our spare time, like iPods and DVDs. An advert for a BlackBerry Pearl offers the chance to 'take all the unproductive gaps out of your day'. It tells us that 'Whether you are in a cab, on the train, or

out and about, you can carry on working with a BlackBerry from Orange, leaving more time for the important stuff in life.' You could, of course, call your kids or another loved one from the back of a taxi but it depends on your definition of productivity.

But even making a two-minute call to our kids becomes a pressured task in a world on a consumer treadmill in which we have to work and spend endlessly. Once we had a vision of a life of leisure because work would eventually be automated. It hasn't worked out that way. Like the bus in the film *Speed*, rigged with a bomb that will go off if we slow down, we cannot take our foot off the shopping accelerator for fear of our world exploding. Time-strapped young executives are paying someone to find them a partner and will pay again to have them dumped. Why don't they go the whole hog and pay someone to have a relationship with their 'partners' to save them the bother and give them more time to spend at work and in the shops?

The British work the longest hours in Europe, on average 1,782 hours a year, which is 301 more than the French, who also get seven days more holiday. And it's worsening. Between 2000 and 2002, the number of people who worked more than sixty hours a week leapt up by a third, to one in six of all workers. We are set to become a round-the-clock society as the number of people contributing to our night-time economy doubles in the next fifteen years. A report by the Future Foundation think-tank suggested that by 2020 a quarter of the UK population – 13 million people – will be 'economically active' between the hours of six p.m. and nine a.m., compared with just seven million now. Why on earth do we want the option to buy anything at three a.m and therefore require someone to be away from their family to serve us? Because, like the rest of consumer society, we want the option when it is presented to us because the option to buy is all there is. Take that away and there is nothing.

Naturally the market, in its dynamic brilliance, can sell us an answer to our lack of time. A drug, Provigil, can now be prescribed in the UK. Formerly only for people with sleeping dis-

orders, it now has looser restrictions. It makes users feel as if they have just had a pleasant nap, even if they have not slept for many hours or even a day or two. Studies have shown that in America 75 per cent of people taking it do so for non-medical reasons. 'This drug enables us to be even more workaholic and obsessed with accomplishments and productivity . . . It takes away the natural checks on that tendency, like needing to go to bed,' says Professor Martha Farah, director for neuroscience at the University of Pennsylvania.

In the last sixty years productivity per worker has doubled. That means we produce twice as much in the same time. But let's put it another way. We could live as we did in 1948 and have an additional six months of the year off to do whatever we wanted, or strike some better balance between time and more things. But this is never the choice that is presented to us. The option is never more time, it's always buying more.

If there is nothing to do but shop, then all there is to do is more of the same – only faster. Fast fashion is what drives the clothing retail sector now. Once, there were two seasons a year; now the retailers cram in as many 'seasonal' changes as they can get away with, all in an effort to increase purchasing frequency. And if you missed the sales, don't worry – another will be along in a minute because it means big profits for retailers. In terms of the law, the 1987 Consumers Protection Act, a 'sale' item is one that has been offered at the original price for twenty-eight consecutive days in the previous six months. But this is easy for retailers to get round. Put some suits at the back of the rack at twice the normal price, then offer them for sale after twenty-eight days at 'half price' and watch them fly out of the shop.

In the past people had to save and enjoyed the delay of gratification. Today it is impossible to be gratified. There is always something more. There must be something more or there is nothing. It's not about being satisfied. Mick Jagger was right: we can't get satisfaction. Satisfaction would end the game. So there is no point in waiting.

Even the nature of the magazines we are buying is changing.

Weekly magazines are doing very well, monthlies are doing badly. According to Louise Matthews, former managing director of publisher EMAP, this reflects the way we view our lives, use our time and the fast culture we operate in. Monthlies, she argues, used to be about 'me time' and there isn't as much of that as there was. A quick coffee break or train journey now serves that purpose. So people operate in shorter time frames with no opportunity to analyse or reflect.

Because of the work-to-consume cycle we have created, we can't slow down. Instead we have to steel ourselves continually for the next round of working more to consume more just to keep up and keep our heads above water . But what now? There is no easy credit and we are in fear of losing our jobs. We might still be earning but the joy of spending has gone. We have built lives that are all consuming but there isn't the means or the confidence to spend. The question is whether we can use the challenge of the crash and have the imagination and will-power to change.

What a waste

Shopping at the speed of light doesn't just mean we have too little time: it also means we have too much waste. There is a simple equation that the more we consume, the faster we have to dispose of what we already own.

I have two tin boxes in my hall, stylish ones from Ikea, of course, one for paper, the other for glass and plastic. The amount of paper I recycle is frightening. Where does it all come from and what fraction do I read? That's the extent of my recycling. Otherwise it's regular trips to the rubbish room in the basement of the block I live in. It's amazing what gets discarded down there. TVs and white goods regularly block the floor. Are they broken or just stylistically past their use-by date?

A packet of plastic razors may flag up its disposability, but ultimately everything we buy is thrown away. Our homes con-

tain, on average, twenty-five electrical appliances. Ownership of such products is estimated to have increased by around 60 per cent over the last five years. The average life of a PC then was ten years. Today it is three. And take our obsession with mobiles, which, on average, we replace after eighteen months when they are designed to last ten years. Over 15 million handsets are thrown away every year in the UK although 99 per cent of them can be reused. They contain, among other harmful substances, mercury, lead and cadmium. But our phone has become an adjunct of our personality. When we upgrade our phone we upgrade ourselves. 'Are you ashamed of your mobile?' the Phones 4Us advert asks. The very fact that we can possibly be ashamed of a piece of technology should be what shames us. And the real obsolescence is not built into the product but into our minds.

The cost of consumption in terms of the waste we have produced has been hidden from our view – the last thing the economy needs is for the consumer to be put off consuming. The shopping cycle must be clean, modern and efficient. Human suffering or filth has been kept out of sight. But behind our view another world now exists in landfill sites on old industrial areas at the edge of towns and throughout the developing world. Where once we made things, now we bury them.

The cycle of effluence from affluence has been increasing in line with economic growth, around 40 per cent over the past thirty years. Britain has become the dustbin of Europe. Every man, woman and child in Britain throws away more than half a tonne of rubbish a year, the weight of a small car. This country produces enough waste to refill London's Royal Albert Hall every two hours. The word 'refill' is interesting: it seems to suggest that all we are doing is putting back what has been taken out of the earth – as if some simple rebalancing act was taking place in terms of natural resources. Replacing like with like. But, of course, that is not what's happening. We are removing the minerals and crops that are used to sustain our consumer lifestyles, and putting back the useless and discarded dreams of those lives.

Our disposable culture hasn't always been with us. Once we used to make do and mend. We had a fix-it culture. My grand-dad never threw anything away. Tape, glue and a fresh coat of paint could fix anything. I think it kept his whole house together. But now things are so cheap it makes no sense to get them fixed. They are cheap because globalized labour is cheap and no price is put on environmental damage. And while the Internet makes finding spare parts for broken goods easy, we've lost the skills to repair things. I used to watch my dad mend the car and he would talk me through it. I knew how an engine worked then, but now they're all sealed units and we either get a new car or pay the garage bills. It's not a skill I'll be passing on to my sons.

It may be too late to pass on car-mechanic skills but all of a sudden the credit crunch means that making do and mending is suddenly back in fashion. Shoe repairers report less well-heeled people getting new soles, not new shoes. Perhaps in the process they are getting new souls. People are repairing their clothes and making presents, but few know how to do it when most people only think of *The X-Factor* when they hear the word Singer. The under-thirty generation has been brought up in a totally dispos-able society. Even society itself can be disposed of when it's become just a collection of consumers whose first instinct is to throw away to create a space for something new. They have no making-do and mending skills to go back to. They will have to discover such talents and pleasures from scratch.

The rapid progress of more things through our all-consuming lives doesn't just mean we throw more away. We have also started to store more. The last two decades saw a huge growth in the self-storage industry, exploding from about thirty outlets in the mid-1990s to around 600 today, an increase of 2,000 per cent. Firms like Big Yellow popped up in garish buildings on orbital roads around the country. Big Yellow's website proudly declares: 'It's just like booking a hotel room!' And it isn't cheap. Big Yellow's inner London rate is £51 a month for a space not much bigger than a large table.

I visited the Big Yellow store on Wick Lane in Bow, east

London. Inside there is something familiar about a Big Yellow store: you see people pushing their consumer goods on trolleys along aisles. But the difference between here and B&Q is that in the latter you pay to take the goods out of the warehouse and in the former you pay to put them in. The important bit for the market, though, is that you pay.

An advert for Big Yellow on TV uses clever computer simulations of waves of consumer goods, from toys to electrical items, cascading over a living-room floor. The pay-off line is 'Get some space in your life.' The image of consumer goods as endless waves we don't have room for is exactly right.

The surge in demand for storage is not because houses are shrinking. The floor area of the average European home is now 87 square metres, up from 83 square metres in 1985, while the average household has shrunk by one person. We have more space than we ever did. The reason for the growth of self-storage is that we are buying more. British householders are using 'self-access' facilities to cope with a day-to-day domestic overflow resulting from greater consumption. William Morris, the Victorian socialist designer, famously said, 'Have nothing in your houses that you do not know to be useful or believe to be beautiful.' This is good advice for those wishing to be both uncluttered and prudent.

But the sin of storage is nothing compared to the shocking waste of food in a turbo-consumer society. Food accounts for 21 per cent of total waste and is the biggest thing we throw away. It is estimated that each year we carry home a staggering 400 bags for every household. We throw away £20 billion worth of the contents in Britain every year – enough to lift 150 million people out of starvation. Almost one in three items we take off the shelves in the supermarket we may as well put straight into the bin.

This is economic and environmental madness. But we keep doing it. Why? Because over hundreds of thousands of years we have been genetically and emotionally conditioned for a harsh life of scarcity. It has been only in the last half-century that we have had a post-scarcity lifestyle. And we don't know how to

handle it. Our eyes and wallets are bigger than our bellies. The market has taken advantage of our emotional weakness and convinced us that our right to choose, shop and discard is now sacrosanct. Meanwhile, some people go hungry in the UK and millions starve in the rest of the world while we discard what we buy but can never hope to eat. And we think we live in a civilized, sane, progressive and modern society.

It took a crash to get us to think and act more carefully. Now the dilemma can't be ignored. The urge to shop is hitting hard up against the means to do so but also the morality and the dire social and environmental consequences of doing so. The global crisis has placed us at a crossroads. We can choose which way to go next. But for some the choice will be harder than for others.

Shopping: the next generation

Today's middle-aged were born into a pre-turbo-consuming world. There were, of course, wants and needs, often spurred by adverts. But life wasn't all consuming, at least not at the turbo rate we have witnessed over the last decade or so. Consuming is all today's teenagers know. They are finely tuned to the consumer society in terms of their expectations. Shopping is hard-wired into them. They'll do anything to fulfil their consumer desires rather than face being ostracized by 'their friends' for not conforming and keeping up. For them the pain of the crash will be more intense because this is all they have ever known. The shock of adjustment will be short and very sharp. As they are the people who will determine whether we can move beyond a life that is all consuming, I wanted to know what they thought.

Emily is seventeen and training to be a legal secretary. Her shopping habits are driven by a simple rule. When you go out clubbing you must have a new outfit. So that means a new outfit every week. She is horrified by the idea that anyone should notice she was wearing a dress or skirt for a second time. It would make her a 'tramp'! Would she realize that someone else

was wearing an article of clothing again? 'Oh, yes,' she says. I ask her what else she would do if she didn't go shopping. 'Watch television,' she offers, as the only forlorn alternative to be grasped in case the shops are ever shut.

I ask Emily and her friends who pays for all this stuff. They are relatively poor kids from poor estates. They are on education maintenance allowance and perhaps have a Saturday job. If they have £50 a week it's a lot. Their parents pay. In part they are nagged into submission. The girls in particular say they are relentless. But it's not just pester power: the parents want their kids to have the 'right brands'; they don't want them to stand out; they don't want to seem unable to look after their children properly.

Then I go to the bottom of the social pile, to a group of teen-agers who are just about hanging on to the kind of consumer society and life we take for granted. Scott is buried in a hood and cap. His mum buys his stuff. Rob admits he nicks stuff. I ask him why. Because he can, is the answer. It may be cakes from Greggs or clothes from bigger shops. It's all opportunistic spur-of-the-moment stuff. They know the shopkeepers are scared of them.

These kids also nag their mums, and sometimes their dads, to buy clothes and trainers for them, but they are more inventive and enterprising about how they get their money. They say they deal weed – which means they all have two mobiles, one for pleasure and one for business. There is some talk of dealing crack and I don't know if this is bravado or for real. I ask what they buy other than clothes. The answer is pretty much nothing except weed and cigarettes. Music they download for free. I ask about books and think about my own trophies on the wall of my flat. They look at me incredulously. I ask them why they buy what they buy. 'It's natural,' says Bobby, as if his particular mix of black baggy jeans with a big white stripe down each side was God-given. Consuming their particular brand of street-wise fashion has become the natural order. They are happy to wear a fake. It falls apart sooner but it looks okay while it lasts. Why

spend £120 on trainers if you can get the same look for £30?

Then a girl, Amanda, says something that genuinely shocks me. I ask what they look for in a potential girlfriend or boyfriend. She says, 'It's the image not the face.' I ask her what she means and she says it's the brands they wear and the way they wear them, not what they look or are like that matters. Of course, we're all attracted by certain looks and styles but to be so blatant and calculating about the power of brands feels like a quantum leap into the heart of an all-consuming society. Perhaps Bobby is right: it is natural. Perhaps consumption is the future of natural selection.

Any downturn in the economy hits those at the bottom hardest. Those living on the edge of poverty feel the pinch first as the trickle-down of money from the top dries up, whether it's legal or illegal. Out-of-work fathers might turn to drink. Their families might turn them out on to the street. The chance of a lifeline through a job in a shop or an office will become much slimmer. More pressing for them will be that they can't spend as they did. When you have little real hope, what you own, when compared with what others own, becomes hugely significant.

The Government is pumping billions of pounds into the economy to get people shopping again, as if that were the answer. I'm not convinced it will help these kids. They were brought up in poverty, not just material poverty but emotional, social and aspirational poverty. Thirty years of free markets and rampant consumerism have taken their toll. Solidarity with and respect for such people has dwindled. Their poverty is deemed to be their fault. Addiction and abuse scar their lives. This is not going to be put right quickly or easily. But more shopping is not the answer. Instead the Government needs to create the conditions for long-term investment in their lives, programmes to ensure they are well fed, free of abuse, schooled properly and consistently, well housed, counselled and guided. If society starts to value their lives, then they will. Their confidence, aspirations and horizons will grow. It's not shopping that will save their lives but the hope of a better and different kind of life.

The future of shopping: it's only just begun

Shopping has hit the buffers. But the extravagances of the last thirty years need not be the peak of shopping madness. We may only have really reached the foothills of the shopping revolution, the tip of the iceberg. If the recovery happens and we go back to 'normal', then the combination of greed, marketing ingenuity and human insecurity can combine in an infinite number of ways to sell us more and more. Retailers are facing the toughest market they have known. But they will be planning for the upturn and the return of consumer confidence. Out of the ashes of the credit crunch will come those who seize the opportunity to sell new things in new ways to more people. The retail revolution might simply be on hold.

Advances in neurology, technology and the use of customer information data put us at the brink of a revolution in the quantity and quality of what we buy. If the object is to get you to part with your money and leave you wanting more, the retail revolution is only in its infancy. Companies worth millions and industries worth billions will do their utmost to ensure that we return as quickly as possible to our old turbo-consuming ways. Tesco is already building a profile of all of us. It is a database called Crucible, of preferences, likes, dislikes and beliefs. This is not just about Tesco shoppers but about all of us. There is no requirement for the company to reveal what information they hold, yet they will sell its contents to the highest bidder and, of course, use it themselves to beat the competition.

Shops and supermarkets are continually reconfigured to maximize sales. We know they put fresh fruit and veg near the door to entice us in. But the future will see more tricks to get us to part with more cash. 'Strategic sound consultants' want to ensure that the right music is pumped into stores to increase sales – up by 10 per cent more, they claim. Companies like Wal-Mart in the US, which owns Asda in the UK, are already changing the whole nature of their stores to cater for key groups

such as affluent shoppers, rural shoppers, empty-nesters and sub-urbanites. Each will be given a target audience makeover. So in future you won't go to any Tesco but to the Tesco that matches your demographic profile.

RFIDs (Radio Frequency Identification) are now widely in use. They are small transmitters that ensure products can be uniquely identified and located. Think of a mix between a bar-code and a satnav system. They were used initially to track batches of products through the supply chain but now there is a move to tag individual products in store and therefore when they leave the store. With tag readers placed in streets and work-places, retailers will know not just who owns what, but where it goes, how much it is used and when it is thrown away.

And shopping centres will pop up in strange places. Already more people go to big airports, like Gatwick and Heathrow, to shop than to fly. Michael O'Leary, the boss of Ryanair, foresees a day when airports will pay him to deliver consumers to their shops, and passengers will fly for free. He talks of an airline in which reclining seats have gone: maybe one day there'll be no seats at all. You'll stand, as you would on a bus going to the local high street.

In the US, where the customer has always been told they were king, shopping and customer service are being taken to the next level. Window shopping can literally be that in New York, when consumers whose attention is caught by the displays at one of Ralph Lauren's Manhattan stores can now buy their clothes with-out entering the premises, using a touch-screen system on the glass. Back in the UK, HSBC sends out Bluetooth messages on its products to the mobiles of surprised passers-by. And as you go down the escalators at many of London's tube stations the old posters covered with chewing-gum are now being replaced with TV-quality pictures that keep the messages moving with you. Soon you'll be offered free television access on your mobile but you'll have to wade through adverts for the pleasure of it. If you see something you like in the shops you'll be able to go into a changing room with any item, and a 'magic mirror' will show you what you and your body will look like in it in 3-D.

What is certain is that the future of consumerism will be online. Etail is set to replace or, at least, transform retail. Ninety-seven per cent of British web users shop online. There are no queues, little guilt and paying feels pain-free; 770,000 people went shopping online, on Christmas Day 2007, spending £53 million in the process. In total £10 billion was spent online in 2006; by 2007 it had reached £40 billion and is predicted to be £162 billion by 2020, according to uswitch.com. It's no surprise given that 80 per cent of retailers still don't offer their goods or services online.

Technology is a huge driver of new wants and creates new ways of buying and selling. One of the most remarkable is the growing market for buying things on MMORPGs, or Massively Multiplayer Online Role-playing Games, like Second Life. There is now a category on eBay for 'virtual sales'. Miami DJ Jon Jacobs spent £57,000 on a space station in the game Project Entropia and has since opened his own nightclub inside it. A large apartment in the city of New Oxford will cost £45 in Project Entropia. Council tax will add a pound a month. A small island in Second Life will cost £800, while the clothing store American Apparel has opened a virtual store in the game. You can get a new shirt for your character for a dollar and pay for virtual flowers to be sent to your virtual friends.[8] What is interesting is how easily we switch from real turbo-consumption to virtual turbo-consumption. Both have an air of unreality.

Google in the US is already recoding what adverts we watch and will release the service here soon, giving advertisers even more information to target us with. And they are ingenious! Digital television recorders mean that 79 per cent fast forward through the adverts but some marketing companies in the US are experimenting with adverts that only make sense when watched at fast-forward speed. Meanwhile, Google and eBay have formed an alliance to create sophisticated personalized promotional links, as Amazon does already. They'll build purchasing profiles and low-cost Internet 'click-to call' communications between the potential buyer and selling companies, making buying faster. Google

revealed in April 2007 that it plans to draw up millions of psychological profiles of online game players, which can then be sold to advertisers. For instance, those who talk more to other gamers might get mobile-phone information or if they know that the gamers have been online for more than two hours they can send them an advert for pizza and Coke.

Powerful computer hubs in the home will allow everyone to enjoy their own entertainment in their own room from the same system, allowing personalized and niche marketing of adverts and commercial messages. Our fridges will soon 'talk' directly to the supermarket via mobile technology to reorder food supplies that are running low. And we might even move about differently. In São Paulo, Brazil, there are 420 helipads, 50 per cent more than in the whole of the UK, as the rich take to the skies to avoid chaos on the roads. Is this the future – at least for some?

Finally, scientists on the west coast of the US are learning how to manipulate the parts of the brain that trigger buying decisions through messages and images. Why bother thinking about what to buy? It's much easier if there's a direct link to the impulses in our neurological systems that will do it for us. If the industrial consumer complex can get its finger on the buy button in our head, the retail revolution will take a quantum leap in terms of its hold on us.

With massive retail investment and innovation in new technologies designed to crank up our consumer desires, together with governments urging us to spend through the recession, it's clear that powerful forces are championing a return to turbo-consumption. But it's not yet the buy button that's been hit: it's the pause button. This is just one possible future for us, though a highly likely one if we don't use the credit crunch and the recession to strike a healthier, more sustainable balance in our lives as consumers and citizens by reassessing what the good life and the good society are. Otherwise, the shopping revolution may have only just begun.

An all-consuming society

A double-decker bus goes by with an advert splashed across the side for *Look* magazine. The question it asks is simple: 'Born to shop?' It seems that we were.

If the thesis of this book is right, that we now live in an all-consuming society, then the first section will have told you what you already know instinctively to be true: that our lives have been dominated by shopping.

Shopping has become addictive because to keep the retail wheels turning at a faster and faster pace we must return to the till to buy more and buy more often. A vast industrial consumer complex has been erected to make this the case. In turn we become little more than consuming addicts. The habit is deeply engrained; companies like Starbucks provide us with our values, Prada our dreams and Coke our authenticity in an endless search for the 'real thing'. Every physical and emotional space has been taken up by the consumption experience. So, when we can't spend we're left with a void.

The blip of the last three decades has filled us with unrealistic consumer expectations. Being a turbo-consumer was all there was to life. But it was never sustainable. Credit could not be endless and house prices could not go up for ever. We suspended belief and hoped that economic laws would defy gravity. We have landed with a hard bump. We only know how dependent we are on something when it's gone. The desire to shop is still there but the means to the ends of turbo-consumerism have been cruelly snatched away. But now what? Will we try to go back or re-evaluate our lives? Right now, whether we can afford to spend or not, force of habit and addiction want us to stay on track and keep spending. But to kick the habit we have to understand it. We have to know how and why we became a society of turbo-consumers.

2. Why it happened

A turbo-consumer society on demand

The society of consumers that emerged in the post-Second-World-War world had deep and rich roots. Today our consuming habits are framed and shaped by research and insights into our psychological and social make-up and then by the exploitation of our deepest emotional needs, anxieties and fears. After all, we must be compliant in this consumption as no one forces us to go shopping or to set so much store by it. As we will see, shopping has been emotionally, culturally and socially grafted on to us. By definition, all life has to consume but we haven't always lived in a consumer society, let alone one operating at turbo speed, and we haven't always defined ourselves primarily as shoppers.

Before we knew ourselves and each other as consumers, we were identified largely by what we did – as makers of things, producers. But today it is what we buy, no longer what we do, that tells people who we are. Our hopes, fears and aspirations are now centred on consumption.

Earlier we met Bobby, the sixteen-year-old who said that what he bought to wear was just 'natural'. For him and all of us that is exactly how we feel. We rarely if ever question our all-consuming life. We make decisions about what we buy but not about why we buy so much. As we will see, it certainly isn't natural. A huge team of highly paid professionals, from neuro-scientists and child psychologists to the best advertising and marketing brains a company can buy, works incessantly to ensure that today's children are born to buy. What is true for Bobby and his younger brothers and sisters is just as true for all of us. We live in a consumer society because it was designed by a set of

interests and has been embedded and sustained to influence every aspect of our lives. Extraordinarily, we live in a world in which we can indeed feel ashamed of our mobile phone. This is something qualitatively different from shopping for necessities, sometimes indulgence and occasionally for luxury.

But it is how and why our desire to desire, which translates as the need to want, increased exponentially over the last thirty years that needs to be explored. How and why did we shift from a consumer society to a turbo-consumer society? We will find the answer in a particular set of political and economic beliefs that took hold of Britain and the US in the 1980s and created the context for the recession we are now in. It was a group of ideas that encouraged a vast new architecture for the consumer industry that deepened and extended our shopping addiction. Unwittingly it sowed the seeds of its own economic destruction, as we are now witnessing all around us.

It would be easy and rather exciting if a James Bond villain, who looked like Donald Pleasance in a Chairman Mao-style suit, sitting in the control room of a large underground bunker, stroking a cat, was the mastermind behind our all-consuming society. Sadly, it's more complicated. But, as we shall see, some people played a key role in unleashing the forces of turbo-consumerism.

It is natural to want to be comfortable, to improve ourselves and to live a good life, but none of that need equate with the turbo-consumerism that has come to dominate the early twenty-first century. Bobby and the rest of us need to understand that that's not natural. It happened for many reasons.

Why we became a consumer society

One factor above all ensured the creation of a consumer society and its turbo successor: it was the shift from a life of scarcity to one based on abundance and therefore choice. The story of the rise of the all-consuming society is about how and why by the

mid-twentieth century there was more to eat, wear and enjoy than we needed to survive.

While it is widely accepted that we live in a 'consumer society', there exists remarkably little consensus about when it first began to emerge. I'd like to think that the life of the first caveman was a bit like Fred Flintstone's – all mod cons but made of rock. The first consumers have been spotted by historians and cultural theorists from the seventeenth century onwards in every country from Italy to the Netherlands, France and Russia. But there is, of course, a longer history.

Goods have been traded, bought and sold, since pre-Roman times. Indeed, a shopping list written by an Italian soldier around AD 75 to 125 was recently found in the north of England near Hadrian's Wall. Since recorded history began, the lives of the rich, which meant kings, queens and their courtiers, were in part about consuming more than those around them. The finery of their clothes, food and homes was part of an élite microcosm of the shopping society to come. But until just a few hundred years ago few people travelled and even fewer could witness the splendour in which their monarchs lived. It was a lifestyle that many believed God had ordained. Society as a whole was still far from being driven by consumerism.

As the end of the Roman Empire gave way to the Dark Ages, from roughly AD 476 to 1000 the shutters on the shops came down. But that began to change. From 900 to 1200 medieval society saw the rise of early merchant capitalism in Europe. This was still an agrarian economy based largely on subsistence farming but the straws of a market economy were in the wind. In 1309, in Bruges, the first commodity market was opened in raw materials such as timber. At around the same time metal currency became more common in Britain for the first time since the Romans, offering a system of purchasing other than exchange and barter. This would be a crucial element in the creation of the consumer society of the future. The exchange of goods and labour for money freed people from dependence on each other and intensified the pace at which things could be traded, bought and sold.

Connections between who made what and how were slowly lost. The consumer society was built on money exchange.

By the 1600s the Netherlands was the Chinese Tiger economy of its day – an economic hothouse that witnessed the creation of the first stock exchange to buy and sell company shares and the first insurance schemes to guard against the accidents or losses traders might face. This would provide the confidence to invest in transport and buildings and set a more entrepreneurial spirit. Trading shares would also create a profit that could be reinvested in the process of production – which would in turn simulate purchasing. In 1636 the world was hit by its first commodity bubble when the price of tulips went through the roof before suddenly crashing back to earth. Investors thought the price would go on and on rising. Sound familiar?

Already the age of discovery and early Empire had kicked in. The Portuguese, out there on the edge of the Atlantic Ocean, were the first to explore and exploit. But rich pickings in the form of plunder and commodities like tea were never going to go uncontested. The Spanish, Dutch, French and, of course, the British all looked for their place in the sun. A world of free riches was there to be taken by whoever claimed it first. An empire meant cheap labour and abundant raw materials that could be turned into even more profitable commodities, like furniture and garments, when brought home. The circle of consumers was still tight and the majority still faced a daily battle for survival, but the tectonic plates of economic and social life had started to shift.

But larger-scale production, in part to add value to the raw materials being imported from the new colonies, could not take place in an essentially farming economy in which production was small-scale and largely home-based. Here, new technology was to play a crucial part in the long road to a consumer society. The advent of steam power meant that production and transport no longer relied on horses and people. Instead large factories could be built and the machines kept working all day and night to turn out much larger volumes of clothes, furniture and pottery

to sell – not just to the British market but back to the settlers in the colonies. New industrial processes, like Taylorism, which specified that each worker did just one simple job, saw efficiency rocket. It was the end of the craftsman and the guilds and the start of the factory ant playing his or her specialist part as a cog in the factory wheel. Investment in production and new technology was made possible because new banks and other financial institutions were created, which started to lend. In 1690 a Quaker family called Barclay opened a bank and offered people credit for investment so that they didn't have to use their own savings. Profitable industrialists eventually became financiers – they wanted somewhere to invest their growing profits – and the era of financial capitalism was born.

The process of early industrialization persisted through the eighteenth century before things took another leap: eventually an important legal barrier was lifted to encourage free trade, commerce and therefore eventually consumerism: the Corn Laws were abolished. Until the 1830s trade was subsidized, monopolies were protected and imports were controlled. In 1846 this ended and Britain became a free-trade nation, accelerating the industrialization process as the volume of trade increased. There was a huge ferment of innovation, production and therefore sales. And with the industrial revolution taking off in the nineteenth century came the biggest leap in human productivity the world had seen. More things were made, more cheaply and at a faster pace than ever before.

But there was one big problem that still had to be overcome in preparing the foundations for a consumer society: the creation of the consumers. The industrialists and wannabe factory owners had a problem: not only were there not enough people to work in their factories but they were the wrong sort of people. Until the 1600s most people still lived in the countryside and the new factories had to be built in the cities because of their proximity to ports and access to steam power. The people were in the wrong place. But rural workers were also lazy by the standard of the new capitalists. Or they had a great work–life

balance, depending on whether you're the CBI or a human being. For generations these traditional land workers had done enough to satisfy their basic needs for shelter, warmth and food, and then they stopped. Why earn more money if there were better things to do with your life that were free – like sleep, daydream and spend time with your family and friends? But this version of the good life was at odds with the demands of the embryonic industrial revolution going on in our cities. So country folk had to be forcefully shifted off the land and transformed into busy worker bees.

The mechanism by which this was achieved was harsh. Hundreds of thousands of agricultural workers were forced off the land and into the factories, primarily through enclosure, first introduced in Tudor times, which confiscated the land they farmed. This was a legal, but immoral, process of fencing off what had been common land that anyone could use to graze their cattle and sheep. Even small strips of private land were taken away or higher rents charged until it was impossible for small-scale subsistence farmers to pay. Land under the control of the feudal manor was turned to large-scale production of cash crops. All of this was bitterly resisted by agricultural workers and was the cause of riots and bloodshed. But the relentless process of displacement meant that the population shifted in huge numbers from the country to the town because the only place in which people could earn a living wage was now the new factories. At the beginning of the nineteenth century only one in five of the population had lived in a town of more than 10,000 inhabitants. By 1850 it was more than one in three.

What greeted the new factory workers was fourteen-hour days, six days a week in the dull drudgery of being human cogs in industrial machines. They could, of course, refuse to work, but that option was made as difficult as possible by the threat of the workhouse – the horrific and degrading alternative to life in the factory. The Poor Laws, which provided some payments, shelter and food for the destitute, had been carefully constructed to distinguish between the deserving and the undeserving poor.

Invalids, the sick, weak and old, who really could not work, were provided with the minimum on which to survive. The rest were dumped in the workhouse – a place of tedious labour, physical abuse, humiliation and degradation. It was the physical stick to get people to work. The emotional pressure came with the establishment of the work ethic, which encouraged unskilled labourers to believe that it was not just a matter of survival to toil all day in factories but their moral duty to God. Work was now the definition of the good life and through it you found the route to salvation.

The work ethic had some effect encouraging diligence but was always a limited motivator in terms of keeping people's noses to the grindstone. A new incentive was needed to keep people in the workplace and to increase their productivity. That incentive was, of course, pay. The physical and emotional sticks were replaced by the carrot. Morality went out of the window and money flew in. Reward through pay meant that the more you earned, the more you could spend.

In the second half of the nineteenth century wages in towns started to overtake price increases – so people could buy more. Family size shrank as child mortality dropped because of better food and sanitation. There was now no need to insure the future with so many children. From seven or eight children on average, the number began to drop.

Instead of waiting to inherit, make do, or go without, people started to buy the new furniture and clothing that were pouring out of the factories. They made purchases based on real need alongside new luxury items like painted ceramics. The upwardly mobile middle classes began to mimic the wants of the aristocracy. By the early 1800s the mass-producing potteries of Stoke-on-Trent ensured that Wedgwood china could be available for an ever-widening band of shoppers. The preserves of the few, like tea, soon became a staple commodity of the many. Changes in dress styles, which had once taken place over generations, now happened within a year.

So, things were being made with the raw materials from the

colonies at the new factories by the factory workers. Through the creation of a class of producers the seeds were sown for a class of consumers, who used their pay packets to buy the things that were being made. But there had to be places to buy these new products.

The word 'retail' comes from the French word *retailler*, which refers to the process of cutting off, clipping and dividing in tailoring. Small specialist retailers and general stores remained common throughout the nineteenth century, but the emergence of all-embracing department stores opened up a new shopping experience. What had started in 1670 with the Hudson Bay Company in Canada, the first store to include departments, was spreading through Europe in the latter half of the nineteenth century. John Lewis, never knowingly undersold, opened its first department store in Oxford Street in 1864, and by the time it got to Manchester in 1880 it had introduced a revolutionary policy of actually allowing customers to browse through displays of household goods, furniture, cosmetics and clothing, instead of being served behind the counter. The department store also offered new customer services never before seen, such as restaurants, cloakrooms, reading rooms, home delivery and wrapping services.

Franklin W. Woolworth, who had opened his first successful five-and-dime store in 1879 in Pennsylvania, in 1907 opened a store in Liverpool, which brought a wide range of new household goods, such as furniture, within the immediate reach of families who could not previously have afforded a new table or bed. By the end of the nineteenth century retailers were offering hire purchase; in the US its use multiplied twenty times between 1918 and 1938. The era of wanting not waiting was born.

The first well-publicized supermarket, Big Bear, popped up in New Jersey in 1932 on the site of an abandoned car plant – the start of serve-yourself food shopping. By then Henry Ford's Model T had reached the masses and they could park and shop. Jack Cohen visited the US from London's East End a couple of times in the thirties and started his own version of the pile-'em-high-sell-'em-cheap store. Tesco was born.

The industrial and consumer revolutions complemented and fuelled each other as a complex network of relationships, events, discoveries and vested interest combined to create excess supply. And the result of all this epoch-making change – the exploration and exploitation, the industrialization and individualization, the morality and the money – was that the fundamental prerequisites of a consumer society were created in the shift from a world based on scarcity to one based on abundance. Throughout the twentieth century, albeit interrupted by wars and recession, life for many stopped being just about survival and started to be about consumption. To consume is to choose and choice demands excess capacity. By the 1950s, for the first time in our history, we were producing enough to allow choice for the masses. Consumer society was truly born. It would be another thirty years before the leap to turbo-consumption but the physical means to underpin our shopping addiction were firmly in place.

But what would keep us buying? Surely enough would eventually become enough and the novelty of abundance would slowly wear off. The law of marginal utility, the economic theory that tells us that the second Mars Bar never tastes as good as the first, would mean that even if there was more to buy we would look eventually for other ways of finding happiness. If we were to go on consuming we would have to move beyond physical needs to emotional desires.

So what keeps us buying?

Shopping as pure emotion

The existence of things to buy is a necessary but insufficient prerequisite for a consumer society. There has to be supply but there must also be demand. But why would we want to buy more and more? Why would we want to keep returning to consume when our physical needs had already been met?

It is relatively easy to get people to do things they don't want to do if their survival depends on it. But how could we be persuaded to buy more than we needed to live? The answer was to structure consumption to meet deep-seated emotional needs in all of us. If consuming could become about feeding our emotions and not just our physical needs, there would be no limit to the amount we could shop for. Only by understanding what drives us as human beings can we understand why we now live in a society that is all about consuming. For shopping to have such a grip on our lives, it has to connect to some of the prime drivers of what it means to be human.

There are two key aspects of this: the need to belong and have security, and its *alter ego*, the need to be free. To thrive we need both and shopping appears to provide them. We are social animals and need to live in groups to survive. We are nurtured and socialized by our parents for years when we rely on them entirely. Contact is an emotional and physical necessity. We understand ourselves in relation to others. Our place in the tribe matters, but belonging to the tribe in the first place matters more. Shopping plays to our need to belong. We wear the same or similar clothes as others in the tribe we choose to belong to. We are fearful of looking out of place, as if we don't belong. So we keep buying to ensure we do. Different labels and brands send a signal to others about whether or not we belong to their tribe. The word 'brand', of course, comes from the marks put on cattle to distinguish one herd from another. We buy to show love and affection, to demonstrate that we care and in return are cared for. Volvo know this and tell us that 'Life is better lived together.' Clothes, shoes, newspapers, haircuts, food, wine, furniture – everything we buy places us exactly where we want to be.

And it's not just what we buy but the act of shopping that is social. As we have seen, Sharon, Sarah and millions of others use shopping as a way to be social, the means to make and build friendships. The 'shopping frenzy', one of the social phenomena of our age, when mobs descend on new fashion stores or at the opening of a new line, is about being part of a collective hysteria.

People need to belong and share 'meaningful' experiences. Shopping is now one of the few ways we feel we can do it. 'It is not simply a matter of whether you're wearing last year's Manolos or passing on this year's Nancy bag,' says Minette Marrin of the *Sunday Times.* 'It makes a big difference to where you position yourself, to your feel for the times, to the people you belong with and the way people treat you. Nobody can ignore that.' [9]

But we have an equally compelling desire to be individuals and express our freedom from others. So, we consume not just to belong but also to be different and to compete to be the best. In a consumer society there is something different for everyone so we can all be 'individuals'. Distinctions are emphasized and extended. Products are segmented so that everyone can find their own happy niche. Let's take our desire for denim as a common example. On one hand jeans represent the democratization of culture and fashion. Everyone can wear jeans, but distinguish themselves by what type – Tesco's finest versus designer Evisu at £199 a go. Denim started out as a cheap and durable fabric for manual labourers. There is nothing intrinsically sexy, cool or subversive about blue cotton. But the millions of pounds spent on advertising and marketing make the right emotional and social connections and, through them, allow for differentiation into social groups. By the end of 2007 the value of the denim market reached £1.51 billion. Sales had increased by 40 per cent in the five preceding years. Eighty-six million pairs of jeans were due to be sold in Britain during 2008. That would equate to three pairs of jeans every second. And the market is not stopping there. Mintel, the market-research company, who made the estimation, predict that there are still parts of the market ripe for development, such as products for those who need to wear larger sizes or those targeted at older consumers.

From jeans to watches and white goods, markets are carefully segmented so that we can make 'spontaneous' choices that 'set us free' and demonstrate our unique identity. And that identity is portrayed in brands as labels or symbols of what we want to be. This notion that identity is shaped by us in an ongoing lifelong

project, based on our buying choices and decisions, is peculiar to consumer society. Before we became a society of consumers, identities were fixed and ascribed; they didn't change over time. Identity was governed by family and occupation. Without such rigid structures, identity has become governed by what we buy and is fluid and ever-changing.

Of course, the urges to belong and to be different are just two sides of the same coin. We can only be different and stand out within the context of others. The retail wheels are kept turning faster and faster by our twin emotional needs for security and freedom as we endlessly switch between the two competing instincts to belong and to be free. Consumption allows us to be different and the same, to stand out and fit in, to seek solitude and solidarity. We are in the same tribe but some tribe members are more important than others – they have more feathers, beads or body paint or, as it is now, better labels and brands. My teenage sons want expensive trainers so that they can be different, express their individuality, but also belong to their particular social group. The youngest and most rebellious wears Vans. His elder brother is more conformist and goes for mainstream brands like Adidas. Like all of us, they want to be 'individuals' but only in a band of other 'individuals', carefully gradated in difference from other groups of consumers.

Consumerism has provided a means by which we struggle for social survival, but the sociological impact appears contradictory. The mobile phone connects us to our friends, family and colleagues – but it also disconnects us from those around us. It means we can switch off from those in the street, shop and train carriage. We talk to each other on our mobiles, not face to face, and see couples walking down the street hand in hand but on their phones to other people – perhaps to other couples performing exactly the same social but individual act. Yet we use the very same mobiles to keep checking for calls or messages to prove to ourselves that someone out there still wants us, that we belong. The *i* in iPod is significant as we retreat from society into our own private world. And yet the very ownership of one confers

status and confirms the need to belong. We live in this ambivalent, fluid state between solid security and the thin air of a life of brands and symbolic meaning. An advert for the now infamous bank Northern Rock says, 'I want a fixed-rate mortgage and I want freedom.' We want it all: to be flexible and fixed, secure and free. Consumer society tries to give us both.

But even deeper human emotions and drivers were exploited by the burgeoning marketing industry in the early twentieth century to get us to buy more. A pioneer in the sphere of public relations and consumer behaviour, Edward Bernays used the insights of his uncle Sigmund Freud on the hidden irrational, sexual and aggressive emotions of our inner self to develop means of controlling the masses of the mid-twentieth century by selling them more than they would otherwise have bought.[10] From the early 1920s he advised big US corporations on how to sell their products through the media and new PR stunts, but he was also developing the way to control the masses that he and other Freudians believed would otherwise cause social breakdown. Using the insights of psychoanalysis, Bernays ran PR campaigns that encouraged people to consume and in the process helped make them, he thought, more docile and less subversive. In *Propaganda*, his most important book, he argued that the manipulation of public opinion was a necessary part of democracy that would, happily for his bank balance and the profits of his clients, replace the ballot box as the means by which society could be governed.

An example of the effectiveness of his work can be seen in his 1920s campaign for the American Tobacco Company to encourage women to take up smoking – which was then a social taboo. Through research and some of the earliest use of focus groups Bernays identified cigarettes as a symbol of the penis and therefore male domination – so we can see how the ideas of his uncle were helpful to him. The notion of the cigarette representing male social power needed to be challenged so that women felt free to buy his client's products. Bernays sent a group of young models to march in the New York City parade. The press was informed that a group of marchers would light 'Torches of Freedom'. At his sig-

nal, the models lit Lucky Strike cigarettes in front of the eager photographers. The whole stunt and the PR it created helped to break the taboo against women smoking in public.

The case of the unsold cake mix also shows off Bernays's astounding handiwork. His client was having a problem getting housewives to buy cake mix. Bernays's ingenious solution was the addition of an egg. In terms of the cooking process the eggs were unnecessary to the mix but his campaign said they were needed. Through careful research, Bernays had found that women felt guilty about not making cakes from natural ingredients. By using the ready-made mix they felt they were failing in their duty as wives and mothers. The simple addition of an egg helped them to make an unconscious connection with their own reproductive system and to feel they were adding something of their real selves to the short-cut process of baking. The sales of packet cake mix soared.

Bernays knew that his client's products were important as symbols of how people wanted to be seen. He recognized that it was critical to encourage and train people to desire new products before the old ones were worn out, or even fully consumed, so that the wheels of industry and commerce could be oiled with faster and faster purchases. He pioneered now common PR techniques, such as celebrity endorsement and product placement, to encourage people to buy more than they needed.

We use the term 'retail therapy' matter-of-factly today. It has lost any pejorative connotations. 'I'm just popping out for a bit of retail therapy' is now a common refrain But the goal isn't to help us manage these needs but to exploit them as a way of ensuring that consumption goes beyond physical necessity to the infinite demands of our emotions and psyche.

From gods to goods

One final change in the emotional jigsaw helped create consumer society: the end of religion as a central organizing force in our lives. Through religion, the world was ordered, and through belief in a

higher being, there was meaning and control in our lives. Indeed, religion was often anti-materialistic. Both Buddha and Jesus assured their downtrodden supporters that only they would find salvation in heaven, given that 'It is easier for a camel to pass through the eye of a needle than for a rich man to enter the kingdom of heaven.' The fall of God and the idea of salvation in the afterlife left us with the worst of all revelations: that we are mere mortals. In place of an eternity in heaven, or hell, a life based on consumption becomes a wonderful distraction from the inevitability of death.

Now it is our possessions that provide us with the illusion of control and mastery of the world around us. We buy security in our homes and cars, protection from the elements and from others. We avoid the thought of death by buying the promises to make us look and feel young. It is one reason why we can't imagine a life without buying — not buying is equated to death. After all, you can't take it with you. There is no higher purpose to life than higher purchase.

The Protestant work ethic provided a divine excuse to seek salvation on earth through what we could buy. But the secularization of society has seen consumerism become one of the world's last great religions. It is practised on us from birth and by us until we die. We all have our shopping Bibles depending on what religion we follow: Prada, Boss or Hermès. Celebrities are our new high priests, the till our altar. It seems we must have something to worship, be it God or Gucci.

The experience of walking into Bluewater, the shopping mall dug from an old Kent clay pit, is nothing less than transcendental. Just like entering a medieval cathedral, the sense of calm, safety, order and other-worldliness sweeps over you — the design similarity of the high peaked ceilings is no coincidence. Like a church, this is a place where we can leave our worries at the door and find salvation by having our hearts lifted by greater things than the mundane drudgery of everyday life. Shopping gives us all that we need: the hope of a better life. If in the past the Church made us pay through guilt or with hard work, today our credit cards will do nicely.

The cathedrals of old were built on the basis of a commitment to a greater good than individual acquisition. Stonemasons would spend their lives toiling to create one window or tower, prepared to dedicate their lives to a higher calling. The elaborate stained-glass windows were meant to give parishioners a brief but spectacular glimpse into the next life – a life full of colour and beauty. Now heaven can be viewed through the elaborate displays in shop windows. As religion and attendance at church once did, shopping takes one out of the dull routine of ordinary life.

Shopping in Bluewater demands a similar sense of belief and dedication but now the focus is on the individual and the here and now, a dedicated pursuit of personal success through shopping. The shop windows give the consumer a glimpse into the world they can have – if they can pay.

The centre is now famous, or perhaps infamous, for banning young people wearing the hooded tops that might intimidate other shoppers. Wearing a hood was once a sign of godliness; now it has become the garment of the excluded. But hooded tops are still on sale in Bluewater shops and it is still possible to try them on without fear of ejection. The decision by the management reveals much about corporate attitudes to 'undesirable' shoppers who might spoil the anaesthetized spirit of the centre. It also confirms Bluewater as a private space run for the profit of a few, not a public space for the benefit of all.

Young people will, of course, subvert the ban. Hoodies have become even more fashionable as a statement of counter-culture and the shops of Bluewater will sell even more of them. Retailers don't care about anti-social behaviour as long as there is profit to be made. A London firm has designed a bulletproof hoodie for £300. Shops have no morality, no principle, and no motive other than selling. Heaven is a world in which the shops never shut and our credit cards never reach their limit.

Perhaps the proof we need of the consumerization of society and its elevation to quasi-religious status can be found in the

commodification of the Church. Andrew Stephen comments
that in the US 'Churches have learnt the basic rule of American
consumerism: give the customer what he/she wants. The mega-
churches have thus become part church, part shopping mall.
One in Tacoma, Washington, even has its own Starbucks. Brent-
wood Baptist Church in Houston has a McDonald's. Those who
attend are passive consumers, entertained by the dazzling audio-
visual systems and by mesmerizing "ministers"; the religious
content may be superficially present, but it is hypnotic, feel-
good public speaking that counts most. I turned on the television the other day and tuned in to a mega-church preacher: "It's
OK to be wealthy," were the first words I heard.'[11]

The souls of turbo-consumers, like those of all other believ-
ers, are up for grabs. That's certainly what marketing guru David
Lewis thinks, as people come to view themselves primarily as
consumers in a global marketplace. He says, 'The marketplace is
their soul and their soul is the marketplace.'[12]

Once again, the objective is not to meet our spiritual needs,
but to exploit them to sell us more things than we would otherwise buy if consumption was just about survival. Just as religion
once permeated every aspect of our lives, now shopping grips us
and does so with a mix of hope and fear. But it needs an ever
more complex architecture of things to buy, ways of persuading
us to buy more, places to buy things and the means to pay for
more.

The industrial consumer complex

Something to buy

Once it has been liberated to buy based on emotional rather
than physical need, a functioning, sustainable and crucially
growing consumer society requires an endless conveyor-belt of
new things to buy, the capacity to make us want them and to
allow us to pay for them. Of course, when shopping is driven

by symbols rather than survival it doesn't really matter what you buy: it's the consuming that counts. And, as we have seen, the quantity and quality of the things we can buy have expanded exponentially.

'What's on the conveyor-belt tonight?' Bruce Forsyth would ask, at the frantic climax of the 1970s light-entertainment show *The Generation Game* as the winning contestant sat behind a procession of cheesy consumer goods, like Teasmades and lava lamps, trying to recall everything they'd seen to take home as a prize. As with these often forgettable items, we buy more things because there are more things to buy and acquiring them feeds our emotional needs and insecurities. But something new and different has to be put on the conveyor-belt. The endless creation of wants that become needs starts with the product. Design, fashion and technology innovation are the fuel that keeps the consumer motor ticking over.

Around the world, in hidden laboratories and offices, vast teams are quietly working away at creating markets for products we never knew we needed until they told us we did. Proctor & Gamble are the masters of product innovation, a multinational manufacturer of brands as diverse as Old Spice, Crest, Dreft and Pampers. They have a renowned system for devising new products that is both rigorous and formulaic. Two parts of the company act in a pincer fashion to squeeze out an endless range of new and improved product lines. Research and Development come up with a new idea, and Marketing know the customer needs. New products take off when there is a congruence between the two. R&D is the place for the white-coated boffins. They might work in plastics, chemicals or technology. Theirs is a life of what-if trialling. They try to find ways of making the unit cost of new products affordable so that technology can meet scale profitably. So, for instance, could a new, cheaper enzyme help create a new product that wasn't feasible at volume when other ingredients were more expensive? Meanwhile the marketing team are constantly in touch with the end user, the customer, looking for new trends and new demands. For example,

they know that family sizes are shrinking, which should mean fewer meals and therefore less space needed to cook. Their data will also be telling them that with PCs in each room, connected up wirelessly to the Internet, family members are spending more time on their own. That means different mealtimes and different meals, which provides an opportunity to reconfigure the design of kitchens and bring in new kitchen-cleaning products.

One innovation that matched technological change to consumer demand was the battery-powered toothbrush. At Proctor & Gamble the boffins found that the tiny motors that drive electric toothbrushes needed less power. Instead of mains chargers they could now be powered by AA batteries. The marketing team knew that many people aspired to electric toothbrushes but couldn't afford them or didn't have the right sockets in their bathroom. So, they invented a new brush that was virtually the same size as the old manual ones that could be stocked in the same place on the same shelves and be sold at six times the price. If one in ten customers switched from the old-style brush to a new battery-powered one, a huge profit could be made. Proctor & Gamble applied the technology of battery-charged brushes, combined with the demand for portability and a tendency towards laziness by some consumers, and rolled out the idea through their product range to other items, like washing-up brushes. Overnight they had created a new market and set a new standard, not for dental hygiene but for what it takes to be a successful consumer in a turbo-consuming society.

The product cycle often starts at the level of high-end yachts because of the demand for luxury and space-saving. It is then applied to the best hotels, then to mass-market hotels. House builders will pick it up for their high-end homes, then Magnet and finally B&Q. What starts with NASA often ends up in Asda. The fabric used in many sports trainers was developed from space-suit technology.

But nothing, especially toothbrushes, is built to last. If it did it would defeat the objective of having to buy more. Redundancy is not so much physical as emotional. The conveyor-belt is, of

course, not real but is in our minds. The old must disappear from our memory to allow room for the new. Vance Packard coined the term 'built-in obsolescence', arguing that obsolescence was based on function, quality and desirability.[13] New designs and technology mean functionality is always changing. PC and software upgrades appear as regularly as clockwork. We use small imperfections in perfectly usable goods as an excuse to buy something new. We will often buy something like a new kettle not because the old one doesn't work but because it doesn't look right or is slightly marked. And, of course, fashion is in constant flux. Even items launched as 'design classics' are soon superseded.

Go to www.coolhunting.com for all the latest must-have designer goods – although the day I did, the home page was dedicated to the kind of barbecue accessories I never knew existed, including this:

Designed by chefs, the Grillslinger is a 'Barbeque Tool System,' or in other words a belt with holster-like pockets for the included knife, tongs and spatula, as well as places to stash salt and pepper, mobile phones, beer openers or anything else you need grill-side. Removable polypropylene inserts for the utensils are dishwasher safe for easy clean-up. It's $100 from Sur la table.

How on earth can any of us manage without the Grillslinger? Many can't. They are not alone. The winner of the Concept Products Award at the *Daily Mail* Ideal Home Show 2008 was something called the Footlume, a rug that lights up when you walk on it. In a previous year a product was on display that baked bread and boiled water simultaneously. Already on the market, you can buy an iPod stereo dock with a toilet-roll holder. But it's not just the manufacturers who are fighting to keep our wallets out. Shops and supermarkets are not designed by accident but to maximize sales. When you go into a supermarket, do you often come out spending fifty pounds more than you'd budgeted for? Why is that? You may have seen someone you

liked the look of with a particular bottle of wine in their trolley, an advert for olive oil on TV last night might have lodged in your subconscious, or the stark bleached floors of the aisles made you think of restocking the cleaning products under your kitchen sink. About 80 per cent of consumer choices are made in the store and around 60 per cent of those are based on impulse. But those impulses are deliberately triggered. 'Every customer presents a minor problem of psychology,' argues shopping historian Rachel Bowlby.[14]

Do you ever get lost or confused in shopping centres? Well, they're designed to confuse and disorient. They don't want you to know what's round the corner but constantly to surprise you. Straight lines allow you to find what you're looking for too easily. Instead, you're forced to walk past as many displays as possible to increase the chances of an extra purchase. This is based on the Gruen Transfer, named after Victor Gruen who opened the first enclosed shopping mall in the US in 1956. It is the moment when a shopper enters a trance-like daze and is then much more likely to make an unplanned purchase. Shopping centres are designed to bring on the Gruen Transfer as quickly as possible.

In the supermarkets the quality and position of all goods are constantly tweaked by computer programs to ensure maximum sales. Cartoon-infested breakfast cereals are placed at children's eye level to boost pester power and thereby maximize sales. Even that comes at a price as companies pay a premium, called a 'slotting allowance', to get their product into the optimum sales position on the shelf. This generates an industry in itself: every week around 150,000 merchandiser visits are made across the UK to audit the position of their company's stock in the shops. At the end of the journey round the aisles, loyalty cards offer a small discount in return for huge amounts of information to sell you even more stuff you didn't know you needed until the persuasion process starts again.

So, what other tricks do retailers have up their sleeves? In clothes shops items are folded so that we have to handle them to

see them in the knowledge that a physical connection makes a sale more likely. Muzak can ensure customers stay 18 per cent longer and make 17 per cent more purchases. The slower the tempo of the Muzak the more we buy. There's Muzak to suit any retail situation: fast-food restaurants play faster music to tie in with the rate at which we chew our food; French music in an off-licence prompts customers to buy more French wine. The Muzak company provides the tapes and programs for stores and businesses to use. They claim that their 'integration of music, voice and sound . . . bypasses the resistance of the mind and targets the receptiveness of the heart. They like it. Remember it. Go back to it. Audio Architecture builds a bridge to loyalty. And loyalty is what keeps brands alive.' What Muzak does for shoppers' hearing, Ecomist does for our sense of smell by selling shops scent-dispensing machines. They claim that 'customers will always respond better to a subtly fragranced environment'.

In different shops assistants will approach you in different ways to use simple selling techniques that play on our emotions and insecurities, techniques like regression and transference. For example, a car salesperson will try to make us feel small, perhaps by using very technical jargon about a car's performance and handling that we won't understand. They then become a parental figure to take us through this threatening alien territory and 'help us' buy what we need.

Nothing about the shopping experience is for us. The massive investment in shops and shopping centres is all about one thing: making as much money as possible. Every aspect of our experience is carefully calibrated to ensure we spend as much as possible. When we walk into a shopping centre we see a cornucopia of places to express our identity and subliminally to meet our emotional, psychological and spiritual needs. The retailers just see us as wallets and purses to be tipped upside down and emptied.

Whether it's gadgets, fashion, food or cars, new products and their adoption curve are growing faster than ever. But supply is only part of the equation. It's demand that really matters and demand is something that can and must be stimulated if society

is to go on consuming. But for demand to be realized, we have to want to buy and then we have to be able to.

The battle for your mind

The consumer has to be mobilized every day in every way to buy. We don't know we want things until we know they're there and are encouraged and cajoled not just to want them but to need them. Of course, traded goods have always been advertised and marketed – stallholders in ancient cities shouted the desirability of their wares. It was the spam of their day. But in this day commercial marketing is ubiquitous. From newspapers, magazines, cinema and TV, advertising and marketing have spilled out beyond billboards and buses to the steps of buildings, shopping-trolley handles, other people's clothing and even their skin.

Researchers have run an experiment to count the number of brand messages we see in a day. Using cameras strapped to people and linking them to a computer that reads and records every brand image, the answer they have come to is a staggering average of 3,500. That's more than two hundred in every waking hour of the day, or 1,277,500 a year. This is how the consumer is being actively mobilized to buy. Commercial messages have been deployed to sell things since the ancient empires of Arabia and Greece. It is generally agreed that advertising began in newspapers, during the seventeenth century, which included classified advertising. But these were simple descriptions with prices. By the late nineteenth century new printing technology meant illustrations could be added, eventually in colour.

It was not until the emergence of advertising agencies in the latter part of the nineteenth century that advertising became a fully fledged institution, with companies like J. Walter Thompson's, now renamed JWT, which grew throughout the last century. These agencies responded to an increasingly crowded marketplace in which manufacturers found that promotion of their products was vital if they were to survive. They sold themselves as experts in the communication of products to customers, leaving

their clients to get on with the business of manufacturing. Companies like film-maker Kodak and the producer of Lifebuoy soap flourished through early advertising campaigns.

The First and Second World Wars saw important advances in mass communication as governments on all sides used advertising as propaganda. We are all familiar with the British posters convincing citizens to fight, and also to persuade the Americans to join in, but the depression of the 1930s and the lack of disposable income meant that commercial advertising only took off again in the 1950s. In that decade consumers bought televisions, and for the next three decades the sets provided the perfect advertising platform, first through programme sponsorship and then the commercial break.

Advertisers made great use of this new, highly visible medium, revealing what made products unique and superior to their competitors. One washing-powder would wash not just white but an even better blue white! Even now some adverts still play to functional attributes – for example, Ronseal does exactly what it says it will on the tin. But sales based on functionality are limited, while purchases based on desirability are boundless. This shift in advertising from the rational to the emotional is best understood in the transition from words to images. An early advertising success story is that of Pears Soap. Thomas Barratt married into the famous soap-making family and realized they needed to be more aggressive about pushing their products if they were to survive. He launched a series of adverts featuring cherubic children that linked his brand with purity and simplicity. The children in the fine-art images he used would be perceived as untainted by commercialism. Barratt's block of soap was much like every other block of soap on the market, but he sold more because his advert made the right connections with his potential customers.

Instead of a USP (unique selling proposition), what matters most now is the image that communicates all of a brand's aspirations and values in one go. Steve Hilton, a branding consultant, says it's now 'all about emotional offerings'.[15] He is now behind the repositioning of the Conservative Party under David Cameron.

The Tory Party, like all major political groupings, has become a brand and what matters for this brand like any other is not so much what it does but the emotion it conveys. Brands like the new-look Conservatives offer a short-cut to meaning. 'Vote Blue, Go Green' was the party's attempt to attract environmentally concerned voters, with lots of images of Cameron cycling through London or visiting the Arctic to be seen watching the effect of climate change on the ice caps. We don't have to take time to get to know someone: we can see who they are from the way they brand and label themselves.

When people buy Coca-Cola it's not just a sugary fizzy drink but the American dream and a vision of corporate citizenship that they're slurping down. Coke is like a friend, part of the lives of millions of people across the globe. It symbolizes what is successful, cool and relaxing. The company producing it has 3,600 people keeping drink diaries so that they can record moments of joy and connections to others whenever they pour it down their throats. The diarists have recorded more than 40,000 occasions when only Coke will do, and their insights will help direct further advertising and marketing campaigns.

Coca-Cola is not really a manufacturer at all: the name is just a brand. The producer holds the formula for the syrup while the rest of the production process is franchised out. So the World of Coca-Cola Museum in Atlanta is just a history of the adverts that created the brand. The brand represents the emotional attachment we have with the product while the filling of the bottles holds little if any value. The share price is based on the brand, not the physical assets of the company. When Ford bought fellow car-maker Jaguar, the physical assets were deemed to be worth only 16 per cent of the total value of the company. Again the key asset was the brand. The marketing industry believes that brand loyalty can start as early as the age of two so there is value in getting them when they're young.

Manufacturers and marketing psychologists know us better than we know ourselves. Charles Revson, the fabled cosmetics king, once said, 'In the factory we make soap, in the shops we sell

hope.' If we can be sold hope in the form of soap, we can be sold anything. They understand the concept of post-decision regret, the niggling feeling that the alternative we rejected might have been better than what we bought. So companies now follow up an important sale with supporting information to keep you feeling good about your purchase. Car manufacturers like BMW, Toyota and Audi send supporting magazines with articles and pictures to make you feel part of 'the family' and stop you going to a different manufacturer next time. The big four-by-four Hummer, the H2, was designed in part with the help of Clotaire Rapaille, a French psychologist, who understood that combat and survival are the most basic human instincts. And what do buyers say they like about the Hummer H2? They say they won't be 'pushed around' in it. But the insights of psychology can be made to work at different levels. The H2 was also made to resemble the armoured Tonka toy to take men back to their youth – an emotional space in which they have the money to buy but without responsibility.

I'm at BMP in Paddington, west London. It's one of the best-established advertising agencies in the UK and I'm here to see its elder statesman, Chris Powell. BMP's reception area is plastered with their latest work for the *Financial Times*. Posters declare, 'We live in financial times.' Indeed we do. Money is now everything. I'm not sure if the posters are meant to make me think I can only really 'live' within the pages of the pink 'un, as the *FT* is known. Perhaps some City and business people feel as if they do. But certainly the message is that if you want to understand these financial times, you should read the *Financial Times*. One advert has Richard Branson transposed on to that iconic image of Che Guevara in beret and beard – a classic marketing ploy that takes a counter-cultural image, like the South American revolutionary, and uses it to sell something. Today Che poses no threat to capitalism – but the echo of rebellion about him is used as a platform for heroism and leadership. Even to sell the newspaper of the capitalist system, the *FT*.

I've come to find out from Chris how advertising works and he takes me through the different jobs and processes that have

generated some of his most famous ad campaigns, from Smash (the country's favourite) to John Smith beer, VW and Walkers Crisps. There are, he says, essentially four jobs in an agency: planner, creative, art director and account handler, each with a specific and skilled role.

First, the planners do the research on what the client's customer or potential customer currently thinks about the product or issue. Most advertising is dedicated to keeping the customers a company's already got, not winning new people. Big brands like Coke spend most, trying to get people to go on doing the same thing by reminding them of why they liked the product in the first place. It's about sustaining brand loyalty. Planners work with focus groups and quantitative data and tend to be young, female history or science graduates. Even when other industries had few places for women, advertising welcomed them because they were making most family purchases; their insights were deemed more valuable than men's.

The planners hand over their findings to the creatives, who use them to come up with the insight or idea that the ad campaign needs to express. This can be largely intuitive. The process of decision-making on what to buy isn't always rational although some economists would like us to think it is. For example, Marlboro cigarettes were sold on the basis of the emotional control they gave the smoker, linking the cowboy image with the taming of the Wild West. The creatives give the idea to the art directors, who produce the posters, television slots or, increasingly, the online campaigns.

I ask Chris which adverts worked best and why. He goes back to Smash, the instant mashed potato that temporarily replaced the real stuff in many households during the 1970s. Planners found that housewives felt guilty about not buying real potatoes, carrying them home, peeling, boiling and then finally mashing them: they felt they were not being proper mums or wives if all they were doing was pouring hot water on to powder and mixing. Of course, this was the same as the eggs in the cake mixture. This time, to get over the guilt, they ran a funny advert, focusing

on the reaction of Martians to the process of making real mash compared with Smash. They chortled their robot laugh and made us feel it was ridiculous to do anything other than reach for the Smash. Mums and wives no longer felt guilty and, for a while at least, Smash took off.

Direct sale through paid-for media, 'above-the-line' marketing, was the principal way in which goods and services were sold and its peak years were the 1960s. Since then there has been a steady move to 'below-the-line' methods of marketing, first through promotions but now through more innovative and ubiquitous forms of marketing. Consumers have become more demanding and wiser: they want to be in on the joke and part of the sale, not a passive recipient of the advertiser's message. So marketing is everywhere: graffiti, cut-outs, wall art, light-bulbs that turn on when we walk past a billboard for the *Economist*, a new full-size Mini in a box like a toy car, images projected on the House of Commons and banners unfurled down the sides of buildings. Below-the-line marketing is craftier and less direct, used to get round customers who are more cynical and less trusting about manufacturers' claims.

Below the line involves techniques, like product placement, that maximize exposure of a client's brand in films or television programmes in the best possible context. According to www.brandchannel.com, a website that counts brand references in films, the 2006 remake of *The Pink Panther* featured more than thirty brands. Probably without noticing you would have seen Apple, Chanel, Holiday Inn, *Newsweek*, Toyota and Viagra among many others.[16] In one study almost 30 per cent of people said they would be persuaded to try a brand after having seen it in a movie, with that figure rising to more than 40 per cent among 15–24-year-olds.[17]

Guerrilla marketing, the use of unconventional and usually low-cost ways of grabbing people's attention, is another below-the-line technique. It is largely unregulated and can be aggressive, and the term works well. A war is going on with fewer and fewer ethical rules being applied as corporations explore new ways to focus our attention. Companies use the built and natural environment to

place products and advertise their campaigns. And if there is
nowhere else to stick their advert, they use people. The patheti-
cally named 'Cunning Stunts' offers students £88.20 a week to
wear a corporate logo on their head for a minimum of three
hours a day – it's a vegetable dye transfer that washes off. These
human billboards join the ranks of the human sign-holders, on
London's Oxford Street and in other busy shopping centres, who
point to back-street 'golf sales' and the like.

Viral marketing signals another turning point: it is the use of
email adverts and other electronic media, such as text messages,
that people are encouraged to pass on to friends. It is part of the
process of new marketing techniques adapting to new and less
deferential times. If we don't believe adverts, we increasingly
rely on people we know to recommend things. Films, music,
restaurants and holiday destinations are often purchased on the
basis of personal recommendation. McKinsey, the management-
consultancy firm, estimates that two-thirds of the economy is
driven by word of mouth, so companies increasingly use paid
advocates rather than adverts to sell – it's called 'buzz'.

Buzz marketing is about the right people saying the right
things about a new product or service. It is relatively new as a
marketing technique, but its roots are pre-Second World War. In
the 1930s a team of researchers invited small groups of employees at a factory to try out various new working conditions in a
bid to improve productivity before rolling them out to the
whole workforce. To the researchers' amazement, the participants seemed to like whatever was on trial to such an extent that
their productivity increased. Then they realized that their results
had nothing to do with what was actually being tried and everything to do with running a research trial. By singling out a
small group of employees to participate in an exclusive trial, the
participants felt valued, special and important. It didn't matter
what was tried, everything worked better because the participants were made to feel special. The research team coined the
term 'The Hawthorne Effect', named after the factory where
the tests took place, to describe the goodwill and advocacy that

research trials generate among participants. The Hawthorne Effect gave birth to buzz marketing.

Paul Marsden, who has written about the experiment, offers some advice: 'If the psychology of the Hawthorne Effect all seems a bit abstract, try it for yourself and see how powerful it is. The next time you want something from someone (a salary increase, a date, or whatever) first do some "research" with them by asking their advice on some matter. It doesn't matter what the matter is as long as you appear to be listening to their advice. Then ask them for whatever you want from them. At a subconscious level they will feel indebted to you for flattering their ego.'[18]

But all of these marketing techniques depend on knowing who to sell to, and for that, market research has always been a vital tool in persuading us to buy. It is the systematic gathering, recording and analysis of information about customers, competitors and the market to boost sales. The industry exploded as information from credit and loyalty cards was gathered on new technology with more than 65,000 employees worldwide and a turnover of around £10 billion. The goal is to secure as much targeted data as possible and use it to profile consumers to know what messages should be sent out and how. Data companies like Acorn offer street-by-street breakdowns of our habits and tastes. If I type in my south London postcode on the Acorn site this is what I get:

Category 2:	Urban Prosperity
Group E:	Educated Urbanites
Type 16:	Prosperous young professionals, flats

You are likely to spend more than £20,000 on a new car, buy wines by mail order. Your key interests are current affairs, fine arts, gourmet foods and wines, snow skiing, theatre, classical music and reading historical works. You will visit a coffee bar more than 3 times a week.

Well, they got the current-affairs bit right but nothing else. It is this type of information that fuels the junk mail industry: 3.4 billion items of junk mail are now received in Britain every year, a quarter of which are never opened – often because they're sent to dead people who get on average eight pieces each month. For some bizarre reason the figure rises to thirteen in Surrey. Never the liveliest county, I guess.

If involving people in 'research' and discussing products is the basis of buzz marketing, now even market research is being turned into a form of below-the-line marketing. Companies pay for people to pose as advocates of their products or find ways of dressing up marketing as research to get the brand bandwagon rolling through opinion leaders. One example is the 'cool hunt', the process by which big companies will go into communities to see what cool kids are wearing or would like to wear. Then they go a step further and use gangs of 'cool' children to push products in their communities, exploiting the power of peer pressure and children's fears of not fitting in. The reward for the cool who have been hunted is to have the new products first and so embellish their status as the hippest kids on the block.

The Dubit website, www.dubitchat.com/, is a prime example of this. You can apply to become a 'Dubit Informer' and get paid between 50p and £2 for completing online surveys, or a 'Dubit Insider' to 'promote brands on the street for free stuff, prizes and cash'. Suggested ways in which young people can do this are 'just talking to your mates about it'; 'wearing or using the gear at certain public events such as concerts which are paid for'; 'flyering or stickering your town or school'; and 'telling everyone on the net about it'. For their troubles, the Dubit Insiders get 'the latest gear to show off to your mates'; 'access to exclusive, inside information and events'; 'freebies, chances to win prizes and some serious cash'; and 'free access to concerts and gigs for the best insiders'.

Why do certain bands suddenly appear on the music scene? In part it's down to radio air play and good PR, but the music industry is leaving nothing to chance by creating 'street teams',

groups of enthusiastic fans who like a particular band so much, and the prospect of free gig tickets or T-shirts, that they will work a bar or a nightclub to drum up new support and create a buzz. One group tells another, they see the band and it spreads. But it's orchestrated rather than spontaneous; a word-of-mouth pyramid system. There is now a word-of-mouth marketing trade association called WOMMA. They spread the word about spreading the word and offer morality too: 'The WOMMA and its members are committed to building a profession that is based on ethical practices.'[19] But how can it be ethical to spread information essentially by deceit?

What lengths will advertisers go to? A campaign to target 'Bridget Jones-type females' for Carte d'Or saw two charismatic female performers in a supermarket, wheeling around a shopping trolley that contained only the ice cream. They told shoppers they were having a girls' night in party and couldn't cook so had decided to serve only Carte d'Or, and went on to describe the flavours in 'tantalizing' detail. They alerted shoppers to the special-offer price. As a result, more than 3,500 tubs were sold, and the exercise generated lots of PR. Sony Ericsson used 'fake tourists' to promote its T68i mobile, hiring teams of undercover buzz agents to pose as tourists and hand the phone to people in the street to take a picture and start a conversation about the phones. In September 2004 *The Times* published an article called 'Trendsurfing'. In it, David Rowan gives the example of Al Fresco Chicken Sausages: the manufacturers have paid thousands of dollars for 'brand evangelists' to talk up its range among those 'who know and trust them'. At the end of any barbecue or social event the agent has to fill in a form. He cites one comment as 'My dad will most likely buy the garlic flavour . . . I'll keep you posted.'[20] I'm not sure if it's the chicken sausages, but something about this leaves a bad taste in my mouth.

So, the world is not necessarily as we think it is. People may not just be other consumers but in effect undercover brand agents. If you are in a bar and a group of hip-looking young drinkers orders some strange-sounding brandy very loudly and

then talks to you about it, just ask yourself whether they're for real. Is the blog you're reading that mentions a new product genuine or contrived? The real trouble with viral and buzz marketing is that they pretend not to be marketing at all. They try to mimic real life and can only end up making us suspicious of every encounter we have. It means that human conversation can now be bought and sold in the pursuit of profit.

As we moved from a consumer society to the more aggressive world of the turbo-consumer the lengths to which marketing firms would go grew longer and longer. What started at the turn of the century with rather gentle and quaint adverts that rationalized and explained the offering to the consumer ended with buzz marketing and guerrilla advertising, directed by teams of psychologists, neurologists, researchers, programmers, copywriters and designers to help us 'meet our needs'. But there was one final ingredient to put and keep in place consumer society. Money.

Money to burn

In the last thirty years people spent more simply because they could. For a number of reasons disposable incomes had risen dramatically. First, many prices had either risen slowly, remained static or even fallen so we could afford more. The internet had increased productivity and the industrial development of countries like China and India, where manufacturing and labour costs are low, kept prices down. In addition we had our homes renovated and painted by cheap migrant labour from Eastern Europe. Flights were cheap, TVs and DVDs cost half what they did in real terms a decade before and computer prices had fallen dramatically.

Second, household incomes had been rising, in part because many more women were going to work and many of us were working longer hours. Some money went on childcare but with unemployment also low more work stimulated growth and spending. The real income of the average household has increased

by £1,000 since 1997. For those at the top the figure was much higher.

But one of the biggest drivers of the consumer boom of the end of the twentieth century and the start of the twenty-first was the unprecedented rise in house prices over the last fifteen years. Between 2005 and 2006 the number of £1 million plus properties almost doubled. As prices rose, £246 billion of this equity wealth has been withdrawn in the last ten years to buy new cars, holidays and home improvements.

Millions of people were remortgaging their properties – pushing up the amount they owed so they could spend more. Sainsbury's Bank estimated that over the final six months of 2006, 6.1 million people were planning to paint and decorate; 2.7 million were aiming to fit a new bathroom, 1.6 million were hoping to put in a new kitchen and 1.26 million wanted an extension. In addition, 720,000 wished to build a conservatory; 645,000 were going for new windows or double-glazing; 420,000 needed a new roof; and 310,000 were aiming at a loft conversion.[21] Every one of those changes acted as the spur to even more spending on fixtures and fittings. It was the biggest house-price boom on record, outstripping in its scale even the Internet bubble of the mid-1990s, and it fed the nation's consumer addiction.

The final reason for the spending boom was even easier access to credit. The advent of credit was a brilliant way of accelerating the consumption process. Why wait to be able to afford things when you can have them now, in an instant? With credit and hire-purchase, the wanting-not-waiting society was born but the liberalization of financial services in the 1980s saw almost endless credit available to almost anyone.

People have always borrowed. Merchants extended credit to those with whom they traded to oil the wheels of commerce. Banks have always lent to the well-off. Building societies sprang up in the nineteenth century as the only way in which poorer people could own their home. Book credit in the local shop was common, and any debt paid on wages day. At the end of the

nineteenth century stores were offering easy-payment and instalment plans, especially for items like clothing and furniture. As we have seen, hire purchase was first used in the nineteenth century; it was a means of enabling carriers to purchase wagons for use in their business. Singer based the sale of his sewing machines on hire purchase. In the 1920s individual firms in sectors like oil and hotels started to issue cards for their products to allow people to buy now and pay later. Then in 1950 the Diners Club card became the first cross-company credit card used to pay restaurant bills. It was followed in 1958 by American Express, launched as a time-saving device. By 1966 Barclaycard had been introduced in the UK. The gradual expansion of credit took off as the financial-services market was deregulated in the 1980s and packs of cards were dealt out to consumers, whether they wanted them or not. It took six hundred years of banking history for household debt to reach half a trillion pounds. By 2009, within just a decade, it has more than doubled.

Credit cards work because of 'coupling', which refers to the degree to which consumption and payment are bound together psychologically. Credit cards decouple the purchase from payment and therefore reduce the pain of parting with money. Cash has a high psychological salience as it's visible and physical. Credit requires a card to be swiped and a simple four-digit pin typed in. Credit bundles purchases and makes them feel easier. Another twenty-five-pound shirt when you already owe £650 is nothing. Before you know it you've spent hundreds. We don't have to think about the whole payment, just the minimum balance at the end of the month. If one card is full, everyone on average has at least one more in their purse or wallet. It's casual, careless, instant and deniable.

Malcolm Hurlston of the Consumer Credit Counselling Service (CCCS) argues that 'The credit card had the great psychological plus of blurring spending and borrowing, so that nobody knows at the moment of purchase which you are doing and indeed you often don't quite know yourself.'[22] A survey conducted in 2003 by KPMG found that a third of people have 'no

idea' how much interest they're paying on credit cards. No one understands APRs – unless they have a degree in advanced maths.

Britain became the credit capital of Europe. So vast had our borrowings grown that by the end of 2008 the total outstanding loans to individuals in the country exceeded £1.3 trillion. In case you were wondering, that is £1,300,000,000,000 – the equivalent of Britain's entire annual economic output. The spending frenzy was increasing personal debt at the equivalent of £1 million every four minutes. The largest amount owed by a caller to the Credit Card Counselling Service was a whopping £225,000. Britons were spending more on their credit cards than the rest of Europe put together, three pounds out of every four. There are 70 million credit cards in purses and wallets across the country. In Germany the figure is just 2.3 million.

Since the unprecedented spending boom events have taken a turn for the worse. Jobs are being lost, house prices are falling and no one is lending anything to anyone. But for a while at least a nation born in the shadow of post-war rationing had never had it so good. The full panoply of a consumer society was now in place. There were the things to buy, the persuasion to buy them and the credit to make it possible. By the 1970s Britain could be understood as a consumer society. We shopped a lot and consuming was how we defined ourselves. But the pace and the extent were kept in check. But over the next thirty years we were to witness an explosion of shopping desires that would see the transformation into a world of turbo-consumption. What it needed was the spark to ignite it.

The road to Surfdom

As we have seen, some people have always shopped and con-sumed conspicuously. The roots of mass consumption are long and deep. But mass consumption is not the same thing as a turbo-consumer society. We became turbo-consumers as a

consequence of a series of economic and political events in the last decades of the twentieth century, which were triggered by a small but determined band of men and one woman.

The story starts in Austria in the early twentieth century at the private seminars of one Professor Ludwig von Mises and ends in the 'I shop therefore I am' culture of Britain today. In the mid-1930s von Mises worked in Vienna for the Chamber of Commerce and Industry, a pro-business pressure group. Every Friday at around seven p.m. a small group of economists, sociologists and philosophers would meet in his office at the Chamber. A paper would be delivered, often by von Mises himself, and discussed by the group. They would go on till about ten p.m., then retire to a small Italian restaurant across the road. Later, the hardier members would adjourn to the Kunstler Café where debate would continue into the early hours.

The main thrust of their discussion focused on the case for a liberal or free-market approach to economics, instead of the government intervention being successfully advocated by the likes of John Maynard Keynes in Britain. They wanted companies and people to be free to spend their money as they wanted and for the state to interfere much less in their lives.

One of those who attended the von Mises seminars was Friedrich von Hayek who, in 1931, was invited to teach at the London School of Economics by Lionel Robbins, himself an influential former student at von Mises's seminars. A few years later, von Hayek wanted to catch the high tide of the post-Second-World-War socialist planning and attack it mercilessly: he could see which way the wind was blowing, from Leninist Soviets, to the Roosevelt New Deal in the US and Fabianism in Britain. In 1944 he brought out his magnum opus *The Road to Serfdom*. In it he argued that all forms of collective action would lead inevitably to tyranny – as they had in Nazi Germany, were doing in the Soviet Union and would, even in their milder forms, in Western Europe. Social spending, as opposed to private consumption, was the road to serfdom and enslavement by the state. It would be much better, he argued, if companies and

individuals were free to spend as they wanted and to compete. Von Hayek was laying the intellectual foundations for our consumer society and the true road to Surfdom, a world in which we could define ourselves by what we bought – even washing-powder.

But the times were against von Hayek and von Mises. The depression that had swept Europe and the US during the 1930s had led to the demand for government action to stop such a deep economic decline happening again. The huge mobilization of people and resources during the Second World War and the shift to the mass systems of production that Henry Ford had instigated had created the conditions in which major central-government projects were the order of the day. Fuelled by Keynesian economics, this was the era of the New Deal in the US to get people back to work, and the creation of welfare-state politics in Britain. The free market was in retreat and for the next two decades the role of the state was not reduced but increased massively.

But that didn't stop von Mises or von Hayek. They became more determined to make their case against big government and in favour of allowing companies and people to spend as they individually saw fit. It was the case for low taxes, a small state and free markets. Ludwig von Mises summed up the essence of his beliefs: 'The development of capitalism consists of everyone having the right to serve the consumer better and/or more cheaply.'[23] By the 1940s, von Mises had moved to an academic post at New York University. Here he developed close ties with the likes of the William Volker Fund, which went on to plant the seeds of Reaganism in the US thirty years later.

Back in Europe the ideas seeped into the pores of a small bunch of right-wing British intellectuals. One of the most important was a chicken farmer, Anthony Fisher. He founded Buxted Chickens, which pioneered battery-farming techniques. He used his fortune, much of which he later lost in an ill-fated project to mass-farm Green Sea Turtles in the Cayman Isles, to fund the Institute of Economic Affairs (IEA) in 1954.[24] This was to be Britain's first proper think-tank and its impact reverberates more than half a century later.

Fisher wanted to make von Hayek's vision of a free-market economy a reality and sought, through the IEA, to make a substantial contribution to the cause. He liked to recall a meeting with von Hayek that went like this: '[Fisher] I share all your worries and concerns as expressed in *The Road to Serfdom* and I'm going to go into politics and put it all right. [Hayek] No, you're not! Society's course will be changed only by a change in ideas. First you must reach the intellectuals, the teachers and writers, with reasoned argument. It will be *their* influence on society which will prevail, and the politicians will follow.'[25]

Fisher recruited the son of a north London bus conductor, Ralph Harris, to become the director of the IEA. Despite his humble origins Harris had got himself into Cambridge and then to a lectureship at St Andrews University. He had developed an almost theological belief in the sanctity of free markets, believing them to be almost God-ordained. Taking their cue from von Hayek, the IEA championed free-market ideas, regardless of their popularity or political acceptability. It was a long slog. For almost twenty years they toiled in the wilderness of the post-war politics that saw both Labour and Conservatives converge on a big government agenda that squeezed out the space for free markets. In this wilderness they published papers on everything from incomes policies to energy markets, monetary controls of inflation and trade-union reform. Then, suddenly, the wind changed and, armed with von Hayek, they were best placed to take advantage.

By the early 1970s the British economy had become sclerotic. Inflation and union militancy were high. The Conservative government of Edward Heath had collapsed in ignominious defeat at the hands of the miners. Harold Wilson and then James Callaghan for Labour tried to pick up the pieces of an ailing post-war settlement based on government from the centre, but the world had moved on. As more confident consumers, people had become less deferential to the state and politicians. The moment was ripe for change.

At this time Keith Joseph, a Tory MP who had been minister for social services under Heath, went to Harris and asked for a reading list. Harris, although wary of politicians and the compromises they forced on anyone close to them, obliged. The Conservative Party was now ready and armed for its switch to radical free markets. Reborn with this mission, Joseph identified an unlikely successor to Heath to lead the Conservatives out of opposition and back into government. She had been education secretary, famous for not much except abolishing free milk in primary schools. Her name, of course, was Margaret Thatcher. To everyone's surprise, she won the leadership contest of 1975 and, in 1979 after the Winter of Discontent, the election with a comfortable majority and a mandate to run the country. The vision of von Mises and von Hayek that would see the state rolled back and free markets allowed to dominate not just the economy but our society and culture was to be realized here in Britain. Mrs Thatcher is rumoured to have carried a copy of *The Road to Serfdom* in her infamous handbag.

The rest is history. Taxes were lowered so people could spend more of their own money; council houses were sold in the name of a property-owning democracy; nationalized industries were privatized so that a wider public could buy and sell shares. At the time, Mrs Thatcher remarked, 'The economy is the means. The goal is to change the soul.' The 'big bang' in the City of London ended import and currency controls, allowing the globalization of capital and its free flow round the planet. Financial services were deregulated and easy access to credit was opened up by the relaxation of lending constraints. Producer interest, in the shape of trade unions, was either smashed or weakened. Now it was consumers who mattered. All the conditions necessary for the creation of a turbo-consuming society were in place. Welcome to the 1980s, the era of *Dallas*, *Dynasty* and designer labels, Sloane Rangers, the Golf GTi, the first mobile phones, multi-channel TV, cheap holiday flights, second homes and fat-cat bonuses.

It was then that the leap was made, the paradigm shift into a turbo-consumer society where the belief that 'greed was good' was

given official sanction by a prime minister who proclaimed, 'There's no such thing as society.' Flexible labour markets meant that jobs that had been for life now offered no such certainty. Industry after industry was allowed to close down and the new jobs sprang up in sectors like retail and financial services. From averaging one job per life we now averaged ten. We would have to fashion our identities not as producers but as consumers. And the barriers to stop the market flooding into the rest of society were lifted: if the market was the best mechanism to distribute goods and services then it should be introduced into the public sector where we would be better served as consumers than as citizens. All of a sudden 'doing the shopping' became 'going shopping' as more malls appeared and an all-consuming society took hold.

Without von Mises there would have been no von Hayek, without von Hayek no Fisher, without Fisher no IEA, and without the IEA no Joseph or Thatcher. And without Thatcher, no turbo-consumerism. Margaret Mead, the cultural anthropologist, once said, 'A small group of thoughtful people could change the world. Indeed, it is the only thing that ever has.' The creation of our consumer society is due in no small part to this group of thoughtful people – not quite the Bond-style villain mentioned earlier but not far removed. And what they unlocked in particular was the ruthless logic of the market and the addiction to shopping that comes with it.

More than anything Thatcherism created the moral and economic space for the retail industry to expand exponentially and take a grip on our lives. A new retail-consultancy industry, packed with costly consultants and brand counsellors, grew up to help the burgeoning retail sector seal an all-consuming deal with the British public.

To find out more about that, I meet Simon, which is not his real name, a management consultant working in the retail sector. I want to know what drives the industry. We all know from our own experience how responsive it has become, how fierce the competition in terms of prices and promotions, how quick it is

to bring in new lines and products. What are the economic factors that keep it on its toes?

The big movers in the sector, Simon says, operate on the basis of high fixed costs, such as rents on shops, labour and the supply chain, which are difficult to change quickly. If costs can't easily be cut then all the focus is on sales. It means that even small changes in sales, up or down, have a noticeable impact on profitability, so the whole sector is based around year-on-year sales growth. Can you make more money from the same fixed costs? 'Like-for-like' sales figures are the Holy Grail of the retail industry. It's what moves the share price and is the basis for management rewards. Simon talks about 'red ocean' competition, where a competitor is 'bleeding' and everyone is feeding on it, and 'blue ocean' competition for new and empty seas. What matters is square footage to pounds spent. He ruminates on whether the industry has reached a ceiling and starts drawing charts and graphs on napkins to show me things like the rate of return on capital invested. All the pressure and all the rewards in the cutthroat world of retail are about making more this year than last. It means that the assets – the space, the people and the products – are sweated as much as possible to secure the greatest returns. It piles on the pressure to get us to part with more and more of our money.

The pressure to perform on like-for-like sales figures has changed our society. It has meant more shops, open for longer, selling more stuff, and has taken shopping online. It led to Sunday opening, an issue now of some confusion: 68 per cent of us are against longer opening hours on Sundays but 60 per cent want to shop when and where they like according to the My Sunday My Choice campaign. I go to their website. They're backed by the likes of Ikea and Asda. They want the restrictions on Sunday opening relaxed. It's interesting that they use words like 'freedom' and 'choice' so liberally. Freedom to shop has become central to our lives. David Ramsden, chair of the campaign, says, 'Today's consumer needs more flexibility and choice.' But what of the freedom and choice not to have to stack shelves in Asda on a Sunday and

instead be with your family? Where do the freedom and choice to shop stop? Should all shops be open 24/7?

But it's not just the market that is built to reward winners and sacrifice losers. Corporations have a legal duty to put shareholders' interests above all else, to put profit before the needs of society or the environment. It means they can't help being at war with their own customers who, for them, exist to be exploited. Now that ownership is separated from control in publicly listed companies, the only measure that matters to the professional and often short-term senior managers is the share price. This is because the share price determines the scale of their pay, bonuses, share options and other rewards. Companies can feel no remorse or regret about what or how they sell because if they don't sell more, someone else will. It is called the free market.

In the 1980s a perfect storm came together to unleash the all-consuming society. We were sold not just abundance but eventually super-abundance. A consumer industrial complex was built up to produce more and to persuade us to buy more. Eventually it was given official political sanction and was encouraged to expand and dominate our world. Our emotions were to be utilized as economic functions, our habits, desires, dreams and anxieties to be mined for the profit of retailers and big business.

No, Bobby, it's not natural. Our turbo-consuming world was made by men and women for reasons of self-interest and ideology. And we are paying the price.

3. The consequences

We've shopped – now we're gonna drop

Caveat emptor! Buyer, beware! The Romans understood the dangers of shopping. But beware of what? Did they mean don't pay over the odds, or something much more worrying? The latter-day version of 'buyer, beware' can be found in the title of the song by the band Johnny Boy – 'You Are The Generation That Bought More Shoes And You Get What You Deserve'. We are and we will.

As shopping has become more and more central to our lives, we have paid not just the pounds on the price tags but a much higher price: myriad emotional and physical costs, to us and the planet, which we try to ignore because to confront them might mean kicking our all-consuming habit. We have become caught up in the social disease of luxury fever and are restless souls, endlessly trying to ape our celebrity heroes, their lifestyles and spending patterns. It has left even the comfortable and affluent middle classes feeling like the struggling poor. Enough is never enough. Someone else has always got more, and that makes us miserable. And that was before it crashed down all around us. Now we are struggling to buy even the basics but all around us are the still tempting trappings of a turbo-consumer society.

But it's not just a diet of perpetual longing and disappointment we're fed: a society defined by consumerism cannot just stop at the high street. Instead, the culture of consuming has to seep into our pores, our bloodstream and DNA, filling as many aspects of our lives as possible. In the process it turns everything that is profitable into a purchasable mush of increasing blandness to maximize economies of scale and global brand recognition. Local and national identities are reduced as far as possible into a

monoculture of styles and tastes. If money can be made from selling public services then they, too, are turned into commodities to be bought and sold. Only those areas from which and those people from whom unacceptable levels of profit can be made will be left outside the consumer society. Later we will see how and why they are excluded. If we primarily understand ourselves and those around us through the prism of consumption, then everything becomes coloured and distorted by the shopping lens.

So, what's wrong with a bit of shopping is that it's never just a bit. It can't be, because an industrial consumer complex seduces and compels us to want more and more. The fear of being excluded from the normality of an all-consuming life is too great. The impact is felt everywhere. Let's start with something quite straightforward: the consequences for the environment. Then we will examine the social impact, and address the way in which consumerism undermines alternatives emerging to challenge its dominance of our culture. Finally, we'll assess the personal impact on lives that are all consuming and how we are coping now the bubble has burst.

Shopping is costing the earth

In mid-January I see the first butterfly of the year hovering outside my bedroom window. My heart lifts – then sinks. It's a wonderful sight that speaks of warm summer days, but in mid-winter is a sign of climate change, and our unwillingness to amend our behaviour to avoid it.

The evidence is now beyond dispute: human activity is driving potentially disastrous climate change and the relentless pursuit of more inevitably has an impact on the finite resources of the planet and its temperature. Economists and the business world refer to such effects as 'externalities' – costs for which companies have no responsibility or concern. And, indeed, that is legally the case. A company's prime and legal responsibility is

to maximize the return for their shareholders. In the long run the destruction of the planet is not so good for the bottom line but business doesn't operate in the long term. As John Maynard Keynes said, 'In the long run we are all dead.' In the short term, managements have to maximize profits, secure the rise in share price that pays the dividends and the bonuses through which they themselves can buy more. If they stop to save the planet, the competition will exploit their weakness, gain the reward and the environment will still suffer. It's called market failure.

Some scientists believe we have gone past the point of no return; that the cycle of climate change is now locked in and has become self-generating. So, no matter how much we reduce carbon emissions the earth will get warmer. Some like it hot! And perhaps that's a good thing, given that temperatures are projected to rise by up to 5.8°C this century, ten times the increase of 0.6°C in the last century. Already we are seeing more floods and, according to the Intergovernmental Panel on Climate Control, deadly heatwaves will occur more frequently, atolls will disappear, coral reefs will be destroyed, oceans will become acidic and snow will melt away from the highest mountains. The more ice that dissolves, the more methane gas is released – and the warmer it gets. Farming will be decimated, along with cities, ports and much of our transport infrastructure. It will be the end of living and the start of survival. At the heart of this impending ecological disaster is our manufactured need to consume more and more. What, then, is so wrong with a bit of shopping?

In one way turbo-consumers are like the butterfly outside my window: we flit from what we have to the next bright object that catches our eye. But we don't pollinate other plants along the way; instead we destroy and distort to the extent that real butterflies appear in deepest winter. At just twenty-two weeks old, an average British baby will have caused the equivalent emissions of the greenhouse-gas carbon dioxide that someone in Tanzania will generate in a lifetime. If every country had Britain's level of consumption, the human race would need 3.1 planets to cope with the

resource demand. Now the levels of consumption we have enjoyed are being copied by China, India and other fast-developing nations. In 2007 the world economy surged at a rate of five per cent per year, pushing consumption of grain, meat, steel and oil to all-time highs. China's fuel consumption shot up by 15 per cent and India's by seven per cent. Not unrelated, last year also brought the largest-ever increase in climate-changing carbon emissions. One image of success, of happiness and what it means to be human now dominates our globe. It's the image of the successful consumer. We have it and they want it.

Like us they want to operate like hunters, who kill and move on with no thought of the consequences and no plan for replenishment of the natural environment. Instead, as Zygmunt Bauman suggests, we should operate like gardeners, who plan, regulate and replenish the soil. But the consumer machine offers no hope of such far-sightedness. Instead it demands the conveyor-belt speeds up so that the earth's resources can be turned into larger profits. Indeed, as we saw earlier, the notion of waste and disposability is central to the reproduction of the consumer society. We live in a throwaway society. According to a report by the Prudential, the insurance giants, 63 per cent of females admitted to buying clothes in sales they had either never worn or only once or twice; 56 per cent had bought shoes they had never worn or only a couple of times.[26] The recession will dent growth and hopefully carbon emissions – but it will be no more than a short downward spike before normal destruction of the planet is resumed.

Tim Cooper and Kieren Mayers have carried out research that investigated the purchase, use and disposal of household appliances in the UK, surveying more than eight hundred households' attitude and behaviour towards product life-span. One-third of discarded appliances were reported to be still functioning. One in five was considered in need of repair, and slightly less than half 'broken beyond repair'. Householders were asked the main disadvantage of purchasing appliances that were 'designed to last a long time'. Almost a third said that such appliances 'may become out of date after a few years'.[27]

At every point our consuming habit is destroying our habitat. Food miles increased by 15 per cent in the ten years to 2002, are still rising and have a significant impact on climate change, traffic congestion, accidents and pollution. Food transport accounts for 25 per cent of all the miles driven by heavy-goods vehicles on our roads. The use of lorries to transport food has doubled since 1974 because we are consuming more from more far-flung places: 19 million tonnes of carbon dioxide were emitted in 2002 through getting food to us, a 12 per cent increase on 1992. Taking into account the time lost due to traffic congestion, wear on the roads, ill health caused by air and noise pollution, and accidents caused by food transport, the cost of food miles is £9 billion a year to the UK. The average distance we now drive to shop for food annually is 898 miles, compared with 747 miles a decade ago.

Air freight, the most polluting form of transport, is growing fastest because of the globalization of the world economy and the manufacture of products in one hemisphere for sale in another. The hike in fuel prices in 2008 has made it temporarily more expensive but we can't rely on market forces to save the planet: we need common sense and human morality to play a leading part.

It is not just our food but our feet we can't keep on the ground. In 1970 British airports were used by 32 million fliers. In 2004 the figure was 216 million. By 2030, according to the Government's most recent forecast, it will have risen to between 400 million and 600 million – which some experts think may be an underestimate. And guess what? It's the rich who fly more, do more damage to the environment and always escape the worst consequences of their actions. In 2003, 96 per cent of the passengers who used Heathrow were from the better-off socio-economic categories A, B and C1. Nationally, households in the poorer C2, D and E categories take five times fewer flights on average. Many poor people have never been in an aeroplane: easyJet is overwhelmingly packed with the prosperous middle classes. The top social groups buy more than three-quarters of

the low-cost airlines' tickets. All of this will be held in check by
the downturn, especially if as predicted it is more of a white-
collar recession than the last one in the early 1990s. But it would
be fatal for the planet if, as soon as we can afford it, we go on
another consumer binge. Of course, people tend to think their
flights are justified and deserved – it's everyone else's that aren't.
And, anyway, what's the point of stopping if no one else does?
Aviation is the fastest-growing source of carbon-dioxide emissions in the UK. One passenger flying from London to Miami
produces as much carbon dioxide as if they had driven a car
12,000 miles. And many fly to Madrid, Milan or Manhattan to
– shop.

We want more exotic food flown to us because that is part of
what defines us as successful turbo-consumers. Not as luxury
but increasingly as perceived necessity. Our tastebuds now
demand out-of-season vegetables and fruit. And we don't just
lose track of the seasons as we tuck into blueberries in January,
flown in from Chile, or organic asparagus that has been air-
freighted from Peru: we lose a bit more of the biosphere that
sustains us. We never asked for these items to be made available
to us and, of course, we enjoy the choice, but the expansion of
the supermarkets into hypermarkets selling everything from
every corner of the globe occurred for no other reason than that
we would buy and spend more

Greenpeace commissioned a report that follows a 7,000-
kilometre chain: it starts with the clearing of virgin forest by
farmers and leads directly to Chicken McNuggets being sold in
British and European fast-food restaurants. It also alleges that
much of the soya animal feed arriving in the UK from Brazil is
a product of 'forest crime', and that British supermarkets have
turned a blind eye to the destruction of the forest. The demand
for other cheap ingredients, found in thousands of products
from shampoo to biscuits, is contributing to the extinction of
the orang-utan. One in ten mass-produced foods on Britain's
shelves is estimated to contain palm oil, a bulking agent and
preservative, from trees that are vital to the survival of Asia's

only great ape. An estimated five thousand orang-utans are killed each year in Malaysia and Indonesia by the burning of vast tracts of virgin forest to supply the world's growing demand for the oil.[28] Our non-essential consumer demands are directly putting at risk the survival of these creatures and others. But to us the products do feel 'essential'. We would 'die' if we were seen in the wrong outfit. The emotional pull of consumption is so strong that we can allow plants and animals to face not just death but extinction.

You may think that we can only eat so much. But we eat five times as much meat as we did fifty years ago. Already there are more than twice as many chickens on the planet as humans, plus a billion pigs, 1.3 billion cows and 1.8 billion sheep and goats – most of which eat more food than they produce. As intensive animal farming increases to cope, more land, water and pesticides are used to grow the soya, grain and other feed the creatures need. One acre of land yields an average 20 kilos (45 pounds) of usable protein from meat, but 35 kilos (78 pounds) of corn and 161.5 kilos (356 pounds) of soya beans. Such inefficiency makes it harder to feed the world's people. But that isn't the object, which is to make as much profit as possible.

In the factories, chickens are allotted the space of an A4 piece of paper for the entirety of their short lives. They fatten so fast that their bone strength can't keep up so many spend their lives sitting in muck and feathers, their legs too weak to carry them. All so that some can enjoy a ready-prepared low-cost roast chicken on Sunday.

The need for speed applies not just to fast food but fast cars. There are two ways in which 'fast' matters: the speed of the car and the speed with which we've been replacing them. Neither does the environment any good. Approximately two million road vehicles are scrapped in the UK every year. Most of them still work. They have just gone out of fashion. The fad of buying four-wheel-drive cars, the so-called 'Chelsea tractors', was particularly damaging to the environment. In 2007, a pollution monitor near London's Sloane Street registered an average

annual level of nitrogen dioxide – a gas that can aggravate lung problems – that was two and a half times the recommended World Health Organization maximum. It was also found that hourly readings breached WHO limits 268 times in the same year.

More cars need more places to park. The growth of controlled parking zones in our cities has a damaging unintended consequence. Instead of paying the parking fees, residents have been ripping up the trees and bushes in their front gardens and paving over to get their cars off the road. The London Assembly calculated in 2005 that the city's love affair with the car has led to roughly two-thirds of its 1.9 million front gardens – an area roughly twenty-two times the size of Hyde Park – being paved. The car is the embodiment of the freedom in the consumer society. Or, at least, the myth of freedom, when the reality is that we drive though our cities not much faster than the horse-drawn carriages of the Victorian era. This, as we will see, is one of the products of the social limits of growth. We sit in cars, often people-carriers made for six or eight, on our own, going nowhere, burning a hole in our pockets and the ozone layer.

But in a consumer society there is always a choice of ways to destroy the planet. In 1906 Willis Carrier, a prodigious and, until then, rather useless American inventor, unwittingly came up with the best means of planetary destruction: the air-conditioning unit. As the planet warms up, more and more of us demand AC for our cars, homes and offices. The US has five per cent of the world's population but uses eight per cent of the world's electricity supply on AC alone; 83 per cent of American households have at least one AC unit, which emits 3,400 pounds of carbon dioxide per year – equivalent to two-thirds of the emissions of an average car in the UK. The more we turn on the AC, the hotter the earth gets. The hotter it gets, the higher we turn the AC and the more units we order. It's a perfect self-reinforcing process. But the market cares nothing for the damage it creates: it just knows there is profit to be made from conditioning air. By the turn of the twenty-first century Carrier Corp showed annual

sales worth $8 billion and could look to expand into new markets in India and China. They want to be cool too.

It's tough coming up with an analogy for our treatment of the planet that brings home the scale and futility of what we're doing. This is the best I can do. When blue sharks are caught in fishing nets, curious fisherman have cut open their stomachs to watch how the smell of their own blood triggers a feeding frenzy so that they gorge on their own entrails. There we have it. Our attitude to the planet. We have become so hooked on consuming that we have been destroying the planet and ourselves. We can contemplate the end of the planet as we know it, or at least the extinction of thousands of species and millions of people through flood and famine brought on by our all-consuming society, but we cannot contemplate cutting down on shopping enough to sufficiently reduce our carbon footprint. The impulse to shop is greater than the instinct for survival. We know in our hearts that this can't go on, that our children and our grandchildren will suffer, but go on it will. I'm unsure if ostriches face extinction from climate change but I'm sure that if they do then, like us, they'll stick their heads in the sand and hope it goes away. It won't. The recession at least gives us a chance to think again, to reassess what matters and what we can live without so that we can go on living. We can't live without a functioning planet.

At no point does anyone compel us to confront the waste created by our consumption, or the energy expended to produce these things and the cost to the next generation. Instead Sainsbury's calls on us to 'Be environmentally responsible – go shopping' to advertise their new reusable shopping bags. And 'You get a striking piece of art for just 50p,' says the bag produced by the Arts Council. Of course, reusable bags are better for the environment than the weaker ones we took at every visit to the supermarket but that's as comforting as the thought of watching the end of the planet in a nice designer outfit from DKNY. The bags exist to make us feel better about packing them with more Sainsbury products that will do more damage to the environment. But remember the commercial pressure the

company is under to improve their like-for-like sales. It's the system that's at fault – a system that allows no time or space for anything but more consumption.

A consumer society was always on a collision course with the sustainability of the planet. But over the last thirty years, instead of steering another course towards less material lives, we jammed our foot harder on the pedal and brought the environmental impact closer through an even wilder bout of turbo-consumerism. The credit crunch has applied the brakes, at least temporarily. But will we be back shopping as soon as we can? It is not just the planet that will suffer the consequences, though that is where the most vital impact will lie, but other aspects of our lives will be damaged too.

Men (and women) behaving badly

A shopper died on Saturday 12 October 1996 in what police described as Britain's first trolley-rage fatality. Gordon Edwards, 71, a retired businessman, clashed with another customer in the car park of a supermarket in Darlington, Co. Durham. 28% of Britain's have lost their rag during a shopping trip.[29]

A new selfishness is at large. It is based on a lack of tolerance, responsibility and, yes, respect for others that is rooted in the aggressive individualism of our age. It is fuelled by our consumer culture. If the consumer is always king, then the concept 'because I'm worth it' easily translates into a world where we are the centre of our own universe. We come first and everyone else nowhere. For the shopper there are no obligations to others, no responsibilities, just rights. All they have to be able to do is pay. This is the dominant mindset of the consumer age and it therefore spills into and contaminates virtually every aspect of our lives and our relations to others.

We are getting angrier and more short-tempered because our real lives don't fit with the myth that the consumer is king, that

we know our rights, have the money and always get what we want. No one else's satisfaction matters. Away from the shops, our social and working relationships have to be negotiated, discussed, built and adapted. We can't all be first or best. We can't all be kings or queens of the high street all of the time or even some of it. We have to compromise and sometimes put others first. The myth of the consumer culture clashes with this reality and we find it hard to cope. We get angry with and intolerant of others because we only understand ourselves as individuals securing the best possible deal with no responsibility for the consequences for others.

Why is noise pollution now one of the most common social complaints, fuelling record numbers of calls to council environmental-health offices? In part it's because everyone has been encouraged to buy their own stereo with as many watts of power as their pennies can buy, but mostly it's because it's our music and it's our right to play it as loudly as we want, whenever we want. Other people's interests and considerations don't count. Personal freedom, to shop, to own and do what you want, is the guiding principle of our age. It is about the creation and re-creation of our identities: what and who we are. It is about the very core of our being. The 1960s have come back to bite us. The reaction to post-war austerity and the dull conformity of the 1950s, the response to the private and public monolithic bureaucracies of the state and big corporations, was the demand for freedom. The hippie movement spawned a sense of personal liberation that started as a counter-culture but was soon appropriated by market forces. Some of this was helpful – attitudes to sexual equality and liberation desperately needed to be overhauled – but there was a dark side, which has begun to seep into every pore of society. The growth of personal freedom and individualism went hand-in-hand with the growth of consumerism. Prioritization of the personal over the social has had a deeply negative effect.

As our commitment to ourselves grows, so our commitment and connection to the society and community we live in diminishes. We started to buy our independence and protection from

others, and the more we bought the more we had to buy. The further away from others we moved, the greater the responsibility we had to take on to provide entirely for ourselves as the old social forms of dealing with risk were diminished. Many people, especially in big cities, have less and less connection with the world around them. They go to work, often in a car on their own or using public transport in which they are in their own iPod world. They communicate with their friends via text messages and emails. They might find their partners via Internet dating agencies. They will go to the gym – but that's a private space. There are few, if any, community ties and therefore few, if any, community obligations. We have become individualized and anonymous. We look for salvation in shops not in society. Mrs Thatcher's words, 'There's no such thing as society' are becoming a self-fulfilling prophecy as we retreat further into ourselves.

In the process everything becomes both transient and impossible to influence and we start to write off the future. The environment has had it. Pensions? Not worth thinking about. Politics offers no solutions. So, why not live for today? Consumer hedonism determines the quality of our social relations and behaviour so we increasingly lie, cheat, rage and vomit at will. Why? Because we can and because there are fewer and fewer moral values or constraints. We demand better and quicker treatment, we know our rights, and if we don't get satisfaction we complain, sue or shout. There is nothing wrong with being assertive: the end of deference is a good thing. But we no longer know where to draw the line. Increasingly we behave like little children who can't get their way so we scream and rant and rave until we do. We are losing control, in part because we know that, as shoppers, we can't really control the world around us. We are sold futility and we keep going back for more. All we can do is run to keep up on the hamster wheel of consumption.

Unsurprisingly shops are one of the worst places for this new selfishness. Shop staff are subjected to unprecedented levels of physical violence, intimidation and foul-mouthed abuse. Figures

from the shop-workers' union USDAW in October 2008 show that the number of violent threats made against retail staff more than doubled in a year with one in ten facing physical assault. The majority of the abuse was of a sexual nature or race-related. Experts blame the yob culture for the rise in retail crime – and have highlighted the new phenomenon of 'refund rage', when customers turn violent over relatively minor disputes, such as a shop's returns policy. Belinda has worked in shops for more than twenty years and has seen it all. Customer rage is frequent and can be explosive. Usually it's low-level, spur-of-the-moment anger – but sometimes it's deliberate. Often people moan at the lone assistant on the till because they have waited so long to be served. It's not the employee's fault that the company wants to stretch its profits by stretching the queues. The customers who complain take up more time and make it worse for the people behind them. Others, though, contrive their anger to get what they want. People will buy items of clothing, wear them out on a Saturday night and try to return them the next week. They will unpick a hem or cut off a button in the hope of getting the full return value for faulty goods. Belinda says it is a combination of the shop's policy on returns, the targets she is set by head office but also her own determination not let people get away with it that means she will always stand up to them. Once a customer said she would shoot her. She says that middle-class women are the worst. The language from some can be quite shocking. It wasn't in one of her shops but she remembers seeing two middle-aged women indulging in a hair-pulling fight over the last carton of single cream in M&S one Christmas Eve.

It's not just in the shops that we can't contain ourselves. Road rage has become, well, all the rage. The car is an extension of us. As we saw earlier, we are what we drive. Pity the person who gets in our way, stops us driving as fast as we want, dents, scratches or even touches our car. In it, we face up to individual versus social considerations at every turn. Small inconveniences – the loss of a few seconds or minutes – are easily magnified into

outrage at our loss of personal liberty in the vehicle we worked so hard to buy and, much more than that, in which we invested ourselves. The gap between the freedom of the car adverts and the reality of the clogged roads could not be greater.

It's the low-level stuff that does the most damage. Swearing, spitting, pushing and littering all corrode the fabric of society. We are more abrupt and less patient. We excuse ourselves because we lead busy lives and don't have time for common courtesies. But it raises the temperature of intolerance and disrespect in a way that makes civility increasingly impossible. Binge-drinking, and the social disquiet it produces in our towns and cities, are not just about cheap alcopops but are a symptom, especially among young women, of deeper anxieties – the pressure to keep up, be normal and especially to be thin. Only when they are blind drunk can they let go and overcome the anxieties of not having the perfect body and the perfect life of their celebrity hero, which is projected on to them. Consumerism offers the promise of happiness but always disappoints – and our only reaction is to consume more in the hope that more will still work.

If we're not raging or bingeing we're cheating. It's become a national pastime. And little wonder. What matters is not how you win but whether you win. The culture of consumerism breeds a psyche of rampant individualism, competitiveness and the desire to look after no one but number one. We learn from our politicians, business leaders, celebrities and sports stars. Businesses spy and steal from each other. Rewards in sport have become so great that drug-taking is habitual among some contenders, such as athletes and cyclists. The logic is irrefutable. If everyone else is doing it – or, at least, you think they are – then the risk of being caught pales into insignificance. Just like the market: there is no moral code to be observed unless society decides to enforce one. Rules are for losers. If we're going to test kids at every stage of their school life and place so much emphasis on exam success, then it should be no surprise that some are going to cheat and that cheating in exams has gone up 27 per cent in one year.

The politicians' answer to the growing culture of disrespect is to blame the parents, blame the individual and crack down hard with policies such as anti-social behaviour orders (ASBOs). The strong state is needed to police the free market. The consequences of the wild hedonism that our consumer culture creates has to be tightly policed to stop it getting out of control to the extent that law and order and profits are under threat. What they refuse to address is the cause of social decay: the rampant individualism and growing inequality fuelled by our consumer society that continually undermines the respect we have for each other.

There was no golden age of society when everything was perfect. Respect for others was often tied to deference and respect for authority because success was to be gained from being part of a social system, not just a lone shopper. But the slide to a society of turbo-consumption has created a new social malaise in which obligations to and even tolerance of others have diminished to dangerous levels. Society can only function on a bedrock of trust and reciprocity. Such values sit at odds with a consumer culture that implants the attitudes of the hunter-gatherer shopper into the family, community and society. It is all take and no give.

Empathy and respect are not values and practices that can be taught via the classroom or an ASBO. Instead they have to be instilled by our experience in the world. We have to build institutions, spaces and processes that allow people to experience each other's lives, where they can be valued as human beings, not just as consumers. But tolerance, affection, compassion and understanding aren't on sale because there is no profit to be made from them. Society is not just corroded but stretched to breaking point as the gap between the successful and unsuccessful consumer widens. The winner-takes-all dynamic of the consumer society creates the basis for a new class division.

The flawed consumers

Society has always been riven by class. The poor have always been with us but the nature of what it means to be poor changes with time. Once the poor were the unemployed, not just because unemployment left you with less money but because, as we have seen, having a job defined what it was to be normal by giving us our sense of purpose. The poor were the opposite of normal and their abnormality was a consequence of their inability to work. If once we were defined primarily as producers and today our role as consumers largely designates our place in society, then to be normal is to be a successful consumer. And so by definition to be abnormal – to be outside the practices, cultures, rewards and trappings of normality – is to be what Zygmunt Bauman, the Polish sociologist, has called a 'flawed consumer'.[30]

A flawed consumer is in many ways just like a successful one. They desire to desire. They want to be seduced, thrilled and intoxicated by shopping. They want to prove their worth by what they buy and create myriad new *me*s through every shopping trip. In this sense they share not just our physical and cultural world but our hopes and dreams. They watch the same television channels, they see the same billboards and magazine adverts. In a consumer society they, like us, want to live the dream. But they have a problem: they can't afford it or, at least, not enough to make them look or feel normal. The flawed consumers are the likes of Bobby and Amanda, whom we met earlier. The consumer society redistributes shame and humiliation on them because they cannot compete on the same terms as the rest of us. They shop but they get it wrong. They buy the wrong things – goods that are too cheap. They don't have sufficient style or consumer acumen. Or they cheat by stealing, or buying fakes.

Unlike the poor of the past, these new poor are unlikely to be in physical peril. In Britain and the rest of the West, they are likely to have shelter and just about enough heat and food to survive. It's not comfortable but they can get by. The new poor

suffer from being in internal exile. They live in a poverty bubble that allows them to see and hear all but not to touch or taste it. Rich and poor share the same cultural oxygen – they want the same things. Burberry is for everyone but the means to purchase it isn't.

Not having money has always blighted lives – more so physically in the past. Now it is the emotional pain that counts. Unlike the poor of the past, this new poor of flawed consumers has no common bond; there is no community of the poor with which to share their plight. Today the notion of a working class has much less social or cultural meaning than it did in the past – although the vast majority of us work by 'hand or brain' and are only one or two payslips from financial ruin. To be the new poor is to live in isolation, unable to share in the spectacle of a consumer lifestyle that is all around you. Like the rest of society, the poor are atomized, living solitary lives, but also beyond the pale – excluded by their failure to keep up. For them the best it gets is perpetual window-shopping.

Richard Wilkinson and Michael Marmot's research on nutrition, lifestyle and environment shows that the new poor live much shorter and less healthy lives than the rest of us.[31] But the very fact that people are poor in today's bloated consumer society makes them ill: the stress and strain of comparing yourselves to others and feeling less than normal means you die sooner. Men in Shettleston in Glasgow die younger than anywhere else in the country. Their life expectancy is sixty-three, fourteen years less than the national average and comparable with Iraq and some countries in the developing world. Their diet, drinking and smoking are a big factor. If those are all the pleasures they have, then it's not hard to see why they over-indulge. But the big stress in life today is not from a high-powered executive post but poverty. And it kills. Worse still, the life-expectancy gap in the UK between rich and poor is getting wider. The poor in some communities, again like Glasgow, are dying eighteen months earlier than they were a decade ago – Britain's first reduction in lifespan since the Second World War.[32]

The new poor don't constitute a temporarily excluded class who enter and exit the labour market *en masse* as they once did in tune with the demands of the economic cycle. Boom meant jobs; bust meant being on the dole. Before, the poor were a reserve army of the potentially employable. To be a reserve is worse than permanently playing the game – but they were still an army and knew that in time they would have their chance. The new poor don't know if their chance will ever come. They are the very long-term unemployed or totally unemployable by choice or by mental or physical illness. Their best hope is perhaps the lottery. That's not much of a hope. What is more, the poor of the past were worth keeping in a physical condition that meant they could become economically active at short notice. They were worth keeping fit to play the game. This meant at least basic housing, health and some education. They were worth some investment.

Today the failed consumers have no economic and social role. They cannot buy so, in a consumer society, they have no purpose. This is one reason why the welfare state is crumbling for the poor and being reoriented towards the people who do matter, who do vote and do consume – the middle classes and so called 'hard-working families', which translates more accurately as hard-consuming families. The Government builds virtually no social or public housing, benefit rates are cut and applied to work availability, record numbers of teenagers end up as NEETS (not in education, employment or training) and health services are oriented around the choice agenda. The Labour Government of the last twelve years has tried to cut child poverty in particular – but in a consumer society it is impossible to achieve. While the economy was strong some progress was made, but targets are now being missed and we are slipping back to the record levels of poverty seen in the 1980s. William Beveridge, the post-war architect of the welfare state, identified 'freedom from want and the fear of want' as one of its goals. That noble intention has now been dropped as risk that was once socialized has become individualized. The trappings of the welfare state still stand, in NHS

hospitals and comprehensive schools, but they operate increasingly on terms dictated by the market – of competition, choice and consumption. There is no reason or room for a welfare state as a safety net, only as springboard to a consumer lifestyle. If you can't make the leap, you have to pay the price of not being able to pay the price. The failed consumers are the ones who got left behind, who can't keep up, who can't make themselves normal.

Perhaps proof that work no longer defines normality comes from the fact that you can work full time and still be poor, and therefore still outside the bounds of social acceptability. The flexible labour market – which is code for the ability of employers to pay as little as possible or fire employees at will – means that many live not just on poverty wages despite working long, gruelling hours, but with the fear of losing even this meagre existence. Legally, people must be paid at least the minimum wage of £5.73. It's not enough to live on – certainly not in London. A report from the Joseph Rowntree Trust in February 2009 found that the majority of children living in poverty had at least one parent in work. Illegally, many employers don't even pay this much – and the Mayor of London's office agreed in 2007 that its London employees should be paid a living wage of £7.50 per an hour. Groups of Eastern Europeans or Africans charge ten pounds for four of them to clean a car, which takes at least twenty minutes. How much are they paid by their bosses? It's the system that's at fault. The pressure to maximize profit and pay the least, and from us to pay the least and buy the most. Then there are the 'board people', who stand on our high streets with signs pointing to sales and discount stores tucked away on sidestreets. They are human message boards: their only value lies in that they can stand up for long periods of time and hold a sign. They slump or try to read. Board people doing bored jobs.

More than anything the new poor are bored. What they have in abundance is time and nothing to do with it – because in a consumer society you can do little that you and others value without paying for it. There are few places to go and there is little to do that doesn't come at a price. The only place to go is the

shops. The children of the new poor end up hanging round the shops, too, but with their hoods up. Being threatening is at least being something. It gets you noticed, gives you an identity and makes you feel powerful. They gravitate to the shops because the ultimate antithesis of boredom is, of course, shopping. Is it any wonder that they collide with the people who have what they don't: the ability to shop.

We are now going back to the Victorian practice of gang-masters – the bosses of casual, virtually slave labour in building, food-processing and farming jobs. Their workers often sleep ten to a room, and are left with about three pounds per hour after all 'costs' are deducted; they toil twelve hours a day, sometimes seven days a week. This is Dickensian misery in our modern, bright shopping nirvana. Indeed, their low wages underpin our ability to buy more cheap goods and services. These new poor suffer a double blight. Their work is miserable and their hours long. They do it to provide the experiences for us that they cannot afford. They work in hotels and see close up the lives of the successful consumers but can never hope to live them. The relentless drudgery makes them even more hungry for the compensating factors of consumerism that they can't afford.

One of my bleakest political moments came when I sat with a Gate Gourmet worker who had lost her job packing aeroplane meals after she had been sacked, along with hundreds of her Asian colleagues, in favour of even cheaper labour from East Europe and Somalia. She had done the job all her working life and it was all she knew. She earned £12,000 per year. There was nothing that could be done to help her: the country's flexible employment laws meant her boss could cast her aside without compunction. But, as with all these jobs, it is in part our fault as well that such people are treated in this way. We want the cheapest deal, and those at the bottom pay the price through insufficient wages or losing their job. We want cheap flights and the lowest-cost car cleaners and builders. Then we can buy more and feel pleased with ourselves that we have driven a hard bargain and found the lowest price.

David Bonderman, the US financial tycoon who founded and runs Gate Gourmet's parent company, spent £10 million on his birthday party in 2002. He hired Bellagio, the most extravagant Las Vegas casino, and entertained his guests with the Rolling Stones and Robin Williams. He is estimated to be worth £15 billion. If he didn't keep his company competitive by paying the lowest possible wages then someone else would and he would lose some of his enormous wealth. That's the way it is. Dog eats dog in consumer society. But it's the poor, like the dignified woman I met who makes our meals, that suffer the most.

But the new poor are not just content to retreat, to give up without a fight. The lure of consuming is too great for that. If they can't be normal by normal means, some will find other means. They may be poor but that doesn't mean they're stupid. They use what resources they do have to 'acquire' the trappings of normality: their wit and cunning, legal or illegal. The younger poor may find an outlet for their creativity through graffiti rather than the high street. The older they get, the more likely it is that some will cheat and steal. What matters is wearing the right clothes and having the right mobile – not the means by which they are secured. The pressure to conform to the norms of a consumer society increases as the ability of people to get out of poverty falls. This declining social mobility set against a deepening consumer culture breeds a new generation of feral flawed consumers, such as those we met earlier.

What matters to the rest of society is not protection for this new poor of flawed consumers but protection from them. As far as possible they are to be controlled, contained and disciplined. We have become tough on crime but indifferent to its causes. Tolerance is set firmly at zero. In the past we were ambivalent about the poor. There was always fear and loathing but there was also pity and compassion. Now the poor are just a drag and a drain on society. This is no longer one nation but two: the successful shoppers and those who fail to make the grade. The flawed consumers are treated at best as outsiders and viewed

with suspicion. At worst they are criminalized rather than treated with compassion. It is one reason why our prison population has increased from 61,000 in 1997 to more than 80,000 today and is set to continue rising. Our jails are now officially full. We exempt ourselves from any moral responsibility for this new poor and, worse, we blame them for their abnormality. It's their fault they don't have the money or the purchasing acumen of the successful shopper.

In the last quarter-century Britain has undergone a series of seismic shifts that have forced a dramatic polarization of society between rich and poor. The income and wealth gap that was being closed after the Second World War has been split open and reached its height in 2007. The Thatcher years did the damage. Rewards for those at the top rocketed. From company CEOs to Russian oligarchs and private equity traders, a new breed of super-rich set the benchmark for the rest of society. In the last fifteen years the number of billionaires in Britain has nearly tripled. These people are the 'untouchables', who have been paying less tax as a percentage of their income than their cleaners and distorting the nation's housing systems because of the exorbitant prices they've paid for properties in London and the South East. There is even now a Cost of Living Extremely Well Index, which measures the price rises of luxury goods; in the bonanza days of HNWIs (high net-worth individuals) it was running at almost twice the normal consumer price index when it was measured on September 2007. Recessions always close the gap as rewards at the top will decline most. But will this just be the lull before another storm of high earnings at the top? Will society try to peg back once and for all the Masters of the Universe who created the crash?

City financiers are one thing, celebrities another. The rich used to be famous for what they did. The self-made person was the epitome of fame. Now celebrities are famous not for what they do but for what they can buy. Madonna is now more famous for buying a baby from Africa and getting divorced from Guy Ritchie than for any of her songs or shows. And perhaps this is

the worst aspect of the new poor: their lack of anyone to hate. The poor of the past had a class enemy in the rich. Today's poor don't hate the rich: they want to be like them because the rich are the apex of a consumer society. They have no one to blame but themselves and no target to get even with, just celebrities to be like – celebrities who are defined and worshipped because of their ability to shop.

Having the right trainers matters far more to the poor when they are surrounded by too little love and too little hope. Brands become the only thing to value. For some youngsters they are worth fighting and stealing for. One study on peer pressure, poverty and brands among a group of 8–12-year-olds in Sheffield found that those who wore the 'right' branded trainers were more popular than those who didn't and were deemed more acceptable as friends.[33] The children would go as far as not to be friends with those who didn't have the right shoes. Another survey by the campaign group Dare to Care found that possession of the right mobile phone was deemed the major determinant among children as to whether or not you were poor.[34] The importance of consumer durables to the poor means that they spend more on them as a percentage of their total income than the rich do. It is compensation for less-fulfilled lives but also the battlefield for status and the new class war.

Today mainstream politicians talk not about class or equality but about social inclusion. But for the majority to be included some have to be excluded. The flawed consumers are the people we contrast ourselves to. They are needed to keep us in check, pounding the treadmill and hungry to buy more because they remind us of our plight if we fail to keep up. Our normality depends on their abnormality.

But the recession will have an effect. All of a sudden we are all slightly flawed consumers. Few of us can keep up in the way we once did and still want to. More of us must count the pennies and go without. Will this be the basis for a re-evaluation between the better and worse off? And not just within our own borders. An all-consuming society requires the globalization of

trade and relies on cheap labour from overseas to sustain the throughput of low-cost items.

And the global poverty you can't see

Because of children's eating habits school uniforms are getting bigger – but they are also getting cheaper. Many retailers will sell you the whole outfit for around nine pounds. Tesco is offering a 'value' uniform for less than a fiver. It's almost half the price it was in 2007. Why pay more? Well, we might not want to pay a higher price but someone always has to. If you buy a school uniform for under a fiver it will show – certainly against a specialist store's uniform or even Marks & Spencer's. The new poor will still look like the poor – even in a bland school uniform that is supposed to make it impossible to tell children apart. Some will always look like more successful consumers than others.

But the losers are not just the poor children in the cheap uniforms: the even bigger losers are the people who have to make the skirts and shirts, the ties and blazers. It's their wages that are squeezed so that we can save a few quid. Wal-Mart now has to fend off a lawsuit from Bangladeshi women to whom they were paying just twelve cents an hour. In the garment factories of China, clothing workers toil for as many as fifteen hours day, often seven days a week for a pitiful return. Mostly they are migrant workers from even poorer nations than China, sending money home so their family can eat. They have to pay exorbitant dormitory fees for the privilege of being exploited. Sometimes the workers can be children younger than the Western kids the clothes are being made for. Children are good as garment workers. Their fingers are nimble and they learn quickly – which is useful with the constant changes: children are more adaptable than machines and therefore more profitable.

The pressure group Labour Behind the Label[35] issued a report in 2006 titled *Let's Clean Up Fashion: the state of play behind the UK high street*. They found that in Thailand one plate of rice, one

cup of coffee, one day's rent and transport to and from work took up 90 per cent of a day's wage. In Bangladesh their estimate of a living wage of thirty pounds per month wasn't even close to the seven pounds per month paid to workers by many of our high-street stores' suppliers. Results from their survey of companies, all of whom belong to the Ethical Trading Initiative, showed Gap and Next doing most to ensure people were paid a living wage, with the likes of Ted Baker, Monsoon and Diesel doing less. In its latest report Labour Behind the Label talks of the 'glacial progress' to a living wage for garment workers. Most still earn half of what they need to meet basic requirements. Ten years after the industry signed up to the campaign for decent wages little has been done to make it happen.[36] Of the thirty big retail groups surveyed none is paying a living wage. It's the same in the toys sector. Mums and dads in the developing world work away from home and their children all year so that ours can have cheap toys at Christmas that they will have forgotten in a couple of weeks.

Unlike the new poor in Britain, the global poor are hungry and cold. But, of course, that needn't be so: 80 per cent of the world's hungry children live in countries with a food surplus – it's just that the excess grain is used to feed the cattle to make the beef for our Big Macs and Whoppers. So, while we are becoming obese and dying of heart-attacks from eating burgers and other fast foods, children around the world are dying from malnutrition because the grain grown in the field next to where they live is being used to fatten us up rather than feed them.

According to the UN Development Agency, less than four per cent of the personal wealth of the 225 richest people in the world would suffice to offer all the poor of the world access to elementary medical and educational amenities as well as adequate nutrition. Would these 225 people really miss having four per cent fewer of the luxuries they now enjoy? Probably not. To them it's the equivalent of the small change the rest of us lose down the back of the sofa. They would probably feel much better about themselves if the money was taken from them in the

form of unavoidable taxation. But it won't be. Because to admit that the rich owe any obligation to the poor, that it is obscene for such injustice to exist when it could so easily be put right, or to suggest that governments have the right to discourage the hard work, initiative and enterprise of top executives, as if this were the case, would undermine the foundations of our economic system and the consumer society that keeps it going. Of course, the 225 could volunteer to give away four per cent of their wealth – but we don't live in an era when the social and cultural conditions exist to enable that to happen. And don't forget that the super-rich are miserable too. They are comparing themselves to people with even more houses, a faster personal jet and their own island. They really need the money – and, of course, they're worth it.

In August 2006 the reality of the consumer bubble of the rich West came home to a group of tourists lying in the sun in the Canary Islands. Eighty-eight immigrants from Africa were grounded on a beach in Tenerife severely dehydrated. The sunbathers helped them to shore, then gave them water and shelter from the sun. It was a moment when their worlds collided and humanity conquered consumerism. Hundreds if not thousands of immigrants never get that far.

A public inconvenience

We don't think about the poor, in part because there is no longer the space or culture to do it. To be a consumer society requires a monolithic infrastructure for shopping that squeezes out the spaces where we don't currently shop or aren't a market. It is easy to forget but only thirty years ago Britain had a mixed economy of public and private industries and sectors. The public realm was the space in which we were primarily citizens, not consumers, and were largely free of the pressures to buy: the parks, libraries and other common spaces we could share.

A consumer society, by definition and necessity, refuses to

recognize such boundaries. Indeed, it is predicated on the assumption that everything is better if the world is one big market of buyers and sellers and that there is no public space. Urged on by the thinking of von Hayek and von Mises, the market, if no one is watching, cares or tries to stop it, will convert every space that's not about buying into one that is if a profit can be made. Every space that is public and not private is a lost selling and buying opportunity.

Just think for a minute about the places that are not about buying and selling, that are outside the marketplaces, like the local park or library. It is in these areas that we are predominantly citizens rather than consumers, where we join, visit, participate, play, volunteer or do nothing – just sit. In these spaces we are valued and welcomed because we are citizens, not because of how deep our pockets are or how good our shopping prowess is. Such places have been under remorseless attack for the last thirty years as the individual and the consumer have dominated society and the citizen.

So what is being transformed and what is being lost? Let's start with the essentials, like public lavatories. Once upon a time, municipal loos were a symbol of civic hygiene, pride, modernity and progress. The Victorians invested heavily in public lavatories. But times have changed. What was good enough for the Victorians is not good enough for us in a consumer society. In the past ten years, the total number of public toilets in England and Wales has dropped from 10,000 to 5,500 and those that exist tend to be between fifty and 100 years old. There is often a charge to use them. When we are out, the only free and easy way to go to the loo is in shops. We are forced into places where we have to spend more than a penny. But the Victorians didn't just take toilets seriously: they invested in the public realm through sewage works, grand town halls and opulent railway stations. They knew that a healthy economy and society required an infrastructure of public investment; we still enjoy the legacy of their enlightened outlook today.

What was once a civic duty is now a job done by outsourced private contractors. If services aren't privatized they are dropped

altogether. With public libraries an expansive state did not just clear up the mess of social deprivation but helped to educate and entertain its citizens. Books weren't commodities you had to own and hoard but were borrowed, read, looked after and returned when the date stamp said they had to be. Libraries were places of cultural refuge where everyone was equal and had access to the great literary classics. All you had to do was be quiet. The air of sobriety, respect and calm was a world away from the competitive hubbub of the high street. However, the march of the market since the early 1980s would not allow these oases of non-buying to last. Between 1987 and 1997 almost 90 per cent of local councils reduced access to their public library services.[37] Instead we have Waterstones, Borders and, of course, Amazon to sell us not just the books we used to borrow but CDs, DVDs, stationery and anything else they can.

It's also getting near to the last post for the Post Office. Almost eight thousand sub-post offices have been closed in the last twenty years and more will share their fate. The one on Bermondsey Street, where I live, shut last year. It was replaced by a café called, wait for it, the Toast Office. You can buy a latte there but you can't send a letter. Thousands of people petitioned against its closure but to no avail. Commerce ruled. Often the Post Office is the centre of a community, providing a range of important services. It might not make a profit – but neither do the police and we don't shut them down. The elderly, disabled, families with young children and those with no access to a car suffer most. We can't put a price on a place for a chat and a friendly face – so the market demands they must shut. Postal services are now being 'liberalized' and opened up to competition between a variety of private companies. Why, though, should one small country like ours have more than one system of sorting and delivering letters and parcels? The duplication of multiple postal networks makes no economic sense. It's a natural monopoly. That was why the Royal Mail was created in the first place. It's the same with gas and electricity supply.

Even when public services aren't being sold off or cut, their

nature is radically altered to fit our consumer culture. Schools are being reshaped to fit consumer society. League tables allow parents, or customers as they are now known, to choose the best, which encourages schools to compete for their custom. Of course the quality of education should be improved. But in the end it's always the best schools that pick the 'best' pupils because there can never be enough 'best' schools. Demand will always outstrip supply. Most parents go through the misery of having to choose where to send their kids to school. Why can't the local school be good enough? Because value is now derived from the best choice – that is, a better choice than everyone else has.

In the right school, fizzy-drinks machines line corridors where a water fountain was once enough. School canteens are closed or the work is outsourced to companies whose profits are as fat as the kids they are creating. At university it gets worse: the introduction of variable tuition fees has created a market in higher education. The best universities will start charging the highest prices. Undergraduates are trained in the art of debt management and the logic of economic rationalism – picking courses to pay back their loans as preparation for the competitive economy and consumer life they now face. The objective is to allow the best British universities to compete with the best in the world and, crucially, to condition students psychologically not just for a life of debt but for a world in which they have to rely only on themselves and no one else. Education for its own sake goes out of the window.

Where education leads the commercialization of the NHS follows. Dentists used to be free. Now four out of ten people in Britain do not go to the dentist because they feel they cannot afford to: free dental treatment on the NHS has decayed to the point of invisibility.[38] We can now choose which hospital to go to – but on what basis? Some crude league table that conceals more than it reveals? I've no idea which hospital is best. I want someone in a white coat with proper training whom I can trust to tell me, someone who is literally operating in my interest and not for a profit.

None of the utilities that were sold off in the 1980s and 1990s has worked for us as consumers. Gas and electricity prices have rocketed in recent years and companies scramble for our lucrative custom by cold-calling at our doors and on our phones. No one really knows which is cheapest. Water came next, and despite all the leaks it's only been the profits of the new water companies that have flowed. Breaking up the railways was not just stupid but dangerous – terrible accidents have occurred, trains are overcrowded and the ticketing system is so complex that for one journey between London and Devon there were more than ninety different price options. People now look back on the old days of British Rail with affection.

Roads are being privatized, too. The M6 Toll Road – formerly known as the Birmingham Northern Relief Road – is Britain's first privately built toll-boothed motorway and runs alongside the public motorway. The average speed between junctions 4 and 11 on the M6 is just 17 m.p.h. Essentially the Toll Road gives you the option of paying and bypassing the traffic, or trundling along beside it. Unlike the London congestion charge, this hasn't been introduced to cut traffic and get people on to public transport but as a private service for those who can afford it.

As our services have become privatized, so have our lives. Nothing highlights the loss of independent public spaces more than what has happened to coffee shops. Coffee houses sprang up around 250 years ago in our newly flourishing cities as places in which people could meet and discuss the public issues of the day; their lodgings were too small to receive guests. The coffee that flooded in from the colonies was a stimulus for ideas and the coffee houses became the focus for long and deep debates between friends and strangers who would become friends. Writers and pamphleteers would test ideas and arguments. The birth of the enlightenment was fuelled by caffeine and the public spaces in which to drink it.

Coffee shops are once again at the forefront of a new age – but now it is the age of the consumer. The independents have largely gone and have been replaced by Starbucks or one of just a few

other chains. What Starbucks represents is not just the ultimate commodification of a once lively public space but the privatization of our hopes and desires. There is little difference between the product of one chain and another. They compete on emotion, and Starbucks wins hands down. Madeleine Bunting, writing in the journal *Renewal*, explains how Starbucks has appropriated the desires and values of the New Age. Founded in laidback Seattle, the home of Nirvana and grunge, they have packaged an 'ethnic feel' that is cosmopolitan and relaxed. Reacting against the culture of fast-food, Starbucks sells us time. Bunting says of its positioning, 'This was building on the *Friends* culture of hanging out. What it cannily perceived was that what a certain type of urban professional wanted above all else was time – and curiously they were prepared to pay for it.'[39] People don't go to Starbucks just for the coffee but for the warmth and sense of community. Only they don't talk to each other like our Friends on the TV and certainly not about public matters. It's a privatized refuge in a once public sphere and Starbucks are making a mint. They buy up all the best locations – ensuring local independents close down. From the corner of Wigmore Street and Regent Street in central London you are within five miles of 164 Starbucks branches. We should wake up and smell the coffee!

But it is not all one-way traffic. There have been some refreshing instances where the public has struck back. I live close to the Tate Modern at Bankside on the Thames. The transformation of this industrial-age power station into an amazing public space speaks to the thrill we get from the public realm. It is a joy to visit. Entry is free and the huge turbine hall is mesmerizing in itself. Its vast scale alone tells us something about being human – that we can build such things but feel so small within them. People wander, sit, stare or read. You can stay as long as you want. Many who visit are tourists and it makes me proud to think they may take the experience of the Tate Modern home with them as at least one definition of modern Britain. The art-and-books shop is, of course, always rammed – but, then, you've got to get your shopping in when you can.

Further along the Thames is the newly refurbished Festival Hall, another great example of the realm of the citizen trumping the world of the consumer. So, too, is Trafalgar Square. Once it was just a glorified roundabout, but Ken Livingstone, the former London mayor, invested in it and now London has a proper central square where people can walk and rest. But these are the exceptions that prove the rule of declining public spaces. For every Festival Hall there is a Millennium Dome that becomes the private O2 centre, or the new Terminal Five at Heathrow airport, which caters for almost 100,000 passengers per day but offers only 700 seats. If you want to sit down you have to go to a café and pay. Heathrow, with an additional 250,000 square feet of new retail space (just think of six supermarkets), has become somewhere to shop *en route* to somewhere else to shop. Jonathan Rutherford, a perceptive cultural commentator, writes, 'Just as early industrial capitalism enclosed the commons of land and labour, so today's knowledge-driven capitalism is enclosing the cultural and intellectual commons, the commons of the human mind and body, the commons of biological life.'[40]

Heathrow, like our high streets, is filled with the same limited range of chain stores. Andrew Simms at the New Economics Foundation has coined the term 'clone towns' to describe these cultural deserts of identical banks, coffee shops, clothing and sports stores. It hit a nerve because it is about our identity and sense of belonging. How can you belong to a particular town when it looks like everywhere else? The notion of coming from Reading as opposed to Rotherham will soon be meaningless because they are all becoming the same. There is no space to develop interesting and different local identities if what surrounds us is corporate blandness. 'This identikit commercial culture isn't just killing diversity in the high street,' says Simms. 'It undermines democracy and attacks our sense of place, belonging and wellbeing. It hands power over to a corporate élite and ultimately pulls apart the rich weave of systems upon which our livelihoods and economy have depended.'[41] Wimbledon was crowned the most extreme example of a clone town with 98 per

cent of shops and restaurants on the Broadway belonging to national and international chains. And in these clone towns it's not just our identities that are being lost but our rights as citizens. New regeneration sites like the Liverpool One development will become no-go areas for some of us. There is no public right of access: they are private property. The young, beggars, *Big Issue* sellers and skateboarders face eviction. The non-consumers will be ejected. To create this new shopping Mecca, thirty-five streets were lost and one public park. With them go the independent stores to be replaced with the new consumer enclosures of cloned shops. The goal: not to create a space where people can live and society flourish, but a site for profit, to wring every possible penny from us.

Here is a tell-tale sign of the shift that has taken place in British society over the forty years as we moved from lives predominantly in a public to a private realm. In the 1958 British film *A Night to Remember*, the sinking of *Titanic* was portrayed as a public disaster with important lessons for passenger safety. In James Cameron's 1997 production, it was presented in terms of a highly romantic personal tragedy. Between these two films, argued journalist Bryan Appleyard, the public realm vanished, to be replaced by the private realm of the authentic self and its fulfilment.[42] But it is more than a pluralistic and public sense of society that is threatened. The march of the market, headed by the vanguard of turbo-consumers into the public realm, poses a threat to our collective ability to decide what kind of society we want. One of the big targets of the steamrolling logic of turbo-consumerism is democracy itself.

Would anyone vote for shopping?

The objective of the 'invisible hand' of the market is threefold: to expand the market so that more things can be sold to more people, to condition people to accept and even welcome, the individualized risk of consumer life and, finally, to rule out any

alternative to consumer society. To do those three things successfully, consumerism has to triumph in the popularity stakes over
democracy and politics.

The relationship between markets and democracy is zero
sum. The more we decide things individually as consumers, the
less we can decide things democratically as citizens. The more
the good life becomes a product of what we buy, the less space,
energy and commitment there is to the collective creation of the
good society through democracy. Democracy is the means by
which we decide when the wider interests of society come
before the narrow interest of the individual or, to put it more
accurately, the desires of the consumer. Democracy allows us to
decide together what can't be done alone and directs the means,
through collective action, to make it happen.

Consumerism now poses a direct and deadly threat to the
future of democracy. The most powerful illustration of this is the
NHS. Before its creation, those who could afford it bought private
health care. It took a collective and democratic decision to provide free-at-the-point-of-need services for everyone through Acts
of Parliament in 1946 and 1947; it was launched in 1948.

The NHS is unacceptable to the market as it denies a space
in which profit can be made, it socializes risk and encourages us
to think and act collectively. It also provides a glimpse of a good
society that isn't based on shopping. So, for a consumer society
to grow as it always must, the NHS and the process that put it in
place, democracy, must be dismantled and replaced by the institutions, processes and belief systems of consumerism.

The method, as ever, is not force or coercion but seduction
and the steady erosion of democratic and collective solutions
with individual consumer responses. The process works like this.
The cultural forces of individual freedom unleashed in the 1960s
are counterposed with the bureaucratic and irresponsive services of the old state. The philosophy of von Hayek and von
Mises is applied to the public sector; only the market is deemed
to be efficient. At the same time the freedom and choice of the
consumer is contrasted to the dullness of the citizen. Far better

to make the public sector like the private world of the consumer. Politics becomes simply an agreement about what should be privatized and consumerized and stops being what it must be: the battle between competing visions of the good society. Democracy stops being about morality and leadership and becomes instead a branch of the retail sector. CEOs, like Terry Leahy of Tesco, are asked to sprinkle their market magic on ailing public services as if being ill or needing to be educated was like shopping in one of their stores.

But it's not just that politics exists to underpin the role of the market and the consumer society: politics must also become like the market. Today we select political parties as we do our supermarkets. Essentially they all sell the same thing: the technocratic management of a consumer society in which the market is dominant. The difference between the parties is one of degree and emphasis: they don't offer fundamental alternatives. The only place we can't have competition and choice, it would seem, is in politics. Personalities are sold rather principles. Soundbites become the political equivalent of advertising slogans. Parties adopt branding strategies and test their policies, as companies do their products, through focus groups. None of this is necessarily wrong in itself. It would be stupid not to communicate effectively. The issue is, for what purpose are they doing it? To build a better society or just reinforce the one we have?

Dick Morris, an election strategist for US President Bill Clinton, marvelled at the way Hollywood film producers would test different endings with the public to see which they liked best. The most popular ending would then be cut into the final edit for general release. Morris applied the same approach to the President's policies. They were tested to see how popular they would be, and what was popular became law. Also in the US, hugely influential pollsters like Mark Penn have started packaging voters by consumer-style labels such as 'young knitters' and 'tech fatales' (women who like technology). The candidates they advise can then target messages at them to win their vote.

And to have a functioning democracy, society needs a balanced

and unbiased system of news reporting. Even that is coming
under threat from the contamination of turbo-consumerism. In
the US in July 2008 McDonald's secured the right to place their
products in regional news programmes. The newsreaders now
have McDonald's 'iced coffee' in front of them. It is a chemical
concoction made to look good under the studio lights and not
melt so none is drunk. But what happens if there is a story about
McDonald's? Will the news programmes be able to report on
them openly and, if necessary, critically? And will politicians try
to hold the company to account if they know they have some
influence over the news agenda?

The result is another vicious circle of decline. The less politicians do, the more people retreat from democracy and see it as
meaningless because it changes nothing. Whoever you vote for,
the answer is more of the same consumer culture. In July 2008
the Government announced a scheme to encourage people to
vote in local elections by entering them in a prize draw to win
an iPod, TV or supermarket voucher. Could you make this up?
Politics gets stripped of its purpose through consumerism and,
understandably, no one bothers to vote, so the politicians respond
by offering the chance to win the latest consumer gadgets as the
electorate's only inducement to get involved!

People have retreated further into their own private shopping
world and become less likely to commit to shared initiatives.
Happiness is found in the small things we buy alone, not the big
things we change together. The good society has become the
consumer society because we operate in the belief that the only
choices and changes we can make to our lives are centred on the
high street. In that sense democracy has been stripped of any
power and transplanted to the shops. It is here that we cast our
votes every day instead of waiting for polling day once every five
years to get what we want. We can have it now, but only if we
can afford it. Meanwhile, political parties simply offer more or
less humane ways of managing the market and the consumer
society it spawns. One New Labour politician, Alan Milburn,
said in the House of Commons, 'Whether we like it or not, this

is a consumer age.' But the point of politics is to believe in something and work to make it happen. What if Churchill had said,
'Whether we like it or not, this is a fascist age'? Would that have
been good enough? Why doesn't Alan Milburn want to fight
them on the beaches for something better than a 'consumer
age'? Instead of making the weather, politicians just try to survive the storm.

But politicians have to justify their existence somehow and
find grounds for competition between them. So, two things
happen. First, politics is used to make consumerism safe and
legitimate. Instead of regulating how far the market spreads, governments increasingly regulate what happens within it. Consumer protection and safety are now of paramount political
significance. The BSE meat crisis, which cost an estimated £3.5
billion, is simply the highest-profile case of Government desperation to win and keep consumer confidence. Britain's farming and meat industries, the retail sector and the reputation of
UK plc, were all too important for the Government to do anything other than spend huge amounts of public money on limiting the reputation damage. Consumer-protection initiatives,
such as anti-rip-off campaigns, are set up. A team of pupils from
Portobello High School in Edinburgh have been crowned Young
Consumers of the Year at a competition in Manchester by the
Office of Fair Trading. The final tested the students' consumer
skills and knowledge, and improved confidence in areas such as
money and finance, food and health, safety and the environment.
The OFT consumer-education department's Paul Burton said,
'The amount spent by young people is enormous and they are
increasingly involved in spending decisions, whether it is mobile
phones, computer games or traditional areas like clothes. Having
a skilled group of consumers shopping around and aware of
their rights benefits us all.'[43]

Second, politicians focus on personal behaviour by addressing
the social symptoms of the spread of consumerism because they
no longer dare to address the cause of our social recession −i.e.,
the consumerization of society. They regulate the social and

personal consequences of turbo-consumerism rather than regulating its causes. This justifies their existence and makes them
look strong. But it tends to victimize the already weak and pow-
erless. It is one reason why ASBOs are popular with politicians
and explains anti-obesity policies aimed at the victims of fast
and fatty food rather than at the profits and marketing campaigns of the companies selling it. The regulation of anything
that underpins the consumer society is off limits.

For the voter, democracy becomes a hollow choice between
parties offering variations on the same consumer theme. Only as
consumers do we have any power and even that is heavily constrained. If we are lucky we can pick and choose this or that item
off the shelf and reinvent our identity endlessly. But that is all we
can do. We can buy any car we want but we don't have a system
to ensure that the roads are clear because public-transport systems are poor. We are free to pick and choose everything that is
laid before us but we can't choose not to choose. But even when
we do engage with the democratic process we do so with the
mindset of the individual consumer.

As consumers we are now demanding unrealistic instant
answers from politicians. We want them to solve all our problems
but don't want to have to sacrifice anything in return. In 2005 a
senior aide to the then Prime Minister, Tony Blair, said that handling voters was like dealing with teenagers – they can't be governed but are unable to govern themselves. They want everything
and hate everyone.[44] The journalist John Lloyd has written that
'We treat politics as we do the cash machine or the supermarket
aisle. Satisfaction must be swift.' He went on, 'Choice, and the
assumed right to have it quickly, is now the hidden engine of
our economies, and thus of our politics.'[45]

One result is that membership of the three main parties is less
than a quarter of what it was in 1964. The fewer members parties
have, the less ideological they tend to be and the less likely they
are to do or say anything that challenges the dominant consumer culture. In 1964, 44 per cent of electors described themselves as identifying 'very strongly' with a political party; this had

dropped to 14 per cent in 2001. Voting at general elections has dropped from almost 80 per cent for most of the post-war period, when the parties competed on more ideological terms, to around 60 per cent today. In 2005 Labour won the election but more people abstained than voted for the party. People stop voting when, regardless of who wins, nothing really changes.

But it is not just that politics and democracy are systematically denied the space to present an alternative to the consumer society: the hope for another vision of the good society is co-opted by the market to get us to buy more. Mikhail Gorbachev sits in the back of a limousine, with a luxury Louis Vuitton bag beside him. 'Retail victims of the world unite,' says Price Runner, a price comparison website, that uses images of Soviet-style workers carrying a banner with the word 'Truth' emblazoned on it. Once, the threat of socialism to the shopping-centred culture of the West was real. Now the threat of rebellion is co-opted, absorbed and deflected to do the very opposite of what these once heroic figures, like Che Guevara, believed in.

Totalitarianism, the accusation levelled against Communism, is a system of control that regulates every aspect of public and private life. Consumerism and Communism are two different versions of totalitarian societies: both offer a pseudo-vision of freedom but operate to systematically reinforce their dominance.

The market continues to co-opt the ideals of democracy. In Boots the chemist, at the end of an aisle a banner above a selection of different goods proclaims, 'Some of the products our customers voted for.' This relates to a poll of customer preferences, which is used to encourage others to follow their buying lead because it is deemed to be democratic. In the designer-outlet site in Ashford, Kent, there is a shop called Autonomy. The word is meant to define the ability to make decisions that allow us to govern our lives. But today the ideal of autonomy is used to encourage women to buy a new dress.

The ancient Greeks called the public realm, where people were citizens rather than consumers, the *agora*. It was here that people could debate and discuss what sort of world they wanted.

They were deemed equal and free and could decide together how to shape their lives and the world around them. In the *agora* they were as free as it is possible to be. Today such spaces are being commercialized, privatized and commodified by market forces and willing political accomplices. Their fear of open public spaces makes them agoraphobics. Today there is no *agora*, just Argos. Or, rather, there is an Agora: it's the name of a chain of slot-machine outlets where you can take your chance of a better life with the hope that three lemons will fall into place.

The ruling out of an alternative way of living, this loss of control and lack of autonomy, or at the very least a way of rebalancing society away from consumerism, is one of the reasons that we are living less satisfying and more miserable lives. As we have seen, an all-consuming life provides sufficient compensation to keep us going back for more but only in the absence of any desirable and feasible alternative. This must be systematically ruled out because it would mean the end of the stranglehold of consumerism on us. In the process it is not just the environment that is destroyed or our social, public and political lives that are commodified: our private and personal lives suffer too.

But, once again, the recession gives us a chance to reassess what is possible. For the first time in decades markets are commonly seen to be failing and the consumer deal of sufficient compensation for a life of endless working and buying is not paying off. But as the government is being forced to step in to prop up the banks and stimulate demand, a new relationship between the state and us as citizens, rather than as consumers, is being forged. All of a sudden huge amounts, around £37 billion, of public money have been found to, in effect, nationalize the banks. Such collective action shatters the myth that the private sector is always good and the public sector always bad. It is creating the space for a more balanced view of what we can do individually as consumers and what we need to do collectively as citizens. If a virtue is made of this necessity, then a new consensus can be built around the role of government in regulating the market in the interests of people and not just the pursuit of

profit. We may begin to identify as citizens, taking a more involved part in shaping decisions and institutions that are important to our lives – not just trying to buy happiness in the shops. Politics is one place in which we need a real choice.

The tyranny of choice

Choice can be a good thing but, as with everything else, too much can have damaging consequences. Personal choice has become the key value of society today. Unless we choose something individually it holds little value for us. It is also the underlying principle of the consumer society. But there are places in which personal choice works better than others. Too much choice or choice over the wrong thing contributes to bad decisions, anxiety, stress and dissatisfaction – even clinical depression. If asked, we will always choose to choose but it doesn't necessarily make us feel better.

Proof of this comes from a series of studies held in the US. In one a food store offered its customers either a limited range of jams or a much more extensive range. Thirty per cent of those exposed to the small array bought a jar; only three per cent of those exposed to the large selection did so.[46] This is because too much choice confuses us. We want to make the right choice but our brains can't cope with the amount of information if too many options are put before us. So instead of deciding we retreat. Indeed, the studies found that people enjoyed products more when choice was limited rather than expanded.

It isn't just jam we have to choose but what medical treatment we want or where to send our children to school. We even have to choose our identity now that it is created by what we buy and not what job we do. Responsibility to choose correctly has become a real burden. We always think we want choice but when we have got it we often change our minds. In one study 65 per cent of people who didn't have cancer said that if they got it they would prefer to choose their treatment. Of those who

actually had cancer, 88 per cent said they would prefer not to choose.

In part, choice has flourished because the rational-choice theory of the free-market thinkers holds that we are all maximizers; that is, we need to be assured that every purchase or decision we make is the best that could be made. But it is impossible to tell what may be the best decision because we can never know or evaluate every possible option. The task we are set, and set ourselves, is so daunting as to be impossible. We can't make the best possible choice, so choice becomes frustrating and annoying.

The alternative to being a maximizer is to be a 'satisficer'. To 'satisfice' is to settle for something that is good enough and not to worry about the possibility that there may be something better round the corner. It doesn't mean we don't think about what we want but it provides the emotional space to be happy with what we've got. That, as we know, is death to the consumer society. The idea of the satisficer came from the Nobel Prize-winning economist and psychologist Herbert Simon in the 1950s. His view was that when all the costs of maximizing decisions are built in, such as time spent, cost of travel and the mental struggle, then satisficing is the maximizing strategy. Indeed, the pursuit of the maximizing strategy opens us to the horrors of post-decision regret: the feeling that we have bought the wrong thing. And then we have the consequences or legacy of these imperfect decisions all around us, no longer new, no longer what we expected of them, no longer holding out the prospect of happiness.

It isn't just choice that disappoints us but the competitive nature of consumer society too. As material affluence spread through the West in the nineteenth and twentieth centuries it led more and more people to want access to a finite source of good and services. Now only two things can happen when things are in short supply. Either not everyone can have them or if everyone does have them the original quality that made them desirable, their exclusivity, becomes impaired. This is why eco-

nomic growth is not tied to increased happiness. How does this work in practice? Let's take the example of wanting a house with a nice view. If it's something you want and value, others will want and value it too. But if everyone builds a house on the same hill, the view for everyone is impaired and the rural location that attracted them is spoiled. The unintended consequences of collective action in a consumer society lead to frustration and disappointment. If everyone stands on tiptoe no one has a better view and everyone gets exhausted in the process. Expectations of fulfilment through mass consumption, the definition of a consumer society, cannot be met. Happiness doesn't stand a chance.

If the shopping, deciding and competing process has an internal logic that is bound to disappoint and frustrate, the impact on our families and private lives of an all-consuming existence brings more yet anxieties. If consumerism knows no boundaries, it is as appropriate and applicable to emotion and intimacy as it is to clothes and cars. If there is a profit to be made, and unless it is stopped, it will seep relentlessly into every aspect of our lives. We have seen how a consumer society exploits our emotions. In a turbo-consuming world, it commercializes those emotions by selling us products and services that replace acts of commitment, love and humanity.

Our nearest or dearest

Natural selection and a few pheromones used to be enough to tie the knot. Now relationships have to be gift-wrapped and tagged as a demonstration of our economic prowess and consumer acumen. Love is big business. If consumer capitalism can tap into our basic animal urge to reproduce, then it really is ker-*ching* time at the tills.

Rachel Greenwald has thoughtfully provided a self-help manual for those women who still haven't made the leap beyond emotion into perpetual shopping when it comes to finding a

partner. *The Program: Fifteen Steps to Finding a Husband After Thirty* [47] is management consultancy for marriage. 'You, the reader, are the product,' and 'The Program is a strategic plan to help you market yourself to find your partner.' Rachel advises the single woman to create a 'personal brand' and to work quickly towards a deal: 'You have to remove or negotiate any deal-breakers such as religious practices or lifestyle differences.' Finally, she must cut her losses if the buyer won't come through: 'Thank him for not wasting your time any further and break up with him.'

This is human relations stripped to the bone of utility maximization and rational-choice theory. It is love without either emotion or commitment. It is love as a deal. It's so cool it's cold. Partners become a series of purchases. The attachment is fleeting, to be consumed, used up, and then we move on. From sex in cars to sex in cyberspace, new technology drives the commoditization of our relationships. The mobile phone and email make no-strings-attached sex as easy and soulless as supermarket shopping. This is the cutting edge of relationship development that will become the norm.

Human beings, especially when they relate to each other, are messy, confused and ambiguous. We are not the calculating machines of the Austrian School of Economists or Rachel Greenwald. That's what makes us interesting. But dating agencies, online dating and now speed dating commoditize and cleanse the whole affair. The risk, the pain, the time, the doubt – the whole messy business is tidied up, sanitized, and comes with a money-back guarantee. If you don't find the date of your dreams in six months then you get the next six at half price.

The new technology and the emerging market for speed and Internet dating offers us more choice – which is the one thing we can't resist. But the easier it is to find a potential partner, the easier it is the reject them. We view potential partners in the same way that we view the possible purchase of a new car: they are sized up and tested, not just on the basis of whether they will be a good little runner but what they will say about us. Will we be viewed as high achievers, go-getters and superior shoppers

with this or that person on our arm? We become partners not in love or devotion but consumption. We want our trophy partner. But all the time bets are hedged. It cannot be until 'death do us part' because desire for the next thing rather than stability is now the emotion that propels our society. No one commits to commitment because it rules out the chance to upgrade to a better, newer model. To be unable to choose is to stop being a consumer and that means we stop being a normal human being in the early twenty-first century. It is as true for the bedroom as the boardroom.

What must be avoided at all costs is the ultimate consumer humiliation of not being chosen, of being rejected. The answer is to give no one the chance. Get and keep the upper hand in all negotiations – just as Rachel advises. Never reveal your hand or expose the weakness of emotion or the need to depend. Keep the exit door in sight at all times as there could always be a better option round the corner.

As we have seen, companies in a consumer society will take just about anything and turn it into a selling opportunity. Let's go back to Ikea, that wholesome blue and yellow friend of the family. It ran an advertising campaign in 2000 to suggest that the cure to the agony, guilt and anxiety of divorce was a trip to one if its stores to furnish a new home and, in the process, create the conditions for new sexual relationships. 'Make a fresh start,' it implored. And to those who were unhappy in their relationships, the advert said they should simply 'walk away'. There are two worrying aspects to this. The first is that it attempts to perpetuate the myth that buying things makes us happy – even in the most extremely upsetting personal circumstances. Anything can be overcome with a bit of a shop. Second, it encourages us to treat relationships as we would commodities – as something eminently and ultimately disposable. Sadly this approach isn't just being applied to humans, who at least have the power to decide and play the consumer game or not. In late 2008 a US company called Flexpetz was due to open a store in London to allow us to hire a pet. That's right: 'A dog isn't for life – it's just

for Christmas.' The animal is delivered and taken away at your and your children's convenience.

In a consumer society our need to belong was used to sell us things that made us feel we belonged to a certain group or tribe. In a turbo-consumer world it is taken a step further. Now the few real relationships we have are found and maintained through a consumerized process. The chances and places to be truly human are diminished still further.

Family fortunes

So you've procured the perfect partner. What's the next investment opportunity in your portfolio? Of course! Organic corporate growth through offspring investment. But the decision to 'start a family' is now just that – a decision rather than, as it once was, a natural consequence of living with or marrying someone. Of course contraception is brilliantly liberating, but the decision to have a family is increasingly based on market values. A family is now a calculation based on the cost of children: what would we have to go without in terms of material possessions or paid-for experiences, like travel, if we were to take on the cost and time of bringing up children? To argue that consumerism is the sole reason for the rocketing age at which couples have children and the declining birth rate would be too far-fetched. Historic issues, such as much higher birth survival rates and the pill, contribute. But the selfish demand for immediate gratification of our consumer society is a big factor in the declining birth rate.

At one level it's not surprising that people are opting out of families, or putting off the decision: bringing up a child in Britain today costs a lot. A 2005 estimate suggested an average of £165,000 per child. The bills are soaring as the numbers of children per family decline – down from the classic 2.4 to more like 1.7 today. Childcare bills have gone up beyond the level of inflation, with some parents paying more than £20,800 each year for full-time care, according to research by the Daycare Trust in

January 2009. A typical full-time place for a child under two is £167 per week – with its parent's average earnings at £497 per week. But let's not forget that the new 'mini-me' is a spending opportunity, to be dressed and transported in the latest designer baby fashions. Children have become an extension of our own consumer desire. Trophy children now stand alongside trophy partners. Proper parents would never allow their baby to be seen in last year's fashions or the wrong brand. Shops such as Baby Gap thrive on our willingness to transfer our consuming passions to newborn babies. They are a reflection of us and would make us look like flawed consumers if they were in the wrong outfits.

But even if we decide to have children, the pressure to spend means that more and more parents are desperate to get back to work to fuel the shopping habit. In 1981, only 24 per cent of women returned to work within a year of childbirth while in 2001 it was 67 per cent and the proportion is expected to continue rising. Men are, of course, worse. Huge numbers never take the paternity leave to which they are entitled. It means we are commoditizing and outsourcing the upbringing of our children to a new and highly profitable childcare industry.

As the need to spend grows, the status of parenting declines. Staying at home is viewed as feckless. The Government keeps announcing schemes to get mothers in particular 'back to work'. The economy needs them and the state doesn't want to have to pay for them. Or, rather, we don't want to pay the state through taxes to ensure that the next generation is raised properly because we have much better things to do with our money. Like buying things that we don't need, rarely use and then throw away. But something deeper is going on. The economy needs to prepare the next generation for a life on the learn-to-earn treadmill. This means socializing children as early as possible to a school-performance system that is measured only in terms of dry academic results. Worker ants that earn the right to be shopping butterflies cannot be left to the vagaries of life at home and parents who aren't paying their way (or, more importantly, buying their way). The

role of the state is to produce the shoppers of the future. Meanwhile parents have to hold down at least one job each and deploy not just 'shift parenting' but sacrifice almost all of the time they could spend together. It's no surprise that the parents who work the longest hours lavish more discretionary spending on their children than those who spend only their time on them. It's down to guilt.

It's impossible to be a perfect parent. But the dynamics of an earn-to-spend existence puts new pressures on families. Either the parents are back at work or when they aren't they're being overly fussy and obsessed with every aspect of their child's development. The demands of success, as defined by purchasing power, filter down to ever-younger children. Once you got serious about work, life and earning in your mid-twenties. Now the pressures can't be applied too soon. 'Helicopter parents' hover over every aspect of their children's lives, interfering with their schooling, friendships and 'leisure' time to ensure they are a success. To get the right house, you need the right job, for which you need the right university and therefore the right set of A-level results, which demands the right secondary school and therefore the right primary, which is dependent on the child having attended the correct feeder nursery. Not every family is like this, but the maximizers set the rules for everyone else. In almost every year of their school life children are now tested and marked, sorted and ranked. We are producing factory-style workers – churned out to be competitive in a commercialized world. Growing depression and burn-out rates among schoolchildren seem a curious price to pay for a consumer lifestyle built to leave us perpetually dissatisfied. But if family life is being pressurized and changed by turbo-consumerism the lives of our children are being damaged to an even greater extent.

The commercialization of childhood

Stella McCartney has become the first 'real' person to feature in a Mr Men or Little Miss book. In the story her character, Little Miss Stella, meets Little Miss Nobody, who is so unfashionable that she is often ignored. But after Little Miss Stella designs a suit for her new friend, Little Miss Nobody is transformed into 'somebody'.[48] What a sweet story about how to make a little girl feel happier. But, of course, that's not what it's about. It's about grooming girls from the earliest possible date for a life of consumption.

'Give me a child until he is seven and I will give you the man,' was the proud claim of the Jesuits, and at eighteen months more children can recognize the McDonald's brand than know their own surname. Socialization always works better if the targets are young. Patterns of behaviour and thinking are more easily set then. As Bobby, whom we met earlier, might say, by the time he is fifteen, what he wears is 'natural'.

There is now a significant amount of evidence and a broad consensus among psychologists that a strongly materialist value orientation is, all else being equal, detrimental to psychological well-being. People who place a high emphasis on material goods and wealth report higher levels of stress and anxiety, lower satisfaction with themselves and their lives, poorer relationships with others, and less concern for the environment. These results have been replicated around the world, for various age groups, and seem to be robust and reliable.[49]

Research for the National Consumer Council (NCC) concluded in July 2005 that 'Children do experience stress from the scale and extent of commercial marketing: young people feel pressure to have the latest "in vogue" items. Girls in particular experience feelings of inadequacy and discomfort as a result of "images of perfection" promoted by advertising. Advertising makes our children unhappy. The more consumerist children were the ones who were "brand aware", cared about their possessions and liked

collecting, the more likely they were to be dissatisfied more widely.'[50]

When I was little I had toys. I would play with Lego for hours, Monopoly games would last for days and soldiers would be lined up all over the house. And, of course, I had my Action Man. I spent entire days playing football, riding bikes and climbing trees. There were no expensive replica shirts so there was not much profit to be made from any of that. What a waste of a profit opportunity for someone. How dramatically things have changed in the last thirty years.

Childhood is not only commercialized: it's sexualized too. Little girls have always aspired to be grown-up like their mothers. They dress up in their mum's clothes and have favourite dolls to look after. But the success of marketers and the media in encouraging children to buy into 'cool' images of how they should look and kitting them out in styles that emulate their celebrity heroines has worrying repercussions: 90 per cent of fourteen-year-old girls now regularly wear makeup. Mintel, the market-research company, recommended that firms should place vending machines for their products (makeup marketed to young girls) in schools and cinemas to target teenage consumers. Five- and six-year-old girls have been reported arriving at schools in sexy thongs and lacy bras. They may start out as the exception to the rule but peer group pressure soon kicks in and makes this activity acceptable.

But it's not just clothing that reflects the sexualization of childhood. Toys are becoming increasingly reflective of this trend. While dolls like Barbie have for decades promoted a stereotypical slim-legged image, today's toys are taking it a step further. Bratz dolls are marketed at six-year-olds and ooze contemporary sexuality: Secret Date Collection pairs each Bratz character with a mystery Bratz Boy, two miniature champagne glasses and 'tons of date-night accessories'. The Miss Bimbo website lets children dress a doll in sexual clothing, have breast implants and keep thin using diet pills. Six-year-olds are having makeover parties. In a survey reported in the 2005 *British Journal of Developmental Psy-*

chology, Mintel found that 60 per cent of girls between seven and ten wore lipstick and 50 per cent of girls between five and eight wanted to be slimmer.[51]

Boys don't escape commercialization. Marketers concentrate on nurturing their competitive instinct by appealing to their inbuilt desires for power, force and control as well as their natural interest in gadgets and technology. The massive computer-games industry is testament to this. Despite age restrictions on computer games, surveys show that large numbers of very young children have played games like *Mortal Kombat* and *Grand Theft Auto III* (rated 18+). Often unsuspecting parents buy computer games with high age ratings for their children because their friends have them. Little if anything is done to stop the march of the market into children's lives. A report by the National Consumer Council and Child Net found 73 per cent of online adverts on children's favourite sites are not labelled as adverts and children often put themselves down as being over eighteen when they are as young as six and often can't distinguish content from commerce.[52]

Pester power is on the increase. Of course, you can 'just say no'. But the point of all the marketing is to make the tantrums and demands undeniable. By 'just saying no', parents quite rightly fear that they are denying their children the consumer symbols that make them normal in the playground. The pressures are enormous and lead to extreme behaviour to try to fit in.

Fiona is forty, a single mum living in Kingston, Surrey, with Holly, her ten-year-old. It's only in the last few years that Fiona has begun to feel the onslaught of pester power. At the moment it's the incessant demand for an iPod Nano, not the Shuffle Holly has got. Fiona thinks the pressure comes from the older sisters of her daughter's friends. They have the latest gadgets and have become the inspirational norm. Holly mentions the Nano several times a week, whenever they go past or near the shop. She also wants an iPhone. But Holly will have a view on a possible new kitchen for the house. Of course, her opinions aren't necessarily heeded but they are heard and they will, inevitably, have

some influence. She likes to think she is involved. Gone are the days in which Fiona would pre-select three T-shirts for her – now Holly chooses most of what she wears. The new battle lines are formed on the issue of over-sexualized clothing. On off-the-shoulder numbers or offensive slogans Fiona will finally stand her ground.

Like many parents, Fiona says she feels guilty. Clothes and gadgets are forms of compensation for missed parenting. Our guilt turns into more presents and more purchasing power as our children influence more of what we buy and another vicious circle is created of working more to pay for the fact that we are working more. Before today's financial crisis, some very rich working parents were shelling out for the Grand Victorian playhouse at a cost of £17,000, or the Cinderella bedroom that came complete at £70,000 – a single pillow case cost £1,200. If the guilt and the pressure were too much, you could hire the services of Practical Princess to keep the house organized round the children. At just £600 per hour.

British children are among the most materialistic in the world, ahead even of Americans, but there remain important warning signs to heed from the other side of the Atlantic. A new trend among American parents is to name their newborns after global brands. Professor Cleveland Evans of Bellevue University in Nebraska stumbled across the trend when surveying 2,000 US social-security records. He found, among other examples, 300 girls called Armani, six boys named after Courvoisier (the cognac), girls called L'Oréal and even one boy named after the sports channel ESPN. Professor Evans attributed this trend to 'a growing desire on the part of parents to mark their children out as different' and said it reflected the material hopes of the parents.[53]

The effects of materialism on children, including emotional or behavioural problems and eating disorders, have been thoroughly researched and documented. The evidence from the Association of Teachers and Lecturers to a Government report on the impact of the commercial world on children's well-being

in June 2008 showed that poorer families put greater emphasis on the importance of branded goods. Among the poor, feelings of being left out led to low self-esteem and insecurity. Children felt isolated and bullied if unable to afford the right fashion items, and 85 per cent of teachers said that branded goods were important to their pupils. One teacher said, 'The need to belong in groups is paramount to young learners and exclusion is something they see as the end of the world.'

And yet, for the market, nothing is ever off-limits. Everywhere is a place to encourage people to buy. Schools have become the new targets of consumerization. In recent years there has been an unprecedented increase in the use of commercial materials in schools, with UK brands spending an estimated £300 million a year on targeting the classroom to increase sales. Several companies sponsor study aids, Shell sponsors an introduction to the oil industry and, of course, there are the vouchers-for-equipment schemes. The Tesco Computers for Schools scheme generously provides a new personal computer worth about £500 if parents are willing and able to collect 21,990 vouchers – representing £250,000 worth of Tesco goods bought. The multimillion-pound 'Cadbury Get Active' scheme targeted children as young as seven to encourage them to buy 160 million chocolate bars, containing nearly two million kilograms of fat, in exchange for school sports equipment to keep them fit and fight obesity. In this scheme children would have had to eat 170 chocolate bars, costing £71, to receive a basketball. By then, though, they would look like a basketball. It's as funny as it's outrageous.

Girls are sold pink and boys blue because the brain latches on to such easy symbols. Hunting and nurturing are part of our genetic fabric. But should companies be allowed to exploit these traits to make a profit from very young children? They are grooming them for a life of shopping, and nothing will stop them unless we decide to. The under-twenty-fives have never known anything but a life of turbo-consumption. They are the easy targets not just because of what they buy and demand but

because of their influence on big family purchasing decisions, like cars and holidays. But children's brains are not yet fully formed and their consumer naïvety is being exploited in the name of profit. If a society refuses to protect its youngest from such untoward influences, then what sort of society is it?

Caring less

As we consume more, we care less. Care, the nurturing of life from cradle to grave, has until recently been unpaid and almost entirely the responsibility of women. But now women are either forced back to work or want to go. Who looks after the small children or the elderly relative? The answer, of course, is the market with the offer of consumerized care. We have ended up with a private care 'economy'. This is not to be critical of women who work: men must take equal responsibility for caring. It is to question whether we want care to be privatized or socialized.

According to research by the recruitment website Gumtree, the amount spent on the domestic-care market is £18 billion a year. Today one in three Britons pays someone else to work in their home, whether gardening, cleaning, housekeeping or childcare, and of those one in four says they couldn't manage without the help they get. Half of all parents are employers of domestic help. Before the downturn, it became a possibility for vast numbers of people who would not have been able to afford it before. We are outsourcing the running of our families. Let me be crystal clear again before my mum, sister and every other woman rightly jumps down my throat. Caring is not the responsibility of women but of us all. And there is nothing wrong with paying for help. But there are consequences for the privatization of care.

In the US there are companies who will write letters to your friends, organize your family photograph albums, and ceremoniously scatter your relations' ashes at sea in your absence. You can already get someone to take away your CD collection and load

them on to your iPod here in the UK. You can pay for someone to visit your elderly parents and have a cup of tea with them or take them out for a walk if you're too busy. And parents who are worried about how well they're performing as family members can call in a professional evaluation company for an in-depth analysis of where they might be able to improve. All of these tasks may be performed efficiently by professionals but in the process we lose out on the intimacy that builds strong and stable relationships.

To be human and to live in society demands that we care for each other. But expressions of vulnerability and dependency are increasingly frowned on. The myth of self-sufficient rational decision-making crowds out the ethic of care and the necessity of dependency. We are living on borrowed time. The care gap will end up as a source of market failure. Where will the well-adjusted workers of the future come from if not well-balanced families and communities? The market has no interest in any of this. Its horizon is just the next big sell in an attempt to drive out the competition and maximize short-term profits. If care sells, then it will be sold. If workers and their families burn out in the process, there will be more on the conveyor-belt – either from home or abroad. Until, of course, there isn't anyone left because exhaustion, depression, stress-induced illness and lack of intimacy have finally taken their toll. And then it will be too late.

This lack of care and the commercialization of relationships at every level is creating a more neurotic and obsessive set of behaviours that find expression in the easiest possible way in a consumer society: through more shopping. For the 'normal' consumer a difficult balance has to be struck. Shop too little and you get left behind, shop and consume too much and you look as if you're addicted and out of control. Food is one of the commodities through which people often lose control.

I predict a diet

Food, and the shape it makes us, exposes many of the worst features of a world that is all consuming. Once, calories were expensive, so only Henry VIII and his chums were fat. Now calories are cheap so it's the poor who are overweight. Once, being rich meant being fat. Now it means being thin.

If being thin is the thing, it will be achieved at any cost, by surgery, stomach stapling, jaw wiring or dangerous dieting. Bob Geldof commented on the Atkins diet that it was brilliant because although you die, you do so thin! It doesn't matter how you get thin or fat, as long as you pay and go on paying. The growth of the fast-food industry goes hand in hand with the diet and keep-fit industries. They rise and fall together, joined at the bulging hip. Consumer capitalism will help you pile on the pounds, then charge you pounds to get rid of them. It's a perfect self-sustaining system. In the West, hundreds of thousands die of obesity every year. In the developing world millions are undernourished and starving to death. Malconsumption and over-consumption sit just a short plane journey from each other. On average, of course, the world is almost getting it right. There are more than one billion overweight people in the world compared to 129,800 million undernourished. There is more than enough for everyone but there is no profit in feeding people who cannot pay. So, people on the same planet, often in the same country, die of too much food or not enough.

If consumerism is at heart the search for a new and better you, there can be little that is more important to a new you than your body. In a diet-obsessed, fat-hating world, the new you is in there somewhere – it just needs the outer layer of the non-you to be shed before it can emerge, butterfly-like, into an adoring world. This is one of the most powerful myths we can be sold, an actual new us, and therefore is one of the most profitable ways in which the money machine of consumer capitalism can be oiled. Thin means self-respect and self-control. The pressure on women is, of course, greatest.

Kate is forty-one and food has been a problem for most of her life. She mentions that her wardrobe is full of clothes in sizes from ten to twenty. Her upbringing, with contradictory messages about food as comfort or good health, doomed her to a yo-yo life of dieting. If consumer society ensures that food is all around her and exploits her emotional problems to sell her more, it will also provide ways of finding 'solutions'. She has joined WeightWatchers and Slimmer's World at least half a dozen times. She is locked into a cycle of buying food and eating excessively, then buying the means to lose weight.

We are conditioned to hate our bodies through the relentless bombardment of perfectly thin images or rippling six-packs that define what it is to be happy and fulfilled in a consumer society. Alongside the perfect, fat people are singled out as idle, weak and, crucially, out of control. Being overweight has become shameful – it is the new social stigma: by targeting this new enemy the thin industry of fashion, diet, cosmetics, surgery and keep-fit can be sustained and rake in billions. Losing weight is praised to the skies and the self-satisfaction of having done so is intoxicating. To be overweight or obese is to become invisible or an object of disgust: the fat are among the social groups that make up the flawed consumers. To be overweight is to have 'let oneself go', to have become almost sub-human. With the cultural pressure to be thin we have a perfect self-sustaining consumer world in which the human body expands and contracts like its own mini-economic cycle. Boom and bust. But always consuming – eating and devouring, whether it's taking in or burning off the calories. In the US a company has produced the 'walk and work desk' so that you can keep earning while keeping off the weight. It costs a thousand pounds.

Choice, the key ingredient of the consumer society, backfires big-time when it comes to food: the overweight are blamed for making the wrong choice or, more precisely, being unable to ignore the choice to eat more. They may be consuming but they are still 'not normal'. They overeat to hide other stresses, strains and anxieties that the social recession of modern life throws at

them. But for the market it's just another weakness to be exploited – a psychological desire to be used as the basis for profit.

Sixty-six per cent of men and approaching 60 per cent of women in Britain are now overweight; 23 per cent of adults are obese, giving the UK the highest fat rate in Europe. And it's going to get worse. Obesity is set to rise to one in three adults by 2010 and there will be a massive increase in obesity among girls under eleven, with devastating implications for life expectancy. The waist of the average boy in 1977 measured 64 centimetres; by 2007 it had reached 72 centimetres, an increase of 12.5 per cent. The average girl's waist has increased by 15.4 per cent. Girls will soon have larger waists than boys. A third of our children are overweight when they leave primary school. Obesity reduces a person's life expectancy by nine years, on average, and increases the risk of a wide variety of diseases, including diabetes and arthritis. Obesity is already responsible for about a thousand premature deaths per week and, based on current trends, will soon become the most common preventable cause of death. Some scientists think we may be fattening up the first generation with a shorter life expectancy than their parents, people facing premature death in their forties because of over-consumption. When something is done to stop kids eating junk, like Jamie Oliver's celebrated campaign, some mums poke doughnuts and chips through the school fence because their little angels are being denied – what? The right to live at least as long as them.

Mintel have found that British women's vital statistics are rising and almost one in five are now size eighteen or over. They predict that if sizes change as much as they have done since the 1950s demographic shifts, by 2011 there will have been a 40 per cent increase of women taking size eighteen or over. This explains why stores cheat on sizes. Manufacturers and retailers indulge in so-called 'vanity sizing', adding a couple of inches or more to waist or hip measurements to allow a size-fourteen customer to fit into a size-twelve dress. They do this for fear that

outraged customers, failing to fit into their size twelve, will walk straight out and into a competitor store where a twelve does fit.

There is no doubt about it: that preserve of rich Dickensian Britain is back. Incidences of gout, an incurable disease, once synonymous with outrageous upper-class over-indulgence, have more than doubled since the 1950s and experts are predicting a further surge as more people enjoy excessive lifestyles at an early age. Dr Michael Snaith of the UK Gout Society has said, 'It is almost inevitable that younger women will start to develop gout because they are getting fatter and binge-drinking . . . I expect to see a lot more women with gout, as they are behaving more like men in their eating and drinking habits.'[54]

We get fat because there is money in it. Food retailers will go to any length to get us to eat more, diet more and exercise more. In the 1960s and 1970s the number of new sweet and snack products produced per year was fairly stable at approximately 250. In the mid-1980s it shot up to 1,000. By the late 1980s it was 2,000.[55] Next time you are in the supermarket make a note of the special offers at the end of every aisle. They won't be fruit or veg but value-added processed junk food – because Tesco or whoever can make more money from a two-for-one offer on Pringles than they can from a parsnip. It's the same with chocolate at the till until there was a big fuss about it and the chocolate had to retreat slightly.

In 2004, the diet food and drink market was valued at £4.6 billion, and is expanding faster than both our waistlines and the regular food and drink market. Ingeniously, diet products are sold alongside 'reward' foods. People are buying Diet Coke, then rewarding themselves with cakes. A tub of own-label sunflower spread costs just 38p per 500g. For thirteen times the price, you could buy Benecol Light, one of the newer brands of spread that are 'clinically proven' to reduce cholesterol. Artificial sweeteners substitute for sugar in existing food ranges; these products run parallel to full-sugar ranges, creating a distinct new line of processed food for people to buy. The food industry is taking out

the nutrients nature provides in the right combinations and sticking some of them into expensive products and pills, then selling them to us at a much higher price.

Portion sizes are getting bigger and the calorie count is getting heavier. The average number of calories in a typical cheese-burger increased from 397 in 1977 to 533 in 1996. Salty snacks jumped by an average of ninety-three calories per serving, and soft drinks went up forty-three calories per serving.

If we continue to follow America – which we tend to do – the next big thing will be competitive eating. The chairman of the US International Federation of Competitive Eating, George Shea, often refers to competitive eating as the country's 'fastest-growing sport'. Does he get the pun? It's mostly poor people who perform for their livelihood by ramming as many hotdogs down their throat as possible in an allotted time. The world record is 53.75 in twelve minutes.

From waxing, tanning, surgery and slimming, to new nails, tattoos and piercings in places I never knew existed, the body has indeed become our temple. A temple to physical consumption. And those temples are getting bigger even though we are constantly sold images of slim perfection. If the market can sell us more junk food and the urge to be slim, they have discovered perpetual eating and dieting motion. The money rolls in and the pounds pile on, while our minds as well as our bodies are paying the price: it's not just excessive food we're becoming hooked on but other addictions, like gambling.

Life's a gamble

Many of us enjoy a flutter once in a while. The Grand National, a bit of bingo by the seaside – where's the harm in it? There's none. But Britain has taken a gamble on gambling. And in its rise we see the dark future of consumerism.

Gambling turnover in the UK is huge. Government figures for 2005 show that £47.7 billion was placed on betting, £1.8

billion on bingo and £4.9 billion on the National Lottery. The numbers are rising quickly. The amounts being bet are going up at a rate of around 10–15 per cent per year. There are estimated to be around 300,000 problem gamblers but it's hard to be accurate, especially given the increase in online betting.[56]

Charlie is a diamond geezer, with the smile of an angel but the betting habit of a devil. He is now in his mid-sixties and has been betting all his adult life. He lives the dream that the next bet will be the big one that comes in. He does the horses and the dogs but it's the casino where he comes alive. Charlie has lost the family home because of gambling debts and now lives in a rented flat with his brother above the Co-op.

Charlie the gambler is the hyper-consumer. The exalted thrill is the speed with which one high follows another, the turnover of emotional peaks and troughs. Gamblers go back to the table like shoppers return to the mall, only much faster and with much greater emotional intensity. It's the same instant hopes, the same desires and adrenalin rush, and the same ultimate disappointment – the house, like the shop, always wins. Gambling and shopping share an endless cycle of repetition and the same manufactured air of conviviality. Malls and casinos are fantasy worlds where the reality of time and debt is lost. For the gambler, every sensation is sharpened, every experience lived at a faster pace. For Charlie, life when he is not at the table is dull. If he won big, would he really be able to stop? The exhilaration at the turn of the wheel, the card or the slot machine magnifies a thousand times the swipe of the credit card. And, as with shopping, there is no end point, no goal, other than to do it all again.

Increasingly, gamblers are becoming socially isolated, on the Internet or the mobile phone – as we are when we're shopping online. The chips are like credit cards – they bear little resemblance to hard cash. Losses become virtual and disconnected from the harsh realities of personal finance. For the shopper, like the gambler, a gulf opens between the value of money in the real world and its value as they purchase, or play.

In the gambler we see the future of the turbo-consumer. Like gambling, the cycles of shopping are getting faster and faster as the need for the hit grows sharper. What matters to the consumer is the thrill of the chase, not the satisfaction of owning and enjoying. Shoppers are heading towards the fate of the gambler and their compulsive but ultimately insubstantial sensations.

But gambling is not just a metaphor for the future of the shopper: it speaks to those whose lives are based on risk, chance and speculation. The notion of the casino is central to our economy and our characters in a consumer society. We live in the hope that our number will come up and save us from ourselves and our dull world, projecting us into lives of fame and fortune. From the national lottery to hitting the phone to get on to *Who Wants to Be a Millionaire?*, we are continually looking for the escape hatch to happiness.

The 'Masters of the Universe' today are not literary or scientific giants who save millions of lives or explain our world and our place in it through their insights. They are the money makers of Goldman Sachs – the glorified Del Boys who wheel and deal – living on the thin air of private equity, hedge funds and derivatives. As the financial crisis of 2008 showed, these people are just officially sanctioned gamblers.

Gambling is now enshrined in our political system. New Labour has allowed the casinos in and has massively deregulated the gambling industry. Why? Because casinos are the basis for local regeneration and therefore jobs and the industry can be taxed. 'We will be the least restricted, most free-market-based regime in Europe,' the Government proudly boasts. Mostly, though, it's the poor who are taxed and the consequences of addiction, ravaged lives and families are for someone else to worry about. The crime and anti-social behaviour that casinos spawn is to be ignored. In mature gambling markets more than five per cent of the population will develop some problem with gambling. Charlie's life and that of his family has been effectively wrecked by gambling. The purpose of a consumer society is to

encourage us to try perpetually to escape through commodities and services that promise what they can never deliver – a new us. Once it was just alcohol and cigarettes. Now it's anything from Viagra to text-messaging to sushi. We are a society of addicts. Our celebrities jostle to explain their addiction on the TV sofas, in the red tops and celebrity magazines. The Priory, once a place for students of God, is now the place where the rich retreat to get back on track before returning to their addiction.

Shopaholics, shoplifters and the debts of despair

It is not surprising that so many lose control in a consumer society because we are not meant to be in control of anything – least of all the urge to shop. Compulsive consumer disorder, or shopaholism, is a growing feature of the modern world. Its causes and consequences are always the same: the belief that buying the next thing will make us happy when it leaves us feeling worse about ourselves, further in debt and unable to resist the urge to do it all again. Shopaholics are the unfortunates who can't compete within the boundaries of normal shopping. They are social misfits – as flawed as the consumers who can't pay.

Studies show that between two and 10 per cent of adults have some compulsive shopping tendencies, with women nine times more likely to be affected than men. One study found that up to half of all fourteen- to eighteen-year-old girls in Scotland, Italy and Spain displayed signs of shopping addiction. Shopaholics tend to spend when they feel down, buying goods that they don't need, rapidly disposing of them, often in their original packaging, and running up large debts in the process. Some can afford it. Elton John once spent £40 million in twenty months, including £293,000 on flowers. But most can't.

Susie can't. She is thirty-eight, has two children and lives in Leeds, a city remade for the purpose of shopping over the last decade. Susie is not her real name but her life and shopping disorder are frighteningly real. I find her through a friend of a

friend and she tells me something about her life in exchange for the promise of anonymity. Susie has been buying too much for about four years. But long before that, for ever it seems to her, shopping had been the central part of her life. Since her teens in the boom years of the 1980s, when the modern shopping revolution kicked off, she says that her life has been defined by fashion. She is unsure when shopping as a leisure activity became a shopping problem. After the kids started at school full time and she didn't have a job, a combination of time and growing loss of self-worth saw her spending more time in Leeds city centre's burgeoning shopping malls.

Susie shops for love, guilt, fear and hope, but mostly insecurity. She says she buys things in a frightening haze, suspended belief and at a furious pace. Like the gambler, alcoholic or drug addict, each shopping hit delivers less and less and she needs the next even faster. It saps her energy and uses up all her free time. Shopping for Susie is a time to forget, for spurious treats, deceits and self-hate.

An ad man called Rod once explained to me why Marlboro promote their cigarettes using the imagery of a cowboy. After lots of research the company discovered why people smoke. Mostly they reach for a cigarette because they are tense, anxious or insecure. Smoking allows them to relax and take control of their feelings. The cowboy is the perfect image of control of the Wild West. The dangers of the frontier, the horses and cattle being tamed by the cowboy, would be linked in watchers' minds to the sense of control that smoking provides.

When she is out shopping, Susie forgets her insecurities. In the department stores of Leeds she is all-powerful. For a moment she is back in control. But the feeling, like the relief of the smoker, doesn't last. So she buys more for the adrenalin rush of being on top. The consequence is the usual array of unopened and never-worn purchases. The clothes she buys don't exist to be worn. It's the buying that matters. She has faced the horror of not being able to pay the minimum balance on her credit card. She has felt the dreadful spiral of guilt of having to tell her hus-

band about another holiday they won't be able to afford, which leads to another shopping spree. Susie knows she needs help to battle her demons.

The madness can grip us all. The shopping compulsion is in all of us, just to different degrees. Temptation is all around us. You can't avoid shops or hide from adverts – on the day I Google 'compulsive shopping', the first site that comes up says, 'Welcome to Shopping Addicts' Menswear sale'.

Credit card in hand, we thought we could swipe our way to happiness. Most of us have resorted to some level of retail therapy, but only the addict is caught in a cycle of repetition that brings with it diminishing returns and horrendous debts. The vulnerable are bombarded with messages telling them that this car or that dress will transform their lives. Then they get the offers of new credit cards and loan consolidations so that they can keep on spending. The weakest people in society are exploited by the most persuasive people on the planet. They are drowning in debt to pay for their consumption habit. The credit crunch will slow the offers, at least for a while, and the Government has called on the credit-card sector to apply more responsible lending criteria. Companies are starting to reduce credit limits drastically, in some cases from £7,000 to a £1,000 when many families were relying on them to make ends meet. But too much easy money can be made from easy credit to stop the sector returning to its bad old ways unless it is restricted by law in terms of how much and to whom they can lend.

As we have seen, credit and debt are now central planks of the consumer society. The social stigma of being in the red has been lifted. Waiting, saving and the link between work and rewards has been broken. The Financial Services Authority found that 66 per cent of us didn't know how much Christmas 2007 was going to cost us. And afterwards 48 per cent were more interested in booking a holiday than paying off debts. More seriously, a million people are paying their rent or the mortgage on their credit card;[57] 400,000 are behind with their mortgage payments, so repossessions and bankruptcies are shooting up. Citizens Advice

dealt with 1.7 million inquiries in the year to September 2007, an increase annually of 20 per cent – and that was before the financial crisis. That is 6,600 debt problems each day. Some of the callers thought that the higher the APR the better it was for them! Every five minutes the UK's personal debt grows by £1 million. As of July 2008 the total household debt was 109 per cent of GDP, the highest level of all the industrialized G8 nations. Meanwhile, the saving rate is at its lowest point since 1959.

To make things worse a new law that was proposed in September 2008 would make it quicker for banks, credit-card companies and other lenders to take action against struggling debtors and could lead to thousands more people losing their homes. The rules will make it easier for lenders to use charging orders to convert unsecured borrowing, such as car loans or credit-card debts, into loans 'secured' against the home of someone who owes them money. Once a charging order has been used to convert an unsecured loan into a secured loan, the lender can then force the homeowner to sell their home to pay back the debt. The political response is to clamp down on debtors but not on those who create the desires and offer the credit deals. Once again it is the symptoms of turbo-consumption that are addressed, not the causes. But there are other worrying symptoms of turbo-consumption.

A 'recovering theft addict' is the post-modern name given to shoplifters by the police and retailers. The average shoplifter steals two to three times a week, gets caught once in forty-eight efforts and is turned over to the police 50 per cent of the time. It is a huge, hidden and rising epidemic. In 2007 shoplifting cost companies £205 million, up eight per cent on the year before, according to figures from the British Retail Consortium. The actual losses are estimated to be at least three to four times as much.

The high incidence of women who zealously over-shop and steal has led to the stark problem of imprisonment. It's not just Winona Ryder who shoplifts. Home Office figures show that a quite remarkable figure of one in three of the female prison

population is there for shoplifting. The figures also show that 80 per cent will reoffend within two years of their release. These people offer no threat to anyone except the profits of the shops – who pass on the costs to us in the form of higher prices. More women are imprisoned for shoplifting than for any other crime. When Tony Blair came to power in 1997, there were 129 female shoplifters in prison; now there are 1,400.[58]

But this dark side of our consumer culture is hardly ever discussed. Prison is an easy way to deal with the symptom but few want to look at the causes of empty lives and useless materialistic hopes. Shoplifters expose the fraud of turbo-consumerism. They don't just lift the goods but the lid on the system, exposing its intent to sell us stuff we don't need by exploiting our anxieties and insecurities. They are what we could be if we don't keep ourselves in check and in some semblance of control. They hold up a mirror to us, showing us the horror of what happens when shopping goes wrong; the ugly, dark and disownable side of the shopping myth.

This madness can't go on

The consumer society was a fantastic success. At least for the industrial consumer complex. Until the financial crash, it was doing precisely what it is supposed to do. It kept us on the treadmill of identity formation through what we buy. But the impossibly high standards we've come to expect of our bodies, homes and lifestyles in pursuit of the perfect consumer have taken their toll. Yet even as we reflect on this problem the market finds a way to win. The term 'status anxiety' comes from a book of that title by Alain de Botton. In a review Steven Poole argues that the irony of the book is the way in which it is presented and beautifully designed 'not as a work of thought but as an object, a status symbol'. Poole goes on, 'If you read it on the train or in a coffee shop, you are declaring that not only are you the kind of sensitive, thoughtful person who reads improving literature, you are the

kind of successful person who can afford to buy it in hardback.'[59]
So we end up with status anxiety over *Status Anxiety*.

And we're all unhappier for it. Each year three million of us
go to our GP suffering from anxiety. One in three of us will suffer from depression. Apart from selling a few self-help books, is
the response of caring capitalism to address the causes of mental
illness and provide psychological support? No. The answer, of
course, is to sell us something. Drugs are one of the big money-
spinning 'solutions'. Global sales of antidepressants total more
than £9 billion, making them the third best-selling class of drugs
in the world. But the fact is that depression has never been so
prevalent since the introduction of antidepressants. There was no
market for antidepressants before the 1960s – before, that is, a
company called Merck was looking to publicize the antidepres-
sant properties of amitriptyline. To do this Merck bought 50,000
copies of a book called *Recognizing the Depressed Patient*, by Frank
Ayd, a psychiatrist, and distributed them among other psychia-
trists and doctors worldwide. Ayd's thesis was that depression, far
from being confined to asylums, could equally well be diag-
nosed in general medical wards and primary-care surgeries.
Merck not only sold amitriptyline, it sold an idea. The company
magnified a problem to sell a product.

In many ways our lives are much better than they were. Just a
few generations ago people worked as servants, had little money,
even less time and virtually nothing to show for it. Some of
them may have been depressed as well. The point is not to argue
for a golden age that never was but to recognize that lives that
inevitably become all consuming at best make us miserable and
at worst drive us mad. We live in an age of abundance and we
don't know how to cope. In particular we don't know how to
cope as individual consumers when we are genetically disposed
to be social actors. The individualization of risk and the loss of
control that comes with it have left us marooned in a private
consumer hell.

In ancient literature monsters have been defined as the self-
sufficient, those who are alienated from others. In *Frankenstein*,

the updated version of this idea, we see the ultimate monster, a creature that lives but is created for someone else's benefit, is separate and alone. We are born dependent but empathy, co-operation and compassion are blunted by the market. The fewer personal bonds you have, the more you are likely to shop. 'It's the image not the face,' Amanda told us earlier . We can choose and change our image in a life of endless consumption, continually attempting to find the 'real me' in what we buy. So we exist, like the human batteries in the film *The Matrix*, not for our fulfilment and pleasure but to reproduce a system that doesn't work for us. In the process we are losing our capacity to be human. We have become our own personal brands – our own monsters.

In 2008 the Joseph Rowntree Foundation published a report of an extensive public consultation to find the ten 'social evils' that afflict British society today. They include: a decline of community, with the rise of individualism and selfishness, the decline of values, the decline of the family, immigration and responses to immigration, poverty and inequality. The last was 'consumerism and greed'. It is consumerism that lies at the heart of our social and environmental problems. As one website participant in the consultation said, 'We are in danger of losing sight of what is important in life, like kindness, playfulness, generosity and friendship. The immaterial things that can't be bought and sold.'

We are told that this is a free country and that in a free country we will be happy. But we have simply the freedom to shop. A freedom that means everything is convenient but we still have no time for what we really care about, that makes us feel like kings as consumers but pawns as citizens, that leaves us picking what we want from the shelves but unable to influence the big decisions that really affect our lives. Our pockets may be deep but our lives feel shallow. We can fly to anywhere in Europe for as little as twenty pounds but we can't guarantee that we can walk our own streets safely at night, that our sons won't be attacked or that our daughters won't self-harm. We have more information than we can handle, more clothes than we can wear and more food than we can eat. But what do we want? More!

This is the monoculture that will dictate our future – a future of more. One astute commentator explained our rootless, restless and over-consumerized lives like this:[60]

You'll be bored with your work, your spouses, your lovers, the view from your window, the furniture, or wallpaper in the room, your thoughts, yourselves. Accordingly you will try to devise a way to escape . . . You may take up changing jobs, residence, company, country, climate, you may take up promiscuity, alcohol, travel, cooking lessons, drugs, psychoanalysis. In fact, you may well lump all these together and for a while that may work. Until the day, of course, when you wake up in your bedroom amid a new family and different wallpaper, in a different state and climate, with a heap of bills from your travel agent and your shrink, yet with the same stale feeling toward the light of day poring through the window.

This is a bleak picture. It is not shopping that is the problem but the creation of a society based on shopping., which by definition means a life of turbo-consumerism. Our lives are out of control because the means of control, collective decision-making and enforcement, have been swept away by the consumer tide. The recession means that the tide is turning once more. The politicians, retailers, producers and marketing consultants that make up the industrial consumer complex want us to return as quickly as possible to such an all-consuming life. We have to make the decision now to counter the forces of turbo-consumerism and find other, more compelling, ways of living the good life.

4. What's the alternative?

Put the basket down!

It would be really funny if you decided now that it was just all too much and the only answer to an all-consuming society was another bout of retail therapy. You could be happy – for a bit. But before you give up and succumb to the dark side of shopping, let's assess whether or not anything can be done to create an alternative that is better than the consumer society. The goal, remember, is not to stop shopping and consuming, which we will always need to do for both physical and emotional reasons. Instead, the answer is to strike a sustainable and rewarding balance between what we do as consumers and a more fulfilling life as citizens, friends, colleagues, community and family members. But by definition there can be no balance in a consumer society, let alone a new turbo variety with go-faster stripes. The free market doesn't do balance – that's why we're in this mess. Consuming has to stop being the prime way in which we define our lives if we are to exert any control over it. So, we have to make the shift to a post-consumer society. But how?

Fundamental social change always requires four things: a strong sense of grievance that something is going badly wrong; a vision of something better that mixes desirability with feasibility; the creation of a group of people big enough and strong enough to make change happen; and an event or turning point that provides the catalyst for a fundamental rethink about the way society is organized and for what purpose. All four of these conditions for change are now in place.

We have seen that there are strong grounds for grievance: not only is consumer society causing psychological harm, social dislocation, physical distress and potential environmental disaster

but the problems are getting worse as, indeed, they are bound to: the industrial consumer complex eats into the ability of society and the planet to be sustained. The crisis of over-consumption would have happened at some point. There is a strong sense of grievance and a lot of people, as we will see, who want change and are making it happen. They and a host of organizations, thinkers and writers have a vision of a different kind of society in which the forces of turbo-consumerism are held at bay. Until now nothing looked as though it could stop rampant consumer capitalism from reigning supreme. Its powers of seduction had effectively bought us off. Now the treadmill has come to a juddering halt. Everything is possible, but only if we decide so. We have our turning point.

The trick is to pull all this together into a coherent project for change. This won't be easy, first because our instinctive response is to want to return to a life of turbo-consumerism. Shopping is still the way in which we define ourselves as being normal members of society. Second, the consumer machine works relentlessly to ensure that everything that possibly can be commodified in our lives is, and in the process any alternative way of living is denied the space and oxygen to exist. Our consumer monoculture makes it very difficult for us to see our way through, round and out of it. It may have been compensation for the 'real thing' but life on the consumer treadmill was good enough to stop the majority of us searching for anything better. But the crash means consumerism is failing to deliver its side of the deal. We are no longer sedated by an endless stream of new consumer purchases. All of that has dried up. The shock has been our wake-up call. What happens next is down to us.

If we don't want to go back, literally, to 'business as usual', we need a convincing vision of a better life and a way of achieving it. There are two ways in which we can make this happen. Both are necessary and interlinked. First, we can start to create an alternative reality on our own. Every day we can make decisions to buy differently and to buy less. Individual action empowers and enlightens us and lots of small changes can make a big difference.

But as well as change from the bottom of society we need change from the top. We need a critical mass of people to act and can't assume they will without some support and awareness that everyone else is playing their part. We need laws and regulations that help create a post-consumer society. This demands we shift from the market state we have now to a social state, whose goal is a world in which a better balance is possible. If consumer society was systematically constructed though ideas, political action and business decisions, it must be systematically deconstructed and a better alternative put in its place. This demands more than taking action alone, it requires that we do things together to put in place the ideas and legal framework that could halt turbo-consumerism and help make a post-consumer world possible. It is the combination of the two, individual and collective action, that will get us what we want.

Going it alone

Since the financial crisis struck, everyone has had to struggle in some way to readjust to tighter financial circumstances. But should we see this as a frustrating blip before we return to the bad old days of consuming too much in the impossible hope that it will make us happy? No one wanted the recession but we can use it as an opportunity to change the way we live for the better. For some time people have been testing other ways of living for the rest of us. They have been doing so from choice, before the economic crash forced the rest of us to readjust and rethink. Welcome to the world of the ethical consumers and downshifters, the people who are shopping better and consuming less. They matter because they give us a taste of life built on controlling and containing the urge to consume rather than allowing it to control us. It's being prefigurative. It's action in the here and now that gives us a glimpse of a future that is qualitatively different from what we have now. Because the ethical shoppers and downshifters are trying to change the system from

within, they may not live totally perfect lives in terms of the inevitable contradictions and limitations that are bound to emerge: they operate within a bubble of a society that is still all consuming, but they could be a bridgehead to a different type of future. One that is more rewarding, free and fun than the world we live in now.

Downshifting

Say the words 'the good life' and anyone over thirty-five will immediately think of Tom and Barbara from the 1970s BBC sit-com. But a good life is one that increasing numbers of us aspire to. According to a British Market Research Bureau survey, carried out in association with Cambridge University in April 2005, 25 per cent of British adults aged between thirty and fifty-nine had chosen to downshift over the previous ten years, earning around 40 per cent less than they did before. By 1997, 1.7 million people in Britain had already 'downshifted', accepting lower pay and more modest living conditions in return for liberation from the drudgery of a full-on work-and-spend life. The number was predicted to reach 3.7 million by 2007.[61] Lots of people are refusing to allow the cult of more to dictate their lives and instead are taking back control to determine a better balance between what they consume and what else they do in their lives.

Prominent among the new breed of downshifters are the TIREDs – Thirty-something Independent Radical Educated Dropouts. Young professionals are increasingly quitting high-powered jobs and opting for more fulfilling lives. New research shows that, as they hit their thirties, many workers in law, finance, technology and the media are suffering from burn-out and want to drop out of the rat race. When they entered the job market in the 1990s, the now successful young thirty-somethings were more worried about their career and money than previous generations had been. But this drive has led to aspiration deficit, a sense of being short-changed by the gruelling work that is the prerequisite of their all-consuming lives.

But they are not alone. What we value is shifting. According to MORI data in 1998, when people were asked if they would prefer more time or money, 42 per cent wanted more time and only 41 per cent wanted more money. The most common reason given was the desire to spend more time with the family. More than one in ten employees, a staggering 2.3 million, would like to work fewer hours even if this involved a cut in pay. But their employment terms and conditions won't allow them to do so.

A 2006 BBC survey suggests the emergence of a large, socially and environmentally conscious set of people whose concerns are far ahead of the decision-makers in power. The survey estimates that around twenty million people share a set of positive values based on fairness, openness, integrity and optimism; 91 per cent of them disagree that money is the best measure of success. They are deeply concerned about the environment, with 86 per cent strongly agreeing that we have to come together for the good of our community and environment. They are seeking change, with 64 per cent strongly agreeing that they are open to new ideas and new solutions. All these people were quietly changing Britain even before the crash.

These surveys dispel the widespread myth that downshifting is confined to a small majority and means selling up in the city and moving to the countryside to live a life closer to nature. While the rural idyll is the route chosen by some downshifters, the phenomenon is predominantly an urban one: the downshifter is more likely to be found next door than in Cornwall. The survey results dispel a second myth about downshifting: it is widely believed that the phenomenon is confirmed to middle-aged wealthier individuals who, having accumulated substantial assets, can afford to take the risk. In fact, downshifters are spread fairly evenly across all age and social groups, although with only a slightly higher proportion among social grades A and B and a lower share among grade E. In a report by Clive Hamilton, when downshifters were asked to assess their new life more than 90 per cent said they were happy with the change, with two in

five saying they didn't miss the extra income at all. Only six per cent were unhappy.[62]

Downshifting is not just happening in Britain. A group of ten friends in San Francisco, calling themselves the Compact, boycotted non-essential consumer goods for a year. Named after the *Mayflower* pilgrims, in 2006 they decided to buy only essential goods, like new underwear, toiletries and food. Instead they swapped, borrowed, traded and built from scratch. It meant they could pay off their mortgages and credit-card bills, and build up their children's college fund faster. These people were not dropping out of society but radically experimenting with downsizing their consumer lives. Some have continued their lives in the same vein and dozens of copy-cat groups have sprung up all over the US and the world.

Downshifting can help make you happier because in terms of balance there is less work and more life. Commuting, stress, workplace disputes, annual pay or bonus worries become more marginal. But it's not just about more time to do what you enjoy or be with those you love. Downshifters know, too, that they are reducing their carbon footprint, doing less harm to the environment, and feel better for it. They are also putting themselves in more control of their lives and gaining a sense of well-being as a consequence. They are determining more of their lives by reducing the impact of external forces like brands and adverts. More of their lives are spent being truly free to do as they please – not just to buy what they were once seduced and compelled into splashing out on. Their whole life orientation has changed: consumption is just part of what they do, no longer their primary activity.

Less can be more. Simple can be more satisfying. Tom Hodgkinson knows this. Tom is Mr Idle. The mantra of the idler is 'Don't just do something, sit there.' I hear him talk on a platform at an event in London about 'Medieval values: why going back will set us free'. In medieval times, Tom explains, overwork was a sign of lack of faith in God. It meant you were taking your fate into your own hands. This is why in Catholic countries like

Spain there is more rest and play than in more secular nations like Britain. It is unlikely that we will ever go back to religious domination but the past gives us a glimpse of what is possible. Before the sixteenth-century Reformation, life in England was a series of festivals, carnivals and holidays. Christmas took twelve days and you were forbidden to work. Candlemas came in early February, then Valentine's Day, Shrovetide, with another ten days off, and Easter. The Hocktide was followed by St. George's Day, May Day, Midsummer's Eve, Peter's Eve, Lammas, Martinmas, Advent and Christmas again. Work was hard but restricted to short, sharp bouts of activity. Often it was only three days a week. You had your own smallholding and practised a craft. Before organized capitalism, production was often based round guilds of apprenticed craftsmen whose focus was on quality, not quantity and profit. The rubbish men were the pigs. Wind was the source of power, as it is starting to become again. Households were highly self-sufficient. Hospitality, neighbourliness and charity were valued. Money-lending was frowned upon. A wake after the death of an aristocrat meant three or four days of partying for everyone.

The notion of idleness came to Tom from within but also from reading the likes of Dr Johnson – the famous essayist of the mid-1700s. Johnson said that work should happen in fits and starts and this was the most natural and productive way of being. His own output was prodigious but it was achieved in bouts of frenzy, then laziness. 'Idleness is our natural order,' Tom argues. 'Just look at the contestants on *Big Brother* who sleep a lot and don't exist around nine-to-five living.'

Does he regret or miss anything? Nothing, he says. He has no pressing material needs except good books. He likes earning and spending but he likes other things more. It is a question of balance but one that Tom has created for himself by turning away from the more culture of turbo-consumerism. Tom and other idlers are proof that we can de-consume our lives and discover a new world of pleasure. Tom is interesting because he uses the past to make us think about our present and possible future. We

can only learn from the past; there is no going back to it. But we can use it to find a new balance between working, consuming and leisure. And through the past we can understand our turbo-consuming world as a blip in the interregnum between a life of scarcity and unsustainable abundance. Tom believes that the only thing stopping us is ourselves. But this is too simplistic: he possessed not only the instinct to be idle but the wherewithal and the confidence. If it was just a simple decision, why aren't even more people making it? It's difficult because the cult of consumerism is now deeply embedded in us. Giving up on the addiction and opting not to be normal is a tough ask for most of us.

I feel like a bit of an idler myself. I once worked from 7.30 a.m. to 8.00 p.m. most days, in an office, visiting other offices. Now I mainly work from home. At home we do more in less time. There's no commuting and it's another set of outfits we don't have to buy. In an office, factory or shop we perfect the art of doing the smallest amount of work in the longest possible time. Four hours of work at home is a whole day in the office. Being self-employed means you are unlikely to have a pension. But the point is to create a life you don't want to retire from. After all, the most important thing we have to give after love is our labour. Why give it away cheaply in the pursuit of more? Not all of us can work from home. We can all make decisions to work less. But we will need help.

To be an idler or a downshifter in a consumer society is to be more subversive than any terrorist or anti-globalizer. Downshifters don't want a deal on land or self-rule, they don't want someone else to stop doing this or that, they just want to do more of what makes them happy. It's not about doing nothing, but doing enough of everything. Downshifters still have to pay their tax bill, they are still part of society, but beyond its emotional and seductive reach, beyond bribes, punishment, control or monitoring. Tom and others have jumped off the treadmill and survived, even thrived, to tell the tale. The Right Reverend Stephen Cottrell is a man of God cast in the same idler's image. He advocates using an egg-timer to be still for three minutes. For most

of us our blood would be boiling after 180 seconds of inaction. But we find idleness doesn't mean that the world collapses around us. Instead we find a life that isn't all consuming. So we can consume less and be happier. But we can also consume differently – and that will make us happier too.

In a recession downshifting is both harder and easier. When times are tough we can retrench and hang on more strongly to the things we have, and desire even more the things we don't. But it is also a possible turning point when we can think again about what matters to us. Events outside our control are reducing our spending money and creating a genuine opportunity for us to reassess what we value. There are some key steps to downshifting: first, understand yourself and what makes you happy, what your values are – for instance, good health might be as important as more time. Then sit down and go through your budget. Work out what feels essential and eliminate at least three items you can easily do without. Cut up at least one of your credit cards. It might not stop you spending more but it's a wonderful symbolic act of defiance. Then donate, recycle or freecycle (www.uk.freecycle.org) any clothes you haven't worn for six months or a year. You are starting to take back control. Eventually you need to find the point of comfort that works for you – a level of income and therefore expenditure that allows you to balance your life properly. This cannot feel like a period of enforced abstinence but a long-term commitment to a different way of living that is more enjoyable and more rewarding.

It will become so when you start to discover new pleasures in doing more things for yourself. Start cooking more meals using organic ingredients and stop buying so many ready meals or going to restaurants. Turn off the TV more often at night and read a book, listen to the radio or play a game with the rest of the family. Start to take yourself away from adverts and the celebrity culture that drives our shopping addiction. Many people have started making things again by rediscovering old crafts and establishing new ones. This has really taken off since the crash as a cheaper way to get hold of new clothes and give

presents. We are seeing the rise of knitting as a cool pastime and craft fairs embracing old-fashioned activities like embroidery and crochet. Making stuff can be fun, social, and is a statement against mass consumerism, uniformity and the damage to the planet. It is a DIY culture that starts to put us back in control.[63] In April 2008 Argos reported that sales of sewing machines had increased by 50 per cent in twelve months. As reasons for this, they cited a backlash against the 'throwaway society' and social and environmental concerns. DIY fashion doesn't transform anything straight away but questions are asked and boundaries shifted. The terms of debate are no longer what they were. Life isn't just about what you buy on the treadmill of consumption but what you can do yourself.

Take small steps to cut down working and therefore earning. Don't work overtime unless you have to and make sure you take all your holiday entitlement. Then you can try to renegotiate your hours of work. Remember, it is now a statutory right to be able to ask for more flexible working. Finally, you might want to switch job completely to work less or differently – perhaps work from home. There is lots of information and help out there about how to downshift: go to www.downsizer.net and if you want to test whether you are ready to downshift try the test at www.pru. co.uk/home/calculator/downshift/. The secret is to be committed to a better life but do a bit at a time. We didn't become turbo-consumers overnight and we won't stop quickly, but a better life is out there for all of us and it's doable if we approach it sensibly.

Ethical shopping

Shopping less is directly linked to shopping better: this is ethical consumption. *Chambers Dictionary* defines 'ethical' as 'not involving the abuse of natural resources or the exploitation of people or animals'. People have been applying this concept to shopping for a number of years. Organic, locally sourced and Fairtrade goods, the principal components of ethical consumption, have

entered the shopping mainstream because of pressure and demand from below, the morality of some retailers and suppliers and, more latterly, the recognition that money can be made from the growing ethical market.

The recession poses a threat to its continued growth and influence. With money tight, some may think they have to cut back on ethical purchases, which sometimes cost more. This need not be the case. Some, such as Fairtrade coffee, may cost more. But the answer is not to give up on ethics but to recognize that the need to sustain the planet and treat developing-world workers properly is as important now as it was before the recession hit. And, as with downshifting, the experience can bring more pleasure to our lives and be more rewarding. Taking care about what you buy, and valuing it, tends to lead us to consume less and therefore spend less. So the downturn is not a moment to turn our backs on ethical consumption but to deepen our resolve to practise it more effectively.

Kate knows this. She has been a reasonably hard-core ethical shopper for about three years. She says it takes more time and quite a bit more effort but she would never go back to normal, uncaring shopping. When she buys food she looks for the lowest air miles, as much organic as she can afford and the least amount of additives and packaging. She gave up her car and now smiles when she walks past petrol stations and sees the prices. But it means walking or cycling to the nearest Sainsbury's or, where possible, the local shops. All the labels have to be read and compared. And you have to take the time to understand what they mean. She makes all her food; there are no ready meals. She grows some vegetables in her garden and gets a delivery of an organic box every week. Waste is composted.

For clothes it's small boutiques to find designs made locally with as much organic cotton as possible. If it's a chain she will check the website www.labourbehindthelabel.org so that she knows how they treat people. She says her wardrobe was full before she started shopping ethically so there is enough to keep her going.

The result is that she feels a lot healthier and doesn't have to earn so much because she buys less. But it seems to be the emotional pay-off that really counts. Kate feels as if she's more in control of her life and isn't functioning to meet the profit needs of the big corporations. As an ethical consumer in an unethical world she knows she can never totally escape from the dominant consumer culture. Images on billboards and in magazines of what is fashionable are hard for her to ignore. But she says her life is so much better now and she would never go back.

She went on holiday to Corsica recently and took the train and a boat instead of a cheap flight. It took a day and half and was about sixty pounds more expensive than the plane but she says it was much nicer. No airport stress, security, delays or baggage-allowance worries. Instead she went by Eurostar to Paris, then another train to the South of France before the ferry to the island. She watched the changing French countryside pass by and felt a different type of pleasure. We are all going to have to take fewer planes but we will gain more pleasure from holidaying ethically. There is no perfect answer from which we can have it all – the quick, cheap flights and a sustainable planet – but we can decide on a better balance in life.

Thirty years ago, ethical consumption did not exist in any meaningful way. It was pioneered by the likes of the late Anita Roddick, founder of the Body Shop. The last ten years have seen a huge rise in it and at some levels it has had a big impact. Most of us are now ethically aware when we shop, even if awareness doesn't always translate into action. Few get on a flight without thinking about the ecological damage and many of us now frown on four-by-fours. Household spending on ethical goods has doubled in the last five years, according to a report on ethical consumerism published in November 2008 by the Co-op Bank. The total ethical market in Britain was estimated to be worth £35.5 billion, up 15 per cent on the year before. In a recession everyone buys less so it's inevitable that the growth of ethical markets slows too. Indeed, this is what the *Ethical Consumer* magazine was predicting in October 2008. In some areas, like organ-

ically produced eggs, there was a dip in demand during the early months of the recession in the autumn of 2008, but that has since stabilized. Many consumers are switching from organic to free range but not returning to battery-produced. People are finding that they can save money by buying ethically. Energy-efficient light-bulbs last longer and therefore cost less. Ready meals are expensive while home cooking can be cheaper and healthier.

Like downshifting, going ethical is better if it's taken in steps and stages rather than a leap into a totally different way of shopping. You can start by shopping locally. If you don't drive you don't pollute. By supporting local shops you build a sense of community and carrying the bags home will do you good. Once you are in the shops look out for Fairtrade marked products, which guarantee that workers have been fairly rewarded for their labour. Sites such as www.soilassociation.org will tell you what has been organically produced. There are labels, too, for non-genetically manipulated (GM) food and the Vegetarian Society symbol, the big V, is always a good guide to ethical production. In terms of wood products look out for the Forest Stewardship Council logo – it's a tree with a tick by it – which verifies sustainable timber and paper products. There are two further steps to take. The first is in ethical money. Save and invest with the Co-op Bank, which has a truly ethical stance, while the Ecology Building Society will only invest in sustainable and energy-efficient housing. Finally, use recycled products from sites such as www.freecycle.org or buy second-hand products from charity shops or car-boot sales. It saves precious resources, reduces the pressure on landfill sites and can save you money.

Being ethical can't be that hard and must induce new pleasures, given the number who are now practising it. Just before the financial crisis another major report for the Co-op Bank called *Who are the ethical consumers?*, by Roger Cowe and Simon Williams, identified five main groups. The largest was called 'do what I can' and made up 49 per cent of the population. They are concerned shoppers but not sufficiently so to make a deep

impact either on their own lives or on the high street. A second group, making up 18 per cent, is more active. They will buy and boycott products on ethical grounds if the process is made relatively easy in terms of the right information. They are matched by 22 per cent who would rather 'look after their own' and have little or no concern for consumer ethics; instead they are interested in value and convenience. The Co-op report identifies two smaller groups. The first is passionately concerned about these issues, going further than the rest of the population to live up to their values. When buying products they are more interested in social and environmental issues than in brand names. They automatically look for recycled, GM-free and Fairtrade labels. Companies' reputations regularly lead them to buy or avoid certain products and many are active campaigners on ethical issues. They will seek out information they need to make ethical choices, and feel guilty when they don't. They are the global watchdogs making up five per cent of the population. Finally there is a group of six per cent who may become the ethical vanguard of tomorrow if ethical concerns continue to shape brand loyalties. So 72 per cent are doing a lot or at least something ethical and a further six per cent are up for grabs. It's a good place to start.

With such numbers, ethical issues can move quickly from the margins of debate to the centre and real influence. Unleaded petrol, energy-efficient light-bulbs and recycling weren't on the radar just a few years ago. Now everyone is doing at least something that is ethical. Freedom Food eggs won an estimated 16 per cent share of the market in just five years and at the beginning of 2008 accounted for four out of every ten eggs sold. It's not enough to put the brakes on turbo-consumerism but, as they say, 'Every little helps.' One in twenty-five has now switched their holiday plans to avoid eco-damage from planes. They have started a new trend. Now it's cool to stay in Britain or travel by train. Camping has become trendy. They are still living an all-consuming life; it's just they aren't doing so much harm to the planet.

Mintel are predicting that that around half of organic-food

shoppers will switch to non-organic alternatives during the recession as they seek to stretch every penny. But organizations like Mintel never predicted the rise in ethical consumption in the first place. Of course there will be some drop-off, but this isn't the time to lose sight of the fact that a more ethical shopping life can be rewarding and cheaper.

So what about me? How ethical am I? The answer is nowhere near ethical enough. I don't eat meat or fish, in part for moral reasons and in part because I know we can feed more people if we don't use land for grazing. I recycle as much as I can and I cycle as far as I can. I won't go near Starbucks or McDonald's but I don't make enough effort to find out whether my clothes come from ethical sources or what kind of air miles my food has racked up. I'm the usual mass of consumption contradictions as I eat my veggie meal on a long-haul flight. I could and will do lots more. In part it is the time and effort that is required to make more informed purchasing decisions but it is more than that. In the past I tended to put more emphasis on changing the context in which we live – the politics of change not the daily practice. I was sceptical of ethical consumption as just another lifestyle choice in which we might end up spending as much and be just as hooked on the addiction of more. But the more I have looked at and understand the 'buycotting' of consumerism, the more sympathetic to it I become. Ethical behaviour can start to push at the boundaries of what it means to be free and live a good life. It's a step on the ladder but a step that introduces new forms of pleasure that could undo the monoculture of our all-consuming lives. 'Be the change you wish to see in the world,' said Gandhi.

An alternative hedonism

Downshifting and ethical consumption can't just be about doing the right thing but about doing more enjoyable things. Only then will the seductive power of turbo-consumerism be challenged. The problem for people who try to describe a different

life from the joy and rapture of consumer society is that they often sound worthy and dull. It feels like one big sacrifice rather than a better and more enjoyable life. Our consciences might be clear but our hearts sink at the thought of hair-shirt do-gooding. The recession is forcing us to tighten our belts but going without and being in denial is not going to get us out of the shops – at least, not for long if we don't change our understanding of what constitutes the good life. A diet from shopping would just lead to a binge at some later stage. We want to have fun and be creative. But can we have fun without consuming so much?

An idea is beginning to blossom called 'alternative hedonism' and is being put into practice by people like Kate who, as we have seen, are not just doing the right thing through ethical consumption but enjoying a better quality of life. Hedonism is pleasure-seeking self-indulgence. It is something we naturally crave and is a perquisite, in an alternative form, of a post-consumer society that is impossible to conceive, let alone realize, if we feel guilty about experiencing pleasure. The self-righteous and self-deniers win few converts. Another Kate, this time Kate Soper, professor of philosophy at London Metropolitan University, has coined the term 'alternative hedonism'. She understands that to counter the seduction of consumption we need a substitute that is equally compelling and seductive.

Like all good thinkers, Kate starts with the problem, if it ain't broke, why bother trying to fix it? Consumer culture is marked, she says, by speed – high speed on high streets – so that much, she argues, has got worse. When I meet her, she mentions railway stations. Even the new ones like Liverpool Street and St Pancras are just shopping malls attached to platforms and ticket offices. Everywhere and everything is an excuse to sell. Victorians, on the other hand, made stations that were more sensual and authentic. It was a joy to be in them to sit and wait. Now there are so few seats that you have to buy a coffee just to sit down. The trains are not part of a grand public service but engines for private profit.

Many more pleasures and experiences have been lost because

of over-consumption and its consequences. Children no longer play unsupervised. Now, only two out of ten kids play in the streets compared to seven out of ten of their parents. It is not just the fear of traffic or strangers that keeps them indoors but the allure of computer games. They live in a virtual and commercialized world. All of us now tend to graze when we eat. Food is fast and boxed in plastic. We are losing the pleasures of time and taste. We take the escalator, not the stairs, and feel less alive and more like plodding robots. Everywhere looks and feels the same. Clothing is cheaper and thinner. Our senses and pleasures are becoming dulled in a joyless economy of call centres.

But Kate says that unknown pleasures are being unearthed by avant-garde groups of consumers, like those identified in the Co-op Bank report, who want a qualitative change in the nature of shopping. It's not, she says, about moving to the countryside because that just means buying new things for new circumstances. Instead we need to find another way of going forward. It won't be easy but there are people who are good at persuading us. I am reminded of Chris in the advertising agency. At the moment some of the best minds in the world are used to make us want to buy things we don't need. What could the same brilliantly persuasive advertising minds do to encourage us to buy things that are necessary, good for us, more sensual, erotic, playful and aesthetic?

An alternative hedonism takes a leap of imagination. It can't be glimpsed in entirety. We can't imagine a totally different society from the viewpoint of the one we are in because we are too constrained, just as no one could imagine a consumer society from the vantage-point of a producer society. But we can experience snippets of an alternative hedonism. If we were to cut down on flights we would cut out noise. If we reduced the number of cars on the road, we would improve the quality of life for people walking and cycling, and more children would be able to live and play in safety. Cycling brings out new pleasures. We see the world around us in a different way and we experience the elements. When I cycle I stretch my legs and my mind.

I see and experience the world in a more intimate way. In the city it's quicker than public transport or the car, and it gives you time to think and reflect. Dumping the car renews local shops and communities and, of course, helps to save the planet. An alternative hedonism would focus on education valued for its intrinsic worth, and knowledge for its own sake. We would have more quality time with our children, family and friends. And an alternative hedonism would be about the rediscovery of the play ethic.

Children's play should not just be about paid-for toys but real imagination and experimentation. Play is not just an essential aspect of growing up but of being human because it teaches us to try things out and learn that it's not the end of the world if we fail. When we play we release our creativity. And just as we have hidden desires to get back to genuine aspects of our youth so we feel the urge to get back to nature too. Millions of us simply want to walk in the countryside or watch birds. Look at the massive popularity of television programmes like *Coast* and the *Nature Watch* series that strike a chord in millions.

If we want a good life then we need hours and days when we refuse to or can't buy things. The choice to go on choosing has to be taken away. It is time to walk, sit, stare, cycle, daydream, watch clouds, rivers or the sea, jog, go to public buildings, read in the library, volunteer, fly a kite, contemplate in a church or listen to the band in the local park. We can do so much that we really enjoy without having to shop. Of course, in a world of alternative hedonism we can and will still buy things. But we will buy less, the importance of what we buy will be diminished and we will invest in durable designs, classic forms of furniture, and clothes that are built to last – both physically and emotionally. An alternative hedonism will involve a beauty that rejects quick fashion and creates lasting desires rather than eternal disappointments.

Happiness

What Tom, Kate and Kate instinctively feel to be right, that more money doesn't mean more happiness, is now being backed up by science. Thanks to the work of people like Richard Layard,[64] happiness can now be measured. We simply have to ask people how they feel, then ask their friends and family for an independent assessment, and by measuring activity in certain parts of their brain, we can rate their happiness. Through interviews, surveys and experiments we can now tell how happy people are, compare them to others and determine some of the key ingredients of what makes us happy.

We know that up to a certain level of income, enough to meet basic survival needs of warmth and food, which can be as low as £12,000 a year, people grow happier as they get richer. But above this level the link between wealth and happiness starts to break down. More money doesn't buy equivalent levels of happiness, and after a certain point it doesn't make us happier at all. We simply go on earning more in the self-defeating race to have more than those with whom we compare ourselves. Beyond that point, the only time that more money makes us feel better is when we spend it on others or give it away. In Britain we stalled on happiness growth in 1975. Since then our real incomes have doubled but the smiles on our faces have failed to keep up. Happiness science turns on its head the whole logic of Western political economy, which is based on the pursuit of more.

So what makes us happy? Happiness science tells us that fulfilment, contentment, status, hope, security, freedom, trust, religious belief, control over our lives and caring for others (people and animals) make us happy, not what we buy. We are more satisfied by making things than buying them. Our identities as producers satisfy our need to create, to build and invent. It is why professionalism and craft skills matter so much and why the loss of them is fuelling the social recession. Our employment status is a badge we can wear throughout our lives – a

symbol of what we have learnt and can do that is useful for us and society. It places us on solid ground where we have more control over our lives. Once you are a qualified plumber or doctor you don't often feel the urge to retrain as something else to acquire a different identity. But as our identities are increasingly a result of what we consume rather than what we produce, we are operating in fast-flowing currents in which survival and security mean making a constant effort to keep up and reinvent ourselves.

One index of happiness for different activities ranks average happiness against the percentage of the day it takes up. It shows how our lives are currently oriented around things that don't make us very happy rather than things that do. At the top came sex at an average happiness of 4.3, taking up two per cent of the day. Second came relaxing, with a score of 3.7 for 14 per cent of the day, and third socializing, at 3.6 for 15 per cent of the day. At the bottom were work and commuting, at 2.3 for 41 per cent of the day and 2.1 for 11 per cent respectively. Shopping came just below the middle at an index rating of 2.8 for three per cent of the day.[65] Not a great score for the activity that determines more than anything what kind of society we live in.

Lasting happiness, like the creation of an alternative to the consumer society, will require more than individual action: it requires a collective response to change the choice of choices we have. Only together can we decide when and where we don't want to choose. Individual unhappiness is the result of collective-action failure and we cannot fix alone a problem we created together. Enough people have to break out of the collective failure of wanting more, and enough people have to put in place ways of regulating and containing the march of the market. So it's important to understand the limits of going it alone and the value of working together.

The limits of individual and ethical action

Buying better is the first step on the ladder to a different way of living. Buying less is the second. Both raise awareness and create pressure for change. They help the planet and make us feel better about ourselves. They are absolutely necessary steps towards a different kind of life. But on their own they are insufficient to put a brake on consumer society and create the conditions for a post-consumer world.

The problem is that 'ethical consumption' can mean whatever we want it to mean. It leaves decisions to individual conscience and morality. Some people may choose to act but what if enough don't? What if the seduction of turbo-consumption is too great for too many? In February 2008 another report from the Co-op Bank found that more people were interested in animal welfare than climate change. The fact that more animals will suffer and die from climate change than from cruelty in the production process hadn't struck them. Despite all the hype, organic purchases still only accounted for 1.6 per cent of farm production in the UK by March 2008. It's not nearly enough to make a difference.

Second, both ethical consumption and downsizing shift the entire onus of responsibility on to the individual when the process can be complicated. Some people are insisting on buying locally to save carbon emission from transport costs. But food miles tell us little except distance travelled. Green beans from Kenya are grown using manual labour not machines. So there is less effect from emissions and people are being paid a wage. And if you drive to the supermarket to buy a packet of beans you can create more carbon emissions than resulted from flying them, with all the other beans, to the UK. Organic farming is less efficient than industrial techniques and takes up more land. There are dozens of ethical trademarks to confuse us and the EU currently has three levels of eco-labelling. The confusion can be seen in a survey the National Consumer Council conducted

into which was Britain's most trusted company. The number-
one response from the general public was Tesco. Asked
unprompted which company they trusted least the answer was
– yes, you guessed it – Tesco. We use different yardsticks all the
time. And as individuals we understandably ask, Why should I
make all the effort if no one else does? There is no guarantee
that others will follow.

Finally, what if people buy more ethically but consume more
so the net effect is that the seductive grip of consumption is
tightened, and in the process we avoid the big issues of creating
a different type of society and the means to achieve it? The danger is that 'ethical' becomes an excuse for guilt-free shopping
with the same consumer mindset – it's just another form of consumption. Anya Hindmarch created a stir when her five-pound
reusable shopping bags for Sainsbury's were snapped up – as a
fashion statement, of course. As you parade around with your
'I'm not a plastic bag' are you making a stand or a fashion statement? Is that the ethical box ticked before you get down to
some serious shopping to fill it? In the decision to 'go ethical'
there is the looming danger of being co-opted to the 'dark side'
in which we end up buying more, or that being 'ethical' becomes
just another lifestyle choice that changes little but eases our consciences.

This is a growing concern because producers and retailers
know that the ethics area is fast becoming a function of brand
loyalty. And we need to remember that their goal is always to get
us to buy more – ethically or otherwise. NetJet, a private airline,
announced in November 2007 that they would insist their customers offset the carbon impact of their flight – but in explaining the rationale, the chairman, Mark Booth, said, 'This will add
a lot of lustre to our brand.'[66] He felt his customers could afford
to pay extra and would enjoy the social credit and bragging
rights it bestowed on them. Their conscience would be clean
even if the planet wasn't.

'Don't throw anything away, there is no away,' runs an advert
in one of the Sunday supplements. It is for Shell, a company not

just responsible for ecological disasters like Brent Spar but whose profits are predicated on the destruction of the planet through petrol-induced carbon emissions. But they often get top marks for being good corporate citizens. Meanwhile some companies are actively snubbing ethical demands. Ford advertises the Fiesta Zetec Climate with the words 'Most people would prefer a hot climate'! And successful ethical firms are inevitably being bought up by profit-maximizing corporations. Rachel's Organics was bought by US Dean Foods, Ben & Jerry by Unilever, Green & Black by Cadbury Schweppes, Body Shop by L'Oréal and Aveda by Estée Lauder. Which begs the question: is L'Oréal's commitment to ethical behaviour just cosmetic and skin deep? To find the answer *Ethical Consumer* rated companies before and after their takeover; the scores are out of twenty and account for their impact on the environment, human rights, animal welfare and political activity. Before takeover, Ben & Jerry scored 15, and after, 1.5; PJ Smoothies also crashed from 12 to 1.5; Prêt à Manger from 13 to 7; Green & Black from 16.5 to 9.5.[67] So there is a serious impact from ethical companies literally selling out.

Nike runs an anti-bullying campaign in schools to boost its ethical credentials, but it is exclusive and expensive brands like Nike that demarcate social acceptance on the poorest housing estates in the country. What trainers you wear determines how much respect you get. Nike helps create a competitive consumer culture by producing more and more must-have designs that lead to envy and bullying. Ninety-nine per cent of FTSE 100 companies have some kind of ethical programme, but until the credit crunch we were buying more and more, the climate wasn't getting any less warm and social inequality was still growing. We need something more than the lone ethics of consumers or companies, which feels too much like relying on 'the invisible hand of the market' to do the right thing. As we have now conclusively seen, this approach is already failing both society and the planet. Expecting individual acts of ethical consumers to transform society is asking too much. They are a vital first step towards a different society, necessary but not sufficient. There are

no purely local and ethical solutions to globally and systematically produced problems. We need systematic solutions that
require collective action to be built on individual ethics.

This is not, and I reiterate not, an excuse to stop buying ethically. There can be no collective solutions without individual
action and no successful individual action without a change in
the context of our social and economic aspirations; that can only
come about if we work together. Change happens in the spaces
of cultural conflict between corporations, government, the
media, citizens and pressure groups. It only comes when pressure from the bottom meets a new paradigm coming from the
top. It is that requirement for a decisive shift beyond an all-
consuming society to which we now turn.

The case for collective action

Consumer society and its turbo-charged successor were not created only by the individual actions of lone shoppers. We became
an all-consuming nation, as we have seen, because groups of
people with political beliefs and self-interest made it happen.
The Enclosures Act, the work ethic, privatization and the ending
of consumer credit controls were political acts to fashion a consuming world. If we want to rebalance our lives and society and
stop the march of the market, individual acts radicalize people,
build confidence and show the way. But it will take concerted
collective action too.

The case for collective action starts with a different way of
valuing ourselves and our lives than the possessive individualism
of consumer society. Here, the work of Abraham Maslow is
helpful if we want to establish a post-consumer society. Maslow
was a psychologist who, in a 1943 paper, came up with the
notion of human beings having a hierarchy of needs. He established a five-stage model. The first and lowest need is biological
and physiological: food, drink, shelter and warmth. From the
bottom rung of the ladder we progress to safety needs, such as

protection, security, and law and order. The next need is to belong to a family and enjoy wider social bonds and relation-ships. The fourth is a sense of self-esteem that comes with achievement, status and reputation. This is where most of us feel we are now. But it's not the highest of Maslow's hierarchy. At the top of the ladder he puts 'self-actualization' of personal growth and fulfilment. This is where it gets interesting. It is at this stage that we become the authors of our own lives, writing our own narratives about who we are, what our place in the world is and, therefore, the nature of that world.

Maslow proposed that people who have reached the stage of self-actualization will sometimes experience a state he referred to as 'transcendence', in which they become aware not only of their own fullest potential but that of human beings at large. And he makes the point that individuals who reach a state of trans-cendence experience not only ecstatic joy but also profound 'cosmic-sadness' at the ability of humans to foil their chance of transcendence in their own lives and in the world at large.

It would be easy to dismiss Maslow's claims of a higher state of human awareness and transcendence if not for one important fact: his work has been keenly interpreted and deployed by mar-keting psychologists to sell us more and more things. It's one reason why adverts now try to appeal to us not on functional performance but on the basis of emotional needs. Coca-Cola is all about belonging to a world citizenship, not about quenching our thirst, because the latter is a higher-order need and therefore more compelling. 'The poorest man is not without a penny but without a dream.' What wonderful and uplifting words – from an advert for www.pokerstar.com, an online gambling website. The 'dream' is, of course, to get rich quickly and easily because being rich means you can buy, and buying is held to be the only route to happiness. This is a constrained version of autonomy or freedom.

Freedom, instead of being the ability to shape the world around you, has become something you buy. The marketing world has grabbed Maslow and turned our higher desires into

higher sales, diverting us from our search for authenticity down the dead-end track of turbo-consumerism. Nowhere is this more apparent than in the deluge of transformation TV shows like *The Swan* and *Extreme Makeover* or *Ten Years Younger*, which define the scope for authenticity as the physical manifestation and transformation of our appearance. A new outfit, new teeth, some plastic surgery and a haircut is all you need to become truly yourself. Of course, that's until we need another physical transformation to become even more like ourselves.

But if Maslow is right, consumerism can only be a pale shadow of living the authentic and self-authored life. We are not writing our own script but following the comic-book pictures in a story written by others that is ultimately and always about the self-defeating pursuit of happiness through what we buy – a painfully limiting and dissatisfying way of being free.

At our core we are about self-survival, Maslow's first step out of the swamp. But at every stage of our evolution we are not just seeking survival but looking to flourish fully as individuals in the only way we can – in a social context with others. Remember Sharon and Sarah's shopping outings? They were purchasing but shopping was an excuse. It was a backdrop to being social, to being with each other, to taking out friends and engaging with others, just as much as it was an opportunity to consume individually and privately. We love the social experience of the shopping event even though the driver is individual self-fulfilment. It is one reason why there are likely to be social limits to what we buy on the Internet. Whether it is queuing to get the latest Harry Potter book or being at the cinema on the first night for the latest James Bond movie, our desire to be social cannot be extinguished but is instead channelled into what we buy. The *Friends* TV series is massively popular not just because it's well scripted and funny but because it offers an idealized vision of a life we would like to lead – full of people like us whom we can rely on. It is our need for friends and the happiness they provide that led Doritos to run a series of adverts calling their snacks 'friendchips'. Not a bad pun but a bag of tortilla chips, even ones

cut into triangles, are unlikely to satisfy our need for real friend-ships. Our desire for authenticity has been derailed by consum-erism. At best we get a proxy for real solidarity. As ever it is compensation for the real thing. At worst it creates a monocul-ture in which we are trapped. It is freedom where, in the words of Jean-Jacques Rousseau, we learn 'to love our own slavery'.[68]

Instead of freedom being an individual pursuit based on what we can buy, we have to redefine it as something we can only achieve together. If freedom is about control of our lives and our society then this, by definition, is something we must strive to achieve together. The job cannot be done alone. Alone, all we can do is choose what has been put before us, making individual decisions about how ethical we are. These can matter enor-mously, but don't take us far enough. We cannot determine a different set of choices or stop competing with each other through what we buy without having created the conditions for an alternative way of living with other people. Vested interests have a strong profit motive that has locked us into a cycle of self-defeating behaviour. We are eternally ratcheting up our expecta-tions as others ratchet theirs up against us. It is a collective-action problem that leaves us insecure, lonely and exhausted, and demands collective action to put it right.

Together we must put a stop to the competition for status through consumption. But to do this we all have to change, or at least a critical mass of us, to flip the system. In part this is instrumental: it is about our own self-interest. We can't cater for our security, health or education alone, only with others. But it is also intrinsic: it is about the quality of the life we want to lead and the society we want to live in. Being with other peo-ple makes us happy. Love, friendship, co-operation and notions of mutual obligation are an essential part of Maslow's hierarchy and come into conflict with the individualizing and privatiz-ing forces of consumerism. To be happy is to have some sense of security, the knowledge that your job will last, that you have a secure place to live, that you have a pension and that you can walk the streets safely at night. A consumer society that

prioritizes private over public spending, that is based on making work as flexible as possible, is about spending now, not saving for later, mitigates against much of what makes us happy. Greater solidarity makes us happier. And as social-capital experts, like Robert Putnam, have found, the more groups we belong to, the longer we live and the happier we are. This is why phenomena such as the online networking site Facebook are interesting. Here people compete not for visible material superiority but for who has the most friends.

We have an instinct to be social and co-operative. What we need is the space and time for these instincts to flourish along-side our undoubted ability to be competitive and individualistic if we are to reach the level of self-actualization. Either that or the five-blade razor is the highest form of human existence. Until, of course, the six-blade razor comes along.

But for real freedom, the freedom to control, with others, the world around us, there are two other requirements, as well as the need to work together. The first is greater equality, and the second is some level of compulsion in some areas of our lives to stop us shopping. Along with our own ethical behaviour, greater collective action, a more equal society and rules about what we should be made to do, in our own interest, create the framework in which a post-consumer society could be established.

The case for greater equality

If a new basis for freedom requires collective action it also demands greater equality. In theory, in a consumer society, you are free to do whatever you like. You are free to buy the most expensive handbag on the planet, but such freedom is meaning-less without the means to pay for it. So our effective freedom to do anything is constrained by how much money we have. If we want to maximize freedom then we should ensure that people have sufficient resources to pay for things. In a society that defines normality by what we can afford to buy growing inequality creates more and more people labelled as abnormal.

We need to find a better way of balancing our resources so that all have the opportunity to express their freedom as fully as possible.

A post-consumer society would be founded on the belief that we are all born equal. That does not mean we are born the same but instead that we all have an equal right to make the most of our lives, regardless of our capacity to achieve. Clearly some are born into richer families than others, with quicker brains, better memories, greater charm, a winning smile or faster legs. Others are born with a disability, are more prone to ill health or to live their lives in poverty. But these are accidents of birth over which we have no control. Why should two babies born in the same place at the same time be expected to face either every advantage or every disadvantage based on the accident of who they are born to and therefore all of the financial, genetic and social implications of that piece of brute luck?

Thankfully, we are all different and we should celebrate that difference. But we should all be able to achieve everything we can. Those born with huge advantages are highly likely to thrive; those born to disadvantage should be given sufficient help to ensure they can live the fullest possible lives too. Everyone has the right to be a fully fledged member of society. But consumer society is based on an eternally competitive view of life, of who is the best shopper, and this takes no account of the luck factor in who our parents are. Indeed, the endless competitive cycle of consumerism exacerbates the luck advantages or disadvantages. Life chances can only be evened up through the collective act of their redistribution – not because we are all the same but because we are all different and deserve the chance to fully express that difference.

The credit crisis offers both opportunity and threat to a move towards greater equality of life chances and outcomes. The threat is that in times of greater hardship people become less generous to others and keener to hang on to everything they have got. But there is an equally compelling case that a recession can be a great leveller. Now more people are experiencing hardship and

know that doing less well isn't their fault. They may not have more sympathy for others who suffer the hardship of poverty but they are more likely to back calls for collective action to safeguard against the perils of an economic downturn. This was the case after the depression of the 1930s, which eventually led to the construction of the equalizing institutions of the welfare state. If the pain of this recession is spread, then it may boost empathy and understanding across class and social division rather than diminish it.

The case for compulsion

But it may take even more than voluntary collective action and greater equality to shift us from our all-consuming habit. The desire to hunt and gather is burnt deep into our souls. If we are still conditioned to live as if survival was based on scarcity then we may have to accept that governments should be empowered to act to force us to stop consuming. Even as we face a period of relative scarcity during the downturn our instinct is still to consume.

In the face of financial chaos and irreversible climate change what will shift our behaviour quickly enough? We can't wait until, as a species, we evolve to cope with abundance. Then it will be too late. If our desire to consume is not quelled we will simply return to turbo-consumption once the economy rebounds. which it inevitably will at some stage. We need mass concerted action now.

To help me find an answer to how this might come about I ask Andrew Simms of the New Economics Foundation (nef), an expert in sustainability. He says that Britain's wartime experience of rationing points the way. Only that level of mass collective social, economic and cultural change may be enough to save the planet, rectify the failures of the financial market and rebalance our lives away from turbo-consumerism. During the Second World War we gave up some freedoms, in particular the freedom to consume, to enjoy others deemed more important. We accepted rationing, blackouts and the evacuation of children because of a greater threat.

In the Imperial War Museum there are displays of the posters used to make the case for rationing and the wider national interest. They are about fun and liberation, not just threats and duty; they are witty, goading and coaxing, not just based on deference or blind fear. And once again we are reminded that the best marketing brains in the world now try to get us to go on buying things we don't need and which don't make us any happier, that we can't afford and which destroy the planet. Surely those brilliant men and women in the advertising industry would be up for the noble task of sustaining society and the planet? The war was about the survival of our liberty against the threat of fascism. Now the threat is about the survival of the planet. In those intervening sixty years we have become seduced into a life of endless shopping. It will be hard to give up. But it took compulsion to fight off Hitler. It's unlikely that people would voluntarily have rationed what they consumed even in the face of the Nazis. It will take another era of compulsion to do what we need to but can't of our own free will.

Sometimes we need to be compelled by law to do what we would fail to do if left to our own devices. 'Don't give people what they want – they deserve better,' remarked the historian A. J. Toynbee. In part this is because we aren't always capable of making decisions that are in our long-term interests, let alone have the will power to act consistently on them. That is why we are compelled by law to do all sorts of things we otherwise wouldn't. We are made by law to wear seat-belts in our cars, drive at certain speeds, and are now banned from smoking in public places because it is good for us and the rest of society and we can't be relied on to do it without legal compulsion.

We are forced by law to pay taxes so that we can be defended by an army and the police, have roads to drive on, schools and hospitals. These decisions are not imposed on us in an arbitrary manner but by a government with a democratic mandate. We may not like every state-imposed restriction on our individual liberty but by and large we accept the constraints because they are arrived at democratically and we know they are serving our long-term interests. By enforcing some constraints on us, like taxing and

banning some activities, other freedoms, like the ability to breathe clean air or walk safely down the street, are strengthened. Publicly we may complain but inwardly many of us are glad that this democratic paternalism forces us to do the right thing.

Even the free market is beginning to agree with the case for compulsion. In November 2007 CEOs from 150 global corporations called for a compulsory and binding UN framework on climate change. Their message was 'Rein us in, please – we can't stop ourselves.' The current financial crisis is making the case for greater government intervention too. Left to its own devices, the banking and financial services industry has turned the money markets toxic. Every economy depends on the trust that allows credit to flow. The case for regulation and compulsory controls of products, salaries and tax evasion has become compelling, as has the case for us to be compelled to buy energy-efficient light-bulbs and drive cars that use non-leaded fuel. We are compelled to do things all the time – for our own good. We need to be further compelled in the future.

The basis for the kind of freedom envisaged by Maslow, the good society if you like, is predicated on greater solidarity, equality and, where necessary, compulsion. It is to the ways in which we can act more effectively together that we now return. The collective failures of an all-consuming society demand a collective response if the market is to be effectively counter-balanced. The last and most important liberty we have is choosing our way of life. We can only do that together. This is how we can make a start.

All together now!

Consumers of the world unite –
you have nothing to lose but your chain stores.[69]

Meaningful and lasting change happens when the desirable meets the feasible; when enough people with a grievance join together to create change from the bottom up and inspire reinforcing

action from the top down. It is the creation of a virtuous cycle of a vision for a better world and a programme to make it happen that will create the basis for a post-consumer society. There are two ways in which we can change things together: the first is through civic action, the second through the state. Civic action involves groups of citizens acting together to make a better world. State action is about what is and isn't legal. Taken together they can help fashion the emergence of a post-consumer society.

Civic action

Consumer boycotts

If we work together as citizens rather than lone consumers we can start to change the context of the choices we make. More Trains Less Strain: people who want to use public transport rather than private cars have organized local fare strikes where travellers use fake tickets and passes because of overcrowding and overcharging. A protest in Bristol led to Great Western putting more carriages on trains. Militant consumer interest like this is born out of personal frustration with the quality of service – but two things are happening. First, passengers are realizing that they can make change happen if they act together. Second, they are reinforcing the place of the public over private consumption. One response to a poor train service would be to jump into a car. But these people know the roads will just get even more clogged and the climate warmer. The only real answer is to work together to apply pressure for a cheaper and better-quality service.

Other protesters have fought back against unfair bank charges and, in the past, there have been high-profile campaigns against companies like Barclays Bank, for its investment in apartheid South Africa, by the Anti-Apartheid Movement, Nestlé formula milk for babies in the developing world, by the Milk Action Group, and Shell, over the Brent Spa oil disaster, by Greenpeace.

In these cases consumers acting as citizens made a real impact. Today it is relatively easy to set up a consumer protest campaign, through emails and websites.

But when it comes to boycotts, we probably don't know how powerful we are or could be. I recall my conversation with Simon, the management consultant. He told me that the retail sector and especially the supermarkets are highly 'geared'. That means their fixed costs, the ones that can't be changed easily, are very high compared to the variable costs, which they can change more easily. So, if revenue starts falling because they are losing customers through a boycott, they can't scale back on costs quickly because they can't dismantle a global supply chain overnight, sell a warehouse or close a store. This is one reason why they are so competitive and want to poach customers from each other through advertising campaigns and price cuts. Small variations in income matter a lot. This makes the big retailers vulnerable not just to competitive pressures but to organized and orchestrated boycotts. It means the supermarkets are incredibly sensitive to collective consumer pressure.

A mass national boycott has never really been attempted against a British supermarket on any scale. In part this is because it has never yet been necessary as the companies have been quick to adjust to new consumer demands very quickly. The best evidence of this was the demand for GM-free food in the mid-1990s. The supermarkets realized very quickly that they should boycott GM foods first because their customers certainly would. Today if one of the big supermarket chains was found to be paying developing world workers much less than they could hope to live on, or their buying activities were recklessly destroying the environment, the effect of a customer boycott could be dramatic. We all have our favourite or most convenient supermarket, but for the majority who live in urban areas there is always another just down the road. Unless you live in a rural community, the sacrifice of going somewhere else would not be that great. But the impact on the company could be huge.

A boycott would not have to be particularly sustained to have a major impact because even a small reduction in revenue would hit profits hard. The evidence suggests the companies would cave in very quickly. The media interest in such a campaign would be huge as the Internet and mobile phones make publicity and communication easy. It would be bad PR for the company affected, which surely prizes its reputation, but more importantly it would hit them directly where it hurts most – in the tills. Their competitors would feel encouraged to emphasize their higher standard of ethical behaviour to persuade disgruntled customers to come to them. The right issues, dealt with in the right way, could bring a supermarket giant to its knees and serve notice to the rest of the sector: behave properly or you're next. The challenge to us is to demand much more in terms of ethical supply of products. Go to sites like www.tescopoly.org or www.ethicalconsumer.org/boycotts/currentUKboycotts.aspx. to find out about international, national and local consumer concerns. If a company based in your community is selling, making or promoting goods that are needlessly commercializing or, worse, sexualizing the lives of children, then a protest outside the store with the local newspaper tipped off would soon get the goods off the shelf.

But you don't have to start by organizing a national boycott. It can begin locally. A supermarket chain may be looking to build a new store on green-belt land or in a community that values its existing independent shops. If enough people protest and let the local councillors know it will swing their vote come election time, then planning permission can be stopped. Tesco used to celebrate the fact that they never lost planning cases for new stores. That is beginning to change. Across the country, from Sheringham in Norfolk to Helston in Cornwall, local people are winning campaigns to decide what shops should be in their community.

Such activity is in essence a collective form of ethical shopping. Like the individual ethical decisions we make, it can and often does lead to buying less. In theory, though, we could go on being turbo-consumers while still making ethical decisions

either individually or collectively. But there are ways in which people are joining together to buy less and buy better by slowing the pace of consumption.

Going slow

Another form of civic action that has been gaining strength is the slow-food movement. This is the soft end of anti-consumerism and came out of Italy in the 1990s as a reaction to the spread of fast-food chains. Its high priest is Carlo Petrini, who campaigned to stop a McDonald's restaurant opening beside Rome's famous Spanish Steps. Petrini castigates the global celebrity-chef phenomenon and wants food to be ethical, environmental and egalitarian. This is quite a recipe. Slow Food UK has more than two thousand member groups and I'd like to say they are growing fast, but I'm not sure that would be the right term!

What the slow movement recognizes is that we can do things that directly challenge and subvert the dominant consumer culture of our age by the way in which we do them. Slow is about a way of life, not just about food. It is about living at human speed and not the frantic pace of turbo-consumerism dictated to us by the expensive watches that we have to work harder and longer to afford. Just try to walk slowly at an even but gradual pace. It's really hard – at least, it is for me – but you can ease yourself into it. Find pleasure in gentle exercise and what you already have. Give yourself time to think and reflect. It helps to stop you worrying about what you don't have. But slow is about more than individual acts of defiance and new pleasure-seeking. Ludlow in Shropshire did this officially because enough people banded together and put pressure on the council to make it happen. Other towns are following their lead because the citizens of Ludlow are happier and it's become a more attractive place for visitors because of its new-found slow status. It is a great example of bottom-up action triggering a top-down response that creates more favourable conditions for other people to alter their lives. You can go to www.slowmovement.com/ to find out more about it.

Slow is about food as pleasure and conviviality, not just as fuel to keep us on the treadmill or a way of demonstrating our consumer prowess by chewing ever more exclusive meals. What the Slow Movement knows is that speed defines modern lives that are out of control. Everything is about time-saving, with faster computers, mobiles, cars and food. But because of speed we taste little and experience less. What matters is the cost and quantity of consumption, not the quality. Slow is about fighting back and reclaiming a pace of life that works for us. It is a way in which we can meet the expectations of Maslow and live a life in which we self-actualize and take control and ownership of our existence.

It all sounds terribly middle class and I guess much of it is. But it needn't be. Access to good quality, locally produced and affordable food should be a right for the many, not a privilege for a few. Access to healthy cheap food is one area in which the case that was made earlier for freedom based on greater equality is particularly strong. New healthy-food co-operatives are springing up in towns across the country. They are small independent retailers and markets that tend to be owned and managed by their staff. The profits they make go back into the shop and the pockets of the workers, not third-party shareholders. They sell produce that, wherever possible, is locally sourced and organically grown. Use them if there is one near you. To find out go to www.truefood.coop/

Caring and sharing

At the moment we waste so much, not just things, as we have seen, but our time in working to buy more without finding happiness. Instead of using everything up we should recycle more, not just things but our time. We can create a virtuous cycle of giving and getting that helps stop climate change and provides us with a much better quality of life.

A brilliantly simple but effective idea is taking off in many communities: the time bank.[70] By donating your own time to the 'bank' to do things you are good at for other people – any-

thing from accountancy to sitting and talking with the elderly, babysitting or gardening – you can withdraw time for things you might need help with, like DIY. It is a mutual-support system that boosts self-esteem, localizes trade, puts people in touch and treats everyone equally. In Peckham in south London time banks are being attached to some doctors' surgeries. The social activity they encourage means that patients are recovering from illness faster and staying healthier longer. And in the process people start to see themselves as local citizens connected to others, not just lone consumers in a hostile and alienating community. You can find out more about time banks in your area and how to start one at www.timebanking.org

But, of course, we can share things too. Websites such as www.mybookyourbook.co.uk is an online library for exchanging books you have finished with.[71] Books can now remain in circulation for ever, passed from one interested reader to another. But you don't have to recycle books on the Internet. The next time you walk through the park check to see if anyone has 'accidentally' left a book on a bench. Book-crossing is a new trend I hope you'll practise. It's simple: you just leave a book you like and want others to read in a place where it can easily be picked up. You can try to leave it in a place where you think it's more likely that someone who will enjoy it can find it. So, gardens for gardening books, etc. Leave a note inside, if you want – even an ID number, and then you can check where it ends up on the site www.bookcrossing.com. Swap parties are also taking off. This is where you take what you no longer want or need and exchange it for something you do. It is cheap or even free, the environmental damage is nil and it is good social fun; www.freecycling.org is another useful site for picking things up someone no longer wants but you might be able to use. Again, it's sensible to swap rather than buy everything from new, saving time and money. But it's the social interaction that counts most, and creating our own networks of exchange makes us feel better about our lives. Collectively we are taking control of our lives as citizens and not having them decided for us as consumers.

Direct anti-consumer action

If going slow and sharing doesn't feel like enough, there is the more militant wing of the anti-consumer movement. This offers much more direct opposition to turbo-consumerism. The Church of Stop Shopping is led by the charismatic white-quiffed Reverend Billy, who looks like Elvis dressed as a preacher, whose gospel is anti-consumerism. A former actor, he hams up the alleluias in a surreal maniac spoof-style tele-evangelism. With dog collar and loud-hailer, he and his disciples storm the likes of Gap, Starbucks and McDonald's and start their anti-shopping sermon. They protest about the commercialization of public spaces that used to join people from different walks of life together. The Reverend Billy and his flock have seen the light. They know that salvation can't be found in shopping; they want to spread the word and win converts. Theirs is a dizzying mix of politics and street theatre in which the congregation is asked to cut up their credit cards as an act of defiance against turbo-consumerism. People like the Reverend Billy, with their media-friendly stunts, are getting others to question their lives and the hold of consumerism on them. As such they play an important role in getting us to question our existence by changing the terms of debate about all-consuming lives.

So do Canada's 'culture jammers', a group who approach anti-consumerism from another, subversive and 'antipreneurial' direction. In their own glossy magazine *Adbusters*, they run spoof adverts for products such as Nike trainers that look like the real thing but subvert the message. They are responsible for the launch of Buy Nothing Day, which does what it says on the lid, and TV Turnoff Week. These are loosely organized events and it's hard to measure the effect of asking people to do nothing. Their impact is more symbolic than actual – but the influence is infectious. Change always requires the terms of debate to be challenged by someone saying something that at first sounds extreme but which confronts dominant beliefs. You can find out more about how Adbusters are doing this at www.adbusters.org/.

Now they are selling their own goods, like trainers, which are ethically produced, to take on the big corporates. This has proved to be controversial with some of their supporters, who argue that they shouldn't be encouraging people to buy anything. The debate points to the problem that any alternative to turbo-consumerism is bound to be contradictory, given that every action must originate from people who live within the turbo-consuming world. Some kids will buy Adbusters 'Blackspot' trainers as an act of defiance, others to look cool. These contradictions will not go away. A post-consumer society will not be a world in which there are no shops and no shopping. It's okay to want to look cool and have an identity: it's just how much it matters, how fast it changes and whether we are in control of the brands or them of us.

It's not just in the US or Canada that activists are subverting the system. In Germany protesters dress as comic-book superheroes to 'liberate' luxury food items from delicatessens to give to the poor. Their argument is that in a world of deep insecurity for so many you have to be a super-hero just to survive. Then there is the practice of Yomango, which is shoplifting as a spectator sport. It involves pinching something, wearing it, then walking back into the shop like a fashion model. Even more surreal is the practice of shop dropping, the opposite of shoplifting. It's an act of defiance that involves placing bizarre items in shops, such as obviously second-hand items of clothing in Topshop, then insisting on buying them. These people are using direct action, disobedience and anti-consumerism all rolled into one to challenge what in a consumer society is deemed to be normality.

At one level such acts sound trivial. But they start to change the terms of debate about our all-consuming lives. They hold up a mirror to our society and mostly they laugh at it. They operate at the fringes but this is where all alternatives come from. Remember von Mises and von Hayek sitting with just a few others in a seminar room in Austria? They had no allies and no influence. It may have taken them thirty years to achieve it but they remade the world in their image because they dared to

believe that something else was better and achievable. These anti-consumer groups tend to involve young people and offer a sense of idealism and action that political parties, the traditional means of changing society, no longer seem to provide. There is a long way for the anti-consumer movement to go and many more ideas to develop, but resistance starts with someone saying 'no'. These people have started.

So, opposition to rampant consumerism is breaking out all over the place, some in terms of soft culture, some in much harder ways. The anti-capitalist May Day marches and G8 protesters grabbed lots of headlines, especially in Seattle in 1999 which was the start of such protests. They created terrible PR for the world's leaders and helped establish third-world debt and climate change as pressing political issues. The more mainstream elements of the protesters are now invited to attend events like the World Leaders Forum in Davos. In part they are co-opted and disarmed by being on the other side of the police lines but compromise, from both sides, is an inevitable and necessary part of making change happen.

More recently we have seen the Climate Change Camp that gathered on fields at the edge of Heathrow in the summers of 2007 and 2008. The protesters gained a huge amount of publicity that will add to public awareness that flying too much is harming the planet and that more and more people care. Ironically the establishment tried to position the activists as a threat to society that had to be rigorously policed, not the companies whose planes are destroying the planet. But they were right. The protesters did pose a threat to society – the society of the consumer. At the end of the week a local resident, campaigning against the extension of the airport, said during a television interview how wonderful the campaigners had been and how over the top the police reaction was. Because of the protest the Government delayed its decision on a third runway for Heathrow until January 2009 when it finally gave the go-ahead; 125,000 more flights a year mean the airport will be responsible for contributing 20 per cent of the country's CO_2 emissions. The

political and business desire for more took precedence over the planet's dire need for less. But the terms of debate have changed again. The Mayor of London, Boris Johnson, will fund through the London Assembly a legal challenge to the decision. Pressure groups like Greenpeace vow the runway will never be built. The Conservative opposition in Parliament say that if they get into power it will be stopped. The flying lobby is on the defensive. This looks like the final big anti-environment decision any government will make. All this has happened in just a few years because some people got together to say no to more. They have shown what can be done.

I meet up with some of the leading lights of Plane Stupid, a non-violent direct-action group campaigning to stop all unnecessary short-haul flights and all airport expansion. Graham, Kitt and Joss are in their twenties and early thirties and mix sharp, serious minds with human warmth. They make you feel just a little optimistic about the future. Currently the Government expects and is preparing for the 25 million passengers travelling annually through the UK to increase to 82 million by 2030. It argues that it is a case of economic necessity for Britain. And in a consumer-driven economy, where growth is essential, it is right. But carbon emissions from planes will be one of the biggest contributors to climate change. Something has to give, either the planet or the amount we fly. Plane Stupid has groups of protesters around the country at every airport, prepared to break the law and face the consequences wherever plans for expansion go ahead. They have no leaders and no hierarchy and are as open and democratic as possible, but have to operate carefully because of infiltration by the police and corporate espionage from the air industry.

What is interesting about Plane Stupid is that the energy for it came from the anti-Iraq war demonstrations. Then millions of people showed that they cared about something deeply and took to the streets to say no. But the politicians didn't listen. People like Graham, Kitt and Joss vowed not to rely on the judgement of politicians again and to take matters into their own hands.

The apparent failure of one campaign led directly to the success of another. Sitting on the runway to stop a flight must be scary but they say it is incredibly empowering.

Alternative ways of living don't start from within the political system but always come from outside. Some of us are more disposed to gentle forms of protest, others to things that are more direct. But what is essential is the realization that there is a chain of activism, with different players doing more and less extreme things. All can do their bit and support each other. We can show that another world is possible by living in it as far as we can, through what we buy as individuals and through campaigning with others to stop things happening and change the terms of debate. But it is still government who can act to legislate or not. Only it can decide what is legal and what is not. Airlines want to fly as many planes as possible and will lobby as hard as they can for more. We won't necessarily volunteer to reduce the number of flights we take. Indeed, we are highly unlikely to do so. It requires decision-makers to step in and take responsibility. Just as in the 1980s the state put in place some of the key legislative steps that helped create our turbo-consuming world, so it will have to pass the necessary laws now to create a post-consumer society.

That is why Plane Stupid have taken their protest directly to Westminster. They made the national news when some of them smuggled banners into the House of Commons protesting about Heathrow expansion and unfurled them from the roof. Some still face possible prison sentences for this act of defiance. On another occasion one managed to get into a reception at Downing Street and tried to glue himself to the Prime Minister. They know that ultimately the political system, too, needs to be changed if we are to secure more balanced lives in which we don't fly our way to environmental oblivion. Through campaigning pressure, Government must be made to act.

Being in a better state

At the moment, though, there is a pro-consumer consensus in politics. All three main parties in Britain treat us primarily as consumers and they see consumerism underpinning their goal of economic growth and thus their ability to win elections. If they can ensure that more people can buy more things, they calculate that they are more likely to hold power. No party is currently willing to face the obvious and increasingly pressing need to break away from consumer-driven politics.

It ought to be the job of politicians to hold convictions, be brave, address difficult issues and show what can be done. The urgent task is to regulate the market to reverse the rise of turbo-consumerism and help create a new moral code that values the good life and the good society in more than material terms. Here, politicians can really take a lead in what they say, not just in what they do. As the elected representatives of the people they can create a moral climate in which it becomes embarrassing once more to accumulate and flaunt obscene amounts of wealth, or not to use the wealth you have for the good of society. The people we champion and cherish should be those who help the community, not just those who help themselves. In the recent boom years we have all read about people who will spend more on one bottle of wine than others can earn in a year. When this is the case, there is something profoundly wrong with our world and it is the job of political leaders to speak out about it.

Saying always prefigures doing. Mrs Thatcher argued that greed was good and created the climate for the rampant materialism of the 1980s. We need a new breed of politicians who will argue for a world in which consumerism is held in check so that we can experience a whole range of other more important freedoms, like time. This is not to pass the buck entirely to politicians. We can't just wait for them to act and cry, 'Betrayal,' if they don't. Instead we have a responsibility to show that if they take a lead we will follow and support them. That is why the examples I have mentioned of individual and collective

action we can take are so important. They create pressure and space for change from the top, space in which state action can ensure we get more from being citizens rather than consumers. We can't organize a boycott every time there is a case of turbo-consumerism going too far. And we can't just depend on individual acts like ethical shopping. We need common standards, rules and sanctions to stop environmental damage or the destruction of the public realm.

Through such intervention and regulation we should be looking to create a social state in which we are stakeholders and citizens with social, economic and political rights and responsibilities, as opposed to the market state that we have today, which is geared towards individualizing risk and commodifying what were formerly social relations. We need the state to act as guarantor of a civic society, not a turbo-consumer society; a state that has the legitimacy to act as a counter-balance to the relentless march of the market and create the underpinning conditions for our freedom – greater equality, collectivism and, where necessary, compulsion.

Rebalancing the demands of the market machine and the needs of society will not happen quickly or easily. There was no blueprint for the creation of a consumer society but, as we have seen, the combination of cultural change mixed with political leadership had a decisive impact on what type of society we now have. From a time when free markets and more shopping were the only solution we are now in a period of flux. It doesn't mean that we will swing back by default to become a more equal, more civic and less consumer-oriented nation. But it does give us the chance if we are determined enough to take it.

Despite the grip of consumerism, people will struggle to create greater freedoms, alternative pleasures, and to be in control of their lives. Indeed, the tighter the grip, the more likely people are to react and fight back. The myth of happiness through consumption is wearing thin for many. The recession is a wake-up call. People are looking for alternatives on their own. They need and want help, and the state should be there to provide it. But to

play this role, a new political class requires a different set of operating principles: the public must be prioritized over the private, the long term needs to take precedence over the short, society over markets, citizens over consumers, care over competition and people over profits. Based on these principles, there are a number of policy decisions that could be made to start the process of rebalancing society away from turbo-consumerism. Here is a shopping list. The first three suggestions are about stopping the damaging influence of turbo-consumerism; the next two are about encouraging good behaviour and activity, and the final four about the time and space to be citizens as well as how we measure the shift to the good society.

1. Restrictions on advertising

Invasive advertising has entered every area of our lives but it is society, not private companies, that should decide when and where market forces are allowed to operate. The market should not be permitted to reach into parts of our lives to cause individual harm and social damage. In particular, one of our duties as a society is to protect children from unnecessary and undue commercial pressures. Other countries have taken action. In Sweden the state banned television advertising to under-twelves in 1991. It allows children the time to grow up free from the calculating advances of marketing professionals. There is no reason why Britain can't do the same.

But we need to go further. The same principle of restricting the creation of what can only be called false desires can be achieved in other ways. In São Paulo, Brazil, the local authority has banned commercial billboards because of the visual pollution they create in the city, making it a place for people to live, not just a realm for profit. The state has successfully stepped in and acted in a way individual citizens would find impossible. If we decide to buy a paper or a magazine with adverts or subscribe to a commercial TV channel, that's up to us. But the public realm should be free of the pressure to buy and it is the state's duty to protect these spaces from private

invasion that none of us individually consents to or can stop on our own.

Another potentially popular step the Government could take would be to ban the worst marketing practices, such as buzz marketing, that rely on the deceitful presentation of products by paid agents who pose as other members of the public. Instead of the decision on what would or would not be included in such a ban being made by the civil servants drawing up the necessary legislation, the public could be involved, through surveys and polls, in the process of deciding what forms of underhand marketing should be outlawed. A statutory code for the marketing industry with hefty fines for infringement would be the basis of effective regulation. And all the time the Government would be sending out signals about the morality of over-marketing and turbo-consumerism – giving companies and the public a lead on how they should live and value their lives.

There is one further step the state can take to reduce advertising and send out the message that relentless material desires are damaging to our well-being: it could tax advertising. The rationale would be that advertising promotes wants without satisfying them and therefore sows the seeds of dissatisfaction while using up scarce resources. If the objective of advertising is to make us unhappy because we're always wanting more, then, like other externalities the market has historically refused to pay for, such as damage to the environment, the Government should intervene to ensure the full social cost of production is met. The money from a tax on advertising could be used to pay for something like a national youth volunteers scheme to encourage the young to get involved in their local communities, improving local parks or looking after the elderly. This would build social capital and promote a wider sense of well-being that can't be gained from more shopping. Only the Government, acting through the legal powers of the democratic state, can restrict the never-ending spread of advertising.

2. Taxing luxury goods

In ancient Greece luxury goods were condemned because they were considered to be a corrupting influence on society. The ancient Romans passed laws to regulate the consumption of certain goods, like spices, precious metals and more expensive clothing. Women were banned from wearing coloured robes, the production and sale of gold and silverware were limited, and foreign wine was banned.

The easy purchase of luxury goods has created a collective-action problem of buying for status. The bar is lifted higher and higher and no one gets any happier through the accumulation of more and more expensive items. A solution to this problem would be the imposition of a tax on luxury goods to discourage their purchase. Of course, the decision about what is and is not a luxury good would be subjective and would have to be decided by either the state or by an annual poll of options by a representative group of citizens. At the end of 2008 the state governor of New York was considering a five per cent luxury-goods tax on items costing more than $20,000. The tax increase would also impact on purchases of cars costing more than $60,000, vessels (including but not limited to yachts) costing more than $200,000 and non-commercial aircraft costing more than $500,000. The outcome of any such tax is bound to be disputed. But this can't stop us taxing goods that are at the core of our consuming habit. We already make lots of complex and difficult tax decisions based on morals and values. There are no easy or uncontentious ways to tax people or things. A tax on luxury goods would reduce their consumption, decrease the competition for status, be progressive as it would apply more to the wealthy, and the proceeds could be earmarked for initiatives such as measures that promote good citizenship.

3. Rationing

We can't go on consuming at the rate we are: the planet cannot take it, and neither can our economy nor our society. If we can't or won't slow down voluntarily then the survival of the earth

demands that we are forced to. Whether we like it or not, growing scarcity is going to make rationing a reality. Much better that
it is agreed, planned, prepared for and any pain shared fairly than
imposed too late and unequally.

In October 2008 the highly regarded Chatham House think-
tank reported that a food crisis is highly likely in the UK, making price and availability central political concerns. The crisis in
supply is likely to be a result of climate change, rising energy
prices and global population growth. They predict that we will
all have to accept a shift from individual shopping preference to
government decisions on food supply. We currently use food at
a rate six times greater than the land and sea available to us can
supply, production relies on the unpredictable supply of migrant
workers to harvest it and is energy-intensive.

Rationing needs to include food and also to restrict other
kinds of consumption that are damaging both society and the
planet. This is not just obvious common sense, as well as being
inevitable, but chimes with people's own expectations. According to an *Observer*/ICM poll of 26 June 2005, 51 per cent of
voters believe that some kind of rationing or restriction on air
travel will be necessary in the future.[72] It would be simple to
allocate to all of us a limit on the air miles we can use each year,
with the total set at an amount that sufficiently decreased carbon
emissions. People who didn't want to use all or any of the air
miles could trade them for money with those who did. Given
it's the rich who travel more, this would have the added bonus
of helping redistribute income to the poor. The principle can, of
course, be carried over to wider carbon-emissions schemes, with
rationing placed on domestic fuel use and car mileage. With new
smart wireless technology, all of these things can be measured
and recorded. According to the International Energy Agency,
global oil supply will peak in 2020. From then on we must dramatically reduce our reliance on oil and diversify our energy
supply, especially through the use of renewables, and prepare for
power to be rationed.

Of course, some will object to rationing, but if it is applied

fairly and to meet clear and present dangers, like climate change, there really is no option. How can the freedom to consume whatever you want without restriction be more important than the freedom to live on a habitable planet? The idea is already winning important backing. The Food Climate Research Network based at the University of Surrey reported in September 2008 that meat must be rationed to four portions a week if the world is to avoid runaway climate change. And, in effect, forms of consumer rationing are already being considered, not just by the state but by the market. Credit-card companies are considering stopping some attempted purchasers if they think the cardholder is spending beyond their means even if they haven't exceeded their limit. If the market can do this in the name of profit, surely the state can in the name of safeguarding society and the environment.

4. Promoting ethical shopping

The problem with ethical shopping is that the entire onus is on the shopper to make the right decisions when information is difficult to obtain and there are few if any universal standards for judgement and comparison. People aren't going to spend an hour checking on the Internet before they buy a T-shirt they have just seen in a shop window. How ethical what we buy is in terms of environmental sustainability and standards of workers' employment is crying out for state regulation. At the moment there is a wide range of ethical kite marks, such as the Soil Association stamp, Traidcraft, Fairtrade and Freedom Foods. On clothing there are no properly established ethical trading marks. The system is so confused and complex that it gives people an excuse not to bother.

The one big labelling success story has been the Food Standards Agency's recommended approach for healthy eating based on the traffic-light system. Green, amber and red labels now appear on many products, drawing attention, for example, to their salt and/or sugar content. It has been immensely popular with consumers because it is clear and consistent. Only an arm

of the state could have achieved this. But the problem is that the system is voluntary, not compulsory. So some companies have opted out of the system because they know that too many of their unhealthy products would end up as red – not least because more salt and sugar get consumers hooked on these products. So, state systems have to be compulsory if they are really to work.

The Government needs to impose a standard of ethical supply to which all producers are required by law to adhere. Correct adherence would enable them to carry one prominent ethical kite mark based on sustainability, animal protection and labour conditions. Those companies in breach of the standard would lose the ethical kite mark, be named and shamed, have hefty fines levied against them and face further restrictions on, for example, the right to open or build new premises. The state could embed ethical production and retail standards overnight.

5. Encouraging environmentally friendly action

The production of waste is central to a turbo-consumer society. The more we consume, the more we have to throw away. Not only should we be more responsible about what we throw away so that it can be recycled, but by being more involved in the process of disposing of our waste we become more mindful of the consequences of our consuming habit. But it takes Government action to bridge the gap between what people think is the right thing to do and what they will actually do. By linking the state, the consumer and companies we can achieve so much more. Government intervention should provide the infrastructure to make it easy to act to save the planet; 63 per cent of us are willing to pay higher taxes to save the environment, according to a *Guardian*/ICM poll carried out in February 2006. It is not just taxes but the action gap that needs to be closed. Nationally we currently recycle around 42 per cent of our waste. In other countries it can be as high as 70 per cent because they have the infrastructure and culture to make recycling much easier. Proper collection of waste, labelling systems and direct charges on households and commercial waste should mean a

zero tolerance to waste. In August 2007 a poll by the Local Government Association showed that 64 per cent favoured a pay-as-you-throw system of collecting rubbish which charged households on the basis of their non-recyclable waste through a council-tax rebate. But it looks as if the Government is backing away from such a scheme because it would be hard to administer. Yet we have to start taking waste seriously if we are to change the climate in a positive way. This demands a change in the climate of opinion that schemes like this would foster. Yes, it would take more time and resources to run. But is there any choice? A host of European countries, like Germany, Denmark and the Netherlands, already operate different ways of taxing waste. So why do we think it's impossible here? The excuse culture has to stop. Ireland's levy on plastic bags has been credited with reducing bag use by 90 per cent. It needs these kinds of incentives and public investment in the right bins, collection services and waste sites, not just private action to create a change in behaviour. And polls now indicate a big rise in the number who agree that air fares should rise to offset damage to the environment; the figure is up from 36 per cent in 2004 to 49 per cent in January 2009.[73]

The new economic foundation (nef) and the National Consumer Council (NCC) have promoted the idea of a sustainable-consumption rewards card along the lines of a successful scheme that operates in Amsterdam. Citizens get points for recycling and buying sustainable products and in return can spend the points on more sustainable goods, public transport or leisure activities, such as going to the cinema. Again, it is the cultural and moral signals we send out that matter, just as much as the encouragement to do the right thing.

Government should take a bigger lead in ensuring that homes and companies become carbon neutral. In February 2007 the Government's monthly fund to help people go green at home with better insulation ran out just ten hours into the month. People are desperate to do the right thing when it comes to the environment – but they need more help. More money needs to be made available. A national home-insulation programme

would cut heating bills, employ an army of people, who would be otherwise unemployed in a recession, and it would reduce carbon emissions. It could be paid for by a tax on the windfall, that is unearned, profits of the energy companies who saw their income soar in 2008–9 because of the rise in wholesale gas and oil prices.

Cars like SUVs should not just be taxed more through petrol consumption and road usage but should come with a government environmental-health warning – just like the ones on cigarette packets. A warning that says, 'This car will damage everyone's health,' would deter some people from buying them and build public pressure against such vehicles. Ex-London Mayor Ken Livingstone wanted to switch the congestion charge to an emissions charge with the biggest gas-guzzlers paying most. It is an idea the Government should take up. The French Government is looking at a tax of up to £3,200 on new four-wheel-drive cars in part because only one in eight SUV drivers has ever driven off road and only two out of five have been outside a city. Research conducted by the NCC shows that the combination of corporate social responsibility, consumer power and Government regulation can change buying cultures and create new social norms. Take as an example the energy efficiency of white goods. An EU ruling to label products was not enough, neither was a price incentive. Only when Comet and then John Lewis refused to stock lower-rated appliances did the market shift.

Much more could be done to encourage cycling with cycle lanes and places to lock bikes up. Public transport could receive more investment. Instead of pumping money into the economy to avert the recession through greater personal consumption at least some of the billions could be spent on a high-speed rail network. This would create jobs and be good for the environment as it would reduce the need for short-haul flights and car journeys. In particular the railways could be brought back into public ownership so that all the investment stays in the system and doesn't leak out through payments to shareholders. Ending the division

between track and wheel through different competing companies would mean that the system could be made more efficient and safer. This needn't cost a penny if the franchises of private train-operating companies are simply not renewed. Once again, we would be acting socially as citizens, experiencing life with each other as the travelling public, not just lone consumers, sending the signal that public can beat private.

In all of this the state has to take a lead if our better instincts and intentions are to be unlocked. Most of us want to do the right thing when it comes to recycling and acting in an environmentally friendly way but we need to know that our efforts are not in vain and will make a difference.

6. Creating a public realm

It is vital that spaces are created and secured in which the values of citizens and the public trump those of the consumer and the private. Beliefs and values resonate within institutions. Private institutions prioritize individual ownership; they are places where money talks. Public institutions are based on need, not the ability to pay. They are open to all and promote compassion and co-operation over competition. The doctor's waiting room and the post-office counter queue are the places in which we are all equal and no private preference can be bought.

To form young citizens rather than budding consumers, schools should be free from commercial pressures. Steps towards this would be easy to implement. Private companies should not be allowed to sponsor equipment or activities at schools: their priority is not the well-being of our children but the maximization of profit. The public should pay for the resources to educate our children properly and we should not have to rely on the marketing departments of firms for computers, books or sports equipment. More importantly, schools should stop being a learn-to-earn treadmill and instead more of the focus should be on education and knowledge for its own sake. An authoritative report in February 2009 by academics at Cambridge University showed just how damaging the target culture and narrow jobs-

based curriculum of our primary schools has become.[74] Students and their parents should stop seeing education as the first preparatory step on the ladder to an all-consuming life but a stage in which knowledge and learning are valued and schools are hubs of their communities offering services to all generations. To stop the middle-class and affluent capture of the best schools, fair selection rules should be applied to ensure a mixed and properly comprehensive local intake. If necessary, ideas like selection by lottery should be introduced to ensure that everyone has a fair and equal chance of attending any school and no one can play the system to secure advantage.

Instead of being genuinely comprehensive our schools have become stuck in a vicious circle of competing with each other for the best students, in order to get the highest possible place on a league table so that they can attract even better pupils. This is a recipe for social division in which only the articulate, confident and affluent do well. Now parents worry about which school is the very best and drive their kids all over town to get them there. But the local comprehensive should have enough investment and offer high enough standards to ensure that it serves all children in its local catchment area. This is not just fair, it enables children of all social classes to mix, understand each other and integrate, laying the basis for their life as citizens. Improvements to schools should not be based on parental competition for the best places but their active involvement in reforming their local school. Instead of a competitive struggle, schools should co-operate and share best practice and the best teachers. We can modernize our public services, like schools, without marketizing them.

If we want to set our young adults up for balanced, fulfilled lives rather than a consumer-driven existence, they should not pay for their higher education through variable top-up fees, which are designed to encourage competition between universities by creating a market in higher education. Variable top-up fees encourage a habit of debt and put off the poor but also promote a view of higher education that is based on financial return

rather than the joy of learning. Because of them, young people are being conditioned to accept more individual risk in going to university. Higher education stops being a social provision and becomes part of the struggle for lone survival. But the recession is hitting the graduate-jobs market hard and many students with huge debts face little prospect of being able to pay them off. Instead of variable upfront fees students should pay a graduate solidarity tax only when they get work. In this way there would be no debts to put people off going to university and the tax payback forms a bond between student generations: after they have had the benefit of university education, they help the next generation.

Because the market knows no boundaries, it will continue to secure any profit it can from the consumerization of public services. From welfare provision, the Royal Mail, education and health to public spaces, such as parks and libraries, the public realm is under constant threat from the march of the market. Too often it has been the market state that has opened the door to different forms of commercialization in the public realm. But the era of this market state might be drawing to an end. The recession and especially the melt-down of the banking sector has seen widespread state intervention in the economy for the first time in decades. Now the tax payer is saving the market from its self-destructive actions. The state has come to the rescue of all of us. This cannot and must not be forgotten or ignored. It is not the state that is being rolled back but the market and the consumer culture that underpinned and supported the era of privatization. All of a sudden it is the state that can't be bucked.

It is not that we should be anti-private sector. Hospitals and schools will continue to be built by the private sector, but private provision and public service have conflicting goals. Often there are much better and cheaper ways of helping people by treating them as citizens rather than as competitive consumers. Take the case of the women recovering from surgery who were given vouchers for a private gym to regain fitness. This is a classic case of a consumer-style answer to health care. It didn't work.

Like most people, they soon gave up on the gym. The only winner was the health-club owner, who happily took the tax payers'
money. Instead the women found they could get fit by walking
and jogging together round the local park. It was fun and socia-
ble and the peer-group pressure kept them going. All the state
had to do was put them in touch with each other. And so it cost
nothing. In all sorts of ways like this collective state-inspired
action can trump private consumption.

We need to confront the myth that there is some way of opting out of society to find personal security through consumer
choices, whether they are within a marketized public sector or
by going totally private. Such actions always create only a few
winners and more losers and the resulting social divisions always
come back to haunt us. We pay the price through the fear of
walking the streets at night and the cost of benefits that have to
be paid out or, worse still, prison for the flawed consumers who
want, like us, to be normal but succumb to breaking the law to
get there. When it costs six times as much to keep a boy in a
young offenders' prison as it does to send him to Eton, we are
making the wrong investment decisions and are all paying the
price: we pay more tax, we still feel insecure and we feel bad
about doing the wrong thing. Until now we have done so
because private consumption has been deemed to be better than
social investment. The recession may help us to understand that
there can be no individual security against the power of global
markets, only social security made possible through state action.

And such social provision needs to be paid for. Tax is the
entry fee we pay to belong to a civilized society. We must be
prepared to forgo some private consumption to pay for public
investment in society and all reap the rewards. To do that we
have to break the emotional hold such consumption has on us.
But we have to move beyond the bureaucratic state of the post-
war years too; it became inefficient and rigid. The market state
has since proved itself not to be the answer as it simply embeds
the culture of consumption. Instead we need a democratic state,
one that is accountable and responsive to our needs as citizens

but which creates genuinely public services that are run for and by us. A better state will be about some personal choices, but would be constructed on the basis that only collective decisions can find answers to the big questions about the nature, quality and extent of the public services we receive. Instead of being passive recipients of welfare services, we can and should become active participants in the creation and co-production of them. This means collaborating with staff and other producers to make those services work better for us. It is, after all, our state.

But education, health and other public services are only part of the public realm. We need plentiful free, open and attractive public spaces where people willingly congregate and gather together to share time. 'We are hard-wired with a desire for congenial places where we can be together,'[75] writes Jay Walljasper, who goes on to say public spaces are where we can 'meet, talk, sit, look, relax, play, stroll, flirt, eat, drink, smoke, sunbathe and feel part of a broader whole. They are the starting point for all community, commerce and democracy.' Public spaces are where we are all equal, all valued, and you cannot buy advantage or status. They are the places in which we can find happiness.

In the past society has created and protected institutions and places that we owned in common. Land where anyone could graze their cattle was called 'the common' until, as we have seen, it was enclosed to force people into the newly industrializing cities. In more recent times the creation of institutions like the NHS gave us something new to hold in common and value. While such old commons should be protected and, where possible, enhanced, it is vital that new commons are not privatized or commercialized. The Internet, DNA sequencing, the human genome and other health and scientific advances should not be the property of corporate interest to make a profit from but should exist for the benefit of all human kind. At the moment the big pharmaceutical companies are trying to buy up the rights to DNA sequencing: they will hold vital information about our genetic makeup so that new drugs can make a profit for them, rather than serve all humankind. The Internet and the

domain names we all use, which are now vital to our ability to communicate, are under threat of ownership from private companies who can then hold us to ransom for their use. Only the state can legislate to stop such anti-social behaviour. Patent laws need to be developed to ensure these new commons stay accessible to all.

Just as we should encourage public spaces we should do more to discourage the extent of inappropriate private spaces – especially shops. If we restricted out-of-town shopping through planning controls and returned to smaller-scale local shops the variety and quality of food and other goods would improve, we would get our communities back and dangerous carbon emissions from cars would be restricted. In the US, in places like Sanibel in Florida, local authorities are limiting the number of 'formula restaurants', such as McDonald's and Burger King, to stop the spread of identikit 'clone towns' and are instigating a community-impact analysis before new superstores can be built. If they can do it, why can't we? But national and local state action must take these steps, a much more effective means by which to strike a balance in our lives between consumption and everything else.

7. The world of work

Our lives will be happier and our planet more sustainable if we rebalance them away from spending and back to making – and not just making more but making better things. Being mere cogs in a machine to 'pile 'em high and sell 'em cheap' or to end up in a McJob as part of the low-wage and low-skill service economy won't provide anyone with a more fulfilling identity than the one they can gain from a new outfit bought at Primark every week. People need jobs that they value, through which they can make a meaningful contribution, not just as a means to an end – to buy more – but as an end in itself. Eventually what we produce influences what we consume and vice versa. If we make things that last, that can be repaired and are well designed, there is no need to buy so much so quickly. A turbo-consumer

society based on the speed of buying means we just have to work harder and longer to keep up. The treadmill keeps getting faster. The quality and substance of work for millions is not a consideration. What people make and do, how they are treated in terms of the hours they work, whether they are trained and well paid – these are some of the key ingredients of a better, more balanced life.

But at the moment there are few controls on working conditions, such as hours. The Government continues to opt out of the EU Working Time Directive, which stipulates that no one has to work more than forty-eight hours per week. Over a third of employers offer no training at all; this covers 37 per cent of the workforce. Among those with no qualifications, only 12 per cent are being trained. Of course, some professions and some companies do train and reward their staff well, but too many firms try to pay the lowest wages and offer the worst terms and conditions. There is a race to get to the bottom in terms of the quality of our working lives because companies on their own feel it is impossible to buck the system, pay well and train more when their competitors are doing the opposite. Too often if a company does invest in training, their best staff are poached by others who have refused to make such a commitment by paying the already well-trained substantially more. The state has to step in and regulate to stop this free-loading and create the context in which work is creative, enterprising and innovative. Work is one of the most important ways in which we are socialized and helps form our identities. A post-consumer society will require us to balance producing better with consuming less. A 'good work' agenda is therefore vital to act as a counter-balance to turbo-consumerism and it is the duty of the state to create the conditions in which work becomes more meaningful and satisfying.

Governments can shape the nature of an economy. They can make tax and investment decisions that give preference to some industries and services over others. The reason Britain has one of the biggest financial-services industries in the world is in part down to Government policy which favoured this sector over,

for instance, manufacturing. Germans make cars and top-quality white goods in part because successive governments there have invested in the necessary technology and training. The Scandinavians are renowned for mobile-phone technology. These things don't happen by accident. Government policy on investment, tax and infrastructure help create the conditions in which certain types of jobs flourish while others diminish. In late 2008 and early 2009 the British state invested billions in the crisis-ridden banking sector. But an economy based on complex financial products and debt is, as we have seen, part of the basis for a turbo-consumer economy. The state could make other investment decisions to favour green jobs, high-tech employment and the care sector. Government-sponsored apprenticeships could be earmarked for industries and sectors that aren't about rapid consumption, such as the public services, social housing and key elements of our infrastructure, such as public transport. The state can and must shape the economy to create the kind of jobs it believes build the good society and the good life to help take us to a post-consumer world.

Once people are in work doing jobs that aren't only about feeding the consumer machine, they should be well trained. One practical idea is the introduction of a national training levy imposed on all companies that refuse to meet a minimum investment level in their staff so that they can't free-ride on other companies that do invest properly. The money would go into a scheme to revive craft skills, like plumbing and motor mechanics, which not only help make people employable but give them a lasting sense of identity from which they can more confidently take their place in the world. You can define yourself for life if you have a craft; it provides a sense of purpose and usefulness, and good prospects of employment. It is a badge of social identity. The scheme could be based around the existing National Employers Skills Survey. In the past, the Government has threatened employers with such a statutory scheme if their voluntary efforts don't shape up. The recession can't be used as an excuse to make cuts to training budgets but should instead

be seen as an opportunity to refocus the country towards a high-skills economy.

The state should also underpin and support the concept of professionalism. In the past thirty years all political parties have tried to undermine professionals because they are deemed to look after their own interests and not ours. Professions like medicine, teaching and even policing fell victim of the same market fundamentalism that afflicted the rest of society. The presumption of free-market thinking is that people only act in self-interest and there can be no altruistic public ethos in which a doctor or teacher dispenses advice and help with a patient's or pupil's best interest at heart. In essence they are all viewed as utility-maximizing individuals who can't be trusted to work in our interest. That is why governments have tried to either dictate to them from the centre, by setting them public-service targets, like waiting times, auditing them through bodies like Ofsted, or to keep them on their toes through the deployment of increased competition, with schools and hospitals competing for patients and pupils.

But it is vital that we retain the notion that through training, education and qualifications there are people we can rely on to educate us and keep us healthy. The consumer is not always king. We don't always know what is best for us. Sometimes there is simply too much complex information for us to make the right decisions. We must learn again that we can and should trust people and that not everyone exists to serve their own interest. There is an important concept called public service. Government should find more ways to give professionals the space to demonstrate such an ethos, enhance their standing as trusted members of society and allow us to have a relationship with them as citizens and not consumers. The growth of targets and the competition should be stopped.

But greater input about what happens in our places of work should be available to all of us — not just to professionals. We are happier, more fulfilled and productive workers if we have some democratic input into the running of the workplace. Left to

their own devices most companies won't put in place the structures to give their workers a voice. Many won't voluntarily recognize the role of free trade unions. The Government should legislate to encourage greater workplace democracy, wherever there is sufficient demand, through the establishment of elected works councils that have statutory rights to information and have to be consulted before big decisions are made about the future of the company. Such councils are already common across the rest of Europe and help build a good work agenda. The insurance giant Allianz, with more than a hundred thousand employees across Europe, has put in place a works council that allows for a large degree of co-determination by the workforce. The economies of countries such as Germany have not suffered from such a power-sharing approach, quite the reverse. In Britain the trade unions should be promoted as a civilizing and equalizing force at work, as well as a crucial building block for democratic engagement of us as citizens. The Government could invest more in trade-union modernization, helping to fund workplace representatives in key areas such as training and health and safety to ensure a good work agenda is fully pursued.

But there is little point in taking any of these steps if people can be dismissed from their jobs too quickly. If we want good work that helps build solid identities in place of the fluid ones we form as consumers, then the flexible hire-and-fire culture of the last few decades has to be addressed. At the moment it's very easy for a company to close one production site and transfer to another location, hiring new staff on worse terms and conditions. Companies have to make a profit but the return to shareholders has to be balanced against the interests of workers who are stakeholders too. It should mean, for instance, that unions can take legal industrial action to stop the race to the bottom of terms and conditions that underpins our consumer culture. The state should look again at the flexible labour-market laws, and in particular agency workers and secondary industrial action, which currently gives the upper hand to companies at the expense of their employees.

Finally, there are three practical steps the state can take to promote a good work agenda. The first is to establish a state-administered and -backed pension scheme, with matched funding from employers. This should be compulsory for everyone who is not covered by a high-standard company scheme. Unlike the private and company schemes that are either collapsing completely or failing to pay the rates they promised, a state-backed scheme could guarantee provision for old age. Such a scheme would help mitigate against the instant-spending culture of turbo-consumerism and reawaken the fulfilment of delayed gratification. The second step should be not just the legal enforcement of the minimum wage, which many employers avoid, but the introduction of a living wage to workers in Britain and in the supply chain in other countries. On the former, the state would be responsible for setting the level of such a wage but some of the cost would be borne by us, the consumers. In some London hospitals and across the Greater London Authority a living wage is being implemented because of campaigns run by a civil society group called London Citizens. The latter can be enforced on UK company-supply chains overseas through the Companies Law Act. We should be paying the right price for goods based on an assessment of what it reasonably costs to live in the places where they are made.

A living wage would ensure that some who need more could spend more. A maximum wage would curtail the spending power of those at the top. The ratio of pay at the bottom and top of company's pay scales has widened hugely in the last few decades. From a ratio of twenty-five to one, many top executives now receive in the order of two hundred and fifty pounds for every one pound that the lowest earners in the company receive. A maximum wage would stipulate the extent of this ratio and ensure that no one could 'earn' such obscene amounts. American football uses a salary cap very successfully and it is being proposed here by UEFA. There is no reason why it can't be extended to the rest of the private sector. The argument against it is that top executives would simply work in countries without

such an earnings limit. But research by the Work Foundation shows there is little global competition for company executives, and if the European Union were to adopt it then standards would apply across the continent. A maximum wage would reduce the consumption of those who already have too much, it would help equalize society and it would send the strongest possible signal that life is about more than spending.

If we want to rebalance our lives away from being all-consuming, it is vital that the world of work becomes more inviting and fulfilling, not so that we work all hours. As we will see, there is a good case for limiting the number of hours we work. But the state has actively to intervene so that work is more rewarding and stable and becomes not a means to more consumption but an end in itself. Properly trained in good work, people could stop relying on what they last bought to shape their identity and instead rely more on how they use what is, after love, the second most precious thing they can give: their labour.

8. Redistributing time and money

In a consumer society there is a strong tendency towards the creation of two distinct social groups: one with money but not much time, the other with time but very little money. Given that recessions tend to hit the poor hardest, this division is likely to be exacerbated in the next few years unless action is taken. All of our lives would be better if time and money could be more evenly redistributed so that we all have access to reasonable amounts of both. The market cannot achieve such balance. Indeed, it creates the imbalance by heaping more financial rewards on the already successful and prosperous. The state must step in.

Some of us need to work less and ensure that we all have the resources to enjoy the freedom of an authentic life. The French have run a reasonably healthy economy based on a statutory maximum thirty-five-hour working week for the last ten years. Economists believe it has had no detrimental effect on economic growth and helped to create 350,000 new jobs between 1998 and 2002. Even now that a more right-wing government is allowing

companies to renegotiate deals with their employees, few are expected to do so. A maximum working week like this enables people to have time to be other things than just harder-working workers so they can be harder-consuming consumers. They have time for family and friends, to take part in community activities and participate in democratic processes as citizens. A maximum working week can be flexibly applied and, in fact, in France people work on average forty-one hours per week, with overtime. But such a law puts parameters around the extent to which we work and therefore consume. The relentless pressure to consume means that we rarely, if ever, think about how long we actually have to work before we earn the money to buy the things that often give us only fleeting satisfaction. Our long-hours culture is not just about consumption. If we are lucky we work because we enjoy the job and the social benefits. But the ability to work longer to shop harder is a vicious cycle that needs to be broken. A limit on the hours we work each week would help to achieve this.

Others have lots of time but not enough money to buy the opportunities to experience the kind of self-actualization that Maslow wrote about. Basic economics teaches us that the poor get more satisfaction from spending an extra pound than the rich. Government should direct its tax and benefits decisions to where it can have the biggest effect in terms of creating the most happiness – at least to the point at which more money doesn't lead to a growing or constant increase in life satisfaction. Such redistribution of income and wealth goes back to the recognition that to be sufficiently free we have to be sufficiently equal. At the moment those who earn most pay less tax as a total of their taxable income than those who earn least. In a civic society you should pay less tax the less you earn and therefore spend. Of course, the rich evade and avoid paying tax to the tune of around £33 billion a year. The state should pursue them more strongly, closing legal tax-avoidance schemes, reliefs and exemptions, like the ceiling on national-insurance payments. The recession is the perfect time to crack down on tax-dodgers. The crash was caused by the greed of some of those at the top, especially in the bank-

ing sector, and the public climate now exists for a new and fairer tax regime that might help curb the extreme consumerism of some and increase the happiness of others.

Money would go to those whose needs are real. Why waste billions in advertising trying to cajole the rich to buy more things they don't really need when a reallocation of resources towards the bottom of society would enable just as much to be bought but more easily and to greater moral and social effect? The Government's tax-credit regime is helping poor families and so is the minimum wage. People should be paid enough to survive normally in the society they live in and so, as already argued, we should promote a living wage. But this could be a building block towards a more transformative policy idea. In the future we could consider combining various state payments, like income support, child benefit, pension and tax credits and the child trust fund, while reducing tax reliefs, to create a citizen's income as an unconditional payment to all citizens as of right. It could be set at an affordable level to start with, then be gradually expanded. Crucially it would confirm our status, above all else, as equal citizens and provide everyone with the security of an income as of right. It would be expensive but is the kind of universal approach that binds society together and could have a transformative social, economic and political impact because it would institutionalize and socialize our status and identity as equal citizens not unequal consumers. Child benefit is akin to a mini-version of a citizen's income. The US state of Alaska has a scheme that redistributes oil revenues to every citizen, while the idea of a citizen's income is being actively considered by the governments in Canada and Ireland. The amount could be set at a fairly low level at first, then increased over time. At the moment we are all paying the cost of social division and wasted lives – a far higher price than the cost of a citizen's income.

If some are time poor but cash rich, while others are time rich but cash poor, the sensible thing would systematically to arrange the redistribution of time and wealth to ensure everyone has enough of each. This doesn't imply that anyone can do

any job, rather that some could work a little less and pay a little more tax so that others could be paid to do more that is socially and environmentally useful. A potential alliance of interests exists between the overworked and highly paid and the underworked and low paid. But it will take state action to unlock such a mutually beneficial alliance by putting in place the mechanism by which people can trade time and money and find a better balance between production, consumption and leisure.

9. Promoting well-being and happiness

We need to be able to measure the state's performance in terms of whether we are getting happier and shifting towards a post-consumer society. The creation of an independently verified general well-being index as the key indicator of national progress would help to achieve this. Currently we measure national economic success on the basis of economic growth through gross domestic production. But such a crude measure tells us little if anything about how happy we are. We can keep producing more but if this brings about catastrophic climate change and adds little, if anything, to our common level of happiness then what is the point? A general well-being index would change the terms of debate about what success and progress looked and felt like, and shift us away from a focus on production and consumption to the quality of our lives.

It would need to measure two things: the physical and the psychological. The physical aspect includes objective measures, such as diet and health. The psychological component measures stress, worry, pleasure and other positive and negative emotional states. One of the most noted quality-of-life measurements is the *Economist* Intelligence Unit's quality-of-life index, which uses subjective surveys of emotional well-being and objective factors to assess well-being across countries. On a regular basis the more equal and less socially stratified Nordic nations of Sweden, Norway and Finland come top. The *Economist* Intelligence Unit is the research arm of the *Economist* magazine, which is the global house journal of free-market

thinkers. Perhaps the writing is really on the wall for turbo-consumerism.

In the UK in 2006 Tory leader David Cameron said in a speech to the Google Zeitgeist Europe conference that the focus of politics should not just be on financial wealth, and argued that there is more to life than making money. He said, 'Well-being can't be measured by money or traded in markets. It's about the beauty of our surroundings, the quality of our culture and, above all, the strength of our relationships.' He went on to say that much of modern consumer culture 'ultimately seems unsatisfactory' because it fails to meet the deep human need for commitment and belonging.[76] But he has said and done little since to embed this approach.

Perhaps, too, we should take the advice of the former Ofsted inspector Sir Jim Rose, who has suggested in a Government-sponsored report that primary-school children should be taught how to lead happy lives as part of a curriculum overhaul. He has said that children should be taught personal, social and emotional qualities essential to their well-being and happiness. If the state can intervene to try to influence issues like people's weight for the better, then why not help make people happier if the knowledge and tools exist to do so? What else is the state there for if not to ensure its citizens lead the happiest possible lives when all the evidence tells us that just consuming more is not the answer?

Just as the state played a decisive role in the creation of the turbo-consuming society, so it must play an equally key role in what kind of society comes next. It will not lead the debate or the campaign. That duty lies with citizens, civil society and campaigning organizations. But it must make the new laws and build the new institutions of a post-consumer world.

10. Changing politics to break the consumer consensus

All of the preceding nine points will help fashion a new society, but at the moment they are impossible to achieve. This is because our electoral system won't allow decisions like this to be made. The first past the post system gives just a few swing voters

in a few swing seats all the power. Political parties only pander to
these few thousand voters. They tend to be the least radical and
the least political people in the community. Like the consumer
world they epitomize they tend to be those who are most likely
to change their minds and demand the most for their vote.
Because of them alternatives are shut down because no one else's
vote counts. The people who are more sceptical of our consumer
culture are ignored. So people who want a more socially just and
environmentally sound politics are frozen out. The political
system is locked into the pursuit of market fundamentalism as
the elites of all three main parties try to get us to leap backwards
to the politics of more. If we want a different and better society,
then we have to have an electoral system in which all votes and
therefore all voices are made to count. We need fair votes if we
want a fair society and a fair chance of avoiding climate chaos.
This last demand is the most important we can make if we want
to rebalance our lives away from turbo-consumerism.

A post-consumer society

Gradually, shopping less and therefore producing less could lead
to a different type of economy: a post-consumer society, not one
based on eternal growth but a steady state economy. In the 1930s
the influential economist John Maynard Keynes believed that by
now, the early twenty-first century, we would have 'solved the
economic problem'.[77] He meant that we would produce enough
not to worry any more about growth or the allocation of
resources. Instead what he thought would preoccupy us was the
quality of our lives, not the quantity of our consumption. What
the architect of post-war full employment failed to realize was
that enough is never enough in a society defined by nothing
more and nothing less than perpetual consumption.

During the intervening eighty years the very notion of modernization shifted. For much of recent history modernization
was viewed as a time-limited process. It had a finishing line.

Modernization was about cleansing, correcting and rebalancing until we reached some kind of steady state in which all lived a fulfilling and sustainable existence. But in a consumer society the notion of modernization has gone from being finite to infinite. Now it is an on-going process, a fluid state of mind, with no end. The modern world is the treadmill of endless and unremitting challenge and change based on consumption. And the question is this: can our energies, our brilliance, our thirst for knowledge and invention, for meaning and new frontiers take other forms than turbo-consumption? Is shopping all there is?

The notion of a steady state economy is based on uneconomic growth. Economic growth can be distinguished from 'economic development', which refers to qualitative change independent of quantitative growth. For example, economic development may refer to the attainment of a more equitable distribution of wealth, or a sectoral readjustment reflecting the evolution of consumer preference or new technology. A steady state economy doesn't mean that nothing changes, that there are no new innovations, but instead that the overall productive capacity of the economy in terms of the resources it takes from the earth is strictly controlled. It means in essence that we turn off the treadmill and focus on the quality of consumption and production, not the quantity.

Concepts and policy ideas, like those listed above, can start to tip the balance towards a post-consumer society. A society in which children are free to be children, devoid of commercial pressures, where education is about the wonder of learning and opening doors in our minds, where work is creative and fulfilling but there is ample time for family and friends, where the guilt of planetary destruction is lifted from the pit of our stomach, where we can live in spaces and places that we are free to enjoy and share with others, where we know each other as equal citizens, and all our lives are valued for the incredible people we are and can be. A good life of caring, playing, dreaming, thinking, creating and feeling – not just consuming.

But such a shift will take a combination of the individual, collective and state action that works best when all three reinforce

each other. Only then will we create the climate of values and beliefs, backed by institutions, organizations and policies, that enables a new sense of what it means to be normal. One not based on buying more but living better. Over the next decade our social and environmental sustainability demands that we create the conditions in which a critical mass defines this post-consumer normality so that we are all able to put the basket down.

Less!

'Lead us not into temptation but deliver us from evil'
The Lord's Prayer

Every thirty years or so, our society goes though a profound transformation of its cultural, social, economic and political make-up.
In the 1940s, after the Second World War, a new collective spirit,
born of the fight against a common enemy, ushered in an era of
social welfare. It was epitomized by the creation of the NHS. This
lasted until the mid- to late 1970s when this consensus finally
broke down and was replaced by the free-market fundamentalism
of von Hayek and Thatcher, which put in place the cultural, economic and legal requirements for a turbo-consumer society. Now,
another thirty years on, the certainties and appeal of that era are
collapsing before our eyes. We stand at yet another moment of
huge potential change: the choice is whether to go back or go
forward in a different way.

The free market and the consumerization of society have
become the problem, not the solution. It is time to roll back
the frontiers of the market if we are to experience the good
society and a good life. As well as the social, psychological and
environmental turmoil that rampant consumerism has created, it is responsible for the recession we are now in. It went
too far and created its own internal collapse through too much
greed for a few and too much debt for too many. But the
recession is a cloud with a silver lining. Regrettably it will
cause misery and hardship but it creates the possibility of a
turning point too, an opportunity to reconsider what we want
from life. Ideas, practices and institutions that one minute
looked and felt as if they would dominate our landscape for

generations to come have crumbled. It is not the end of history after all.

All of a sudden everything is being questioned and new possible futures revealed. The crash can change everything. But it may not. Powerful forces want us to go back to the turbo-consuming status quo. The politicians stretch every sinew to get us back into the shops and buying again. Then, they think, it will all be okay. But they are locked into the old paradigm of more. If they cannot get to grips with why the crash happened, it is impossible for them to find a way out of our problems. They look at the symptoms of the crash, not the causes. They are looking in the wrong place. Meanwhile, the industrial consumer complex is gearing itself up for a make-over of the high streets, with new products, shops and concepts. They are already preparing new formats to get us back on an even faster treadmill. Coffee shops are to be replaced with tea houses, chain pubs with gastro-pubs; clothes will shift to the Internet, along with music and computer games. But the idea that an economic catastrophe will be averted by more of the behaviour that got us into this mess is absurd. But a turbo-consuming world is absurd.

My mind goes back to Amanda and Bobby. Remember that Amanda said that when she looks for a potential boyfriend what matters to her is the 'image not the face'? Her goal, it seems, is to go out with a brand, not a boy. This can only be because she sees herself as a brand, not as a young woman. It is a marriage of the brands she seeks. Bobby said that his look, and presumably everyone else's look despite his obvious disapproval of them, is natural. It is natural that he wears a particular make of jeans with a wide white stripe down the side. To him and now millions of us, the fact that we micro-select each item of clothing in preference to the thousands of other options that are placed before us and end up with 'our' look is somehow an act of nature, something organic that has evolved in a Darwinian struggle for the survival of the fashion fittest.

This might have been the ultimate victory of the industrial

consumer complex: the impression that a world of brands within which we willingly enslaved ourselves is somehow natural. The clever, determined and well-paid men and women with their clipboards, psychology degrees, focus groups and advertising tricks must have thought their work was done. It isn't.

We have had a wake-up call and been given a way out. An over-stretched turbo-consuming society has created the moment in which it can be transcended to a post-consumer world – but only if we take the right path and refuse to go back. We will do that if we feel a strong enough sense of grievance with the world as it has been and act as individuals, as well as through civil society and the state to make change happen.

'Say what you will, this is a free country.' It's a refrain you sometimes hear as the last defence of our way of life in a consumer society. But how free are we if we haven't been able to choose to stop consuming when we know it doesn't make us any happier and is destroying our planet? And what sort of freedom is it that ends up with everyone on the same treadmill, buying minute variations on the same fashion themes? Surely a society that was truly free would lead not just to different styles and tastes but to a totally different way of living. Instead what we have is a consumer monoculture. We are no longer born free but born to buy. Our minds are conditioned to believe, as Bobby does, that a life that is all consuming is natural.

Perhaps it's no surprise that we allow ourselves to believe such things. Soon after birth we are imbued with the knowledge that we are going to die. Apart from thumbs it's what separates us from the rest of the animal kingdom. For many, God and the afterlife have gone. In their place all that we have had left is shopping. So the trap of the myth of more is sprung. We divert our attention from our mortality through a life spent on the consumer treadmill.

Who dies wishing they had bought more clothes, cars or TVs? Only the most heartless and callous. No, we die wishing we had spent more time with the people we love. I want to die with dignity and freedom, knowing that I had experienced the pleasures

and fulfilment of a life I made with others. I want the freedom to shape my world, and to do that I know I must work with others. I think we're worth it. Life is short and precious, and to spend it just spending fails miserably to allow us to reach the incredible potential that each of us has. Why live a chloroformed consumer existence, dressing ourselves like glorified Barbie and Ken dolls in the latest must-have outfits, buying our identities and succumbing to the frivolous and the banal? I have news for you – Coca-Cola is not the real thing: it is an expensive sugary and sickly drink that uses up precious water resources in the developing world. The real thing is a world in which we are in charge of our destiny because we work together and enjoy greater equality. And to maximize the benefit of the greatest and most important freedoms we will need sometimes to be constrained from actions that undermine our ability to be properly autonomous.

What I hate more than anything is the notion of waste. Not just the physical waste of consumption in the shape of discarded packaging and pollution but the biggest waste there is: the waste of human lives. There has to be something else, something more than a hundred new shirts, tonnes of new gadgets, another new car or even a second home. Life as a series of purchases is a life sucked from us. Human progress cannot just be measured by more. This cannot be the end of history.

This sense of anger at the opportunities being lost and the lives being wasted can now find expression in a world in which the consumer dream has imploded. But it means we have to question, challenge, fight, struggle and protest for something different, something better. And the anger needs to be combined with the hope of better life: of love, courage, friendship, wisdom, compassion, beauty, creativity and nature. Here the concept of Utopianism is helpful to us. Utopia describes the perfect world. But the notion of Utopia has fallen into disrepute. To be Utopian is to be a bit of a dreamer, an airhead. The belief in something different and better was purposefully knocked out of us by the monoculture of consumer society. This was as good as it could get.

But we live in a Utopia. It's just not our Utopia but that of von Mises, von Hayek, Thatcher and the industrial consumer complex that their ambitious vision spawned. It's a Utopia of free markets and big rewards for the few while the rest of us consoled ourselves with the compensation of buying what we could. Of course, in a life confined to such narrow and exhausting limits, who wouldn't choose to buy as much as possible? It's a Utopia without end because there could be no conclusion to life on a treadmill. But their Utopia has come crashing to earth. It is becoming a dystopia. Now we have the chance to replace it.

To be realists, we must first be visionaries. We have to know what we are being realistic about. A world in which we do more than buy is not impossible to visualize and start to create. The demand is not an end to consuming but a rebalancing of our lives. But rebalancing won't happen voluntarily or naturally. Consuming society is geared to ensure that shopping monoculture flattens the earth. To strike a healthy and sustainable balance to life means we have to create the political, legal and cultural barriers to ensure society is not overshadowed by the market.

That is why we have to take action. First we have to take the steps as individuals to buy less and buy better. We need to downshift and rebalance our lives as best we can and we need to take the time to shop as ethically as possible. If we do it, others will follow. Millions are already taking steps to control and limit what they spend. Millions more want to. We can build momentum for change from the bottom up. This is not just necessary for the future of the planet but will bring more pleasure and fulfilment into our lives. We would have to work less but, crucially, buying less and better will help to put us back in charge of our lives. The recession is already opening up spaces for new ways to live and be free. There is a boom in take-up of allotments: economic necessity and land availability are combining to encourage the real-food movement. Meanwhile artists are moving into the free spaces being vacated in high streets where shops have closed down to open up 'creative squats', galleries and studios.

However, we can't do it all on our own. We have to work together. We have to organize, protest and practise a different way of living with others. We have not yet realized how powerful we are when, as consumers, we take collective action against retailers and others whose products and practices we don't like. Through civil-society action we can recycle, swap and help each other outside the distorting influence of market and consumer relations. So the role that we as citizens play in civil society is of critical importance.

But we need the state to act too. Just as political decisions gave life to turbo-consumerism in the 1980s, so Government action is required to establish a post-consumer world. First, the state can stop harmful consumer practices by restricting advertising, taxing luxury goods and rationing scarce resources. Second, it can help foster good buying behaviour and activity by making ethical shopping and recycling easier. Finally, through our democracy, we can create spaces in which markets are restricted and effectively regulated, so we can be citizens, not just consumers, to help us forge more durable and satisfying identities as workers while providing us with the time and money to live more autonomous lives. All of this can be measured and progress assessed through the creation of a general well-being index.

All of this interlocking action, at the levels of the individual, civic society and nation state, could create the basis, over the next few years, for the transformation of our society. And here the principle that means shape ends is vital. By doing these things in the here and now we challenge the principles of consumer society head on: that we are better off alone than together, that private is always good and public bad, and that the needs of the market should come before those of society.

The future is not something we enter, it is something we create, but only if we do it together. If we stand alone as consumers then too little changes, except the fashions and fads that keep us on the treadmill. As citizens nothing is beyond our control. I want a future where people are truly free to create their own

world and not just their own look. A world in which we value social attachment, authenticity and sustainability more than what is stocked in the shops. I want more, but it has to be the right kind of more. The treadmill has come to a halt. All we have to do is step off together to regain our freedom.

The thirty years of free-market supremacy and turbo-consuming are coming to an end. They can cling on for a little longer if we allow them to. But they can't meet the challenges of the future because they are all collective problems that demand collective solutions, from affordable housing to overcrowded transport, from poor education and insufficient health care to climate change. We can't buy ourselves out of these problems and when we try the problem just gets worse. If we didn't accept that fact before then we have to now.

If we look back at history, regimes, cultures and societies that appeared impregnable and immovable always changed, adapted or crumbled. Nothing lasts for ever. The trouble is that the impossible begins just beyond the possible and we rarely see it coming. But things can change very quickly. Dissent, discontent, unhappiness and frustration with consumer society is no longer just marginal but widespread. The global credit crunch and financial turmoil that rocked the world in the autumn of 2008 places us on the cusp of a post-consumer society. All we have to do is step off the treadmill. How tantalizing is that?

'Less is more,' wrote the pioneering modern architect Ludwig Mies van der Rohe. But 'Less is only more,' responded his fellow architect and educator Frank Lloyd Wright, 'where more is no good.' And centuries before, the German philosopher Meister Eckhart had said, 'The more we have the less we own.'

A shopping list of policies for lives that are more than all consuming

1. **Restricting advertising:** we must place the needs of society before the market by banning all adverts in public places, stopping advertising to under twelves, taxing adverts and heavily regulating buzz marketing.

2. **Tax luxury goods:** we must signal that status can and must be gained in other ways than buying top end goods.

3. **Ration key goods and services:** we know that supply of oil and other minerals and goods will reduce dramatically. Either we decide to rationalize them effectively and fairly now through democratic decisions or the market will decide for us – unfairly and inefficiently.

4. **Promote ethical consumption:** through one government standard kite mark that tells us categorically a product is good for people, animals and the environment.

5. **Promote environmentally friendly action:** by taxing waste and using the revenue for a national home-insulation programme – thus creating thousands of jobs to help get us out of recession.

6. **Create a public realm:** by ending privatization, banning companies from schools and making modern community schools work for everyone to stop the competition for places. Protecting new commons like the Internet and DNA sequences and making the case for the taxation of income and, especially, wealth as the basis for more efficient and effective public consumption.

7. **Making work as important as shopping:** by introducing a national training levy, enabling workplace democracy and introducing both a living wage and a maximum wage to create a sense of fairness and justice in the workplace.

8. **Redistribute time and money:** to ensure a better balance between those who have too much time and too little money and their alter egos by introducing a thirty-five-hour week and moving towards a citizen's income.

9. **Make happiness the priority of all governments:** by measuring their success through a general well-being index.

10. **Break the consumer consensus:** by introducing a system of proportional representation that makes everyone's vote count.

Notes

1 From Charles Dickens, *Oliver Twist*.

2 Figures from Alert Data, www.uk15000.co.uk/4968.htm

3 NFPI, *Hard Sell, Soft Targets*, February 2004.

4 *GQ*, May 2006.

5 J. K. Galbraith, *The Affluent Society*, Penguin, London, 1999 (first published 1958).

6 C. Hamilton, *Overconsumption in Britain – A culture of middle-class complaint?*, Australian Institute, Canberra, Australia, 2003.

7 Nicholas Georgescu-Roegen, *Energy and Economic Myths*, Pergamon, Oxford, 1976.

8 J. Bray, 'Castle, non-existent, yours for £50,000', *Guardian*, 26 September 2006.

9 Minette Marrin, 'Why fashion matters', *Sunday Times*, Style, 2 March 2008.

10 I am indebted to the Adam Curtis BBC documentary *Century of the Self* for this information.

11 A. Stephen, 'America', *New Statesman*, 23 August 2004.

12 D. Lewis, *The Soul of the New Consumer*, Nicholas Brealey, London, 2000.

13 Vance Packard, *The Waste Makers*, Van Rees, New York, 1960.

14 Quoted in Rachel Bowlby, *Carried Away: the invention of modern shopping*, Columbia University Press, New York 2002, p. 168.

15 'Branded – a special investigation', *Guardian*, G2, 9 July 2001.

16 http://www.brandchannel.com/brandcameo_films.asp?movie_year_az=2006#movie_list

17 http://www.bandt.com.au/news/d8/0c01f1d8.asp

18 From Paul Marsden, 'Seed to spread: how seeding trials ignite epidemics of demand', in Justin Kirby and Paul Marsden (eds), *Connected Marketing: the viral, buzz and word-of-mouth revolution*, Elsevier, London, 2006.

19 From their website, www.womma.org

20 David Rowan, 'Trend surfing: Buzz marketing', *The Times*, 4 September 2004.

21 Cited http://www.homebuying.co.uk/homeimprovements/diyProfits.htm, accessed on 18 August 2006.

22 Tim Adams, 'Give me some credit', *Observer*, 18 April 2004.

23 www.mises.org/quotes.aspx

24 For a more detailed but readable account of the rise of the new right in

Britain, see Richard Cockett, *Thinking the Unthinkable: Think-Tanks and the Economic Counter-Revolution 1931–1983*, HarperCollins, London, 1994.

25 Quoted in The Reader's Digest condensed version of *The Road to Serfdom* from the introduction by John Blundell, 'Hayek, Fisher and The Road to Serfdom', 1999, http://www.iea.org.uk/files/upld-publication43pdf?.pdf, p. 20.

26 Prudential, Soggy Lettuce Report, 2004.

27 Tim Cooper, 'Inadequate Life? Evidence of Consumer Attitudes to Product Obsolescence', *Journal of Consumer Policy*, 27 (2004), 421–49; Tim Cooper and Kieren Mayers, 'Prospects for Household Appliances', E-SCOPE, 2006.

28 *Independent*, 23 May 2006.

29 C. Williams, 'Rise of the Botox Battleaxe', *New Statesman*, 16 May 2005.

30 Z. Bauman, *Work Consumerism and the New Poor*, Open University Press, Maidenhead, 2005.

31 Richard Wilkinson, *The Impact of Inequality: How to Make Sick Societies Healthier*, New Press, New York, 2006; Michael Marmot, *Status Syndrome: How Your Social Standing Directly Affects Your Health*, Bloomsbury, 2005.

32 'You'll be lucky to live to 60 here. But it's not the third world . . . it's Glasgow's East End', David Smith, *Observer*, 14 March 2004.

33 Richard Elliot and Clare Leonard, 'Peer pressure and poverty; exploring fashion brands and consumption symbolism among children of the British poor', *Journal of Consumer Behaviour*, vol. 3, no. 4 (June 2004), pp. 347–59.

34 Lucy Ward, 'No mobile, means poverty say children', *Guardian*, 19 September 2007.

35 www.labourbehindthelabel.org/resources/reports/20/257-lets-clean-up-fashion-2008

36 www.labourbehindthelabel.org/resources/reports/20/257-lets-clean-up-fashion-2008

37 Researchers at Sheffield University's Centre for the Public Library in the Information Society, 1999.

38 Mary Kenny, 'Tooth and Sale', *Guardian*, 6 March 2004.

39 Madeleine Bunting, 'From socialism to Starbucks', *Renewal*, vol. 9, no. 2/3 (2001).

40 Jonathan Rutherford, 'Cultures of Capitalism', papers for Soundings debate, 2007.

41 A. Simms, 'The gaudy sameness of Clone Town', *New Statesman*, 24 January 2005.

42 Quoted in David Lewis and Darren Bridger, *The Soul of the New Consumer: Authenticity – What We Buy and Why in the New Economy*, Nicholas Brealey Publishing; new edition, London, 2001

43 http://www.oft.gov.uk/news/press/2007/94-07

44 Patrick Wintour, 'Voters act like teenagers, says No.10 policy analyst', *Guardian*, 22 December 2005.

45 John Lloyd, 'We want it, and we want it now', *New Statesman*, 10 January 2000.

46 Barry Schwarz, *The Paradox of Choice: why more is less*, HarperCollins, London, 2004.

47 Rachel Greenwald, *Find a Husband After 35 Using What I learned at Harvard Business School*, Random House, London, 2003.

48 As reported in O. Stallwood (2006), 'Say hello to Little Miss Macca and co', *Metro*, 5 October 2006.

49 See *The Commercialization of Childhood,* Compass, 2007.

50 NCC, *Generation X*, July 2005.

51 *Observer*, 24 August 2005.

52 NCC and Childnet, *Fair Game*, 6 December 2007.

53 BBC News, 'US Babies Get Global Brand Names', 13 November 2003, http://news.bbc.co.uk/go/pr/fr/-/1/hi/world/americas/3268161.stm

54 Stephen Khan, 'Galloping gout hits a new generation', *Observer*, 18 January 2004.

55 Greg Critser, *Fat Land*, Allen Lane, London, 2004, p. 39.

56 Figures from Gamecare, www.gamcare.org.uk/publications.php?category= Reports

57 www.dailymail.co.uk/news/article-488032/More-1million-using-credit-cards-pay-mortgage.html

58 Statistics from Simon Jenkins, 'Britain's prisons reek of a wretchedly backward nation', *Guardian*, 20 June 2007.

59 Steven Poole, review of de Botton, *Status Anxiety*, *Guardian*, 27 March 2004, p.12.

60 Joseph Brodsky, 'In Praise of Boredom', in *On Grief and Reason*, Farrar, Straus and Giroux, New York, 1995, pp. 107–8.

61 Ben Summerskill, 'Focus: The downshifters', *Observer*, 20April 2003.

62 Clive Hamilton, 'Downshifting in Britain: A sea-change in the pursuit of happiness', Australia Institute Discussion Paper, no. 58, November 2003.

63 See sites like www.castoff.info or www.crafster.org for more ideas and insights.

64 Richard Layard *Happiness: lessons from a new science*, Allen Lane, London, 2005.

65 Richard Layard, 'The Secret of Happiness', *New Statesman*, 3 March 2003.

66 Dan Milmo, 'Private jet firm makes carbon offsetting mandatory', *Guardian*, 13 November 2007.

67 David Teather, 'Branded for life?' *Guardian*, 25 October 2007.

68 Quoted in Benjamin Barber, *Consumed: how markets corrupt children, infantilise adults, and swallow citizens whole*, W. W. Norton, New York, 2007.

69 With apologies to Karl Marx and Friedrich Engels, *The Communist Manifesto*, Penguin Classics, London, 2002

70 See www.timebanks.co.uk

71 See www.bookcrossing.com

72 http://observer.guardian.co.uk/carbontrust/story/0,,1515572,00.html

73 John Carvel, 'Takeoff time for guilt over air travel', *Guardian*, 28 January 2009.

74 news.bbc.co.uk/1/hi/education/7896751.stm

75 Jay Walljasper, 'The future of the human race depends on public spaces', *New Statesman*, 15 August 2005.

76 news.bbc.co.uk/1/hi/uk_politics/5003314.stm

77 J. M. Keynes, 'Economic Possibilities for our Grandchildren', in *Essays in Persuasion*, W. W. Norton, New York, 1930.